BOUNDARY AREAS
IN SOCIAL AND DEVELOPMENTAL
PSYCHOLOGY

BOUNDARY AREAS IN SOCIAL AND DEVELOPMENTAL PSYCHOLOGY

Edited by

John C. Masters

VANDERBILT UNIVERSITY
INSTITUTE FOR PUBLIC POLICY STUDIES
NASHVILLE, TENNESSEE

Kerry Yarkin-Levin

ADVANCED RESEARCH RESOURCES ORGANIZATION
WASHINGTON, D.C.

1984

ACADEMIC PRESS, INC.

(Harcourt Brace Jovanovich, Publishers)

Orlando   San Diego   San Francisco   New York   London
Toronto   Montreal   Sydney   Tokyo   São Paulo

ACADEMIC PRESS, INC.
Orlando, Florida 32887

United Kingdom Edition published by
ACADEMIC PRESS, INC. (LONDON) LTD.
24/28 Oval Road, London NW1 7DX

Library of Congress Cataloging in Publication Data

Main entry under title:

Boundary areas in social and developmental psychology.

   Includes bibliograhies and index.
   1. Developmental psychology--Addresses, essays,
lectures. 2. Social psychology--Addresses, essays,
lectures. I. Masters, John C. II. Yarkin-Levin, Kerry.
BF713.5.B68 1984   302   83-15146
ISBN 0-12-479280-4 (alk. paper)

PRINTED IN THE UNITED STATES OF AMERICA

84 85 86 87   9 8 7 6 5 4 3 2 1

Contents

1

Boundary Areas in Psychology

JOHN C. MASTERS, KERRY YARKIN-LEVIN, AND WILLIAM G. GRAZIANO

2

Some Observations on the Study of Personal Relationships

WYNDOL FURMAN

3

Microsocial Process: A View from the Boundary

G. R. PATTERSON

4

Why Marriages Fail: Affective and Physiological Patterns in Marital Interaction

JOHN M. GOTTMAN AND ROBERT W. LEVENSON

5

Social Support Processes

SHARON S. BREHM

6

Children's Peer Relationships: An Examination of Social Processes

SHERRI ODEN, SHARON D. HERZBERGER, PETER L. MANGIONE, AND VALERIE A. WHEELER

7

A Developmental Approach to Social Exchange Processes

WILLIAM G. GRAZIANO

8

The Influence of Group Discussions on Children's Moral Decisions

THOMAS J. BERNDT

9

Inferences about the Actions of Others: Developmental and Individual Differences in Using Social Knowledge

W. ANDREW COLLINS

10

A Distinction between Two Types of Relationships and Its Implications for Development

MARGARET S. CLARK

11

Self-Evaluation Maintenance Processes: Implications for Relationships and for Development

ABRAHAM TESSER

Contributors

Numbers in parentheses indicate the pages on which the authors' contributions begin.

THOMAS J. BERNDT (195), Department of Psychology, University of Oklahoma, Norman, Oklahoma 73019

SHARON S. BREHM (107), Department of Psychology, University of Kansas, Lawrence, Kansas 66045

MARGARET S. CLARK (241), Department of Psychology, Carnegie-Mellon University, Pittsburgh, Pennsylvania 15213

W. ANDREW COLLINS (221), Institute of Child Development, University of Minnesota, Minneapolis, Minnesota 55455

WYNDOL FURMAN (15), Psychology Department, University of Denver, Denver, Colorado 80208

JOHN M. GOTTMAN (67), Department of Psychology, University of Illinois, Champaign, Illinois 61820

WILLIAM G. GRAZIANO (1, 161), Department of Psychology, University of Georgia, Athens, Georgia 30602

SHARON D. HERZBERGER (131), Department of Psychology, Trinity College, Hartford, Connecticut 06106

ROBERT W. LEVENSON (67), Department of Psychology, Indiana University, Bloomington, Indiana 47405

PETER L. MANGIONE (131), Max Planck Institute, Munich, Federal Republic of Germany

JOHN C. MASTERS (1), Vanderbilt University, Institute for Public Policy Studies, Nashville, Tennessee 37212

SHERRI ODEN (131), Graduate School, Wheelock College, Boston, Massachusetts O2215

G. R. PATTERSON (43), Oregon Social Learning Center, Eugene, Oregon 97401

ABRAHAM TESSER (271), Institute for Behavioral Research, and Department of Psychology, University of Georgia, Athens, Georgia 30602

VALERIE A. WHEELER (131), Department of Psychology, University of Illinois, Champaign, Illinois 61820

KERRY YARKIN-LEVIN (1), Advanced Research Resources Organization, Washington, D.C. 20814

Preface

Over the past decade there has been a gradual movement in psychology toward interdisciplinary approaches to understanding social phenomena. This is apparent from the increasing number of psychological conferences as well as the content of many edited volumes and articles on interdisciplinary research (e.g., Harvey, 1981[1]; Harvey & Weary, 1979[2]; Dunnette & Fleishman, 1982[3]). (The present volume is based largely on the proceedings of a conference at Vanderbilt University in June 1981.) The present volume extends this emerging commitment to identifying, examining, and fostering interfaces that have already begun to develop among areas of specialization within psychology. It brings together scholars known for their work in areas of social and developmental psychology, whose views actually fall at a conceptual or methodological interface between these two subdisciplines of psychology.

These scholars examine the internal complexity of psychology that has fostered the evolution of theoretical issues and research problems that cross conventional demarcations separating traditional areas of specialization, and they are convinced of the increasing significance of boundary areas (see Chapter 1 for a more complete discussion of boundary areas in psychology). One of the goals of the present volume is to highlight some examples (surely not exhaustive) of research that illustrate facets of the important boundary area between social and developmental psychology. A second goal is a more selfish, interactive one: to enhance the degree to which we ourselves appreciate how our own empirical research or theoretical speculation falls into a boundary area. Each author was charged with describing the boundary nature of his or her own work or of research and theory in the general domain of her or his interest. The intent of this second goal was twofold: (1) to allow descriptions of theory or research on various boundary issues to serve as a model to others, and (2) to encourage development of boundary aspects of other current and future work.

[1]Harvey, J. H. (1981). *Cognition, social behavior, and the environment*. Hillsdale, NJ: Erlbaum.

[2]Harvey, J. H., & Weary, G. The integration of social and clinical training programs. *Personality and Social Psychology Bulletin*, 1979, *5*, 511–516.

[3]Dunnette, M., & Fleishman, E. A. (Eds.). *Human performance and productivity* (Vol. 1). Hillsdale, NJ: Erlbaum, 1982.

This volume is a true product of group interaction, including both a seminal meeting of all senior authors of the chapters and more than a year's subsequent interaction, exchanging drafts of chapters, providing mutual critiques, and in general contributing to one another's continued thinking about boundary issues as well as to the chapters that follow.

The first chapter deals with the broad issues of boundary areas in psychology, ending with specific consideration of the boundary between social and developmental psychology. The broad consideration of boundary areas establishes a context for the importance of the specific area between social and developmental psychology, for while there has been some prior concern with other boundary areas (e.g., Harvey [1981], who dealt with the boundary between cognitive, social, and environmental psychology) in the 1970s and 1980s, that between social and developmental is perhaps the most flourishing and interactive boundary. Developmental researchers tackle questions of attributions and group interaction in children and adolescents, while social psychologists ponder the developmental origins of particular processes and behavior and extend their thinking to include the behavior of individuals at various developmental levels.

Following this introductory chapter, Wyndol Furman considers several general propositions regarding the importance of integrating concepts and methods from social and developmental psychology in the study of social relationships. Next, G. R. Patterson shows how integrating social and developmental considerations can assist in the understanding of relationships between parents and children, including those that involve behavioral pathologies. John Gottman and Robert Levenson discuss another family relationship—marriage—and extend developmental and social concepts to identify and study some of the aspects of the marital relationship that may lead to its dissolution. In a similar vein, Sharon Brehm provides a theoretical treatment of social support processes in adults, including factors that may influence the development and use of systems of social support.

Chapters 6–11 deal with boundary area issues focusing primarily on children's social behavior. Sherri Oden and her colleagues discuss the complexity of social processes inherent in children's peer relationships, particularly the development of such relationships. William Graziano theoretically and empirically examines an important and basic area of research in social psychology—social exchange processes—raising questions and speculations about their role in social relationships from infancy to adulthood. Thomas Berndt turns his attention to cognitive and social aspects of group influence processes and considers the different perspectives that social and developmental psychology bring to both theory and research on group influence. Andrew Collins addresses a fundamental issue that illustrates the importance of integrating social and developmental perspectives in the study of social behavior and knowledge: the way in which children's understanding and cognitions about the social world change with development. Margaret Clark considers the factors that may lead to different developmental histories for different types of relationships between children and adults; specifically, she examines the development of communal and exchange relationships. In the final chapter, Abraham Tesser discusses the developmental questions and issues relating to the important social phenomenon of self-esteem maintenance processes. His chapter represents the worthy attempt of a social psychologist to consider developmental processes that may impinge on a phenomenon previously regarded as being squarely in the domain of social psychology.

For such a group endeavor to be successful, many people must work long hours and contribute in a variety of ways. We extend our appreciation to John H. Harvey, who planted the seed that has blossomed into a series of interdisciplinary conferences at Vanderbilt University. We also thank the many others who assisted in the logistics involved in the conference and subsequent interactions among conferees. In particular, the continued assistance provided by Elyse Schwartz Felleman and Charles Carlson is very much appreciated.

1

Boundary Areas in Psychology

JOHN C. MASTERS

KERRY YARKIN-LEVIN

WILLIAM G. GRAZIANO

INTRODUCTION

The discipline of psychology is complex and contains a number of sub-disciplines, each with an identity of its own. Indeed, individual scientists within the field have long tended to label themselves by reference to their area of specialization, and graduate training programs typically include "tracks" that represent the subdisciplines into which the field is commonly divided. In addition, as a profession, psychology has initiated formal certification procedures for some specialty areas, and many states have licensure or certification laws that designate specific subdisciplines as formal and legitimate areas of expertise.

This pluralism within psychology is not particularly surprising—at least not to those who appreciate the depth and breadth of the field in terms of the many classes of behavior that have been studied, the varied contexts in which behavior may occur, the factors that may influence it, or the way it may change over time. Initially, the designation of specialization areas or subdisciplines served the important purpose of limiting a focus of study to manageable size for the generation of meaningful theory and informative data—and this is still an important function. There are other consequences, however, that are not so positive. Prominent among these is a degree of insularity between subdisciplines, perhaps fostered initially by limitations in the scope of theory or data and later preserved by elegant, complex, and yet highly focused theories and associated rosters of empirical findings.

1

BOUNDARY AREAS IN SOCIAL
AND DEVELOPMENTAL PSYCHOLOGY

We do not intend to develop an argument against specialization within the broad field of psychology. To the contrary, without some kind of focus, the generation of empirical research would be a wandering and almost random process and the development of meaningful theory would be impossible. However, we wish to deal with issues relating to the existence of independent and relatively insular subdisciplines within psychology and speak to the timeliness and importance of building bridges linking them. There are two simple reasons for this. First, a natural consequence of formally defined subdisciplines is the occasional parallel development of concepts, methods, or theories that may have different names or other designators but that, in fact, reference concerns that are similar on a conceptual level. Another consequence of formally defined subdisciplines is the existence of some mutually agreed-upon perimeter, a judgmental limit for what are deemed to fall within the subdiscipline as "legitimate" concepts, methods, categories of behavior, and so forth, and what are not. So a second consequence of specialized subdisciplines is that periodically, and with greater frequency as a subdiscipline develops a good armamentarium of theory and data, investigators begin to tackle problems that approach this consensually defined perimeter and start to have relevance for subdisciplines that are normally out of bounds.

Thus, as subdisciplines within a field evolve, like cultures, contact begins to develop between them, either at points where there has been parallel evolution or where mutual progress in research and theory generates questions of interest that relate in new and creative ways to theoretical and behavioral domains that hitherto may have been defined arbitrarily as falling within another subdiscipline. We term these areas of contact *boundary areas* in psychology.

FACTORS INFLUENCING THE DEVELOPMENT OF BOUNDARY AREAS IN PSYCHOLOGY

Obviously, we see boundary areas as a natural consequence of disciplinary evolution in psychology (and perhaps, by extension, within any science). To some extent, we are simply arguing that the evolution of the field proceeds, in part, by a process of nonrandom assortment as concepts and methods from various subdisciplines are integrated with one another. But there is more to it than this, if only because the definition of specific subdisciplines in any field creates issues of turf and fosters a myopia that concentrates attention on questions that are considered central within the area and away from those at the edge. This creates problems in working at a boundary, and we discuss some of them here later. For the moment, let us consider some general precepts about the natural history of individual boundary areas and the pressures and processes that draw investigators into them. Readers should remain mindful, of course, that a boundary area cannot actually exist without investigators or theoreticians to provide the data, method, or theory that define it.

What are some of the factors leading to the development of boundary areas? We have already discussed relatively accidental ones, the parallel evolution of concepts and methods, and the gradual development of research and theory that approach the perimeter of one subdiscipline and touch on questions relevant to another. Harsher factors are also analogous to processes of natural selection. When there is heavy competition for academic or research positions—that is, overpopulation—individual investigators may develop interest in questions that are less typical or stereotypic of a given subdiscipline, broadening the number of vocational niches for which they may qualify. In doing so, these investigators also bring to those niches the basic thrust of their subdiscipline of origin, in effect moving toward or into a boundary area or even creating one. To take an example, there is population pressure today within the subdiscipline of social psychology, and one consequence has been increasing interest among social psychologists in questions relating to personality (Kenrick & Dantchik, in press) or in developmental issues that touch on standard social psychological concepts (e.g., the present volume).

To some extent, the development of boundary areas may depend on the individuals who first venture forth. These are likely to be those who *see* the parallels between subdisciplines or *realize* potential interrelationships that have not yet been explored. Consider the "new look" in perception research, illustrating that social, personality, and cognitive variables influenced processes of perceptual judgment (Bruner & Postman, 1949). Contrariwise, consider the use of methods from perceptual discrimination research in studies of social perception and parent–child relations (Holleran, 1982). Implicit in this is the notion that parallel evolution between two subdisciplines may require an inferential leap on the part of a particular investigator before it becomes effective in producing a boundary area of research or theory.

One factor influencing the development of boundary areas within psychology may be the nature of the field itself. It has been proposed that the entire field of psychology began as a boundary area between physiology and philosophy (Boring, 1950). If that is so, then psychology illustrates one potential future for a boundary area—namely, development into a core discipline (or subdiscipline) of its own. This may have happened within psychology for the area of personality, as distinct from clinical–abnormal and from social. In a more contemporary vein, we are now seeing the gradual independence of pediatric psychology as a subdiscipline distinct from clinical, from child–clinical, and from developmental psychology.

This is not to imply that boundary areas are destined to be independent, eventually resulting in a psychology that is burgeoning with subareas of specialization. Another, perhaps more common, natural history for boundary areas may be that they simply cease to be boundaries, sinking back into the core areas of each of the contributing subdisciplines or perhaps only to one. Thus, social perception becomes an accepted focus within social psychology, or reinforcement an accepted process in both animal learning and social learning approaches to normal and abnormal behavior.

PRESCRIPTIONS AND PROSCRIPTIONS: PROBLEMS INHERENT IN BOUNDARY AREA RESEARCH

One of the major problems besetting boundary area research is political—put more gently, it is a problem of fairly rigid judgments by fellow scientists about what does and does not constitute relevant, significant, or state-of-the-art research. In his seminal paper on interdisciplinary relationships in the social sciences, Campbell (1969) noted that partisans working closer to the supposed core of a discipline may exert pressure on the boundary researcher either to move closer to the disciplinary core or to move out of the discipline altogether. Direct judgments may be made about the relevance of boundary research or the degree to which it reasonably fits within the discipline: "that is not X-ology—it even comes close to being Y-ology."

There are several reasons why this might happen. First, persons in specific disciplines share many basic assumptions about the nature of the entity they study. For example, most psychologists believe that the fundamental unit of analysis is the behavior of individual organisms, whereas most sociologists would not accept this assumption. As a researcher moves from the core toward the boundary, basic assumptions begin to be challenged, and such challenges can be threatening to persons working near the core because the challenges threaten the rationale for core research. In many cases, the basic assumptions are not unreasonable for people working near the core, so the challenges are often dismissed by core researchers as products of faulty thinking or rebelliousness.

Another factor influencing the approval and acceptance of boundary area researchers relates to their teaching role. It becomes more difficult—or at least more arbitrary—to teach graduate and undergraduate students "fundamental X-ology" when there is no consensus on fundamental or core phenomena or assumptions. Boundary researchers may not be trusted to teach important core courses because they will offer an unorthodox approach and corrupt young, impressionable minds. That such pressures are brought to bear on research scientists is an interesting social development phenomenon in its own right and may also tell us something about the importance and pervasiveness of labeling a person as a member of this or that group. Such processes are obstacles to scientific innovation, however, and boundary researchers may be especially likely targets.

Consider also the problems of publishing boundary research. When research manuscripts are submitted to journals, reviewers are selected to evaluate the submissions. Because these reviewers are likely to be selected for their competence in dealing with core disciplinary issues, we can anticipate differences in the way reviewers might react. The reviewer from one core area may note the missing references to the classic work of Z, or may consider the author's alternative explanations to be due to the unusual method employed by the boundary researcher. The reviewer from a different core area may make similar observations but be concerned about the missing work of W, not Z, and have his or her own reservations about the method employed. Although citing different literatures, each reviewer would agree with the others that the method is faulty and important previous work is overlooked. The editor then finds that the two reviewers agree in finding conceptual and methodological problems, though they may differ somewhat in the specifics, and declines the paper. While this scenario is perhaps somewhat harsh (and we mean to cast no aspersions on the general wisdom of the system of review by one's peers), it illustrates the problem of peer judgment when boundary area research is concerned.

A potentially problematic misconception about boundary area research is that it requires total mastery of more than one area of specialization, in effect approaching what could be considered a Renaissance man conceptualization of the knowledge base required for effective research. This is not so; and to the extent it is accepted as necessary, it may serve as an impediment to the development of interest or activity in boundary area research. Campbell (1969) discussed the problems associated with *Leonardesque aspirations* in psychology, this being his term for the desire for complete mastery of several disciplines demonstrated by Leonardo da Vinci.

First, Campbell proposes that such aspirations inevitably lead to failure, as they tend to produce a shallow, lowest-common-denominator breadth at the expense of intense specialization that is one of the essentials of scientific productivity. Victims of Leonardesque aspirations may attempt to meld the different approaches into a convenient model, suitable for a single new conceptualization of a research project but having limited potential for long-range theoretical or empirical development. Indeed, the melding may produce a mutant monster that reflects an eclectic accommodation between constructs of differing natures and levels of abstraction that may, in the long run, fail to deal adequately with the phenomenon that attracted the researcher to the boundary area in the first place (see Overton & Reese, 1973). One is reminded of an apocryphal story related by statistician Maurice J. Kendall (1949):

> A friend of mine once remarked to me that if some people asserted that the earth rotated from East to West and others that it rotated from West to East, there would always be a few well-meaning citizens to suggest that perhaps there was something to be said for both sides, and that maybe it did a little of one and a little of the other; or that the truth probably lay between the extremes and perhaps it did not rotate at all [p. 115].

To some extent, it might be argued that the most productive researcher in a boundary area would be one who wandered into that area without any premeditation, an X-ologist who became interested in phenomenon Y but not from the point of view of Y-ology. This would then bring to the attention of Y-ologists the relevance and advantages of an X-ological approach to Y, either in terms of borrowed concepts or borrowed methods. Contrariwise, astute X-ologists would recognize a new extension of their field and begin to relate phenomenon Y to other X-ological concepts and methods.

This is easily said but not always easily done. Consider, for example, Dollard and Miller's (1950) translation of classical psychoanalytic theory of personality development and psychopathology into the then-current terms of Hullian behavior theory. Historically, this may be seen as an important transitional phase in the development of social learning theory (see Bandura & Walters, 1963), though it is roundly (and deservedly) criticized for being uncritical in its acceptance of psychodynamic constructs for translation. In a more contemporary vein, recent studies of experimentally induced emotional states in children and adults, coming from a cognitive, social-learning theory approach to personality, have been followed by studies of induced emotional states on learning and memory (Bower, 1981; Masters, Barden, & Ford, 1979), which are certainly at the boundary of standard learning theory and experimental psychology. Another good example of boundary work is that of Walton and Sedlak (1982), who attempted to describe children's social interactions, using a rule-of-occurrence model that is extrapolated from transformational grammar systems used to describe language (see Chomsky, 1957).

To some extent, it behooves the boundary area researcher to develop the importance of his or her research at the boundary, noting the advantages of adapting constructs or methods from one subdiscipline to another. This means that it is important to be aware when one is in a boundary area. This is the stuff of which *Psychological Bulletin* and *Psychological Review* papers are made. Walter Mischel, for example, in the development of *cognitive* social learning theory, denoted and discussed its development in an important review paper (Mischel, 1973). The boundary area character of Walton and Sedlak's use of transformational rule systems to describe social behavior was also developed in commentary that followed the publication of the article in which the technique was actually used (Masters, 1982). This illustrates another method for delineating boundary areas that allows such delineation to proceed through the efforts of individuals other than the boundary area researchers themselves.

Consistent with the considerations discussed so far is a simple message: Boundary area researchers should not lose sight of their own special expertise from their own (sub)discipline while attempting to study a somewhat alien construct or to use a somewhat alien method in a creative way. It is this expertise that allows the proper creative selection of the construct or method under study, such that between the question and the method there is a complementarity that advances understanding in a new direction, rather than simply further along the same road. One might characterize boundary area research as providing disjunctive increments to knowledge, as contrasted to the conjunctive increments that occur from significant but mainline (sub)disciplinary research.

A CASE IN POINT: THE BOUNDARY AREA BETWEEN SOCIAL AND DEVELOPMENTAL PSYCHOLOGY

The remainder of this volume is devoted to theoretical and empirical contributions describing examples of boundary area considerations between social and developmental psychology. This particular boundary merits some discussion in the present chapter, too, because it provides a good illustration of some of the general points we wish to make about boundary area research in general.

At first, one might think that developmental psychology would foster boundary area research, if only because it may be seen to exist *only* at the boundary of other subdisciplines of psychology: for example, social development, language development, personality development, physical–physiological development, cognitive development, and so forth. In fact, however, these boundaries are present largely in name only. For example, research in social development does not consistently adapt developmental methods or concepts to the study of aspects of social behavior commonly studied in social psychology; nor does research in cognitive development address that corpus of research problems currently of interest in experimental studies of thinking and cognition. There is, of course, movement in this direction—hence this volume, illustrating and exhorting research at the boundary of social and developmental psychology.

There are, however, a number of obstacles to cooperative interchange between developmental and social psychology and between developmental and social psychologists. Casual perusal of handbooks, textbooks, and jounals reveals profound differences between the kinds of theories and methods employed in each of the two disciplines. In his classic article on the two disciplines of scientific psychology, we suspect that Cronbach (1957) would even assign the two disciplines to different categories. Because people cannot be assigned randomly to different developmental levels, developmental psychology would be classified as a variety of *correlational* psychology, while social psychology seems to fit into the category of *experimental* psychology. It is likely that such theoretical and methodological differences can be traced to the substantive nature of the topics typically investigated within each discipline. For example, a researcher whose substantive interest is group dynamics or attribution processes is less interested in material causation and stability of behavior across time than is a researcher whose substantive interest is intellectual development.

Another obstacle is the different metatheoretical assumptions and unstated preferences found in the two disciplines. There are different disciplinary concerns with the stability, as opposed to the mutability, of behavior; different choices of physical as opposed to biological models; there are differences in the emphasis on and search for immediate proximal—efficient causes, as opposed to distal—material—formal causes. All of these differences seem to have at least part of their origins in *founder effects*. That is, some assumptions and preferences seem to be attributable to the influence of founding figures such as James Mark Baldwin, Alfred Binet, G. Stanley Hall, Fritz Heider, Kurt Lewin, Jean Piaget, and Heinz Werner (Allport, 1968; Cairns, 1983; Hendrick, 1977; Sears, 1975). Whatever their origins, the different types of metatheories, theories, and methodologies found in the two disciplines offer legitimate procedural solutions, especially for researchers working within one discipline near its core. It should be recognized from the outset that little is to be gained by trying to produce a general resolution of such differences, and that the cooperative interaction between researchers from both groups can occur without such a resolution.

It should also be recognized, nonetheless, that such differences of opinion between groups can lead to problems for the researcher who actually works in the boundary area between the two disciplines. For example, Feldman and Ruble (1981) discuss the different approaches social and developmental psychologists take to the phenomena of person perception. Social psychologists usually employ a hypothesis-testing approach, and they focus most frequently on processes underlying person perception, particularly the role that motivation plays in these processes. Dependent measures usually involve relatively precise paper-and-pencil measures, but often little attention is paid to the content of the responses produced. In contrast, developmental psychologists have approached person perception largely from the perspective of cognitive development. More attention is paid to the role of age-related ability differences and the content of responses than to motivational processes. Dependent measures often involve a less constraining but less precise free-description methodology. Given these different approaches, the boundary researcher is faced with some basic decisions. Should the primary focus of a developmental person perception be on hypothesis-testing or on a description of developmental patterns? Should there be any attempt to assess or to manipulate motivational states? How should dependent measures be collected?

We have noted how the boundary researcher should strive for the maintenance of a clear area of specialization, focusing on a single aspect of a contiguous discipline. Further, the boundary researcher should *not* seek complete mastery of all aspects of the contiguous disciplines. It is likely, we think, that boundary area researchers will find themselves concentrating on a general substantive process or phenomenon that is of common interest to two or more contiguous disciplines. For example, the phenomenon of school desegregation is of interest not only to social and developmental psychologists but also to anthropologists and sociologists. To study this phenomenon, or to take advantage of it to study processes of social behavior or behavioral development, or to consider sociological or anthropological questions, it is not necessary for a researcher to master the entire literature on attribution, attachment, or physical anthropology. We would not argue, of course, that parts of the attribution or attachment literature are irrelevant to school desegregation, or more generally that ignorance is better than knowledge. However, a *little* ignorance may help one break free from expected patterns and creatively invoke concepts or moethods that would seem counterindicated by some additional knowledge. In this case, the most interesting initial questions about attribution processes in racially mixed and segregated schools may be those that do not address nitty-gritty issues in attribution theory, but rather adapt more molar questions to the context of interaction among children of different races at different ages, integrating aspects of the attribution literature with that on the development of racial awareness and developmental changes in social reasoning.

A *phenomenon-based* approach to research is much maligned, especially by traditional social psychologists. It is criticized as being excessively inductive and empirical and in contributing to fragmentation of scientific knowledge. An example is provided by Hendrick (1977) in his thoughtful critique of social psychology as an experimental science. Hendrick notes that research on interpersonal attraction has sought to uncover the way a variety of empirical variables (e.g., attitudinal similarity, physical attractiveness, propinquity) bear on attraction, with little or no concern for theory development. Such a phenomenon-based approach can produce long lists of variables that influence a particular phenomenon without illuminating the basic processes underlying the phenomenon itself, or the way the phenomenon is related to other phenomena.

Critics of the phenomenon-based approach to research argue that such an approach forces an excessively narrow focus on specific events that are the result of more general principles. For example, Cairns (1979) notes that many aspects of the phenomenon of attachment in both sheep and human infants are the result of more general principles of contiguity learning. Furthermore, there are some important similarities among such apparently diverse phenomena as attachment, aggression, and depression that might remain unnoticed but for the presence of the overarching learning theory. For another example, Walster, Walster, and Berscheid (1978) note that many aspects of the phenomenon of attraction are the result of more general principles of interpersonal exchange. There are important similarities among such seemingly diverse phenomena as romantic attraction, business partnerships, marital infidelity, and parent–child relations that would not be apparent but for the presence of equity theory.

Critics of the phenomenon-based approach also note that many phenomena are regarded as trivial, or even go unnoticed, until some theoretical system provides an integrating context. Prior to Purkinjie's work in 1825, for example, how many people regarded as significant (or even noticed) the relative changers in color vision from daylight to darkness? Interestingly, it took over 70 years to verify anatomically Purkinjie's theoretical assertion that the retina must consist of at least two different components.

Despite the limitations of the preceding phenomenon-based approach, this approach may be a productive beginning for the researcher working in the boundary area between developmental and social psychology. For domains in which little is scientifically known, premature theorizing may actually inhibit the growth of knowledge. Once some reliable pattern of outcomes can be found, theories become more useful as predictive and summarizing tools. There are recurrent, reliably produced, empirical phenomena or empirical themes common to the two disciplines, and critical comparative evaluation of different approaches to these empirical regularities may contribute a great deal to the advancement of our scientific knowledge about them (Cook & Campbell, 1979; Meehl, 1978; Popper, 1959, 1972).

Another factor we have noted is how the boundary researcher should seek to identify complementary theoretical formulations or methodological approaches from contiguous disciplines. Ideally, the formulations should address similar substantive phenomena or processes, but the theoretical formulations should offer a sufficiently different perspective on a phenomenon or process to generate some conceptual conflict and some innovations in the researcher who uses them. Such an attempt was made by Feldman and Ruble (1981), who identified the complementary theoretical accounts of person perception provided by social and developmental psychologists. There are many other processes and phenomena that could be subjected to this type of analysis. By juxtaposing complementary theoretical accounts, gaps in knowledge and assumptions about phenomena become more apparent, and innovative hypothesis generation is facilitated.

There are, of course, other techniques for generating innovative hypotheses. McGuire (1973) suggested nine different techniques: the intensive case study, accounting for a paradoxical incident, use of analogy, use of the hypothetico-deductive method, the search for the adaptive significance of behavior, analysis of the practitioner's rule of thumb, accounting for conflicting results, accounting for exceptions to a general rule, and reducing complex relationships to simpler component relationships. Some of these have been used extensively by developmental and social psychologists, but they have rarely been employed systematically. In general, we would expect that the use of these techniques would be related to their compatibility with the central concerns of each subdiscipline.

One of the central goals of developmental psychology is the discovery of patterns of behavior change over time, and the technique of the intensive case study is compatible with that goal because it seeks to array events carefully in sequence. The intensive case study has a long history of use by developmentalists (e.g., Piaget's intensive study of his own children's cognitive development), and information so derived has been a rich source of developmental hypotheses. A central goal for social psychologists, on the other hand, is the precise specification of the immediate antecedents of behavior. The intensive case study is less compatible with this central goal than are some other techniques. Several classics of social psychology have used the intensive case study (e.g., Mrs. Keech's Doomsday group, studied by Festinger, Riecken, & Schachter, 1956), but these are notable exceptions. The technique of accounting for conflicting results, however, has been used extensively by social psychologists (e.g., the various attempts to reconcile cognitive dissonance and self-perception studies), and these attempts have been a rich source of hypotheses for social psychology. In general, we argue that the choice of a technique for generating innovative hypotheses should not be prescribed normatively, but should be chosen with an eye to the central concern of the specific research program.

Social and developmental psychology are particularly good candidates for boundary research because they share areas of substance as well as some common conceptual approaches to research issues. Both disciplines encompass strong interest in interpersonal relationships. The classical topic areas in developmental psychology include attachment, peer relations, independence and achievement, and moral development, to name the most obvious (see Masters, 1981). The classic topic areas in social psychology include persuasion and conformity, communication, attraction and affiliation, leadership, altruism, and group dynamics (see Berkowitz, 1980). Both disciplines claim the interpersonal relationships inherent in imitation, aggression, and social cognition (e.g., Hartup, 1978, 1983). Furthermore, both disciplines take a similar approach to relationships. Both devote a great deal of empirical activity and journal space to the issue of the *functional significance* of relationships for individual persons (e.g., Ainsworth, 1979; Duck, 1980, 1982). Both disciplines also stress the embeddedness of any particular behavior within a larger context, and the potential application of basic research findings to the improvement of conditions for the disadvantaged and the handicapped (e.g., Furman, Rahe & Hartup, 1979; Rosenfield & Stephan, 1981; Woody & Costanzo, 1981). Though boundary area research is not an easy undertaking (see the final comments of Patterson, Chapter 3), the boundary between social and developmental psychology seems to be more hospitable than most. Indeed, the chapters that follow confirm both the hospitability and the fruitfulness of research and theory at this important boundary and, by implication and illustration, underscore the importance of fostering boundary area research within psychology at large.

REFERENCES

Ainsworth, M. D. S. Infant–mother attachment. *American Psychologist,* 1979, *34,* 932–937.

Allport, G. W. The historical background of modern social psychology. In G. Lindzey & E. Aronson (Eds.), *The handbook of social psychology* (2nd ed., Vol. 1). Reading, MA: Addison-Wesley, 1968.

Bandura, A., & Walters, R. H. *Social learning and personality development.* New York: Holt, Rinehart & Winston, 1963.

Berkowitz, L. *A survey of social psychology* (2nd ed.). New York: Holt, Rinehart & Winston, 1980.

Boring, E. G.*A history of experimental psychology* (2nd ed.). New York: Appleton, 1950.

Bower, G. H. Mood and memory. *American Psychologist,* 1981, *36,* 129–148.

Bruner, J. S., & Postman, I. On the perception of incongruity: A paradigm. *Journal of Personality,* 1949, *18,* 206–223.

Cairns, R. B. *Social development: The origins and plasticity of interchanges.* San Francisco, CA: Freeman, 1979.

Cairns, R. B. The emergence of developmental psychology. In P. Mussen & E. M. Hetherington (Eds.), *Carmichael's manual of child psychology* (4th ed., Vol. 4). New York: Wiley, 1983.

Campbell, D. T. Ethnocentrism of disciplines and the fish-scale model of omniscience. In C. W. Sherif & M. Sherif (Eds.), *Interdisciplinary relationships in the social sciences.* Chicago: Aldine, 1969.

Chomsky, N. *Syntactic Structures.* The Hague: Mouton, 1957.

Cook, T. D., & Campbell, D. T. *Quasi-experimentation: Design and analysis issues for field settings.* Chicago: Rand McNally, 1979.

Cronbach, L. J. The two disciplines of scientific psychology. *American Psychologist,* 1957, *12,* 671–684.

Dollard, J., & Miller, N. *Personality and psychotherapy.* New York: McGraw-Hill, 1950.

Duck, S. W. Taking the past to heart: One of the futures of social psychology? In R. Gilmour & S. W. Duck (Eds.), *The development of social psychology.* London: Academic, 1980.

Duck, S. W. *Personal relationships* (Vol. 4): *Dissolving personal relationships.* London: Academic, 1982.

Feldman, N. S., & Ruble, D. N. The development of person perception: Cognitive and social factors. In S. S. Brehm, S. M. Kassin, & F. X. Gibbons (Eds.), *Developmental social psychology.* Oxford: Oxford University Press, 1981.

Festinger, L., Riecken, H. W., & Schachter, S. *When prophecy fails.* Minneapolis: University of Minnesota Press, 1956.

Furman, W., Rahe, D. F., & Hartup, W. W. Rehabilitation of socially withdrawn preschool children through mixed-age and same-age socialization. *Child Development,* 1979, *50,* 915–922.

Hartup, W. W. Children and their friends. In H. McGurk (Ed.), *Child social development.* London: Metheun, 1978.

Hartup, W. W. The peer system. In P. H. Mussen and E. M. Hetherington (Eds.), *Carmichael's manual of child psychology* (4th ed., Vol. 4). New York: Wiley, 1983.

Hendrick, C. Social psychology as an experimental science. In C. Hendrick (Ed.), *Perspectives on social psychology.* Hillsdale, NJ: Erlbaum, 1977.

Holleran, P. A., Littman, D. C., Freund, R. D., & Schmaling, K. B. A signal detection approach to social perception: Identification of negative and positive behaviors by parents of normal and problem children. *Journal of Abnormal Child Psychology,* 1982, *10,* 547–558.

Kendall, M. G. On the reconciliation of theories of probability. *Biometrika,* 1949, *36,* 101–116.

Kenrick, D. J., & Dantchik, A. Interactionism, idiographics, and the social psychological invasion of personality. *Journal of Personality,* in press.

Masters, J. C. Developmental psychology. In M. R. Rosenzweig & L. W. Porter (Eds.), *Annual review of psychology* (Vol. 32). Palo Alto, CA: Annual Reviews, 1981.

Masters, J. C. Ecumenism in psychology or "lessons my grammar taught me": A commentary on Walton and Sedlak. *Merrill Palmer Quarterly,* 1982, *3,* 541–544.

Masters, J. C., Barden, R. C., & Ford, M. E. Affective states, expressive behavior, and learning in children. *Journal of Personality and Social Psychology,* 1979, *37,* 380–390.

McGuire, W. J. The yin and yang of progress in social psychology: Seven koans. *Journal of Personality and Social Psychology,* 1973, *26,* 446–456.

Meehl, P. E. Theoretical risks and tabular asterisks: Sir Karl, Sir Ronald, and the slow progress of soft psychology. *Journal of Consulting and Clinical Psychology,* 1978, *46,* 806–834.

Mischel, W. Toward a cognitive social learning reconceptualization of personality. *Psychological Review,* 1973, *80,* 252–283.

Overton, W. F., & Reese, H. W. Models of development: Methodological implications. In J. R. Nesselroade & H. W. Reese (Eds.), *Life-span developmental psychology: Methodological issues.* New York: Academic, 1973.

Popper, K. R., *The logic of scientific discovery.* New York: Basic Books, 1959.

Popper, K. R. *Objective knowledge*. Oxford: Oxford University Press, 1972.

Rosenfield, D., & Stephan, W. Inter-group relations among children. In S. S. Brehm, S. M. Kassin, & F. X. Gibbons (Eds.), *Developmental social psychology*. Oxford: Oxford University Press, 1981.

Sears, R. R. Your ancients revisited: A history of child development. In E. M. Hetherington (Ed.), *Review of child development research* (Vol. 5). Chicago: University of Chicago Press, 1975.

Walster, E., Walster, G. W., & Berscheid, E. *Equity: Theory and research*. Boston: Allyn & Bacon, 1978.

Walton, M. D., & Sedlak, A. J. Making amends: A grammar-based analysis of children's social interaction. *Merrill Palmer Quarterly*, 1982, *3*, 389–412.

Woody, E. Z., & Costanzo, P. R. The socialization of obesity-prone behavior. In S. S. Brehm, S. M. Kassin, & F. X. Gibbons (Eds.), *Developmental social psychology*. Oxford: Oxford University Press, 1981.

2

Some Observations on the Study of Personal Relationships*

WYNDOL FURMAN

EDITORS' INTRODUCTION

In the present chapter, Furman presents four propositions regarding the proper study of both the nature and the development of social relationships. The propositions are developed citing research in both social and developmental psychology and illustrated with data from his own research. For example, it is proposed that one needs to incorporate the perspectives of both outsiders to and participants in a relationship, to examine multiple facets of the relationship, and to employ a variety of methodological tools (e.g., interviews, questionnaires, observation). The importance of longitudinal data is stressed for describing the developmental course of a social relationship, and an example is presented with respect to the development of children's friendships. Furman points out how this kind of multifaceted research is important in studying relationships because it allows the identification of the sequences of development and of the transitional stages of a relationship (see Duck, 1982) and also enables the investigator to examine such factors as the interdependence and basic structural properties of personal relationships (Kelley, 1979). Overall, the consistent theme both in the theoretical and methodological arguments and in the data that Furman presents is that personal relationships

*Portions of this research were supported by grants from the National Science Foundation (BSN-3014668), National Institute of Child Health and Human Development (1RO1HD16142-01), and the Biomedical Research Grant Fund (BRS-S07RR07138). Appreciation is expressed to Thomas Berndt and William Graziano for their comments on an earlier draft.

simply cannot be understood fully unless one adopts a perspective that is both developmental and social, conceptually as well as methodologically.

INTRODUCTION

If asked what is important in their social life, most people would probably describe a close relationship with another person, such as a spouse, friend, parent, or sibling. In fact, the question is rather trivial. It seems obvious that such personal relationships are the core of social life for both children and adults.

Yet, much of the literature in social and developmental psychology has not been concerned with these close relationships. For example, the early work in social psychology was composed principally of studies of interactions between strangers. Similarly, in the developmental field the study of children's social behavior has had a long history, but relatively little attention has been paid to children's personal relationships except with parents. Research on social development has centered instead on different types of social behavior such as aggression, play, or prosocial acts.

Although valuable, characterizations of the *general patterns* of social behavior cannot do justice to the complexity of interpersonal interaction. It is necessary to describe such patterns of behavior within the context of the *specific relationship* in which they occur. That is, we not only need to be concerned with the child's general tendency to behave in a prosocial manner, but we also need to consider the child's prosocial behavior in his or her interactions with mother, father, a close friend, a sibling, or some other significant person.

Since the early 1970s, research on personal relationships has grown significantly. Research with adults has become more concerned with long-lasting relationships, particularly romantic ones (Berscheid & Walster, 1978; Burgess & Huston, 1979; Duck, 1982; Duck & Gilmour, 1981a, 1981b, 1981c). Studies of infants' social behavior now focus principally on their attachments to specific others (Ainsworth, Blehar, Waters, & Wall, 1978). In the domain of peer relations, investigators have come to recognize that peers are not a homogeneous group of social objects. Consequently, research has begun to be concerned with specific relationships such as friendships (Asher & Gottman, 1981; Foot, Chapman, & Smith, 1979; Furman, 1982).

As a result of this trend, social and developmental psychologists have found a common interest: personal relationships. Unfortunately, the two fields have remained relatively separate. Few investigators are familiar with the body of literature in the other field or keep up with progress in that area.

Consequently, the data bases, methodological approaches, and conceptual frameworks are not well integrated. The purpose of the current chapter is to promote such an integration by discussing some general considerations for conducting research on personal relationships.

Four propositions are put forth:

1. If one is to understand a personal relationship, one must examine multiple facets of that relationship.
2. One needs to incorporate the perspectives of both outsiders and the participants themselves. Each perspective should be examined with a variety of methodological tools.
3. Relationships are in a constant process of change or development. Hypothesized temporal changes should be incorporated in theories of relationships.
4. The fundamental unit of interest should be the relationship.

The present chapter points out how each of these propositions are applicable to both developmental and social psychological research. The chapter also includes a discussion of how the insights of social psychologists can be useful in developmental studies of relationships. Conversely, it indicates how a developmental perspective can be valuable in understanding social psychological processes in relationships.

MULTIPLE FACETS OF RELATIONSHIPS

Proposition 1. *If one is to understand a personal relationship, one must examine multiple facets of that relationship.*

Almost all personal relationships serve multiple functions. Consequently, any relationship is likely to be characterized by different patterns of behavior in different contexts. Research on a single facet or function can provide valuable information about that aspect of the relationship, but it cannot capture adequately the complexities or multifunctional nature of the general relationship.

Much of the initial research on relationships was composed of univariate studies. For example, early research and theory on adult relationships concentrated primarily on a few variables, such as similarity (Byrne, 1971). self-disclosure (Goodstein & Reinicker, 1974), or rewards and costs in interpersonal interactions (Homans, 1961; Thibaut & Kelly, 1959). Similarly, research on parent–infant interactions has focused principally on the security of the attachment bond (Ainsworth *et al.*, 1978), whereas research on interactions between parents and older children has been concerned mainly with disciplinary style (Baumrind, 1971, 1973). Research on peer relations has not been as focused, but most studies have examined only one facet of the relationship at a time (Furman, 1982; Hartup, in press).

Certainly good rationales exist for examining only a limited number of variables at a time. Not only are such projects more feasible, but also they are often appropriate for addressing the questions of interest. During the 1960s and 1970s most investigators were interested in testing specific predictions derived from some minitheory of interpersonal attraction; consequently, it was appropriate to conduct a univariate study using a familiar experimental paradigm. Since this time, several investigators have called for multivariate research that provides a more complete description of the phenomena of interest (Altman, 1974; Hinde, 1979). In fact it appears that the field is changing from being theory-centered to being phenomena-centered (Markman, Alvarado, Buhrmester, Furman, Reis, Shaver, & Sorell, 1982). That is, investigators are becoming less concerned with finding or creating phenomena that are consistent with a theory, instead, they are more concerned with being true to the phenomena that actually occur in relationships. Multifaceted research is consistent with this trend because it can provide more comprehensive pictures of the characteristics of personal relationships.

It is important to note that *multifaceted* (as opposed to multivariate) research involves more than just the inclusion of several independent or dependent variables. It involves studying a relationship in many contexts or examining the multiple functions a relationship may serve. For example, some studies of parent–child relationships incorporated more than one variable—such as the strictness, consistency, and warmth of disciplinary efforts—but the selected variables typically reflected only one facet of the relationship: disciplinary interchanges. A multifaceted study would not only examine these aspects of discipliary encounters but would also examine the relationship in other contexts, such as when help or advice is needed or when the two are engaged in leisure activities. Unfortunately, our knowledge of parent–child and most other relationships is limited principally to a few facets of each. Moreover, studies of different types of relationships have tended to focus on different facets, making it difficult to obtain an integrated picture of children's or adults' social networks.

The importance of a multifaceted approach is illustrated in several of our recent projects. In one, we conducted unstructured interviews with late-elementary-school-aged children about their sibling relationships (Furman, Buhrmester, & Ritz, 1982). The children's descriptions were rich, commonly including a diversity of characteristics such as affection, caretaking, and quarreling. Table 2.1 presents a list of the facets commonly mentioned by the children. Each of these characteristics except competition was men-

TABLE 2.1

Factor Pattern Coefficients of *Sibling Relationship Questionnaire* Scales[a]

	Factors			
Features	Warmth/closeness	Relative status/power	Conflict	Rivalry
Intimacy	70			
Prosocial behavior	83			
Companionship	78			
Similarity	70			
Nurturance by sibling	28	−77		
Nurturance of sibling	26	85		
Admiration by sibling	67	25	−29	
Admiration of sibling	69	−28		
Affection	69		−36	
Dominance by sibling		−65	55	
Dominance over sibling		80	41	
Quarreling			88	
Antagonism			92	
Competition			63	36
Parental partiality				96

[a]Scores are factor loadings on a principal components analysis with a general promax rotation. Factor loadings below .25 are not presented. Factors are minimally correlated (−.20 > r < .20)—except Conflict and Rivalry (r = .35).

tioned by at least 20% of the children, and most were mentioned by the majority. Apparently, even children recognize the multifaceted nature of their relationships.

Next, a self-report questionnaire assessing these 15 qualitative features was developed and administered to 198 fifth- and sixth-grade children. A principal components analysis revealed four underlying factors: (1) Warmth/Closeness (2) Relative Status/Power, (3) Conflict, and (4) Rivalry (see Table 2.1). The four factors correlated minimally with one another excepting Conflict and Rivalry (r = .35). The first two factors seem similar to the affection and status dimensions that have emerged in previous studies of social interaction (Wiggens, 1979). Interestingly, the third factor of Conflict seems relatively independent of the degree of Warmth/Closeness. Apparently some siblings both quarrel frequently with and feel close to one another. The fourth factor, Rivalry, is also relatively independent of Warmth/Closeness and of Relative Status/Power, although Adlerian conceptions of sibling relationships have stressed the centrality of competing for parental attention (Adler, 1924). Clearly no single motivational factor can account for the multifaceted nature of these relationships.

Subsequent analyses revealed that sibling constellation variables, such as birth order, age spacing, or gender, were *not* strongly related to any of the four factors except Relative Status/Power; not surprisingly, older children were accorded higher status and power. Thus, these findings illustrate the multifaceted nature of sibling relationships and suggest that the characteristics of these relationships are determined by factors other than static constellation variables.

Children also differentiate among different types of relationships. In another project, children of late elementary school age were asked to characterize their relationships with each family member, their closest grandparent, closest friend, and teacher (Furman & Buhrmester, 1982). Based on Weiss's (1974) theory, six relational provisions were examined: (1) reliable alliance (permanence of the relationship), (2) affection, (3) reassurance of worth, (4) instrumental help, (5) companionship, and (6) intimate disclosure. Additionally, children rated the degree of conflict, relative dominance over the person, overall importance of the relationship, and overall satisfaction with the relationship.

As can be seen in Table 2.2, each of the relationships was differentiated from the others. Over 80% of the comparisons of scores in pairs of relationships were significant (Tukey's test, p's < .05). In general, relationships with mother were described in the most positive terms. She either received the highest ratings on each of the six relational characteristics or shared the highest ratings with another relationship. More conflict, however, occurred with mother than with friends or teachers. Relationships with father were also rated positively, although the ratings of companionship and intimate disclosure were lower than those with mother. It is interesting to note that these are the two facets in which the mother–child and closest friendship ratings did not differ. Relationships with grandparents received relatively high ratings on affectively based facets, such as affection, alliance, and reassurances, but much lower ratings on facets involving regular contact, such as instrumental help, companionship, and intimate disclosure.

A mixed picture of sibling relationships is presented. Like other family members, siblings were thought to have reliable or permanent relationships with the subjects, but feelings of affection were lower. In fact, unlike the parent–child relationships, the feelings of affection tended to be less strong for siblings than for closest friends. Similarly, children turned less often to siblings than to friends for reassurance of worth or for the disclosure of intimate feelings. Conflict was particularly high in sibling relationships. The relative age of siblings also affected ratings. Not surprisingly, older siblings were perceived as being more dominant and more frequent sources of help than younger ones; there was also a tendency for older siblings to be less frequent companions.

TABLE 2.2

Children's Perceptions of the Characteristics of Their Social Relationships[a]

	Reliable alliance	Affection	Reassurance of worth	Instrumental help	Companionship	Intimacy	Dominance	Conflict	Importance	Satisfaction
Mother	4.43	4.54	4.01	3.77	3.34	3.22	1.69	1.94	4.70	4.22
Father	4.38	4.49	3.95	3.87	3.06	2.79	1.59	1.89	4.62	4.09
Grandparent	4.12	4.27	3.73	2.82	2.17	2.17	2.19	1.24	4.33	3.84
Older brother	3.94	3.49	3.11	3.21	3.05	2.38	2.14	2.83	4.11	3.60
Younger brother	4.08	3.43	2.97	2.07	3.22	2.29	3.84	3.09	4.21	3.42
Older sister	4.00	3.67	3.14	2.87	3.03	2.73	2.34	2.63	4.06	3.57
Younger sister	4.02	3.51	2.92	1.81	3.23	2.26	3.89	2.89	4.17	3.45
Closest friend	3.67	3.32	3.47	2.99	3.28	3.39	2.97	1.77	4.03	3.93
Teacher	2.54	2.70	2.72	3.15	1.49	1.44	1.51	1.66	2.89	2.78

[a]Scores can range from 1 to 5 with higher scores indicating more characteristics. As a rough guide, differences in relationship ratings of .22 or more are usually significant (Tukey's test, $p < .05$).

Closest friendships were also described positively but in a different manner than parent–child relationships. That is, the ratings of affection, alliance, and reassurance of worth were lower for friendships than were comparable ratings in parent–child relationships, but the ratings of disclosure and companionship were higher than those in father–child relationships and comparable to those in mother–child relationships. Additionally the children reported less conflict with friends than with mothers and perceived their friendships to be more egalitarian than relationships with their parents. These data support the common contention that friendships and parent–child relationships serve different functions for children.

Finally, children did not perceive their relationships with teachers to be characterized by affective features such as affection. They did, however, perceive teachers to be a frequent source of instrumental help—more frequent, in fact, than most siblings.

The marked differentiation of relationships was also evidenced in the relative ratings of features within a relationship. For example, the facets of companionship and intimacy between parents and children were rated much lower than most other facets of these relationships, but in friendships, these facets received ratings comparable to the other characteristics. Similarly, the ratings of affection and alliance are comparable in parent–child relationships, but in sibling relationships affection ratings were substantially lower than ratings of alliance.

In summary, these findings illustrate that children do differentiate among their relationships in terms of a number of different facets. Moreover, the areas of differentiation differ for various pairs of relationships. These differentiations appear to be based on a number of underlying factors, such as the relative age of the person, whether the relationship is a voluntary one or a kinship relationship, and the degree of daily contact.

In any multifaceted research, investigators must decide how many and which facets to examine. On the one hand, if only a few facets are examined, important ones can be missed and a misleading picture can result from combining facets that are actually distinct. On the other hand, the inclusion of many different facets leads to obvious pragmatic problems in conducting the research and interpretive problems in making sense of a complex pattern of results.

One promising solution is a multitiered approach in which both a series of molecular facets and a few broad dimensions underlying these facets are examined. This is the approach we used in studying the characteristics of sibling relationships.

The most important guideline, however, for either differentiating or combining variables is theory. Although the importance of theory seems obvious, it is not always evident in developmental research on children's relationships. In particular the selection of categories in observational studies often is based not on theory but on simple intuition. The fact that one can develop distinct operational definitions for two categories does not, however, reduce the necessity for providing construct validity for the distinction (Furman & Drabman, 1981). Clearly the current emphasis on providing careful descriptions of the multiple facets of relationships should not be translated erroneously into adherence to blind empiricism (Markman *et al.,* 1982).

Once the investigator has selected the variables and collected the data, several analytical techniques exist for demonstrating that the combination or differentiation of two potential facets of a relationship is warranted. The technique used most commonly is factor analysis. Factor-analytic studies have tried to identify orthogonal factors. Although there are some distinct statistical advantages to orthogonal factor scores, it may be erroneous to assume that the common factors underlying a set of variables are independent unless the theory specifies that they should be. We suspect that many positive facets of relationships may be distinct factors but positively related.

Factor analyses are also not the only way to provide evidence that two facets are distinct. Although two facets may load on the same factor, they may differ in terms of relative mean level in different relationships. For example, in our factor analyses of facets of sibling relationships and friendships, we found that companionship and intimacy load on the same factor of Warmth/Closeness. Yet we believe that the distinction between companionship and intimacy should be retained because the pattern of mean scores differs in different relationships. Ratings of intimacy are much lower than ratings of companionship in sibling relationships, whereas ratings of the two are comparable in friendships. Analytical tools, such as Gollob's (1968) Factor Analysis of Variance (FANOVA), may prove to be valuable means of examining this kind of differentiation.

Clearly the problems involved in identifying and studying different facets are complex and cannot be solved with certainty. Yet it is important that we try to examine multiple facets of a relationship. Such research will help us to develop the rich descriptive base necessary for understanding relationships. Similarly, multifaceted research is needed to determine how a specific type of relationship is different from others; the differentiation occurs on different facets for different pairs of relationships. Theories of personal relationships need to recognize the multifaceted nature of relationships. Any theory that only addresses one facet of a relationship will prove to be too simplistic.

MULTIPLE PERSPECTIVES

Proposition 2. *One needs to incorporate the perspectives of both outsiders and the participants themselves. Each perspective should be examined with a variety of methodological tools.*

TABLE 2.3

Four Types of Research Methods[a]

Reporter's frame of reference	Type of data	
	Subjective	Objective
Insider	Self-report methods	Behavioral self-report methods
Outsider	Observer subjective reports	Behavioral methods

[a]Taken from Olson, 1977, by permission of University of Massachusetts Press, copyri§ 1977. All rights of reproduction reserved.

In a classic paper, Olson (1977) differentiated between the perspectives an insider and of an outsider. An *insider* was considered a participant member of the relationship being studied, whereas an *outsider* was someo not involved in the relationship. Typically outsiders are social scientis Olson also drew a distinction between subjective and objective data. *Subje tive data* referred to rating scales, whereas *objective data* referred to beha ioral observation procedures. The combination of these two differentiatio yields the four cells depicted in Table 2.3. Most methods of data collectio can be incorporated into this table. For example, most self-report instr ments would be classified as subjective insider measures. A similar rati scale completed by a social scientist or other nonparticipant would be co sidered a subjective outsider measure. A typical behavioral observatior procedure would fall into the objective outsider category, whereas su observations conducted by a member of the relationship would constitu an objective insider measure.

Few studies of relationships have incorporated more than one form data collection. The two used most commonly are subjective insider me sures (e.g., self-report questionnaires) and objective outsider measures (e.; behavioral observations). The use of objective insider measures or subjecti outsider measures has been uncommon, although the development of se monitoring procedures by behavioral psychologists has increased the use the former (Ciminero, Nelson, & Lipinski, 1977).

Olson (1977) observed that the selection of an approach seems to depei on one's professional discipline. Family sociologists have relied principal on subjective insider reports, whereas social psychologists have depend on observations or other forms of objective outsider data. In the develo mental field, the selection seems to depend on the age of the child. Typicall observational procedures are used in research regarding infants and your children, but self-report procedures continue to be the measures prevalent used with older children and adolescents.

Three major arguments can be made for the inclusion of multiple perspectives. First, such efforts would foster the integration of research in different disciplines. Second, hypotheses would receive strong convergent validation if similar results were obtained with different approaches. Third, the various methodological approaches and perspectives are fundamentally different; each type can provide unique information about the relationship.

We believe the third argument is stronger than the second, because convergent validation is uncommon. For example, Olson (1977) reviewed the literature on power techniques by family members and found that two measures from the same cell (e.g., two self-report measures) usually corresponded but measures from different cells commonly yielded discrepant results. Sometimes these discrepancies may reflect undesirable method variance, but we believe they often reflect meaningful differences in the approaches.

Consider the distinction between insider and outsider data. Meaningful differences between insiders' and outsiders' interpretations of behavior can exist for several reasons, including the information each has and the kinds of comparisons they make in their judgments. As a result of interacting repeatedly with the person, insiders would know much more about the person than would outsiders. Behaviors can develop some idiosyncratic meaning in the course of an ongoing relationship. For example, a seemingly innocuous nickname, such as "Toots," could become either a sign of affection or a derisive comment. An insider would be aware of the private meaning of a behavior, but an outsider can rely only on the culturally shared set of symbols and meanings for interpreting an act. Differences in the amount of knowledge and awareness of idiosyncratic meanings may lead to differences in the interpretations of behaviors by insiders and outsiders. It may appear that the judgments of insiders are preferable because they are based on greater knowledge of the person. The insider's involvement with that person may lead, however, to some biases in judgment. Certainly all of us are less likely than outsiders to see flaws in ourselves or in those whom we love.

Insider–outsider differences may also occur because the reference points for comparisons can be different. Outsiders may interpret a behavioral event by comparing it with their observations of other people in similar situations. On the other hand, the insider may determine the meaning of that event by comparing it with his or her experiences with that person in other situations or at other points in time. In other words, the outsider is usually limited to comparisons *across* different relationships, whereas the insider may make comparisons *within* that relationship as well as across relationships. Each form of comparison seems valuable.

It should also be recognized that one can differentiate not only between the perspectives of insiders and outsiders but between the perspectives of different insiders. All relationships have at least two insiders, and their views are likely to differ. For example, Gottman, Notarius, Markman, Bank, Yoppi, and Rubin (1976) asked distressed and nondistressed couples to engage in a simulated conversation using a communication box. In this task, one member made a statement and then rated the *intended* valence of the comment. Then the partner rated the valence of the statement's *impact*. Distressed and nondistressed couples did not differ in intended valence, but they did differ in the valence of the impact of the comments. Gottman *et al.*'s approach resulted in a picture of the distressed couples' communication difficulties that is more precise than could have been obtained by asking for either the senders' or receivers' perceptions alone.

The inclusion of both subjective and objective data can also provide a more comprehensive picture of a relationship. Olson's selection of terms may seem to suggest that subjective measures are inferior to objective data, but Olson did not mean to imply this. In effect, subjective measures involve a greater degree of inference or interpretation by the raters. At times the inferences and interpretations may be either necessary or desirable.

Consider the factors that affect the degree of subjectivity or inference in a measure. First, variables that principally have covert markers are more subjective than those with clear behavioral markers. For example, the concept of affection seems to refer to individuals' underlying feelings; therefore, it seems almost necessary that affection be measured subjectively. Perhaps one could try to measure affection objectively by observing the number of physical gestures such as kisses or hugs. These overt markers, however, seem to be less valid indexes of a person's feelings than a report of their underlying feelings. Perhaps the ideal solution is to collect both forms of measurement and see how such subjective perceptions are manifested objectively.

The degree of subjectivity of a measure is also affected by the size of the unit of rating. Measures that group behavior into molecular units are likely to be more objective than those that group behavior into global units. For example, judgments of the amount of social interaction in the last minute are likely to be more objective than judgments of the amount of interaction in the last week. The difference in unit size is one of the major reasons that observational measures are considered more objective than questionnaires or clinical judgments. Typically observational measures are based on molecular units, whereas questionnaires are based on global units. Questionnaires could be based on molecular units or observational procedures on global ones, but we know of very few such instances.

Global and molecular measures tend to index different properties of the interaction (Cairns & Green, 1979). Global rating procedures are designed to measure the stable qualities of an interaction. In contrast, molecular measures, such as observational procedures, assess both stable and unstable characteristics because they are more sensitive to and more influenced by contextual or situational factors. Sequential patterns of interaction can also be assessed more readily by molecular approaches. Thus the purposes of global and molecular measures are different.

It may appear that molecular measures are preferable because one can derive global scores from them by summing the molecular units. For example, one could add up the number of instances of requests or commands to derive a measure of general dominance. In contrast, it is not possible to derive molecular from molar units.

The argument that molecular units are preferable is not compelling, however. First, the greater costs of collecting molecular types of data—particularly observational data—are well known. Second, the sensitivity of molecular measures to unstable characteristics is both an advantage and a disadvantage. When using a molecular measure, an experimenter may need longer periods of observation to ensure that the scores are reliable estimates of *stable* rather than unstable characteristics (Moskowitz & Schwartz, 1982).

Third, the summation of molecular observations into a composite score is based on the assumption that a global measure should be a simple linear composite. Perhaps, however, some instances of behavior are more important than others. For example, a command may be a stronger index of dominance than a simple request. One could include separate categories for commands and requests, but pragmatic considerations restrict the number of categories that can be included. It would be difficult to include categories for very low base-rate behaviors, but such behaviors may be particularly strong indexes of the presence of some characteristic. That is, one may be more likely to infer that a person is dominant if he or she yells a command than if he or she makes a simple, polite request.

Additionally, the timing of commands may influence perceptions of a characteristic. For example, a series of commands early in an interaction may be thought more indicative of dominance than an equal number interspersed throughout a session. Of course, one could argue that such differential weighting of instances reflects judgmental biases that should be eliminated. On the other hand, one could argue that these biases should not be discarded because one is interested in how a person's behavior is interpreted—not how it really is; that is, the interpretation, biased or not, will affect how the observer responds. In essence, the issue here involves the classic debate between phenomenological and behavioral approaches (Wann, 1964)—a topic far beyond the scope of this chapter. Empirically speaking, the decision to aggregate does not have major implications. Simple linear models are remarkably strong predictors of judgmental processes

(Dawes, 1979; Wiggens, 1973). As was the case for insider and outsider data, when possible, the inclusion of both molar and molecular measures is preferable because the strengths of each can be exploited.

Multiple forms of data were incorporated in one of our projects on the process of acquaintanceship in children (Furman & Willems, 1982). Dyads of unacquainted or acquainted third-grade children interacted in a laboratory playroom for 25 minutes. During this period, the children's interactions were videotaped through a two-way mirror. Two different sets of measures were derived from the videotapes. Objective outsider measures were developed by coding the children's play and conversations using standard behavioral observational schemes. Subjective outsider measures were developed by having two naive judges, observe the tapes and rate such facets of the encounter as the overall amount of mutual play or self-disclosure.

Additionally, the children were taken to separate rooms after the session and asked to describe the experience. In particular, they were asked to rate the same facets of the encounter rated by the naive judges. Thus these data would be considered subjective insider measures.

The pattern of correlations among the three types of measures is presented in Table 2.4. First, consider the correlations for the combined conditions. On both variables, the correlations between the global outsider and molecular outsider measures were relatively high (mutual play, $r = .60$; self-disclosure, $r = .62$). The size of these correlations is particularly noteworthy in light of the fact that the judges were naive, untrained observers. If the judges had received instructions or training in rating procedures, higher correla-

TABLE 2.4

Intercorrelations of Different Measures of Acquaintanceship[a]

	Subjective outsider–objective outsider	Subjective insider–subjective outsider	Subjective insider–objective outsider
Combined conditions			
Self-disclosure	.62**	.42**	.37*
Mutual play	.60**	.39*	.41*
Unacquainted condition			
Self-disclosure	.69**	.69**	.52*
Mutual play	.63**	.45*	.56**
Acquainted condition			
Self-disclosure	.50*	.10	.16
Mutual play	.37	.37	.25

[a]Subjective outsider refers to observers' global ratings of interactions. Objective outsider refers to observers' molecular ratings of interactions. Subjective insider refers to children's perceptions of their own interactions.

*$p < .05$. **$p < .01$.

tions might be expected. These findings suggest that at least in some situations, subjective outsider measures may serve as inexpensive substitutes for objective outsider measures. Correlations between the subjective insider and subjective outsider measures were also significant but lower (mean $r = .40$). Interestingly, the subjective insider measures correlated equally with the objective and subjective outsider measures. This pattern suggests that the reason objective outsider and subjective measures tend not to be highly correlated is because of the difference in the perspectives of insiders and outsiders, rather than the difference in the amount of interpretation involved.

An interesting picture emerges when the correlations among measures are examined separately for the two conditions. In three of the four instances, the correlations with the subjective insider measures are greater in the unacquainted condition than in the acquainted condition. This differential pattern of correlations can be understood in terms of the kinds of comparisons the children may have made. In the unacquainted condition, the children have no other experience with that person and thus probably compared their mutuality of play or degree of self-disclosure to that in their interactions with other children. This comparison is similar to the one underlying the observational data, and thus high correlation can be expected. On the other hand, children in the acquaintance condition also may have compared the present interaction with previous ones with that child. Such a within-relationship comparison is different from the cross-relationship comparison underlying the observational data; thus the correlation should be lower. While this interpretation is inferential, the inclusion of multiple perspectives does seem to enrich our understanding of the perceptions and interactions that occur in relationships.

THE DEVELOPMENT OF RELATIONSHIPS

Proposition 3. *Relationships are in a constant process of change or development. Hypothesized temporal changes should be incorporated into theories of relationships.*

All relationships have a history. Often, in fact, this history spans years of interaction, as in the case of parent-child relationships, marriages, or long-lasting friendships. During their course of development, relationships are likely to undergo a series of changes. Consequently, the study of relationships must include not only a description of the current patterns of interaction but research on how the relationship has developed or changed over time. The previous history is interesting in itself and is likely to be an important determinant of the current state of the relationship. Research is also needed on participants' expectations regarding the nature of future interactions, because these expectations will affect both current interchanges and subsequent development of the relationship (Berscheid, Graziano, Monson, & Dermer, 1976; Danheiser & Graziano, 1982; Darley & Berscheid, 1967; Monson, Keel, Stephens, & Genung, 1982).

Only a limited amount of work has examined the different stages of relationships. Huston and Levinger (1978) observed that 90% of the social psychological studies conducted in the mid-1970s focused on initial attraction. Research on children's relationships with peers or parents has been similarly limited. For example, research on age differences in the nature of friendship has been conducted (Furman, 1982; Hartup, in press), but little is known about the temporal course of a friendship at any specific age. Fortunately, the situation is changing. Volumes by Burgess and Huston (1979) and Duck and Gilmour (1981b, 1981c) describe ongoing work on the development and deterioration of adults' relationships. Similarly, such investigators as Gottman and Parkhurst (1979), Oden and colleagues (this volume), and Furman and Willems (1982) have begun the task of describing the process of acquaintanceship and friendship formation. Despite these new developments, however, most of the research is still being done on early stages of relationship development. Only in the case of marriages do we seem to know much about the deterioration and termination of relationships.

One way to study relationship development is to compare different levels of relationships. For example, one could compare the pattern of interaction of friends and acquaintances or that of premarital couples and married couples. Such comparisons yield information about the different types of relationships and have important implications for theories of relationship development. For example, because all friends were once acquaintances, comparisons between friends and acquaintances can provide information about how the relationship changes as a friendship develops.

Alternatively, longitudinal studies can be particularly useful for studying temporal changes. In particular, such studies can assess directly the dynamic processes involved in the development of relationships. Cross-sectional comparisons of various relationships can indicate differences in phases of relationships, but they do not reveal what *effect* a variable has on the development of a relationship. Often the differences observed in cross-sectional comparisons can be secondary in importance—in fact, they can even present a misleading picture of the processes involved. For example, acquainted children are more critical of each other than are unacquainted children (Furman & Willems, 1982). It seems unlikely, however, that criticism promotes the development of friendly relationships. Instead, the difference may reflect an increase in the acceptability of expressing feelings in the relationship. Neither explanation can be evaluated, however, by cross-sectional data. The dynamic processes involved in relationship development can be delineated only by manipulating a variable experimentally or examining the pattern of relationships across time.

Longitudinal studies can also be valuable for identifying the sequence of events in the emergence of relationships. Different facets of a relationship are not likely to emerge simultaneously. Instead, the various processes and patterns of behavior associated with an intimate relationship occur at different times. Similarly, some patterns of behavior may characterize a relationships for only a short period. Although costly and pragmatically difficult, longitudinal studies are essential if we are to identify these sequences of development and transitional stages.

Finally, cross-sectional comparisons of different relationships are limited by a problem analogous to the general problem of cohort effects in cross-sectional studies of development. Differences between types of relationships may reflect either the level of the relationship or differences in the characteristics of the participants involved in the relationships. Not everyone will have a spouse, be a parent, or even have an intimate friendship. Thus observed differences between the interaction of friends and strangers could be a function of the relationship, but it could also reflect differences between the characteristics of people who are or are not likely to develop friends. Although one could try to equate the characteristics of people involved in different relationships, such an approach would result in the general problems of matching ex post facto groups (see Furman & Childs, 1981; Meehl, 1970, 1971).

Several points concerning the merits of studying relationship development are illustrated in a study on the emergence of children's friendships during a week-long summer camp (Furman & Childs, 1981). The camp environment provided an ideal setting for a longitudinal study of relationships. Most children were unacquainted at the beginning and interacted intensely during camp. Consequently, it could be anticipated that numerous dyads would progress through many of the early stages of acquaintanceship in a relatively brief time.

In this study, 139 preadolescent and adolescent children were asked to characterize their relationship with each of their cabinmates on the second, fifth, and seventh days of camp. Since each child had an average of nine cabinmates, we were able to obtain longitudinal data on the development of approximately 1250 relationships. On each of the three days of data collection, the children were asked to describe six facets of each relationship using a series of 7-point Likert items: (1) prosocial support, (2) intimacy, (3) companionship, (4) similarity, (5) affection, and, (6) quarreling. The first five were selected on the basis of previous research indicating that they were

TABLE 2.5

Ratings of Relationships as a Function of Time, Level of Acquaintanceship, and Level of Friendship at End of Camp[a]

Facet	Friendship level	Previously unacquainted			Previously acquainted		
		Day 2	Day 5	Day 7	Day 2	Day 5	Day 7
Prosocial support	Low	2.98	2.79	2.84	3.20	2.67	3.33
	Medium	3.66	4.07	4.15	4.59	4.67	4.63
	High	4.39	5.08	5.39	5.62	5.62	5.65
Companionship	Low	2.61	2.67	2.64	3.46	2.88	3.24
	Medium	3.57	4.10	4.07	4.62	4.84	4.66
	High	4.47	5.32	5.31	5.82	5.87	5.77
Intimacy	Low	2.70	2.57	2.63	3.22	2.43	2.86
	Medium	3.34	3.77	3.84	4.36	4.42	4.43
	High	4.23	5.01	4.92	5.29	5.40	5.28
Similarity	Low	2.79	2.58	2.67	3.40	2.54	2.79
	Medium	3.42	3.74	3.90	4.36	4.36	4.39
	High	4.22	4.71	4.96	5.23	5.29	5.42
Affection	Low	3.62	3.47	3.08	4.00	3.40	3.12
	Medium	4.49	4.86	4.79	5.27	5.37	5.17
	High	5.40	5.86	5.68	5.95	6.09	5.99
Quarreling	Low	2.25	2.90	3.25	2.64	3.72	3.61
	Medium	2.13	2.48	2.60	2.45	2.68	2.92
	High	2.26	2.35	2.31	2.40	2.67	2.76

[a]Minimum rating = 1. Maximum rating = 7. Significant effects are described in the text.

central facets of friendship (Furman & Bierman, in press), whereas the last one (quarreling) was included so as to provide information about antagonistic interactions.

Table 2.5 presents the longitudinal trends. These trends were examined separately for children who first met at camp and those who were previously acquainted; scores were also examined separately for children who received low, medium, and high ratings of friendship on the seventh day of camp. Some children had rated more than one friendship as low, medium, or high. To eliminate this dependency in the data, mean ratings were derived for each kind of relationship, resulting in a sample of 390 cases.

The children differentiated markedly between their relationships with those with whom they were acquainted and unacquainted. In particular, previously existing relationships received higher ratings on all six characteristics, including quarreling. Apparently the process of acquaintanceship results in an increase or intensification of both positive and negative interactions. More interesting is that the ratings of new relationships increased over the time span, whereas the ratings of acquaintance relationships remained stable—except on quarreling, where ratings of both types increased over the time at camp. These findings indicate that the new relationships were undergoing a more rapid process of development than were more established ones.

The children also provided different descriptions of their interactions with children they liked and did not like. In fact, their descriptions of children subsequently rated as high, medium, and low friends differed significantly after just one day of contact. On each of the five positive characteristics, the children gave the highest ratings to their relationships that subsequently received high ratings of friendship and the lowest ratings to relationships that subsequently received low ratings of friendship. Conversely, relationships receiving low ratings of friendship were characterized by greater quarreling than were those receiving medium or high ratings. Apparently children are quick to form impressions about others. Moreover, the relations between these early ratings and subsequent ratings of friendship suggest that all of these facets are significant factors in determining the course of relationship development.

Although the children were quick to form impressions, the degree of differentiation among friendship levels increased as the days passed. In particular, for the five positive characteristics, the ratings of high and medium friendships increased over time, whereas the ratings of low friendships decreased. In contrast, the ratings of quarreling increased in the low and medium friendships but remained stable in the high friendships.

Moreover, the increasing differentiation among friendship types seems more characteristic of new relationships than established relationships. Consider the characteristic of prosocial support. For the new relationships the ratings increase over time in the high and medium groups and decrease in the low group; in contrast, the ratings were relatively stable in the three groups of acquainted children. For the other characteristics, the interactions among time, friendship ratings, and acquaintanceship status were not significant, although examination of the means suggest that there were trends in this direction. Again, these findings illustrate how the new relationships are undergoing more rapid change.

Finally, these data illustrate how longitudinal data provide a more accurate picture of dynamic processes than do cross-sectional data. The cross-sectional comparisons indicate that acquainted children—including friends—quarrel at least as much as unacquainted ones. Yet on examining the relation between quarreling scores and later ratings of friendship, low ratings of quarreling are found to be associated with the subsequent development of close friendships.

Although 7 days is not a long time, Furman and Childs's data illustrate the potential value of longitudinal studies of relationship development. Of course, research spanning a longer period of time is needed to understand the evolution of friendships or any other relationships.

We also believe that a temporal perspective would enrich our theories of relationships. Many of the early theories of interpersonal attraction focused on the role of static characteristics of individuals, such as physical attraction or similarity. Because relationships change over time, the role of these characteristics can also be expected to change. For example, different processes may be central in the initiation and maintenance of relationships (Graziano & Musser, 1982). Moreover, a temporal perspective requires that we incorporate dynamic processes and not just static properties. In fact, if static properties are included, we must talk about how these characteristics are discovered and how they affect subsequent interactions—not just whether or not they are present. For example, one would want to discuss how similarity is found through interactions and how the discovery of similarity affects interactions, rather than merely hypothesizing that preexisting similarity may foster attraction.

It should also be noted that our theories of relationship development are still based principally on commonsense observations and simplistic developmental models. The insights of developmental psychologists should prove useful in formulating more sophisticated theories. Although many of the specifics of a theory of development remain unknown or in dispute, developmental psychologists have learned what topics must be addressed. Classic issues such as the nature of stages, quantitative and qualitative changes, phenotypic and genotypic continuities, and the complexities of growth curves are as relevant to the task of describing relationship development as to the task of describing individual development. Certainly, the analogy between individual and relationship development can be overstated. One should not expect to observe the consistency and orderliness in a relationship's development that one hopes to see in an individual's development. That observation, however, does not decrease the significance of the developmentalists' insights; it only underscores the difficulty of the task of describing the development of relationships.

THE RELATIONAL UNIT

Proposition 4. *The fundamental unit of interest should be the relationship.*

So far, three major propositions have been put forth: (1) Research should examine multiple facets of a relationship; (2) multiple perspectives and modalities of data collection should be employed; and (3) relationships are in a constant process of change and development. Each of these points can be incorporated into our final and most general proposition: (4) The focus of research should not be on social behavior or even on patterns of social interaction, but on the relationship.

How are relationships different from social behaviors or social interactions? Burgess (1981) provides a useful set of distinctions. *Social behavior* is defined as the behavior of one person that is influenced by the behavior of another, but the influence is unidirectional. *Social interaction* refers to the mutual influence of two or more people on each other's behavior; that is, interaction involves bidirectional social behavior. In a *social relationship* the participants know each other and have interacted frequently over time, and their current behavior is influenced by their previous history of interaction. Thus the relationship incorporates more than just the current pattern of interaction. The relationship is a superordinate construct that serves as the context for specific interactions and determines the nature of interchanges.

The implications of the concept of a relationship are rich. Because it serves as a framework for specific interactions, the context of the relationship can affect the meaning or impact of a behavior. That is, the same behavior can have different meanings in different relationships; conversely, different behaviors can fulfill the same function in various relationships. Several investigators have found that the effect of a behavior is dependent on the relationship in which it occurs. For example, friends express less gratitude for help from a friend than for help from a stranger; conversely, more resentment is felt when help is refused by a friend (Bar-Tal, Bar-Zohar, Greenberg, & Hermon, 1977). Dyads of friends and strangers also react differently to a situation in which one person has been made to feel obligated to the other (Weinstein, DeVaughn, & Wiley, 1969). The obligated stranger reacts by offering help to the partner and assuming leadership. On the other hand, the obligated friend responds by perceiving himself or herself to be in greater need of help and defers leadership to the partner.

Children's behavior is also influenced by the relational context. Perhaps the best illustration is Youniss and his colleagues' study of the effect of violating a trust (Cabral, Volpe, Youniss, & Gellert, 1977). Children were asked what effect telling a secret would have if it were done by a friend, an acquaintance, and a parent. The children thought that if a friend were to do so, it would seriously damage and perhaps end the relationship. They thought it would be acceptable for an acquaintance to violate a trust, but such an act would probably preclude the development of a friendship. If a parent told a secret children believed it was "for their own good" and this would not damage their relationship.

Because the meaning or impact of a behavior can vary depending on the nature of the relationship, the central processes and their specific manifestations may not be the same in all relationships. Wright (1969) argued that investigators have erred in treating the attraction variable as if there was a high level of uniformity in either the benefits of different relationships or the determinants of attraction in the different relationships. Although the data are piecemeal, Wright's position has been well supported. Many results obtained in research on one type of relationship have not been found to be applicable to other types of relationships. For example, Banta and Hetherington (1963) found that women selected different types of men to be friends and fiances; moreover, women chose female friends who shared similar needs, but men chose friends with few similar needs.

We do not mean to imply that all relationships are inherently different. Some of the central processes and important patterns of behavior are likely to be the same in various relationships; others may differ. The point is simply that one needs to be sensitive to the potential impact of the relational context on the organization and meaning of different behaviors or processes.

Relationships as Systems

In addition to being contextual determinants, relationships should be conceptualized as organized entities. This point is best described within a systems theory framework (Bertalanffy, 1969; Buckley, 1967, 1968; Sroufe & Waters, 1977; Watzlawick, Beavin, & Jackson, 1967). According to this framework, individual components are organized into a coherent whole; different facets or patterns of behavior are integral parts of a broader relationship. As such, they display the property of nonsummativity. That is, the different facets of a relationship are not independent of each other; changes affect other facets or the whole. The specific effects are determined by the feedback loops that interrelate the different facets.

Thus in a systems theory framework, the organization of the relationship is of central interest. According to the principle of equifinality, the organization may be the critical determinant of behavior outcome. The same result can emerge from different behaviors because the outcome will be determined by the organizational parameters of the system. This point is similar to the idea that different behaviors may serve the same function, or that when the system parameters are different, the same behavior may serve different functions. Functional similarity or difference is determined by and analytically related to the organizational whole.

Although promising, a systems framework has yet to be explored extensively. The simple assertion that the various facets of a relationship are interrelated is scientifically unsatisfactory. The specific nature of the interrelations needs to be delineated. As yet, however, most systems theorists have not attempted to specify the interrelations. and very little empirical work has been generated from this approach. Perhaps the systems framework will prove its value in the years to come.

Interrelations among the Four Propositions

As may be evident, Propositions 1–3 can be incorporated into Proposition 4. First, the principle of nonsummativity points out the need for multifaceted research. That is, because the different facets are interrelated, studies that focus on one facet of a relationship can tell us about a specific pattern of interaction, although they cannot provide much information about the relationship as a whole.

The need for multiple perspectives can also be incorporated into the final proposition. Relationships involve more than simple patterns of interaction. By including multiple perspectives, different pictures of the relationships that underlie such interactions can be obtained. Insider data can be especially valuable for identifying instances in which the meaning or function of a behavior is dependent on the context of the relationship.

The present emphasis on the concept of a relationship also underscores the importance of a temporal perspective. One of the fundamental differences between a relationship and a social interaction is that the behaviors in a relationship are influenced by the past history of interaction. The meaning of a behavior and the organization of different facets emerge and change over the course of the relationship. In fact, the concept of a relationship is important even in the earliest stages of development. As Morton and Douglas (1981) aptly observed, "two people do not simply get fully acquainted using individualistic intrapsychic processes and then suddenly enter a state of 'we-ness.' They are in a relationship almost from the beginning and relational constructs must be introduced at that point to explain their individual cognitive/affective/behavioral activity and the synchronization of their relational behavior" (p. 26).

Future Directions

Research is needed on several issues central to the concept of the relational unit. First, basic taxonomic studies are required to determine the most appropriate means of classifying relationships. Some research has tried to delineate the principal dimensions of relationships (e.g., Marwell & Hage, 1970), but this work has focused primarily on the differences between personal and role relationships. The dimensions underlying different forms of personal relationships are not as well known. Similarly, typological approaches have commonly relied on laypersons' concepts of types of relationships. It seems unlikely, however, that broad categories such as friendship are a homogeneous cluster. Additionally, the relative merits of dimensional and typological approaches to relationships have not been examined.

Research on relationships can also benefit from recently developed analytical techniques. Early observational work was principally composed of static descriptions of participants' behavior. With the development of techniques such as sequential analysis or time series, work has started on the more difficult, but essential, task of describing the pattern of interaction in the relationship (Cairns, 1979; Lamb, Suomi, & Stephenson, 1979; Sackett, 1978).

Two types of research are required to exploit more fully a systems framework approach. First, work is needed on the functions relationships may serve; such theorists as Sullivan (1953) and Weiss (1974) proposed theoretical models of the functions of relationships, but few empirical studies have been conducted (Furman & Buhrmester, 1982). Second, research on the interrelation of different facets of a relationship should be undertaken. Such research is essential for identifying the organization underlying a relationship.

Research on relationships also must take into account theoretical processes and their specific content. Social psychological research on personal relationships has focused principally on social processes. That is, most investigators have been interested in studying penetration, similarity, social exchange, or other general processes hypothesized to occur in most relationships. Little is known about the context in which these processes occur. To argue that social exchange is an important process in most relationships is not sufficient; the specific commodities or subprocesses must be identified. As noted earlier, the relationship in which a process occurs will be an important determinant of the form in which it is manifested and its significance to the relationship.

With the emergence of ethological perspectives, developmental psychologists have made marked progress in obtaining descriptive information about the specific patterns of interactions in various relationships, but developmental theories about underlying processes of relationships are rudimentary at best. Such theories are needed if developmental psychologists are to go beyond simply describing what occurs to explaining why it occurs. Thus it is essential that research on relationships focus not merely on process or content but on their interplay in relationships.

Finally, it should be noted that relationships are open systems. Any relationship is influenced by factors external to that system. In particular, a relationship is affected by and affects other personal relationships. The interdependence of the various dyadic relationships has been recognized in conceptualizations of the family (Bronfenbrenner, 1979; Feiring & Lewis, 1978; Lerner & Spanier, 1978). This recognition is an important conceptual advance, but it is only the first step. Further progress will require that much empirical research be done on the social networks in which we all are involved.

CONCLUSION

It is hoped that the foregoing discussion of Propositions 1–4 will foster further work in the study of personal relationships. In this chapter I have tried to draw on research and theory in both the developmental and social psychological literatures; therefore, some of the points will be familiar to developmental psychologists and others, to social psychologists. Unfortunately, few social scientists are well acquainted with both literatures, and the fields have learned little from each other. The issues and problems in studying relationships, however, are common to both. Perhaps this and other chapters in this volume will foster greater integration of our efforts.

REFERENCES

Adler, A. *The practice and theory of individual psychology.* New York: Harcourt, Brace, & Co., 1924.

Ainsworth, M. D. S., Blehar, M., Waters, E., & Wall, S. *Patterns of attachment: Observations in the strange situation and home.* Hillsdale, NJ: Erlbaum, 1978.

Altman, I. The communication of interpersonal attitudes: An ecological approach. In E. L. Huston (Ed.)., *Foundations of interpersonal attraction.* New York: Academic, 1974.

Asher, S. R., & Gottman, J. M. (Eds.). *The development of children's friendships.* Cambridge. Cambridge University Press, 1981.

Banta, T. J., & Hetherington, M. Relations between the needs of friends and fiances. *Journal of Abnormal and Social Psychology,* 1963, 66, 401–404.

Bartal, D., Bar-Zohar, Y., Greenberg, M. S., & Hermon, M. Reciprocity behavior in the relationship between donor and recipient and between harm-doer and victim. *Sociometry,* 1977, 40, 293–298.

Baumrind, D. The development of instrumental competence through socialization. In A. D. Pick (Ed.), *Minnesota symposium on child psychology* (Vol. 7). Minneapolis: University of Minnesota Press, 1973.

Baumrind, D. Current patterns of parental authority. *Developmental Psychology Monograph,* 1971, 4 (1, Part 2).

Berscheid, E., Graziano, W., Monson, T., & Dermer, M. Outcome dependency: Attention, attribution, and attraction. *Journal of Personality and Social Psychology,* 1976, 34, 978–989.

Berscheid, E., & Walster, E. H. *Interpersonal attraction* (2nd ed.). Reading, MA: Addison-Wesley, 1978.

Bertalanffy, L. v. *General systems theory: Essays in its foundation and development.* New York: Braziller, 1969.

Bronfenbrenner, U. *The ecology of human development: Experiments by nature and design.* Cambridge, MA: Harvard University Press, 1979.

Buckley, W. *Sociology and modern systems theory.* Englewood Cliffs, NJ: Prentice-Hall, 1967.

Buckley, W. *Modern systems research for the behavioral scientist.* Chicago: Aldine, 1968.

Burgess, R. L. Relationships in marriage and the family. In S. Duck & R. Gilmour (Eds.), *Personal relationships 1: Studying personal relationships.* New York: Academic, 1981.

Burgess, R. L., & Huston, T. L. *Social exchange in developing relationships.* New York: Academic, 1979.

Byrne, D. *The attraction paradigm.* New York: Academic, 1971.

Cabral, G., Volpe, J., Youniss, J., & Gellert, B. *Resolving a problem in friendship and other relationships.* Unpublished manuscript, Catholic University of America, 1977.

Cairns, R. B. (Ed.). *The analysis of social interactions: Methods, issues, and illustrations.* Hillsdale, NJ: Erlbaum, 1979.

Cairns, R. B., & Green, J. A. How to assess personality and social patterns: Observations or ratings. In R. B. Cairns (Ed.), *The analysis of social interactions: Methods, issues, and illustrations.* Hillsdale, NJ: Erlbaum, 1979.

Ciminero, A. R., Nelson, R. O., & Lipinski, D. P. Self-monitoring procedures. In A. R. Ciminero, K. S. Calhoun, & H. E. Adams (Eds.), *Handbook of behavioral assessment.* New York: Wiley, 1977.

Danheiser, P. R., & Graziano, W. G. Self-monitoring and cooperation as a self-presentational strategy *Journal of Personality and Social Psychology,* 1982, *42,* 497–505.

Darley, J., & Berscheid, E. Increased liking as a result of the anticipation of personal contact. *Human Relations,* 1967, *20,* 29–40.

Dawes, R. M. The robust beauty of improper linear models in decision making. *American Psychologist,* 1979, *34,* 571–582.

Duck, S. *Personal relationships 4: Dissolving personal relationships.* New York: Academic, 1982.

Duck, S., & Gilmour, R. *Personal relationships 1: Studying personal relationships.* New York: Academic, 1981. (a)

Duck, S., & Gilmour, R. *Personal relationships 2: Developing personal relationships.* New York: Academic, 1981. (b)

Duck, S., & Gilmour, R. *Personal relationships 3: Personal relationships in disorder.* New York: Academic, 1981. (c)

Feiring, C., & Lewis, M. The child as a member of the family system. *Behavioral Science,* 1978, *23,* 225–233.

Foot, H., Chapman, T., & Smith, J. (Eds.). *Friendship and childhood relationships.* London: Wiley, 1979.

Furman, W. Children's friendships. In T. Field, G. Finley, A. Huston, H. Quay, & L. Troll (Eds.), *Review of human development.* New York: Wiley, 1982.

Furman, W., & Bierman, K. L. Children's conceptions of friendship: A multimethod study of developmental change. *Developmental Psychology, in press.*

Furman, W., & Buhrmester, D. *A motivational approach to the study of personal relationships and social networks.* Paper presented at the Second International Conference on Naturalistic Studies of Social Interaction. Nags Head, North Carolina, 1982.

Furman, W., Buhrmester, D., & Ritz, W. *Qualitative features of sibling relationships.* Paper presented at the International Conference on Close Relationships, Madison, Wisconsin, 1982.

Furman, W., & Childs, M. K. *A temporal perspective on children's friendship.* Paper presented at the biennial meetings of the Society for Research in Child Development, Boston, 1981.

Furman, W., & Drabman, R. Methodological issues in child behavior therapy. In M. Hersen, R. M. Eisler, & P. M. Miller (Eds.), *Progress in behavior modification* (Vol. II). New York: Academic, 1981.

Furman, W., & Willems, T. *The process of acquaintanceship in middle childhood.* Paper presented at the International Conference on Close Relationships, Madison, Wisconsin, 1982.

Gollob, H. F. A statistical model which combines features of factor analytic and analysis of variance techniques. *Psychometrika,* 1968, *33,* 73–115.

Goodstein, L. D., & Reinecker, V. M. Factors affecting self-disclosure: A review of the literature. *Progress in experimental personality research* (Vol. 7). New York: Academic, 1974.

Gottman, J., Notarius, C., Markman, H., Bank, S., Yoppi, B., & Rubin, M. E. Behavior exchange theory and marital decision making. *Journal of Personality and Social Psychology,* 1976, *34,* 14–23.

Gottman, J. M., & Parkhurst, J. F. A developmental theory of friendship and acquaintanceship processes. In W. A. Collins (Ed.), *Minnesota symposia on child psychology* (Vol. 13). (Hillsdale, NJ: Erlbaum, 1979.

Graziano, W. G., & Musser, L. M. The joining and parting of ways. In S. Duck & R. Gilmour (Eds.), *Personal relationships 4: Dissolving personal relationships.* New York: Academic, 1982.

Hartup, W. W. The peer system. In P. H. Mussen & E. M. Hetherington (Eds.), *Carmichael's manual of child psychology* (4th ed. Vol. 4). New York: Wiley, in press.

Hinde, R. A. *Towards understanding relationships.* London: Academic, 1979.

Homans, G. C. *Social behavior: Its elementary forms.* New York: Harcourt, Brace & World, 1961.

Huston, T. L., & Levinger, G. Interpersonal attraction and relationships. *Annual Review of Psychology,* 1978, *29,* 115–156.

Kelley, H. H., *Personal relationships: Their structure and processes.* Hillsdale, NJ: Erlbaum, 1979.

Lamb, M. E., Suomi, S. J., & Stephenson, G. R. (Eds.). *Social interaction analysis: Methodological issues.* Madison: University of Wisconsin Press, 1979.

Lerner, R. M., & Spanier, G. B. (Eds.). *Child influences on marital and family interaction: A life-span perspective.* New York: Academic, 1978.

Markman, H. J., Alvarado, A., Buhrmester, D., Furman, W., Reis, H., Shaver, P., & Sorell, G. *Recent trends in the study of close relationships: Are we about to reinvent the wheel?* Paper presented at the International Conference on Close Relationships, Madison, Wisconsin, 1982.

Marwell, G., & Hage, J. The organization of role relationships: A systematic description. *American Sociological Review,* 1970, *35,* 884–900.

Meehl, P. E. Nuisance variables and the ex-post-facto design. In M. Radner & S. Winoker (Eds.), *Minnesota studies in the philosophy of science IV.* Minneapolis: University of Minnesota Press, 1970.

Meehl, P. E. High school yearbooks: A reply to Schwarz. *Journal of Abnormal Psychology,* 1971, *77,* 143–148.

Monson, T. C., Keel, R., Stephens, D., & Genung, V. Trait attributions: Relative validity, covariation with behavior, and prospect of future interaction. *Journal of Personality and Social Psychology,* 1982, *42,* 1014–1024.

Morton, T. L., & Douglas, M. A. Growth of relationships. In S. Duck & R. Gilmour (Eds.), *Personal relationships 2: Developing personal relationships.* New York: Academic, 1981.

Moskowitz, D. S., & Schwartz, J. C. Validity comparison of behavior counts and ratings by knowledgeable informants. *Journal of Personality and Social Psychology,* 1982, *42,* 389–588.

Olson, P. H. Insiders' and outsiders' views of relationships: Research studies. In G. Levinger & H. L. Raush (Eds.), *Close relationships: Perspectives on the meaning of intimacy.* Amherst, MA: University of Massachusetts Press, 1977.

Sackett, G. P. (Ed.). *Observing behavior* (Vol. III): *Data collection and analysis methods.* Baltimore: University Park Press, 1978.

Sroufe, L. A., & Waters, E. Attachment as an organizational construct. *Child Development,* 1977, *48,* 1184–1199.

Sullivan, H. S. *Interpersonal theory of psychiatry.* New York: Norton, 1953.

Thibaut, J. W., & Kelley, H. H. *The social psychology of groups.* New York: Wiley, 1959.

Wann, T. W. (Ed.). *Behaviorism and phenomenology.* Chicago: University of Chicago Press, 1964.

Watzlawick, P., Beavin, J. H., & Jackson, D. D. *Pragmatics of human communication: A study of interactional patterns, pathologies and paradoxes.* New York: Norton, 1967.

Weinstein, E. A., DeVaughn, W. L., & Wiley, M. G. Obligation and the flow of deference in exchange. *Sociometry,* 1969, *32,* 1–12.

Weiss, R. S. The provisions of social relationships. In Z. Rubin (Ed.) *Doing unto others.* Englewood Cliffs, NJ: Prentice-Hall, 1974.

Wiggens, J. S. *Personality and prediction: Principles of personality assessment.* Reading, MA: Addison-Wesley, 1973.

Wiggens, J. S. A psychological taxonomy of trait-descriptive terms: The interpersonal domain. *Journal of Personality and Social Psychology,* 1979, *37,* 395–412.

Wright, P. H. A model and a technique for studies of friendship. *Journal of Experimental and Social Psychology,* 1969, *5,* 295–309.

3

Microsocial Process: A View
from the Boundary*

G. R. PATTERSON

EDITORS' INTRODUCTION

Gerald Patterson's self-identity is that of a research clinician, a psychologist interested in clinical questions involving pathologies of behavior and social interaction. He astutely recognizes that this places him at a complex boundary, that between clinical, social and developmental psychology. Thus, the present chapter presents a model for viewing antisocial behavior in children from both a developmental and a social perspective. A bilateral, interactionist position is developed in which the child and parent have mutual impact on one another's ongoing behavior, including its initiation, continuation, and cessation. A social interactional analysis is presented that includes consideration of the dispositions to act that a child or parent bring to a situation as well as the dispositions to react that each may bring.

The chapter provides an excellent methodological framework to illustrate the conceptual points that are made about the development and maintenance of family interaction patterns. From a social psychological perspective, this work represents an examination of the impact of familial settings and personal dispositions on small group processes (e.g., the family network). Developmentally, issues are raised regarding the continuity of behavior on a molar level as well as the

*This research was supported by NIMH Grant MH 32857 through the Section on Crime and Delinquency. I gratefully acknowledge the editorial contribution of J. B. Reid, who also has contributed to all of the ideas outlined in this chapter.

BOUNDARY AREAS IN SOCIAL
AND DEVELOPMENTAL PSYCHOLOGY

factors that come to elicit specific instances of action and reaction, something that Patterson terms "microsocial process." The methodology used to measure antisocial behavior takes into account the variables outside the immediate family environment (e.g., illness, unemployment), those inherent to that environment (e.g., parental child-rearing practices) and the dispositions of the actors. Thus Patterson's "bidirectional" orientation, examining as it does the role of microsocial processes in interpersonal interaction patterns, is an outstanding example of the breadth and depth that can be attained in research that truly falls in a boundary area, and his comments about the difficulties of such research are worth heeding.

INTRODUCTION

Many of the questions that preoccupy a clinical psychologist place him or her in the boundary areas that define one area of specialization or another. The very nature of clinical phenomena is so complex that no one specialty is likely to be sufficient to the task. Given that one is wedded to the idea of understanding a particular kind of deviant behavior, then one is quickly placed in the role of perpetual wanderer from one specialty area to another. The search is for one specialty's shift in perspective, another's mechanism or construct, another's assessment device, and another's laboratory technique—each of which, one hopes, can be fitted together to form a mosaic that explains the clinical phenomenon. As a clinical researcher, I have so frequently sampled from the areas of developmental and social psychology that I could properly be categorized as a wanderer, a transitional person who belongs to no particular discipline at all. The reason for this lies not in a deep commitment to eclecticism but rather in a sequence of reactions to necessity.

The present chapter briefly outlines a model for viewing antisocial behavior in children that draws heavily from concerns typically ascribed to developmental and social psychologists. In this model the construct of microsocial process plays a key role. On the one hand, it serves as an explanation for how families train a child to become antisocial; this, of course, has been the traditional concern of the child psychologist. These same microsocial variables are thought to reflect sensitively the impact of variables that impinge from outside the family. The matrix in which the family lives can alter the interactional sequences and, in so doing, initiate a process that results in fundamental changes in the family itself. The impact of settings on group process has, of course, been the traditional concern of the social psychologist and the sociologist. From the perspective of the model, it is these forces from outside the family (such as crises, illness, and unemployment) that help us understand why family structure changes over time. Because of the central role played by these variables, a section of this chapter briefly reviews some of the methodological studies relating to issues concerning reliability, sampling, and validity of these measures.

OUTLINE OF A MODEL

The goal is to construct a performance theory that will facilitate understanding antisocial behavior in children. The most salient characteristic of a performance theory is that the contributing variables are evaluated in terms of variance accounted for over a spectrum of criterion measures for antisocial behavior. Variables that cannot be measured or that do not contribute significant amounts of variance, either directly or indirectly, were dropped from the model.

The model outlined here is based on 15 years of field observation and clinical efforts to intervene in the lives of several hundred families with antisocial children. The effort led to the development of a theory about coercive process in families (Patterson, 1982). This was followed by the development of a number of new assessment instruments that measure the model more adequately, describing how antisocial behavior develops (Patterson, Loeber, Stouthamer-Loeber, & Dishion, n.d.). The model itself was designed to be tested formally in a longitudinal study, which is currently in progress. The function of this chapter is to present an outline of the model as an example of boundary research and to explore briefly some of the characteristics of microsocial variables.

Several characteristics of antisocial behavior are now well accepted; their complexity demands a great deal of flexibility from anyone who proposes to explain the phenomenon. The characteristic of primary interest is the continuity of antisocial behavior in children. Extremely aggressive children tend not to outgrow the behavior (Eron, Walder, & Lefkowitz, 1971; Robins, 1966). In fact, the majority of adult offenders have histories of antisocial behavior as juveniles (Robins & Ratcliff, 1978). The second characteristic of the research findings is a rather persistent—albeit low-level—correlation between certain child-rearing variables and antisocial child behavior (McCord, 1979). The combined set of findings seem to point directly to the research expertise of the developmental psychologist. However, any formulation that emphasizes the relation between parent child-rearing practices and child antisocial behavior must also explain a third set of findings that is equally as consistent and compelling as the first set. Although there is indeed continuity, it is also the case that about half of the extremely antisocial youths do *not* continue their antisocial behavior or become career offenders. It is also the case that roughly half of the chronically offending adolescent youths were not extremely antisocial when of elementary school age.

A careful review of the recent findings by Loeber (1982) emphasizes three phenomena, all of which demand an explanation. Antisocial behavior is a developmental phenomenon in which many of the extreme individuals continue the process, some drop out, and others join late. Any given model must then explain all three phenomena. The developmental investigator who believes that child-rearing practices determine antisocial behavior must also explain why these practices change over time so that some would-be career offenders are deflected from their course. The investigator must also explain why some parents alter their formerly adequate practices. The model must make some provision for continuity; it must also make some provision for change.

As shown in Figure 3.1, forces from outside the family are thought to affect microsocial variables. These variables measure the reaction of one family member to the behavior of another. The last 10 years of our micro-analytic work have focused on the patterned sequence of irritable reactions (Patterson & Cobb, 1973; Patterson, 1977, 1982). The implicit assumption, however, is that there would be analogous patterned reactions for warm, supportive exchanges among family members. Presumably an analysis of such exchanges might facilitate our understanding of such so-called products as the feeling of being loved, of having a satisfying relationship, of self-worth, and so on. It is also assumed that these positive reactive patterns can be increased significantly by positive forces that impinge from outside the family, such as the family being sent on an extended vacation or a parent receiving a promotion. As we will see, the term *microsocial* refers to the probability of a certain reaction, given that the family member behaves in a certain way. Implicit in Figure 3.1 is the idea that the father's promotion will, on that evening, slightly increase his affectionate initiations to his spouse and children, as well as being associated with an increased likelihood of his reacting affectionately to their positive initiations to him.

The other path described in Figure 3.1 is based on a similar metaphor. This time, the assumption is that there are threshold changes, day by day, in the inclination to react irritably to another family member. This bit of conventional wisdom receives strong empirical support from the programmatic laboratory studies by Knutson and his colleagues (Knutson, Fordyce, & Anderson, 1982). Their first series of studies showed that irritable reactions in animal subjects covaried significantly with both the number and the intensity of prior aversive experiences. In the next series of studies, Knutson and Viken (in press) also demonstrated convincingly that there were individual differences in reaction to mild aversive stimulation, which in turn

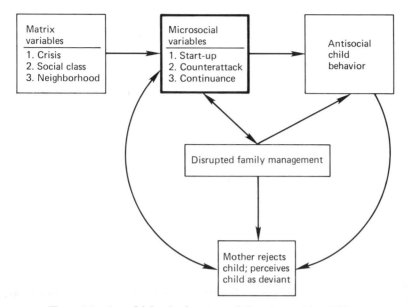

Figure 3.1 A model for the functions of the microsocial variables.

covaried with irritable reactions to cage mates. Again, the assumption is that aversive events from outside the family, such as an extended illness, unpleasant interchanges with a neighbor or coworker, and any or all of the daily unpleasantries of family life, may in the aggregate alter the threshold for reacting irritably to another family member.

The significance of a slight shift in probability of an affectionate or irritable reaction is of little moment—a psychological note, as it were. Studies of family process, however, point to the fact that repeated minor shifts of this kind, or a minor shift that extends over a period of time, can initiate a process that quickly gets out of control, particularly if the participants are relatively unskilled. Three components of this process are responsible for changes that may be of some clinical significance: synchronicity, extended chains, and escalation (Patterson, 1982).

Cairns (1979) used the term *synchronicity* to refer to the statistical coordination of the behavior of one person with that of another. As I use the term here, it refers to coordination between actions and reactions in which the content of the two events is similar. At present we know very little about why the content of action and reaction may be matched (i.e., synchronous). It could be that this pairing of events is an operational definition of modeling or imitation; but then one wonders why all social behaviors are not paired in this fashion. Research findings from field and laboratory studies demonstrate that some social behaviors, such as smiling, are often synchronous. For example, in a study by Margolin (1977), wives smiled in about .01 of their interactions with their husbands, but if the husband smiled, the conditional probability that the wife smiled increased to .07. Unfortunately for the human condition, aversive content is much more likely to be synchronous than are affectionate responses (Patterson, 1982). Mothers' reactions to target children in 36 normal and 37 matched families of antisocial children showed a strong likelihood of a synchronous reaction in the child to an aversive action of the mother. If the target child reacted in any of 14 coercive categories, the mothers were likely to respond in kind. The conditional probability value for normal families was .387 and for families of antisocial children, .407. Raush (1965) also found that normal and clinical populations of adolescent boys interacting in a residential setting showed equal likelihood of reacting in an unfriendly fashion to unfriendly overtures by peers.

In the present context, given that the irritability threshold has shifted for the caretaker, it is likely that the family member will *respond in kind*. The irritable mother will elicit irritable reactions, particularly from the problem child, who is significantly more likely than normal children to counterattack. It is assumed that the longer the mother's irritable state continues, the more likely she is to start conflicts and to receive synchronous aversive reactions, particularly from the one or two members of the family who tend to be selected as targets. The frequent irritable exchanges in these dyads lead to a quantitative shift in another interaction pattern; each person tends increasingly to persist in his or her irritable reactions, which in turn produces increasing numbers of extended coercive sequences, or coercive chains. Comparisons of normal and clinical samples showed that members of families of antisocial children were significantly more likely than their normal counterparts to engage in extended coercive exchanges (Patterson, 1976, 1982).

Extended chains are of special interest because they provide the setting in which either member of a dyad may learn to escalate the intensity or amplitude of his or her coercive behavior. According to Patterson (1982), negative reinforcement can function as the mechanism that strengthens this disposition (i.e., one member attacks, the other person counterattacks, and the initiator withdraws from the fray). Laboratory studies by Viken and Knutson (in press) provide strong support for the hypothesis that negative reinforcement can strengthen high-amplitude attack behaviors.

In summary, crises external to the family may alter the irritability threshold for the caretaker. Irritable actions are met with synchronous irritable reactions, particularly from one or two family members. Over a period of time, these exchanges become extended and increase in frequency. During these extended interchanges, first one member then the other learns that sudden increases in amplitude pay off (e.g., the child stops fighting with his or her sibling when struck by the mother). In some families escalation of this kind on the part of one member will be met with a synchronous reaction by the other, so that the escalation must be extreme before it works. The dyad is now at risk for serious injury. There are also by-products of these changes in process that feed back into the social interaction sequences, ensuring their long-term maintenance and further exacerbate an already worsening situation.

As shown in Figure 3.1, one by-product of alterations in the microsocial process is disruptions in family management practices. Gradual increases in the amplitude of the caretaker–target child exchanges make it difficult to discipline the child or to monitor his or her whereabouts (e.g., a query about when he or she will return home in the evening can lead to a major conflict). Efforts to intervene in conflicts between siblings can actually worsen the situation. Similarly, family efforts to discuss mutual problems may quickly break down into irritable exchanges. Details of the relationship between crises external to the family, disrupted microsocial process, and disrupted family management practices have been explored in a series of multivariate and causal modeling analyses (Patterson *et al.*, n.d. Patterson & Forgatch, 1982).

Changes at the microsocial level in the quality of parent–child exchanges presumably can lead to disruptions in family management practices if they get out of hand. As shown in Figure 3.1, the altered microsocial process provides a kind of direct basic training for overt aggressive behaviors for the target child. Our causal modeling analyses (Patterson & Forgatch, 1982; Patterson, in press) showed that the microsocial variables also make an indirect contribution to physical fighting via the disruption in discipline (and parental monitoring as well).

There are many other by-products of these shifts in caretaker–child exchanges and the concomitant disruptions in family management practices. As Figure 3.1 shows, the caretaker may come to perceive the child as deviant and to reject him or her. These cognitive and affective shifts feed back into the coercive process to maintain it and probably to make it worse. Although we have not as yet tested this hypothesis in a longitudinal design, the causal modeling analyses of cross-sectional data are consistent with this formulation (Patterson & Forgatch, 1982). Other by-products not shown in Figure 3.1 but thought to be of clinical significance are the increased depressed reactions of the caretaker, the target child's lack of self-control, and the child's perception of being rejected by his or her parents. The coercion model emphasizes that long-term disruptions also place the child at risk for failing to acquire a wide spectrum of social survival skills necessary to adjust to peers, academic requirements, and the work world (Patterson, 1982). Again, the empirical findings are consistent with this hypothesis.

It should be noted that the general model is derived primarily from clinical contacts that focused on efforts to assist the families in changing themselves. *The key to understanding the antisocial child lies in an understanding of the bidirectional relation between microsocial process and family management practices.* According to the model, long-term change in the antisocial child will occur most consistently if one manipulates the family management variables, which in turn will alter the microsocial process. This formulation reflects findings from both laboratory and field studies of antisocial boys. The data demonstrate consistently that attempts to reinforce prosocial behaviors that compete with antisocial behaviors and/or to use so-called extinction schedules are not successful in altering antisocial behavior. Only the use of such punishments as time out, work details, or loss of privileges has been effective. Similarly, parent training that focuses on supervising parents in their use of this kind of discipline has been demonstrated to be effective in a series of studies that employed random assignment to comparison and treatment groups and used observational data collected in the home as criteria for evaluating outcome (Patterson, Chamberlain, & Reid, 1982; Walter & Gilmore, 1973; Wiltz & Patterson, 1974). Presumably it is the parents' failure to use effective discipline that permits the child's irritable reactions to escalate. If the parents apply effective discipline, they will effectively reduce the child's disposition to react irritably to parents and siblings. This, in turn, is followed by overall reduction in the level of coerciveness for all family members.

Another implicit assumption relating to the model is that clinical efforts to change directly other by-products of the process, such as caretaker depression, the child's lack of control, or the child's lack of social skill, are probably meaningful clinical goals. However, success in treating caretaker depression or in teaching social skills probably will not alter the rates of antisocial behavior, because caretaker depression or lack of social skills was not the cause of antisocial behavior-both are simply by-products of the process that produced it. In the same vein, one could think of other manipulations that might have a direct effect on child antisocial behavior. For example, medication given to either the target child or to key family agents (mother and sibling) would certainly produce an effect; at least one would expect an effect from the model. Reducing the irritability of either member of the dyad should reduce the overall level of the child's antisocial behavior. I suspect, however, that the effects would be short-lived; this would be of interest to test empirically.

The larger model described by Patterson *et al.* (n.d.) places the mother and the sibling in the role of providing basic training for coercive skills. Given that the child learns to be extremely coercive in his or her interactions with family members, it becomes increasingly likely that he or she will generalize these behaviors to other settings, such as the school or neighborhood. Fighting and stealing accompanied by a lack of social and academic skills make it increasingly likely that the child will be rejected by the majority of his or her peers (and family as well). This in turn increases the likelihood that when he or she reaches the age at which parents grant more unsupervised free time (ages 10 to 12 years), the child will drift into a deviant peer group. From this developmental model, the latter commitment is a major step that places the child at risk for later official delinquency. A recent application of structural equations to data for 106 adolescent boys offered strong support for the model: Disrupted parental monitoring is associated with lack of social skills and commitment to a deviant peer group. Both of these in turn place the child at grave risk for delinquent activity. The model accounted for 59% of the variance in multiple indicators of delinquent activity (self-report, police records, mother report).

So many assumptions and products are generated by the model that it is difficult to imagine any single study that would permit us to reject it. The longitudinal studies now under way will provide a reasonably straightforward test for the assumption that crises or other disruptors at Time 1 should be associated with an altered microsocial process at Time 2, as well as concomitant changes in family management and antisocial child behavior. The model could also be rejected if training parents in effective discipline did not reduce the child's irritable reactions, or if treating caretaker depression and the target child's lack of social skills led to reductions in child antisocial behavior. Similarly, the fate of the larger model could be jeopardized by demonstrating that the bulk of chronically offending delinquents did not come from homes where monitoring was disrupted, or that the majority were not socially unskilled and/or involved with deviant peers. The key assumption is that only the parents (or parent figures) can monitor and discipline antisocial child behavior effectively, because only they have the time and commitment to the child.

Whatever the eventual fate of the model itself, microsocial variables define one of the key constructs. The remainder of the discussion focuses on some of the properties of these variables. How does one go about measuring irritable reactions? What are the stability and validity of these measures? Do the properties of the variables vary as a function of the sample? The answers to these questions will help us to decide how well the measures fit the requirements of the microsocial construct.

MICROSOCIAL VARIABLES

Background Assumptions

Before examining the microanalytic variables themselves, one should note several background issues—for example, the assumption that the reactions of significant others function as the prime determinant for some social behaviors. This would mean that warm, affectionate children come from warm, affectionate families. Conversely, aggressive children must come from families in which other members are aggressive. If aggressive children do not come from systems in which significant others are aggressive, then efforts to obtain precise measures of aggressive reactions would hardly seem warranted.

The examination of either assumption requires that one construct a code system that will describe sequences of behavioral events reliably and sensitively. To achieve this purpose, for 3 years we observed normal and antisocial children in their homes (Reid, 1978). In doing so we developed 14 categories that described the aggressive behaviors exchanged by family members occurring most frequently (e.g., tease, disapproval, physical negative, yell). We added 15 categories that described, though rather inadequately, 15 prosocial behaviors (e.g., talk, work, play).[1]

A semistructured format was used (no TV, everyone present, etc.), and generally the session occurred just prior to the supper hour. Every 6 seconds, the observers recorded the behavior of the target subject and the family members' reactions to what he or she did. Every 5 minutes a new target subject was selected randomly. Each person served as target twice in each session. At minimum, data were collected for six sessions for each family; roughly 1200 events were recorded per session. The samples included a large number of father-absent and blue-collar, working-class families.

The problems of observer agreement, observer training, relation of interaction complexity to observer reliability, observer bias, reactivity to observer, and validity of the code system have been evaluated in a long series of studies reviewed in Reid (1978) and updated in Patterson (1982).

The Total Aversive Behavior (TAB) score was designed to measure the overall level of family members' coercive behavior observed in the home. The TAB score was based on the summary of each of the following 14 code

---

[1]The other FICS categories are as follows:
    Prosocial Behaviors: approve, attend, comply, indulge, laugh, play, physical positive, touch, and talk
    Neutral Behaviors: normative, no response.

categories: disapproval, dependency, destructive, hyperactivity, humiliate, cry, command negative, ignore, noncomply, negativism, physical negative, tease, whine, and yell. Each variable was converted to a standard score. The mean of the 14 standardized scores constitutes the measure of TAB. For a sample of antisocial children, the test–retest correlation for the TAB score across a 2-week period was .78. For a small sample of normal children the test–retest correlation across an 18-month interval was .74 (Reid, 1978).

Do Aggressive Children Live in Aggressive Families?

The TAB score was used to test the hypothesis that aggressive children live in aggressive families. The traditional clinical literature suggests that an equally plausible hypothesis would be that the child's behavior was in reaction to a cold, distant home presided over by an authoritarian martinet who permits no aggression.

The hypothesis was tested by comparing the mean TAB scores for family members from three different samples (Patterson, 1982). Two samples consisted of families of antisocial boys and one of families of normal boys. The samples were matched for age of target child, father presence or absence, and parent occupation.

The data summarized in Table 3.1 attest to the fact that, indeed, members of families of children referred for antisocial behavior were significantly

TABLE 3.1

Mean Coercion Levels by Family Members for Three Samples[a]

Family member	Mean TAB[b] scores by samples			F Value	Duncan
	Social aggressors (SA) (N = 34)	Stealers (St) (N = 37)	Normals (N) (N = 37)		
Problem child	.98	.36	.17	25.12**	St vs. SA SA vs. N St vs. N
Mother	.87	.89	.45	11.51**	SA vs. N St vs. N
Father	.68	.50	.34	4.51*	SA vs. N
Siblings[c]	.66	.53	.31	5.00*	SA vs. N

[a]From Patterson, 1982.
[b]Total Aversive Behavior score from home observations.
[c]Mean for all siblings age 3 years or more.
*$p < .01$. **$p < .0001$.

more coercive than were their counterparts from normal families. Generally, members from families of social aggressors were the most coercive, normals were the least, and members of families of stealers were intermediate. The data offer consistent support for the hypothesis that aggressive children come from aggressive families. Note that in the clinical samples, it was the *problem child* and the *mother* who were the most coercive.

The mean values do not clarify which family members were involved in the conflicts with the target child. It is conceivable that the problem child's conflicts were evenly distributed among parents and siblings. A test of this hypothesis was based on a sample of 20 normal and 30 socially aggressive children matched for age of target child, parent occupation, and father presence (Patterson, 1982). The target children were divided into younger (less than 8.5 years) and older groups. The dependent variable was the proportion of the target child's coercive episodes that involved the parent as initiator or reactor. The conflict could have been initiated by a sibling or by the target child, but if the parent was involved at any point it was so tabulated.

The data showed that one or more of the parents was involved in about 80% of the target child's coercive episodes; the differences between normal and clinical samples were not significant, however. The parents were no more likely to be involved with younger than with older target children. A second analysis showed that the siblings were involved in about 60% of all the target child's coercive episodes. This in turn indicates that there was a great deal of overlap between parent and sibling involvement. Roughly 40% of the time parents and siblings were drawn into the same conflict with the target child. This vortex effect seemed to characterize particularly the episodes in which the antecedent was neutral (e.g., the parent or sibling was engaged in something, such as reading the paper, when the target child launched an attack).

The possibility exists that in families of antisocial youngsters, the parents tend to become overly enmeshed, not just with the target child but with siblings as well. The alternative hypothesis is that the parents' interaction with the siblings lies within the normal range, but it is their interaction with the problem child that contributes to the child's deviant status. To test this hypothesis, the interactions of family members in clinical samples were compared to normal samples given the presence or absence of the problem child (Patterson, 1983). The comparisons clearly identified the problem child as having special status as a "storm center" for interactions with the parents. When parents in the clinical samples interacted with siblings or with each other, their rates of coercive behavior generally were not different from normals. The one exception to this was fathers and male siblings, whose rates were significantly higher for the clinical than for the normal sample. Parents of problem children permit siblings to be four or five times more deviant than siblings of normals. This level was not significantly affected by the presence or absence of the problem child. In interactions with the problem child the parents become significantly more coercive than normals. There seemed little doubt that in these clinical samples, the identified problem child has a special niche. He is differentiated from his highly coercive siblings by *the manner in which his parents react to him.*

To summarize, there is some support for the assumption that the aggressive child lives in an aggressive family. Our analyses to date also suggest that a microsocial analysis should focus particularly on the reactions of the mother as a prime contributor to the process. The next issue to be addressed is the extent to which the immediately prior behavior of the other person serves as an important determinant for the ongoing behavior of the child.

The Moment-to-Moment Influence of One Family Member's Behavior on Another

The microsocial variables that measure the functional relationship between the behavior of one family member and another are based on conditional probability values derived from sequential observation data collected in the home. Certain sequential interactions between two people recur in a predictable fashion. In a probabilistic sense, the behavior of one person serves as a reliable cue for a specific reaction on the part of the other. In the analysis, each member is cast in the role of both reactor and initiator.

Most current studies of parent–child interaction sequences search for structure. This means that the behavior of the child is predictable in two difference senses (Gottman & Bakeman, 1979; Patterson, 1982). On the one hand, there is a predictable correlation between what he is doing at Time 1 and, if the interval is a few seconds, what he will be doing at Time 2. This is called *intra-individual structure.* There is also a modest amount of structure found by studying the interindividual connection between the behavior of, say, the mother at Time 1 and the child's reaction at Time 2. Note here that the child's behavior at Time 2 is determined by both inter- and intra-individual structure components, a point now well accepted in the social interactional literature (Martin, Maccoby, Baron, & Jacklin, 1981).

How does the fact that some social interaction is structured relate to deviancy training? The key concept is defined by the term *bilateral trait* (Patterson, 1982). Stated in its most general form, the idea is that the reaction of the other person determines the level, rate, or frequency with which deviant behavior is performed. The reactions also determine where and when the behaviors will be performed.

It is traditional to view a trait score as a summary of past commerce between the child and his or her social environment. In keeping with that tradition, the present formulation holds that a molecular analysis of what a child is reacting *to* (i.e., the social environment) would provide a kind of mirror image of what is meant by any given social trait. Analysis of how these structures change over time would also define what is meant by deviancy-generating mechanisms. In the case of a trait such as child aggression, a molecular analysis of sequences of family interaction would identify each member in the role or reactor and initiator. Each person, then, is embedded in a context defined by the reactions of other family members. Measures of each member's disposition to react aggressively and to initiate aggression constitute a description at a molecular level of the social environment with which the child must cope.

If one proceeds to define aggressive reactions and initiation by both members of a dyad, then in an important sense the behavior of one person constitutes a list of the determinants for the behavior of the other. At one level, this means the aggression scores for a dyad must intercorrelate. This, in fact, is the case for samples of both normal and antisocial families (Patterson, 1982). At another level, such a bilateral definition for a trait implies that the level at which a trait is performed could be altered by changes in the disposition of the *other* member of the dyad either to initiate aggression or to react aggressively to the first member's aggression. This altered definition of a trait provides a means for studying the impact of variables from outside the dyad.

There are three measures of irritable reactions that are pertinent to the present discussion. The first variable, *start-up,* describes the likelihood that conflict will start. If one person, such as the problem child, is being neutral or prosocial, how likely is another family member—perhaps the mother—to initiate an aversive exchange? The second variable is *counterattack.* If the other member initiated an attack, how likely is the subject to react aversively? The third variable is *continuance.* If the subject initiates an aversive exchange, how likely is he or she to continue being aversive? Problem children and their mothers were significantly more likely than their normal counterparts to respond in all three ways (Patterson, 1982). One can, of course, continue to search for such structure through as many junctures in interactional sequences as the data will allow. Each additional step, however, introduces an increasing number of zero entries in any sample of sequences (particularly for normal children and their families). For this reason, most of our variables describe a maximum of three sequential events in the irritability cycles for each member of the dyad.

It is thought that these dispositions define a *fight cycle.* One variable defines the likelihood for start-up. The next defines the likelihood that the other will continue by reacting aversively. The last one defines the disposition to continue a fight no matter how the other person reacted. As noted earlier, families of antisocial children are characterized by more fight cycles and by cycles of longer duration (Patterson, 1976; 1982).

Sampling and Reliability of the Irritability Measures

The first assumption relating to the network of hypotheses about microsocial variables is that irritable reactions are significantly more likely for mothers of problem children than for mothers of normals. The complimentary hypothesis is that the target children with whom each is interacting are similarly disposed. The first major test of these related assumptions was based on comparison of the two clinical and one normal sample described earlier (Patterson, 1982). As summarized in Table 3.2, the findings provided strong support for the hypothesis. In each of the comparisons involving start-up, counterattack, and continuance measures, the reactions by members of the clinical samples were significantly more irritable than were those from the normal sample.

Careful examination of the data for individual subjects, however, suggests that the mean conditional probability values for a sample reflect a combination of two different pieces of information. This in turn relates to the fact that for the individual, a conditional probability value of 0.0 may mean two entirely different things. A conditional probability has as its given that Person A interacts with Person B. Suppose, for example, that Person A

TABLE 3.2

Mean Irritability Scores for Three Samples of Mothers[a]

Irritability variables	Samples of mothers			
	Normals $(N = 37)$	Social aggressors $(N = 37)$	Stealers $(N = 38)$	F Values
Mother's reaction to target child				
Startup	.021	.047	.041	11.00**
Counterattack	.150	.228	.164	4.12*
Continuance	.122	.266	.217	15.00**
Target child's reaction to mother				
Startup	.007	.040	.027	8.00**
Counterattack	.093	.274	.156	20.82***
Continuance	.125	.321	.238	13.86**

[a]Adapted from Patterson, 1982.
$*p < .05.$ $**p < .001.$ $***p < .0001.$

never interacted with Person B. Then the calculation is based on zero for the denominator, and by definition the conditional probability value will also be zero. Now let us suppose that Person A interacts 112 times with Person B; the denominator for our calculation will now be 112. If this describes the likelihood of X, and X never occurs, the 0/112 will provide a conditional probability value of zero. Zero values, then, can mean that the dyad never interacts, or that they do interact but are not involved in a particular kind of exchange (e.g., they interact but are never irritable with each other).

It seemed reasonable, then, to begin analyzing carefully what zero values meant and the extent to which this possible confound could influence our efforts to measure microsocial process. At the same time, we were interested in the amount of data sampling required in order to obtain stable (reliable) estimates of each of the microsocial variables.

First, data were examined for a sample of 21 families of normal boys that had been observed in the home for six sessions and then 4 months later for three additional sessions. The data were taken from the protocols of both members of the mother–child dyad. The findings are summarized in Table 3.3 for the mother–child dyad. For the start-up variable, the denominator for the probability value describing mother–child would be the given: Child is interacting in a prosocial or neutral fashion with mother. As can be seen from the column, all 21 of the boys interacted with their mothers; in fact, the values ranged from 21 to 580. For most such conditional probability variables, the expected values were less than .25 (Patterson, 1982). This means that one must have, on the average, at least five givens to get one target sequence. Thus protocols with fewer than five target antecedent events were excluded from the analysis. It will be shown later that such a decision rule can have some rather serious consequences.

As before, the mothers were more likely to start conflicts with the child than the child was with the mother. The reason for the appreciably larger mean values for start-up in this normal sample as compared to the findings in Table 3.2 presumably lies in the fact that the target children are younger, and coercion rates for child and mother have been shown previously to vary as a function of age (Patterson, 1982). The stability correlations for the relatively brief 1- or 2-week intervals were satisfactory for both the mother and the child (.83 and .64, respectively). Notice, however, that the stability for the mother–child start-up variables is questionable when the interval was 8 weeks or more.

Examination of the data for the counterattack and continuance variables brings the problem into clearer focus. To calculate the probability value for mother counterattack requires that the (normal) child initiate at least five coercive attacks on his mother. The range here was from a low of 0 for one boy up to 111 attacks for another. As can be seen from the second column

TABLE 3.3

Stability Correlations for Irritability Variables for Mother–Child Dyads from a Sample of 21
Normal Families

Irritability variables	Mean[a]	N	Stability correlations	
			2 Weeks[b]	8 Weeks
Startup				
Mother–child	.055	21	.83***	.39*
Child–mother	.029	21	.64**	.71***
Counterattack				
Mother–child	.284	15	.26	.54*
Child–mother	.235	19	.31	.44*
Continuance				
Mother–child	.278	18	−.06	.37
Child–mother	.398	13	.44	.65*

[a]The mean describes only those subjects (N) who have five or more appropriate events in the denominator.

[b]The intervals are approximate. Generally the baseline of six observation sessions requires 2 weeks, but for some it may be as many as 3. The stability correlation is based on the mean for the first three sessions against the mean for the last three and the six baseline sessions against the three follow-up sessions.

*$p < .10$. **$p < .01$. ***$p < .001$.

of Table 3.3, there were six boys whose attacks were so infrequent that the probability for mother counterattack could not be estimated reliably. The mean probability for mother counterattack for those boys who did initiate conflict five times or more was .284. Most of the mothers were coercive five or more times with their sons, so only a few dyads were lost in the estimations of the means. Notice, however, the counterintuitive findings for the stability coefficients. The data showed that the test–retest correlations for the longer, 8-week or more interval were a modest but perhaps acceptable .44 and .54, whereas the correlations for the shorter interval were an unacceptable .26 and .31. My interpretation of these findings is that for normal samples that demonstrate low rates of aversive interchanges, three home observation sessions simply do not give a sufficient sampling of the events (particularly those that go into the denominator). Correlating a score based on three sessions with another score based on three sessions is not as good, from the sampling viewpoint, as correlating a score based on six sessions with another score based on three sessions.

The same kinds of problems seems to manifest themselves in estimating the continuance probabilities. The range of child attacks was more restricted: from 1 to 37. As shown in Table 3.3, only 13 of the boys mounted

attacks with sufficient frequency to provide even a minimal basis for estimating the conditional probability value. The findings from the stability
correlations are again consistent with the interpretation that three sessions
is too few and that even six sessions may be barely sufficient for the estima-
tion of probability values for the continuance variable.

For this normal sample, it seems that three in-home observation sessions
represent an absolute minimal amount of sampling to establish stable estimates of start-up for mother–child dyads. Somewhere between three to six
sessions are apparently necessary for the adequate sampling for counterattack and continuance.

Dyadic Trait for Irritability

Each of the three microsocial variables is thought to contribute in a
different fashion to the likelihood of extended coercive chains; indirectly,
each makes a differential contribution to escalations in amplitude of aggression. Each measure is thought to assess a different facet of the same underlying construct: irritability. If so, then the three measures should covary significantly with each other. Second, the two members of a dyad should train
each other to function at roughly comparable levels for each of the three
variables: It should then be the case that the across-person correlations for
each variable would be significant.

In a study by Patterson (1982), the hypotheses were tested by combining
the data from the two clinical and one normal sample. The correlations are
summarized in Table 3.4, which shows that the data provide support for
both hypotheses. The median intercorrelation for the child was .67 and for
the mother, .50. In both instances, the three measures of irritability inter-
correlated at a level such that one could speak of a trait for irritability for
the child and a similar trait for the mother. Incidentally, knowing the problems involved in event sampling and stability for normal samples, one might

TABLE 3.4

Intercorrelations among Irritability Variables for Mother–Child Dyads[a]

Child's irritable reactions to mother	Mother's irritable reactions to child		
	Startup	Counterattack	Continuance
Startup	.31	.49	.50
Counterattack	.74	.33	.56
Continuance	.57	.67	.58

[a]Adapted from Patterson, 1982a, any correlation over .20 is significant at $p < .05$.

consider using the start-up variable as a single indicator for the irritability construct for these samples.

There is only modest support for the convergence in traits across members of the dyad. Although the convergence correlations were significant for both start-up and counterattack, it is obvious that knowing the level of either variable for one member of the dyad did not account for much of the variance in comparable measures for the other.

A more powerful test of the hypothesis that the measures define a trait for a member of the dyad would require that on days when the individual engages in high rates of start-up, she or he also engages in concomitantly high rates of counterattack and continuance. In a pilot study by Patterson (1983), five mother–child dyads were each observed in their homes for a minimum of 12 sessions. The three microsocial measures were calculated for each of the mothers for each session. Correlations among the three variables were then calculated for each mother for all sessions. The median of the resulting 18 correlations was .55 (range −.01 to .71). For the five caretakers, the variables that tended to covary most consistently were counterattack and continuance. Both the across-subjects and the across-sessions correlations provide support for the hypothesis that the three measures of irritability tap the same underlying trait.

Validity of the Irritability Measures

There are three hypotheses to be considered regarding validity. I suggested earlier that the irritability exchanges between mother and target child and between siblings and target child function as a kind of basic training for overt aggression. One would expect, then, that measures of the child's irritable reactions to the mother and to the sibling would correlate significantly with summary measures of his or her aggressiveness in the home. Second, it was assumed that the effects of this training generalized from the home to the school. This being the case, one would then expect measures of child irritability to covary significantly with measures of aggressiveness in settings other than the home, such as the school. Third, the bilateral trait hypothesis strongly emphasized that the irritable reactions of mother and sibling would be major determinants for the level of the target child's aggressiveness. It should be the case, then, that measures of mother and sibling irritability in their exchanges with the target child would covary with a wide spectrum of measures of the target child's antisocial behavior.

The first test of the bilateral trait hypothesis was based on data from a heterogeneous sample of normals, stealers, and social aggressors who had been observed in the home using the Family Interaction Coding System

(FICS) (Patterson, 1982). In that study, the irritable reactions of mothers, fathers, and siblings were calculated and correlated separately by family agent with the problem child's TAB. The multiple regression analyses showed an R of .506 ($p < .001$) for the mothers; .471 ($p < .05$) for the fathers; and .382 ($p < .01$) for the siblings. It should be noted, however, that the analyses were based on a heterogeneous sample of clinical and normal cases. This would tend to inflate the magnitude of the correlations. Furthermore, the dependent and independent variables were derived from the same data set.

A second analysis in the same report provides a more rigorous test of the hypothesis. Parents' daily telephone reports of the occurrence or nonoccurrence of specific antisocial child behaviors was used as the criterion. The mean daily frequency for a range of antisocial behaviors correlated with the same promising independent variables (irritability measures) used in the previous analysis. The criterion scores were available for only a limited segment of the sample, but even so the multiple regression value of .52 ($F = 2.12$, $p < .10$) was of borderline significance. In the same report, all measures of the target child's irritable reactions to the mother correlated significantly with both the TAB score from home observations and measures of child aggressiveness from parents' telephone reports. The child's irritable reactions to the father and the sibling showed less impressive support for the hypothesis. No data were available for testing the contribution of irritable exchanges in the home to aggressiveness in other settings.

The next study was designed to test all three hypotheses. It was based on six different measures of antisocial behavior from a combined sample of 84 normal boys from the fourth, seventh, and tenth grades (Patterson et al., n.d.). A new behavioral coding system was also used (Toobert, Patterson, Moore, & Halper, n.d.). Both the dependent and independent variables were standardized by grade. The three irritability values were derived, describing the irritable reactions of each family member to the target child and his irritable reactions to them. In this study, the three measures of irritable reactions were standardized and combined to form a composite score for the target child to each family member, and vice versa (Patterson, in preparation).

The target child's irritable reactions to mother, father, and sibling correlated with a composite score measuring fighting in the home and in the school. The data provided significant support for the across-setting hypothesis. The criterion fighting score was a composite based on ratings of physical fighting by mothers, by peers, and by teachers. The correlation between the composite score for target child irritable reactions to siblings against the fighting score was .47, $p < .001$; the comparable correlations for irritable reactions to mothers was .30, $p < .01$, and to fathers, .22, $p < .10$. The greater the child's irritable reactions to mother and sibling at home, the greater the likelihood that others perceived him as engaging in frequent fighting at home and at school. These findings replicate and extend the support provided by the prior study, which showed that the child's irritable reactions to mother covaried with her telephone reports of his antisocial behavior.

The bilateral trait hypothesis also received some support. The irritable reactions of the mother to the target child correlated .23, $p < .05$, with the fighting score; the comparable correlation for siblings was .31, $p < .01$; for fathers the correlation was not significant. Note that in this study only boys from normal families were used in the analyses. This probably results in a restriction of the range of scores and reduces the magnitude of the correlations; but as these findings stand, there is strong support for the idea that siblings' and mother's irritable reactions to the target child covary significantly with his disposition to fight at home and in school.

Thus far the emphasis has been on the role of microsocial processes in the production of antisocial child behavior. The second hypothesis raised earlier about microsocial variables relates to their role in reflecting reliably forces from outside the family, such as crises. We have completed only one preliminary test of this hypothesis so far. Data were examined for a sample of five mother–child dyads, each of whom participated in 12–20 days of assessment (Patterson, 1983). The analyses showed covariations across days between the probability of mother continuance and a measure of familial crises collected on a daily basis. The data for three of the mother–child dyads provided strong support for the idea that on days when the mother was subjected to more crises, she tended to be more irritable in coping with her preschool child. The correlations for these three mothers were .45, .61, and .58. Two other mothers, however, showed just the opposite reaction: On days when there were more crises, they tended to be more distant and less irritable in interacting with the child. The correlations for these two mothers were −.45 and −.70.

Clearly the relation between irritability and crises is not a simple one. In the next study, the network of variables was expanded to include measures of support and mood shifts was well as microsocial measures of irritability (Patterson & Forgatch, 1982). In addition, 11 different measures of crises, stress, and martial conflict were factored to demonstrate that the concept of family disruptors is composed of several different dimensions. Although this analyses is still in progress, the data provide strong support for the general model outlined in Figure 3.1. Certain multiple indicators of familial crises do covary significantly with microsocial measures of caretaker irritability; these in turn contribute significantly to disruptions in family management.

The first attempts to measure microsocial variables suggest that the enterprise is feasible but complex. The network of empirical findings also supports the functions ascribed to microsocial variables in the general model. The variables do seem to relate to criterion measures of antisocial child behavior, which underscores their potential contribution to deviancy training. That they also relate to measures of family disruptors and to family management variables in the manner prescribed in the model emphasizes their potential contributions to change in family structure. The network of findings is consistent with, but does not confirm, the model presented here.

IMPLICATIONS

Most of us are trained to investigate entities that are viewed as static (e.g., personality traits in the child, child-rearing practices). Even when examining phenomena that by their nature are dynamic, such as group and family process, we tend to restrict our view to a single slice, a single sampling. The rising popularity of short-term longitudinal designs should do much to alter this provincialism among both developmental psychologists, who seldom study change, and social psychologists, who rely on single samples of group process to understand groups.

Change is a fact of life in child development. But where are the models that make even the most feeble effort to study the mechanisms by which changes occur? Even in interchanges such as the conference at Vanderbilt, where participants were selected because of their nonparochial stance, it was noteworthy that those who talked about development in the sense of change presented very few data. Part of the reason for the sparse coverage of this and other topics in the boundary area lies in the overwhelming methodological problems to be found there. For example, how does one go about measuring change? Most of us have been taught to avoid the use of any index that describes the magnitude of change for measures collected at Time 1 and again at Time 2. The difficulty has been known for several decades; its solution is not readily available.

I think another reason most of us avoid the boundary areas is that we tend to retain a maximum degree of comfort in pursuing the limited set of skills bequeathed by our major professors during graduate training. I can be convinced that this is not true, but in my experience it is true much more often than it should be. Exploring boundary areas is fine at the hortatory level, but in practice it is seldom engaged in because of the individual effort required to learn new concepts and techniques. I think those of us working with the concept of families and questions about how they change over time will come increasingly to generate a perspective that could well be labeled "boundary area." Given that these efforts are productive, they should provide new ways of looking at areas such as developmental or social psychology.

REFERENCES

Cairns, R. B. *Social development: The origins and plasticity of interchanges*. San Francisco: Freeman, 1979.

Eron, L. D., Walder, L. O., & Lefkowitz, M. M. *Learning of aggression in children*. Boston: Little, Brown, 1971.

Gottman, J. M., & Bakeman, R. The sequential analysis of observation data. In S. Suomi, M. Lamb, & G. Stephenson (Eds.), *Social interaction analysis: Methodological issues*. Madison: University of Wisconsin Press, 1979.

Knutson, J. F., Fordyce, D., & Andersen, D. The escalation of irritable aggression: Control by consequences and antecedents. *Aggressive Behavior*, 1982, 6, 347–359.

Knutson, J. F., & Viken, R. J. Animal analogues of human aggression: Studies of social experience and escalation. In R. Blanchard & J. Hovey (Eds.), *Aggressive behavior*. in press.

Loeber, R., The stability of antisocial and delinquent child behavior: A review. *Child Development*, 1982, 53, 1431–1446.

Margolin, G. *A sequential analysis of dyadic communication*. Paper presented at the annual meetings of the Association for the Advancement of Behavior Therapy, Atlanta, Georgia, December 1977.

Martin, J., Maccoby, E., Baron, K., & Jacklin, C. The sequential analysis of mother–child interaction at 18 months: A comparison of several analytic methods. *Developmental Psychology*, 1981, 17, 146–157.

McCord, J. Some child-rearing antecedents of criminal behavior in adult men. *Journal of Personality and Social Psychology*, 1979, 9, 1477–1486.

Patterson, G. R. The aggressive child: Victim and architect of a coercive system. In L. A. Hamerlynck, L. C. Handy, & E. J. Mash (Eds.), *Behavior modification and families (Vol. 1): Theory and research*. New York: Brunner/Mazel, 1976.

Patterson, G. R. *Coercive family process*. Eugene, OR: Castalia Publishing Co. 1982.

Patterson, G. R. Stress: A change agent for family process. In N. Garmezy & M. Rutter (Eds.), *Stress, coping and development in children*. New York: McGraw-Hill, 1983.

Patterson, G. R. A three-stage functional analysis for children's coercive behaviors: A tactic for developing a performance theory. In D. Baer, B. C. Etzel, & J. M. LeBlanc (Eds.), *New developments in behavioral research: Theories, methods, and applications*. In honor of Sidney W. Bijou. Hillsdale, NJ: Erlbaum, 1977.

Patterson, G. R. Training for aggression: The contribution of siblings. In J. Block, D. Olweus, M. Radke Yarrow (Eds.), *Development of antisocial and prosocial behavior*. Academic, in press.

Patterson, G. R., Chamberlain, P., & Reid, J. B. A comparative evaluation of a parent training program. *Behavior Therapy*, 1982, 13, 638–650.

Patterson, G. R., & Cobb, J. A. Stimulus control for classes of noxious behaviors. In J. F. Knutson (Ed.), *The control of aggression: Implications from basic research*. Chicago: Aldine, 1973.

Patterson, G. R., & Forgatch, M. S. *Impact of crises and support on family process and deviancy*. Proposal prepared for National Institute of Mental Health, October 1982.

Patterson, G. R., Loeber, R., Stouthamer-Loeber, M., & Dishion, T. J. *Understanding and predicting delinquent behavior*. Unpublished manuscript (NIMH proposal being prepared as SRCD monograph).

Raush, H. L. Interaction sequences. *Journal of Personality and Social Psychology*, 1965, 2(4), 487–499.

Reid, J. B. (Ed.). *A social learning approach to family intervention* (Vol. II). *Observation in home settings*. Eugene, OR: Castalia Publishing Co., 1978.

Robins, L. N. *Deviant children grown up: A sociological and psychiatric study of sociopathic personality*. Baltimore: Williams & Wilkins, 1966.

Robins, L. N., & Ratcliff, K. S. Risk factors in the continuation of childhood antisocial behavior into adulthood. *International Journal of Mental Health*, 1978, 7(3–4), 96–116.

Toobert, D., Patterson, G. R., Moore, D., & Halper, V. *Measurement of Family Interaction (MOFI)*. Unpublished instrument, Oregon Social Learning Center.

Viken, R. J., & Knutson, J. F. The effects of negative reinforcement for irritable aggression on resident–intruder behavior. *Aggressive Behavior,* in press.

Walter, H. I., & Gilmore, S. K. Placebo versus social learning effects in parent training procedures designed to alter the behavior of aggressive boys. *Behavior Research and Therapy*, 1973, 4, 361–377.

Wiltz, N. A., & Patterson, G. R. An evaluation of parent training procedures designed to alter inappropriate aggressive behavior in boys. *Behavior Therapy*, 1974, 5, 215–221.

4

Why Marriages Fail: Affective and Physiological Patterns in Marital Interaction*

JOHN M. GOTTMAN
ROBERT W. LEVENSON

EDITORS' INTRODUCTION

John Gottman and Robert Levenson provide a thorough and careful treatment of the literature on marital satisfaction and dissatisfaction, critically examining both methodological and conceptual aspects. In a detailed review of the literature, they illustrate the importance of construing relationships molecularly, interactively, and across time as the relationships develop and dissolve. The authors make a clear case that the social interactions in a close relationship, such as marriage, should be viewed as integrated patterns of social behavior and affective responding that can be construed as ongoing, active systems and as both the product and context of mutual social learning. The relevance of psychometric considerations from both a social and a developmental perspective is well demonstrated, especially in their thorough review of measurement techniques designed to investigate marital satisfaction among distressed and nondistressed couples. Gottman and Levenson's work takes into account the growing literature in social psychology on close relationships (e.g., Kelley, 1977, 1979) and the problems leading to marital dissolution (e.g., Levinger, 1976; Duck, 1982; Harvey, Weber, Yarkin,

*This chapter was supported in part by NIMH Research Scientist Development Award 1K02MH00257 and NIMH Research Grant MH 29910.

BOUNDARY AREAS IN SOCIAL
AND DEVELOPMENTAL PSYCHOLOGY

& Stewart, 1982), as well as relevant methodological and conceptual contributions from developmental psychology (e.g., Lamb, (Soumi, & Stephenson, 1979;
Hetherington & Martin, 1972). They provide a thorough treatment of the role of
affect in the interactions that occur within close personal relationships and argue
that a symmetry in emotional responding underlies closeness in satisfactory
marriages.

INTRODUCTION

By far the oldest research question in the study of marriage is why some
marriages are sources of misery, stress, and unhappiness whereas others
bring fulfillment and promote harmony. Many psychologists are unaware
of the excellent psychometric foundation the literature has built for further
inquiry. It is important for psychologists to become aware of what is currently known because psychology has some unique contributions to make in
our understanding of how marriages function.

THE MEASUREMENT OF MARITAL SATISFACTION

Burgess, Locke, and Thomes (1971) assembled a thorough introductory-
level review of the measurement of marital satisfaction. Initially researchers
included a variety of dimensions of marital functioning in their assessment
instruments, including couples' judgments of permanence, happiness, adjustment, general satisfaction, specific satisfactions, consensus, love, the
quality of the sexual relationship, companionship, compatibility of temperament and personality, and the number of marital problems. However,
the questionnaires constructed to assess each of these apparently different
concepts correlated very highly. Burgess and Wallin (1953) then concluded
that a general factor they called *marital success* could be defined on the basis
of correlations in the high 80s and low 90s between Locke's measures of
happiness and the Burgess–Cottrell measure of adjustment. Subsequent research has borne out their conclusion.

For example, a measure of the extent to which a couple reported having
problems correlated highly with the Burgess–Wallin scale of marital happiness in one study of 984 Catholic couples (Matthews & Milhanovitch,
1963). Also, the independent criterion of whether or not a family is seeking
psychiatric assistance (not necessarily for marital distress) correlated .90
with Locke's Marital Relationship Inventory (Locke & Williamson, 1958;
Navran, 1967). Terman and Wallin (1949) found that their inventory of
marital happiness had moderate success ($r = .47$) in predicting marital

stability. Except for Markman's (1977, 1981) work, this is the largest correlation establishing predictive validity in this area. In ratings of marital happiness that were obtained under conditions in which pairs of raters could not collaborate, Burgess and Cottrell (1939) found that when the ratings of outsiders were compared to the ratings of the couple, "of the 272 pairs of ratings only 24, or 8.8 percent, show a disagreement by two or more scale steps. The tetrachoric coefficient of correlation . . . is .91" (p. 31).

In measuring marital satisfaction, two short inventories are in common use: the 15-item Locke-Wallace (1959) inventory and the 22-item factor-analyzed Locke-Williamson (1958) inventory. The two correlated highly (see Gottman, 1979); however, the Locke-Williamson self-administered forms and face-to-face interviews were employed by Locke (1951) in his classic validity study. Furthermore, the personal interview format tolerated various modifications in order to elicit the cooperation of spouses. Locke (1951 p. 19) wrote that

> sometimes the interview took place in a bedroom; at other times it was in the interviewer's car or at the office. One divorced man was located in a tavern, and was induced to go to the university. Then he was talked to until he was relatively sober. . . . Two were interviewed in prison and two were questioned in the woods with the subject sitting on one stump and the author on another. The author played rummy with one man to get him into the spirit of cooperating. Another man was shearing sheep, and the interview was carried on in this situation.

Modifications in the phrasing of questions were also made according to the respondent's degree of literacy and religion, as well as to minimize the obtrusiveness of the items on sexual functioning, especially with elderly respondents.

Of the 15 items contained in the Locke–Wallace inventory, 14 were among those found on the marital adjustment test factor-analyzed by Locke and Williamson (1958) in another classic study in this area. The interview format for this study included personal inventories. The 14 Locke-Wallace items were among the 19 found to have significant loadings on one or more marital adjustment factor.

In 1959, Locke and Wallace published a report on a research project whose aim was to develop a shortened version of the marital adjustment tests used in previous research. By omitting redundant items and including only those items with the highest discriminative validity in previous studies, they derived a 15-item Locke-Wallace inventory. The questionnaire was then administered to a sample of so-called adjusted and maladjusted married persons and was found to differentiate "clearly" between these two groups.

During the 1970s, the Locke-Wallace inventory was used with self-administered formats in research on marital interaction and therapy. Marital satisfaction scores on the inventory are predictive of spouses' self-reports of home marital interactions (Gottman, 1979; Wills, Weiss, & Patterson, 1974) and spouses' and observer's descriptions of marital interaction at home and in the laboratory (see Gottman, 1979). In our laboratory we recently compared a telephone-administered form of the Locke-Wallace with a self-administered form with good results.

Scores on these two inventories appear to be robust, reflecting favorably on the procedures of administration. The history of the items contained on both the Locke-Williamson and the Locke-Wallace inventories reveals that differences in item phrasing and administration have been tolerated without sacrificing their psychometric properties. These items first appeared on Locke's (1951) 29-item marital adjustment test and were among the items found to discriminate between a divorced group and a happily married group of husbands and wives.

Every few years a new inventory of marital satisfaction appears in the literature, either to focus on a more specific construct, such as communication (Navran, 1967), or to control for some variable, such as traditionality or presumed secular changes in the conception of marriage. Usually subsequent research discovers that these new inventories correlate very highly with the Locke-Wallace and Locke-Williamson, and the new inventories usually have higher test–retest reliability than the Locke-Wallace. The Locke-Wallace appears to be a better measure of *current* attitude toward the marriage than the Locke-Williamson and hence has lower test–retest reliability. This is because more items on the Locke–Williamson than on the Locke–Wallace refer to the unchanging past of the couple, and because one item on the Locke-Wallace that rates general marital happiness is more heavily weighted than the other items assessing more specific areas of marital functioning. Nonetheless, most new inventories are hardly better measures than the Locke-Wallace or Locke-Williamson. For example, the new Spanier measure of marital satisfaction (Spanier, 1976) correlates .86 with the Locke-Wallace (1959) measure. Our experience indicates that if a couple is unhappy, they will agree that almost any dimension of marriage that could be negative is in fact negative. All such dimensions will correlate highly if a sufficient range of marital satisfaction is sampled.

Thus it is reasonable to conclude that the constructs designed to assess various aspects of marital functioning converge to form one dimension, and that current questionnaires provide a reasonably good psychometric network with more-than-acceptable levels of reliabilities and validities. The term "satisfaction" seems more acceptable and less pejorative than the family sociologist's term "success." The major task now is not to design a better measure of this construct, but to account for variation in marital satisfaction in a coherent, theoretical manner. It is satisfying that this pre-liminary psychometric foundation is reasonably solid and need not be re-done; it lays the foundation for more interesting work. We now review the history of concomitants of marital satisfaction.

HISTORY OF RESEARCH ON MARITAL SATISFACTION

The first report on marital happiness and unhappiness was published in 1938 by Terman, Buttenweiser, Ferguson, Johnson, and Wilson. They stated their goals as testing what they called the "chaos of opinion on the determiners of marital happiness." They were referring to a set of strongly held beliefs about the importance of such dimensions as "the effect of shock at first intercourse on the wedding night." Today these opinions sound quaint and anachronistic—except possibly to those who yearn for the sim-plicity of a bygone age of innocence. More important, even at that time Terman and his associates found that most of these opinions were wrong. Their findings were subsequently borne out by a series of other studies.

Terman and his associates were in for some surprises of their own. Armed with the psychometric devices of early twentieth-century personality theory, they hoped to discover the ideal psychological profile of the happy mar-riage. They found no such profile. There were no relationships between personality traits and marital satisfaction. Subsequent research has found very low (albeit sometimes significant) correlations between personality var-iables and marital satisfaction and only for specific kinds of personality variables, which we discuss later in this chapter.

Terman *et al.* (1938) were amazed by their negative results. They found, for example, no relationship between the frequency of sexual intercourse and marital satisfaction. They wrote, "One might suppose that a high de-gree of congeniality between mates would tend to express itself in a rela-tively high frequency of copulation, a lack of congeniality in a relatively low frequency" (pp. 275–276). Early researchers on marriage were also amazed that there was no relationship between demographic variables and marital satisfaction. For example, Burgess and Cottrell (1939) intensively studied 526 couples, once again with questionnaires, and their results were largely consistent with those of Terman *et al.* (1938). They were particularly sur-prised to learn that "the economic factor, in itself, is not significant for adjustment in marriage" (p. 346).

However, these early investigations were by no means characterized by negative findings. For example, in the area of sexual intercourse, Terman and his associates did find a strong relation between the *discrepancy* be-tween desired and actual frequency of sexual intercourse and marital happiness. Their findings led them to recognize the importance in predicting marital satisfaction from variables that describe the marital relationship. For example, they reported, "The highest ranking item is the one about avoiding arguments. From these data it appears that among the 545 items the greatest single danger to marital happiness is for one spouse to like and the other to dislike to argue" (p. 29). In their investigation of "domestic grievances," they were amazed at the amount of consistency in their data. The rank-order correlation between seriousness of grievances between husbands and wives was .76. They found that of 220 comparisons between happy and unhappy couples (based on a median split), all but 7 were statistically significant. From a long list of gripes, the following were cited the most frequently across all marriages: *husbands*—insufficient income, wife's feelings too easily hurt, wife criticizes me, in-laws, wife nervous or emotional; *wives*—insufficient income, in-laws, husband nervous or impatient, poor management of income, husband criticizes me. They thus discovered a remarkable consistency in these results.

This consistency was echoed in subsequent investigations that employed questionnaire and interview methods. For example, although Burgess and Cottrell (1939) found no relation between income and marital satisfaction, they did find that "the outstanding features in marital adjustment seem to be those of affection, temperamental compatibility, and social adaptability. The biological and economic factors are of less importance and appear to be largely determined by these other factors" (p. 349).

The major conclusion that emerged from these investigations was that most important were variables describing the relationship in accounting for variance in marital satisfaction. Burgess and Cottrell's findings were also largely corroborated in Burgess and Wallin's 1953 longitudinal study with 1000 engaged couples. In both cross-sectional and longitudinal research, the same patterns of results emerged. The point is critical because a research tradition grounded in individual personality theory was paving the ground for the study of relationships and demonstrating that the two modes of thinking (individual and relational) are by no means identical.

The point cannot be made too strongly. For example, let us consider research directed at the study of personality in marriages. Studies comparing happily married with unhappily married couples found low to moderate correlations between self-ratings of happiness and personality indices. For men, these correlations ranged from .28 (Dean, 1966) to .39 (Burchinal, Hawkes, & Gardner, 1957). For women, the correlations were slightly higher, ranging from .35 (Dean, 1966) to .42 (Burchinal et al., 1957; Terman et al., 1938). However, the variables that characterized happily married spouses tended to be interpersonal rather than intrapsychic in nature. For example, in Burgess and Wallin's (1953) summary of the earliest investigations dealing with the relationship between marital adjustment and personality scale variables, happily married couples were characterized as emotionally stable, considerate of others, yielding, companionable, self-confident, and emotionally dependent.

Dean (1966) noted that the personality variable with the highest correlation with both husbands' and wives' marital adjustment scores was wives' positive rating of their husbands' emotional maturity. Thus it seems that the *perception* of a personality dimension by the spouse predicts marital satisfaction better than the dimension itself. Corsini (1956) noted that the only significant correlation between marital happiness and interspouse Q-sort predictions occurred when the wife predicted the husband's Q-sort. The Q-sort is a task in which a set of statements about someone's personality are sorted into categories ranging from "extremely characteristic" to "extremely uncharacteristic." In a Q-sort prediction, one person predicts how the other will describe himself or herself. Corsini's findings are consistent with Tharp's (1963) review of interpersonal perception among spouses: Tharp concluded that marital happiness is related to the wife's perception of the husband being congruent with his self-perception. This, again, may be interpreted in terms of the predictive value of perception of personality rather than of personality variables per se.

In the late 1930s the point that relationships could not be understood by reference to individual personality theory was not well understood. For example, the prominent means of therapy for distressed marriages was individual therapy. As late as the 1950s it was considered unethical for the therapist to see husband and wife together, and questionable practice for the same therapist to see both partners individually. Such was the influence of individual personality theory (for a review, see Gottman, 1979, chap. 14).

One lone voice challenged these assumptions. As early as 1937 Ackerman suggested that two neurotic individuals could have a happy marriage and that the focus of therapy should be on *interaction patterns* (Ackerman, 1937, 1954; Ackerman & Sobel, 1950). Ackerman was eventually joined by a group of maverick psychiatrists led by Gregory Bateson. They published an extremely influential paper on the relation between a type of family communication called "double-bind messages" and schizophrenic symptoms in children (Bateson, Jackson, Haley, & Weakland, 1956).

The double-bind hypothesis paper stimulated a great deal of interesting thinking about marital and family interaction patterns. The basic motto of this literature was "the whole is greater than the sum of its parts," by which its authors meant that an *interactional system* is not capable of being understood by isolating its separate parts (for example, see Watzlawick, Beavin, & Jackson, 1967).

The point was forcefully made and it has become largely accepted as truth, despite the fact that no consistent scientific evidence exists supporting the original double-bind hypothesis (for example, see Beels & Ferber, 1969; Olson, 1972). Ten years after the double-bind paper was published, a paper by Mishler and Waxler (1966) about the hypothesis humbly noted: "Our persistent concern with whether we had fully understood the meaning of one or another concept is obviously related to what we feel to be an unnecessarily high level of ambiguity and imprecision in their writings" (p. 409). In the same journal, Bateson (1966) responded as follows:

> The authors have been generous and—so far as this was possible—have been understanding in their critique of the "double-bind" theory. They say with some justice that the phrasings of the theory are sometimes ambiguous. They might have gone further and said that (like much psychoanalytic theory) the double-bind theory of schizophrenia is *slippery*—so slippery that perhaps no imaginable set of empirical facts could contradict it. . . . [U]nfortunately, but necessarily, there is a basic formal truth about all abstract premises, namely: *The more abstract the premise, the more likely it is to be self-validating* [pp. 415–416; italics added].

Despite the dead ends of general systems theory, by the 1960s it became clear that the study of interaction per se might be valuable in understanding how *systems* functioned or malfunctioned. By the mid-1960s a great deal of observational-based literature existed suggesting how social groups functioned (e.g., Bales, 1950) and also suggesting that groups with an interactional history were different from groups of strangers (Hall & Williams, 1966). A great deal of interactional research had been done on families; furthermore, some consistencies existed in this literature. Unfortunately, these consistencies were largely ignored. For example, Riskin and Faunce's (1970) decade review paper suggested that one consistent finding was that agreement-to-disagreement ratios greater than 1.0 characterized normal families and that ratios less than 1.0 characterized distressed families. This consistent finding was dull and unglamorous; perhaps it even seemed somewhat circular. Researchers tend to be more charmed by and attracted to complex conceptualizations such as Leary's (1956, 1957) circumplex model or what might be called Laing, Phillipson, & Lee's (1966) "meta-meta-etc." model of interaction. To conclude that distressed marriages disagree more than they agree hardly seemed profound.

It is often the case in the history of science that valuable results are overlooked by everyone except those whose thinking is somehow childlike and simple. This was certainly the case in the history of physics. Galileo's observations of changing shadow patterns on the moon convinced him that the moon had mountains and did not give off its own radiance but reflected the radiance of the sun. The same data were available to anyone with a telescope. Newton's observations of the oval instead of circular pattern of light coming through a round hole in a curtain and through a prism led him to propose the wave theory of light. His colleagues could not see the point for many, many years.

The point that agreement-to-disagreement ratios were consistently different for distressed and nondistressed families was not lost on Patterson and Weiss at Univeristy of Oregon, whose work has been motivated by the integration of general systems theory and social learning theory. They had been intrigued by cybernetic, or "general systems theory," concepts, but only after they had come to value the importance of measuring observable behavior and of producing testable hypotheses, and after they had come to value the elegance of simplicity. Perhaps more important were the methodological advances made by the Oregon group—in particular the Family Interaction Coding System (Reid, 1967; Patterson, Ray, Shaw, & Cobb, 1969) and the Marital Interaction Coding System (Hops, Wills, Patterson, & Weiss, 1972). These methodological advances led to thinking about relationships as interacting systems, which led to a search for interaction patterns that characterized distressed marriages.

THE SEARCH FOR PATTERN

In an excellent review of the relationship between family interaction and child psychopathology, Hetherington and Martin (1972) wrote:

> Most of the studies of family interaction have yielded separate frequency measures of parent and child behavior recorded while they were interacting. However, investigators are usually actually interested in the etiology, contingencies, and sequencing of these observed behaviors and often generalize to such questions on the basis of inappropriate methodology. . . . *Such studies should look sequentially at interchanges involving chains of interpersonal exchanges* and should investigate shifts in probabilities of response in one family member to the specific behavior of others [p. 36; italics added].

Until recently most research on interaction ignored sequence and collapsed data over time. For example, whereas all the hypotheses of pathological family interaction concerned the patterns of interaction, none of the 57 research studies reviewed by Jacob (1975) was concerned with pattern. They all presented analyses of the differences in rates of various behaviors. By their data-analytic methods, these studies therefore assumed that the more of something good, the better and the more of something bad, the worse. This was a tenuous assumption because, for example, not all interruptions in a dialogue may be the same; interruptions may initiate one kind of sequence, such as a negative affect cycle, in distressed families and a different kind of sequence, such as humor, in nondistressed families. In other words, the vast majority of research on family and marital interaction has not always analyzed the relation between codes over time, and this seems to be a major shortcoming.

This state of affairs, until the 1960s, also characterized the research on marital interaction. For example, perhaps the most influential hypothesis about marital interaction is the quid pro quo hypothesis suggested by Jackson (1965). Jackson cited a study of Leik (1963) that found that "the traditional male role (instrumental, nonemotional behavior) appears when interaction takes place among strangers. These emphases tend to disappear when subjects interact with their own families" (p. 145). As one example of a quid pro quo, Jackson (1965) suggested,

> If A says to B, let us do X, spouse B assents because they have established a time-bound relationship in which the next move would be B's. The husband may suggest to his wife that they go to a movie; she says yes, and then she has the right to say, we can have a beer afterwards [p. 1538].

In 1968 Lederer and Jackson published an influential book in which they elaborated on the quid pro quo concept and suggested a form of therapy called *reciprocal contracting* as a treatment for distressed marriages. Note that the quid pro quo interaction pattern had never been carefully established as a phenomenon by quantitative, observational research as characteristic of marriages that both partners consider mutually satisfying or as failing to characterize distressed marriages. The quid pro quo concept nonetheless was so intuitively appealing to behavior-oriented therapists that it was rapidly adopted. In 1969 Stuart published a paper on four couples reporting that a reciprocal contract had been established with all four. In 1976 he reported, rather briefly and casually, that he had obtained high rates of success (approximately 84%) with a large sample (200 couples), measuring improvement with his own Marital Precounseling Inventory. Therefore the reciprocal contract, despite its lack of strong empirical support, began to be the treatment of choice of behavior-oriented marriage counselors (see also Jacobson & Martin, 1976). The treatment was, however, considerably modified by adding training in negotiation and in other communication skills (e.g., Jacobson, 1977; Patterson, Hops, & Weiss, 1975; Weiss, Hops, & Patterson, 1973).

This clinical theorizing ignored existing research that pointed to the potential importance of describing sequential patterning in marital and family interaction. Among this work was Haley's research on a variable called "*R*-deviation." This research was based on the most primitive of all possible coding systems; it contained only two codes for each family member: talk and silence.

Haley (1964) studied talk patterns in three-person (two parents and a child) "disturbed" and "normal" families. The disturbed group of 40 families included those in which some member (1) was diagnosed schizophrenic; (2) had committed a delinquent act; or (3) had been referred for a school problem. Also included in the disturbed group were families in which a member sought help for "a neurotic problem" or in which the parents sought marriage or family therapy. They were considered normal because they had not come to the attention of the community as having problems. Children ranged in age from 10 to 20 years and were living at home with their natural parents.

The process measure that resulted in the greatest separation of disturbed or normal families on Haley's tasks was obtained by using the Family Interaction Analyzer devised by the Alto Scientific Company of Palo Alto, California. Using lavaliere microphones, the interaction analyzer automatically records the frequency with which each member's talk is immediately followed by that of another family member. When father speaks, for example, nothing happens until mother speaks; then a click is recorded on the father–mother (FM) counter.

Haley's process measure, called R-*deviation,* was the extent to which the sum of the percentage of speech in each of the six categories (FC, FM, MF, MC, CM, CF) deviated from what would be expected in a random talk pattern (16.66 in each category). Note that the R-deviation measure is a naive approximation to an information theory search for "digram structure." *Digram structure* means that immediate temporal linkages exist. Haley is not controlling for imbalance in the frequences of M, C, and F. Haley hypothesized that one would expect to find greater rigidity, more limited response alternatives chosen, and therefore greater R-deviation scores in pathological families.

The results of this experiment were provocative. Haley's hypotheses were supported. Furthermore, Haley found that analyzing individual sequences of three, four, five, six, and seven speech patterns (the series of three would be FMC, FMF, etc.) in terms of R-deviation produced significant but weaker differentiations of the two groups than in terms of the digram R-deviation.

Haley's (1964) results did not extend to four-person families with two children, considered in a later study (Haley, 1967; selected on the same criteria as the 1964 study). In fact, if one reanalyzes Haley's results in the 1964 study for only those families with marital problems, there is a mean R-deviation of 21.45, which is not significantly different from the normal mean of 19.16, since the critical difference value of R-deviation is 4.42 for two speech sequences.

Waxler and Mishler proposed a T-statistic that may be a more useful measure than R-deviation with well and problematic family triads in four-person families. Using the task of the family's discussion of questionnaire items, Waxler and Mishler (1970) also did not succeed in replicating Haley's (1964) results. They suggested a procedure for controlling for relative participation rates and again found (as did Haley, 1967) that there was no difference in predictability of talk sequences. However, there was one important exception. "The exception occurs," they wrote, "when the parents of a schizophrenic child interact with that child (rather than with a well child from their own family). In this case the sequence of *three* speakers is more predictable than that for normal families" (p. 219). Thus it may be that with respect to potentially conflict-producing interaction, distressed families have developed structured interaction rules for family subgroups and that *R*-deviation (or Waxler and Mishler's *T*-statistic) is tapping this interaction structure.

Here we have an example of a program of research that suggests that the presence of a temporal structure is associated with distress in families. This would contradict the quid pro quo hypothesis, which suggests that greater temporal patterning is characteristic of *well-functioning* families. More descriptive detail is, of course, necessary because the quid pro quo hypothesis discusses the functional aspects of *positive* reciprocity, and a simple talk–silence coding system cannot provide such information.[1]

How should positivity and negativity be coded and defined in the study of marital interaction? This is not an easy question to answer. A clue to its answer lies in the remarkable consistency that has been found in the differences between people's interactions with their spouses and opposite-sexed strangers.

Ryder (1968) asked the question, "What, if anything, is demonstrably distinctive in interaction between husbands and wives?" Using a decision-making task (The Color Matching Test), he paired husbands with their wives or with female married strangers and found:

> Husbands are more likely to take the lead in conversations with their wives than with strangers, suggesting more task orientation with wives. Wives laugh less with spouses than with strangers; but they also use more disapproval of spouse, as do husbands. . . . The differences between married and split dyads seems much better described by noting that Ss treat strangers more gently, and generally more nicely than they do their spouses [p. 237].

[1]It should be noted that in a recent paper Sackett (1980) invented a brilliant system for using lag-sequence analysis with a simple talk–silence coding system in a large group. By using sequence analysis Sackett was able to describe complex patterns that *do* relate to positiveness. For example, some dyads stimulate one another; that is, when one person speaks, the other is more likely to speak than he or she ordinarily might. Some dyads are asymmetrical; that is, one person stimulates the other, but this person inhibits the partner. And so on. Sackett's innovation demonstrates the conceptual power of sequential methods even with a simple coding system.

The effect was replicated by Birchler, Weiss, & Vincent (1975) for a high-conflict problem-solving task (the IMC) and for simple conversation in a comparison of stranger dyads and nondistressed couples.

Winter, Ferreira, and Bowers (1973) used their standard decision-making task to study interaction in married and unrelated couples. Replicating Ryder (1968) and Birchler et al. (1975), they found that "unrelated couples were more polite to each other than were married couples" (p. 91). They also found that married couples intruded on and interrupted each other more often than did unrelated couples and that unrelated strangers listened respectfully to one another, whereas married couples were often rude. Also, interruptions in married couples decreased subsequent talk by the spouse who was interrupted, whereas in strangers interruptions increased subsequent talk.

The concept of "nice versus nasty," rudeness, or negative affect appears to emerge from this literature. In fact, it has turned out to be extremely profitable to invent categories that globally coded interaction along this type of positive–negative affect dimension. Birchler et al. (1975), using the Marital Interaction Coding System, combined their categories of positive verbal and nonverbal behavior and negative verbal and nonverbal behavior. They were able to discriminate distressed from nondistressed couples on the mean rate per minute of negative codes in both a problem-solving (IMC) task and in conversation. They were also able to discriminate distressed from nondistressed couples on positive codes, but only on the problem-solving task. These findings are consistent with other research on family interaction. There is more humor and laughter in nondistressed families (Mishler & Waxler, 1968; Riskin & Faunce, 1970), and there is more support and less defensiveness in nondistressed marriages and families (Alexander, 1973a, 1973b; Caputo, 1963; Cheek, 1964; Mishler & Waxler, 1968; Riskin & Faunce, 1970). Alexander (1973) found that parent–child interactions in families without a delinquent child were more positive ("supportive"), or less negative ("defensive"), than in families with a delinquent child.

In a study of couples' behaviors at home, Weiss, et al. (1973) computed a "pleases to displeases" ratio using a behavioral checklist kept daily by couples as an outcome measure of their marital therapy program. They reported that the seven couples seen in their program (who were shown to have improved on other variables) increased their pleases:displeases ratio. Wills et al. (1974) showed that pleases and displeases were able to account for substantial portions of the variance in a daily global one-item rating of marital satisfaction in seven nondistressed married couples. They also reported that pleases and displeases are essentially unrelated, and they found no relationship when these events were further classified as instrumental

(e.g., helping with household chores) or affectional. Affectional event records were kept with a wrist counter worn by each spouse, as these events
were considered too brief to be remembered for subsequent recordings on a
checklist. Wills *et al.* (1974) found that instrumental and affectional behaviors over 14 days accounted for 65% of the variance in the global daily
rating of satisfaction, but that pleasurable behaviors accounted for only
25% of the variance. They also concluded that "husbands tended to emphasize the instrumental dimension and wives the affectional" (p. 807).

To summarize, in reviewing literature on family interaction, there is remarkable consistency in the general conclusion that distressed couples and
families are far more negative toward one another than nondistressed couples and families, and there is some (though less) support for the conclusion
that distressed couples and families are less positive toward one another
than their nondistressed counterparts. We may also conclude that it makes
some sense to code interaction on a positive–negative dimension.

Two issues remain to be addressed. First, what about *pattern?* The quid
pro quo hypothesis is not about the amount of positive interaction, but
about its *temporal reciprocity.* Second, a great deal more precision is now
possible in the study of affect than a simple positive–negative dimension.
We turn to a brief review of both issues. First we discuss how pattern should
be studied, then how affect should be studied.

The Detection of Sequential Pattern

The basic concepts of sequential structure were elaborated by Shannon
(1949) in a classic monograph on information theory. The basic notions of
information have to do with choice and redundancy. What is information?
A doorbell is a two-choice information transmitter; it may ring or be silent.
A doorbell that never rings is perfectly predictable, and it obviously sends
no information. One doorbell provides us with an information channel that
can transmit one bit (a binary unit) of information. Viewed as a group, three
doorbells that can or cannot ring independently present the eight possibilities for transmitting a more complex set of codes. There are eight
possibilities, or $2 \times 2 \times 2$, in this system composed of elements, each of
which has one bit of information. If we counted the number of 2s in the
product above, we could define the information of the three-doorbell system
as the sum of the information of its elements, for a total of three bits.
Carrying this mode of thinking further would suggest that an information
system with a total of n equally likely messages would have information of
the power to which we needed to raise 2 to get n—that is, $\log_2 n$. To
understand this better, consider how many (yes–no) questions we would

have to ask to find out on which particular square of the 64-square chessboard someone had placed a king. It would take a minimum of 6 yes–no questions such as, "Is the square on the left half?" to locate the king, and 6 is the $\log_2 64$, because $64 = 2^6$. Each answer provides one bit of information by reducing the remaining alternatives to half. The information, H, is thus $\log n$, where n is the number of equiprobable alternatives.

If the messages were not all equally probable, the total amount of information would have to be weighted by the probability of each message.

In analyzing a stream of codes obtained by classifying interaction units of some kind, one searches for repetitive patterns. The task is similar to deciphering a code. To illustrate this notion, consider the approximations to English that Shannon generated. The first approximation was the random one in which all the symbols of the alphabet occur with equal frequency:

XFOML RXKHRJFFJUJ ZLPWCFWKCYJ FFJEYVKCQSGHYD QPAAMKBZAACIBZLHQD (p. 43).

This looks very little like an English sentence. If we next assume that the symbols are temporally independent but occur with the frequencies they have in a usual English text, we might obtain

OCRO HLI RGWR NMIELWIS EU LL NBNESEBYA TH EEL ALHENHITPA OOBTTVA NAH BRL (p. 43).

Now if we add such rules as U follows Q, we create the lag-one dependency characteristic of English spelling, and we might obtain

ON IE ANTSOUTINYS ARE T INCTORE ST BE S DEAMY ACHIN D ILONASIVE TUCOOWE AT TREASONARE FUSO TIZIN ANDY TOBE SEASE CIISBE (p. 43),

This lag-one dependency is also called a "digram structure." If we add the trigram structure of English, we might obtain

IN NO IST LAT WHEY CRATICT FROURE VIRS BROCID PONDENOME OF DEMONSTURES OF THE REPTAGIN IS REGOACTIONA OF CRE (p. 43),

In each case we get closer to the English code, although we may never be able to generate an interesting passage without understanding the structure among larger units (e.g., words).

The fundamental notion of communication is thus related to temporal structure in the following way: A behavior of one organism has communicative value in a social sense if it reduces uncertainty in the behavior of another organism. This means that, for example, if the quid pro quo hypothesis were correct, if we know that a husband in a happy marriage has just been positive toward his wife, we would have a greater chance of predicting that she would subsequently be positive toward him, and that this would be less characteristic of couples in unhappy relationships. The test statistic must involve a comparison of a conditional probability of $(W+|H+)$, read "the probability that she will be positive right after he has been positive," with an unconditional probability, $p(W+)$, "the probability that she will be positive regardless of what occurred previously."

What is the evidence on the truth of the quid pro quo hypothesis? Unfortunately, most research has not employed the temporal contingency-based notion of reciprocity that is necessary. Let us compare the uses of the concept of reciprocity in theoretical writing with the empirical assessment of the concept. Patterson and Reid (1970) wrote, "Reciprocity describes dyadic interaction in which persons A and B reinforce each other, at an equitable rate. In this interaction, positive reinforcers maintain the behavior of both persons" (p. 133). There are several components in this use of the term *reciprocity*. It is apparently still possible in this definition to judge reciprocity from the interactions of one dyad. This is consistent with the use of the term in other literatures. A seemingly new addition is the term *reinforcer*, but by definition, for a behavior emitted by one person in the dyad to be a reinforcer, it must first *follow* the behavior of the other person; second, it must alter the probability of that behavior's taking place. Hence the two definitions of reciprocity are equivalent so far. However, the notion of equitable rates is a new concept, and Patterson and Reid (1970, p. 140) further explicate this idea as follows:

> [Reciprocity] would require that, over a series of interactions, two persons reinforce or punish each other for approximately the same proportion of behaviors. For example, if person A reinforces B for 50 percent of the interactions which B has with A, then A, in turn, will *receive* about the same proportion of positive reinforcers from B.

This concept is really one of similar rates of positive behaviors in the two members of the dyad, and this concept is logically independent of the notion of contingency that is central to other uses of the term reciprocity. The similar rate idea is one that Patterson and Reid (1970) called "social economics" (p. 139) in referring to behavior exchange theory (Thibaut & Kelley, 1959).

Stuart (1969) had a similar concept in mind when he described the quid pro quo arrangement. He wrote,

> In effect, a quid pro quo or "something for something" arrangement underlies successful marriage (Jackson, 1965, p. 591). The exchange of rewards in a marriage may be viewed as a quasi-legal contract affording distinct safeguards to each partner. Whenever one partner to a reciprocal interaction unilaterally rewards the other, he does so with the confidence that he will be compensated in the future [p. 675].

In addition to the difference between a *rate-matching* definition and a *probability change* definition, the time periods involved in the two definitions are vastly different. Brazelton, Koslowski, and Main (1974) referred to a more moment-to-moment definition, whereas Stuart (1969) proposed the following illustration: "For example, if the husband agrees to entertain his wife's parents for a weekend, he does so with the expectation that his wife will accompany him on a weekend fishing trip at some time in the future" (p. 675).

Researchers have at times discussed the concept of reciprocity as a probability change definition but measured it by rate-matching. For example, Azrin, Naster, and Jones (1973) wrote,

> The strategy may be summarized as "reinforce the reinforcer (person)." . . . Since the nature of the reinforcing interactions is changeable, each partner must continuously rediscover the reinforcers. Secondly, *the relationship must be contingent:* the reinforcers are to be given when, but only when, reinforcers are received. This contingent relation is adequately described by the term "reciprocity," a concept which was also central in Stuart's (1969) marital counseling procedure [p. 267; italics added].

Weiss, Birchler, and Vincent (1974) described their intervention procedure with married couples as a means for developing *"mutual gain or reciprocity"* (p. 211; italics added) but never assessed it by probability change methods.

The two definitions of reciprocity are not equivalent. It is easier to see this if we consider nonsocial behaviors, such as eating or typing. A husband may eat or type at a rate similar to his wife's without any contingency between these two activities; they may, for example, have similar physical tempos. In this case, we would merely report that eating or typing took place at similar rates, not that they were reciprocal. If a mother smiles at a rate similar to her infant, their interaction may nonetheless be totally unconnected and noncontingent; the mother's smiling and her infant's smiling would be considered reciprocal only if the acts were somehow connected in the probability change sense.

The two definitions would be similar only if the term *reinforcement* were used strictly in the sense of altering probabilities *within* a dyad. In fact, in research on reciprocity by social learning theorists, the term has been used to mean positive behavior defined as positive on a priori grounds. There has been no demonstration that positive behaviors are reinforcers in the probability change sense. Furthermore, in every case but one the empirical test of reciprocity has been inadequate: Husband–wife correlations of the rates of positive act *across* couples or correlations between family members *across* families were calculated. This test of reciprocity has abandoned the individual dyad in the definition. The correlation of husband–wife rates of positive behaviors *across* couples also does not deal with base-rate differences of positive behaviors between couples, and it is thus invalid as a test of a reciprocity hypothesis.

Birchler (1972) found a husband–wife correlation of .97 across 12 nondistressed couples for mean frequencies of positive items checked and .74 in 12 distressed couples; the correlations for negative items checked were .26 and .54, respectively. Alexander (1973a) analyzed his data in a similar manner. He obtained high correlations between father-to-son supportiveness and son-to-father supportiveness (.69) across families, and a similarly high correlation for mother-to-son supportiveness and son-to-mother supportiveness (.59); however, the equivalent correlations for defensiveness were not significant. He concluded, "to have developed and maintained these differential rates, the families would have had to reciprocate supportiveness but not defensiveness, which was exactly the finding of the present study" (p. 616). In fact, rate differences between families, not reciprocity, was exactly what was tested by the correlations. The point is similar to one that states that analyses of husband–wife correlations across couples is an inadequate test of a reciprocity hypothesis. Gottman, Notarius, Markman, Bank, Yoppi, & Rubin (1976) wrote,

> Although nondistressed couples may seem to be reciprocating positive behavior more frequently than distressed couples, that may only be an artifact of the higher probability of positive behaviors in nondistressed couples. By emitting more positive responses, nondistressed couples increase the probability that one partner's positive response will be followed by the other partner's positive response [p. 14].

High (noncontingent) positive frequencies in some couples and not in others could also be an artifact of many other variables, such as similar physical tempos (couples are more similar to one another than they are to strangers on most variables), or an artifact of the amount of time spent together (for couples who spend more time together each day, both husband and wife will have more items checked on their behavior checklist than will couples who spend less time together).

The only test of correlations of positive and negative checklist items *within* couples was made by Wills *et al.* (1974), who correlated these variables for seven nondistressed couples between each husband and wife across 14 days. Husbands had been instructed (as a validity check) to double their output of positive affectional behaviors on Days 13 and 14. Wives' recording of their husbands' behaviors on these days showed a significant increase in pleasurable instrumental events as well as in pleasurable affectional events. In six of seven couples, there were no significant correlations between husbands' and wives' records of pleasurable behavior, but in four of seven couples there were significant correlations between husbands' and wives' records of displeasurable behavior.

The Wills *et al.* (1974) study concluded that there was evidence for the reciprocation of displeasurable but not of pleasurable behaviors. They wrote: "The within-couples analysis provides an index of immediate reactions to behavioral events and indicates that in day-to-day affectional interaction, a displeasurable behavior is more likely to be reciprocated than a pleasurable behavior" (p. 809). There is thus evidence to support negative reciprocity but no evidence to support the positive matching or quid pro quo model of nondistressed marriage proposed by Azrin *et al.* (1973), Patterson and Reid (1970), and Stuart (1969).

The within-couple analysis of displeasurable events for these four nondistressed couples also does not constitute support for the conclusion that the *matching* of displeasurable events across days is necessarily related to marital dissatisfaction. This test has never been conducted; however, Murstein, Cerreto, and MacDonald (1977) reported that adherence to a quid pro quo belief—particularly by husbands—was related negatively to marital satisfaction. The correlation between an exchange orientation and marital satisfaction was $-.63$ ($p < .01$) for men and $-.27$ ($p < .06$) for women. The correlations between each person's exchange orientation score and his or her partner's marital satisfaction score were also negative and significant.

The Study of Affect

Anyone who seriously investigates emotional communication in the flow of conversation must come to the conclusion that affect is conveyed in every possible channel of communication—linguistic, paralinguistic, facial, gestural, and proxemic. Furthermore, it rapidly becomes obvious that these channels of emotional communication cannot be isolated, separately investigated, and then later reintegrated. Birdwhistell said it nicely: "Studying nonverbal communication is like studying noncardiac physiology" (quoted in Knapp, 1972, p. 3). Birdwhistell was challenging the additive channel model of nonverbal communication that is currently mainstream.

To see the truth in Birdwhistell's point, consider the vocal channel for a moment. Current scientific methods require the removal of content from speech in order to isolate vocal components of emotion. This is done either by electronic filtering of high frequency cycles or random splicing (see Scherer, 1981). There are problems with each method. Emotional communication has been found to occur precisely in high frequency shifts of the voice (Rubenstein & Cameron, 1968), which suggests that electronic filtering may be eliminating the information of interest. Random splicing techniques lose temporal form so that an angry moment characterized by steadily rising volume will be spliced randomly, rendering its temporal shape unrecognizable.

There is a logical reason for agreeing with Birdwhistell. Suppose you tell your secretary, "I'd like this as soon as possible." Stressing the word "soon" communicates impatience; stressing the word "possible" communicates that you are not in a hurry. Any content filtering will lose the emotional flavor of the *interaction* of paralinguistic cues with the words. A bit of experience with conversation will convince the reader that the argument can be generalized to other cues in the voice, such as pause, whine, and so on. Experience with film or videotape will convince the reader that this is the case for physical cues from every channel of nonverbal communication: *Emotion is communicated by a nonadditive gestalt of channels.* You cannot take Humpty Dumpty apart, study the separate pieces, and even hope to learn about Humpty Dumpty.

This is *not* to say that physical cues of nonverbal behavior do not provide reliable emotional information independent of language. The researcher of emotional communication must know all channels well.

Consider the face. The study of facial expressions was discredited in psychology in a review by Bruner and Tagiuri that appeared in 1954. However, Ekman, Friesen, and Ellsworth (1972) critically reevaluated the evidence before and since the Bruner-Tagiuri review and made several points. First, the research evidence was misrepresented and distorted by Burner and Tagiuri. Ekman *et al.* (1972) wrote that "Bruner and Tagiuri were factually incorrect and misleading. They enhanced the credibility of negative findings on accuracy by saying that all of those experiments utilized photographs of real emotion elicited in the laboratory. This is true only of Landis and Sherman" (p. 78). Second, the studies in which subjects could not identify emotion accurately from facial expressions suffered from several methodological weaknesses. For example, early investigators of facial expressions expected to find an isomorphism between emotionally arousing situations and universal facial expressions. However, several factors may intervene to ruin this one-to-one relationship. For example, not everyone laughs at a standard set of jokes; nor does everyone react with fear to the threat of shock. Therefore, the assumption that a particular experimental event will produce the same internal state in all subjects is unwarranted. Third, in some studies (Landis, 1924, 1929) the subjects were colleagues of the experimenter, and he marked their faces with burnt cork to highlight facial features. They were thus aware of what was being measured, and in most situations (even suddenly placing excrement under their noses) they produced the same expression—a pained, polite smile. Given that subjects were asked to pick out which situation produced which photograph, it is predictable that they did no better than chance. Fourth, the situations followed one another in rapid succession, which may have contributed to subjects' producing blends of various affects. Ekman *et al.* (1972) show that when these methodological problems are controlled, subjects can identify facial expressions accurately. This result has been replicated in many investigations by several researchers (for example, Izard, 1971).

The state of the art in measuring facial action is Ekman and Friesen's (1978) anatomically based Facial Action Coding System (FACS). This system is a significant scientific tool because it avoids the use of emotional-laden adjectives in describing facial motion. To explain the great clarity that will eventually be gained by using FACS, consider one category that many researchers use: the smile. Some researchers (e.g., Brannigan and Humphries, 1972) distinguish among various kinds of smiles (e.g., Brannigan and Humphries describe the "simple smile," the "upper smile," and the "broad smile"); often these distinctions are based on adjectives (e.g., "tense smile"). For a comparison of facial coding systems, see Ekman (1982). Most of us think we know what a smile is. Most investigators have simply specified that the lip corners turn up in a smile and that the mouth is shaped somewhat like a U. But this is not sufficient to describe a smile. In a number of different types of smiles the lip corners turn down. This smile is often seen in coy, playful, or flirtatious interaction; it looks like the person is working hard *not* to smile. The FACS would describe this smile in terms of the "action units" (AUs) that are involved in creating the facial configurations that involve upturned corners of the mouth but that are often indexes of negative affect. For example, the symmetrical or asymmetrical configurations produced by AU14—the dimpler—resemble the proper reaction to a bad pun or a common contempt expression. In short, a smile is not a smile; it depends on the specific facial configuration. For an excellent discussion of the variety of possible emotional and conversational functions of brow movements, the reader is referred to Ekman (1979).

Historically, the major concern of the field of nonverbal communication was the communication of emotion. In 1872 Charles Darwin published a book in which he attempted to specify a set of facial expressions and gestures that represented primary, biologically adaptive emotions. He also explored the phylogenesis of these expressions. For example, the emotion of disgust, he suggested, which involves wrinkling the nose, is adaptive because it functions to shut the eyes and nasal passages so that a noxious odor will not harm the individual. Similarly, fear involves widening the eyes so that individuals can increase their ability to perceive a threatening stimulus. Darwin's major interest was facial expression. In fact, study of the evolution of social behavior in primates reveals that the evolution of the facial musculature accompanied the evolution of social communities that function in relative physical proximity (see Chevalier-Skolnikov, 1973).

Darwin's emphasis on biologically based, species-universal expressions and gestures that are isomorphic with internal emotional states has been modified to some degree to take into account cultural display rules (see Ekman, 1971; Ekman & Oster, 1979; Eckman & Friesen, 1972). It is now clear, however, that facial expressions can be measured reliably (see Ekman *et al.*, 1972; Scherer & Ekman, 1982), though many basic questions about emotion still remain.

The voice is as important a channel of emotional expression as the face. Although the precise set of physical cues that relate to specific emotions has yet to be discovered, a number of physical cues are important, such as shifts in fundamental frequency (see Scherer, 1979, 1982), speech disturbances (Mahl, 1956), and a variety of other cues including amplitude variation, tone changes, and key shifts, (e.g., major to minor; see Scherer, 1974).

Research on other channels of nonverbal behavior also have produced interesting cues that may suggest emotional states. For reviews of these literatures see Harper, Wiens, and Matarazzo (1978) and Scherer and Ekman (1982). It should be clear at this point that researchers who are interested in studying affect in marital interaction have to become familiar with an important body of literature on emotion. Unfortunately, this familiarity is rarely displayed in the literature on marital interaction.

THE EVIDENCE ON PATTERNING

What, precisely, has been discovered to date about the interactional differences between happily and unhappily married couples? In this section we summarize some of the principal findings of a program of research reported in detail in Gottman's (1979) book *Marital Interaction*.

Based on a review of the literature, Gottman (1979) proposed a model of marital interaction called the *structural model*. It has three dimensions: a positive–negative affect dimension, a negative affect reciprocity dimension, and an asymmetry in emotional responsiveness dimension. Four hypotheses comprise the structural model.

Hypothesis 1: *Degree of Structure.* There is more patterning and structure in the interaction of dissatisfied couples than in the interaction of satisfied couples.

Hypothesis 2: *Positiveness.* Satisfied couples are more positive and less negative toward one another than dissatisfied couples. The differences should be greater for negative than for positive interaction, and greater for nonverbal than for verbal behavior.

Hypothesis 3: *Reciprocity*. The reciprocation of negative behavior will discriminate dissatisfied from satisfied couples, with more reciprocity of negative behavior in distressed than in nondistressed couples. Similar discrimination is *not* predicted in the reciprocation of positive behaviors. Such discrimination would be predicted by quid pro quo theory.

Hypothesis 4: *Asymmetry*. The interaction of dissatisfied couples will show more asymmetry in predictability than will the behavior of satisfied couples. This greater asymmetry of predictability, which is in itself a type of patterning in interactions of dissatisfied couples, is also consistent with the hypothesis regarding the differential degree of temporal structure in the two groups.

These hypotheses were confirmed in one study and were replicated in a second. The results generalized across the issues couples discussed in attempting to resolve an area of disagreement in their marriage, and the results generalized across settings (from the laboratory to the home). Also, in a series of training studies it was found that couples who changed along the dimensions specified by the structural model also changed in marital satisfaction. The most central of Gottman's (1979) interactional results have been confirmed by work in other laboratories: in Oregon and California by Margolin and Wampold (1981); in New Jersey by Ting-Toomey (1982); in Germany by Revenstorf, Vogel, Wegener, Hahlweg, and Schindler (1980); and in the Netherlands by Schaap (1982).

Gottman's coding system made it possible to describe differences in the way couples resolve conflict. Basically these differences can be described by using the analogy of a chess game. A chess game has three phases: the beginning game, the middle game, and the end game. Each phase has characteristic good and bad maneuvers and objectives. The objectives can, in fact, be derived inductively from the maneuvers. The goal of the beginning phase is control of the center of the chessboard and development of position. The goal of the middle game is the favorable exchange of pieces. The goal of the end game is checkmate. Similarly there are three phases in the discussion of a marital issue. The first phase is the agenda-building phase. The objective of this phase is to air the issues as they are viewed by each person. The second phase is the arguing phase, whose goal is for partners to argue energetically for their points of view, and for each partner to understand the areas of disagreement between them. The third phase is the negotiation phase, and its goal is compromise.

It is possible to discriminate the interaction of satisfied and dissatisfied couples in each phase. In the agenda-building phase, *cross complaining* sequences characterize dissatisfied couples, while *validation* sequences characterize satisfied couples. A cross complaining sequence is one in which a complaint by one person is followed by a countercomplaint by the other person (e.g., *Wife:* I'm tired of spending all my time on the housework. You're not doing your share. *Husband:* If you used your time efficiently, you wouldn't be tired.). A validation sequence recognizes the potential validity of the other person's viewpoint before complaining (e.g., *W:* I'm tired of spending all my time on the housework. You're not doing your share. *H:* I suppose you're right. If you used your time efficiently you wouldn't be tired.).

In the middle arguing phase, *without the use of the nonverbal codes, the two groups of couples would essentially be indistinguishable.* The nonverbal codes distinguish the two groups throughout the interaction. In the negotiation phase, *counterproposal* sequences characterize the interaction of dissatisfied couples, while *contracting* sequences characterize interactions of satisfied couples. In a counterproposal sequence the proposal is met immediately by another proposal by the partner, whereas in the contracting sequence there is first some acceptance of the partner's proposal.

There were interesting negative results that disconfirmed cherished clinical beliefs about the role of the quid pro quo (or positive reciprocity), the role of metacommunication (i.e., a statement about the processes of communication, such as "You're interrupting me."), and the role of self-disclosure in discriminating the two kinds of marriages. The quid pro quo hypothesis was simply wrong. It is the deescalation of negative affect and not the reciprocation of positive affect that discriminates the two groups. Metacommunication tends to be what is called in Markov model theory an *absorbing state* for unhappily married couples—that is, it becomes nearly impossible to exit once having entered. For satisfied couples metacommunicative chains are brief and contain agreements that lead rapidly to other codes.

Self-disclosure is rare during conflict resolution conversations. Instead, couples *mindread*—that is, they make attributions of emotions, opinions, states of mind, and so on to their spouses. The effect of mindreading depends entirely on the affect with which it is delivered. If it is delivered with neutral affect or with positive affect, it is responded to as if it were a question about feelings; it is agreed with and elaborated on, usually with neutral affect (e.g., *H:* You always get *tense* at my mother's house. *W:* Yes I do. I think she does a lot to make me tense.). If it is delivered with negative affect, it is responded to as if it were a criticism; it is disagreed with and elaborated on, usually with negative affect (e.g., *H:* You *always* get tense at my mother's house. *W:* I do not. I start off relaxed until she starts criticizing me and *you* take her side.).

A critical role is played by the agreement codes. In effect, satisfied couples continually intersperse various subcodes of agreement into their sequences. In the agenda-building phase this is primarily a simple nonverbal *assent* form of agreement, as in "Oh, yeah," "uh huh," "I see," whereas in the negotiation phase this is primarily direct agreement on actually accepting the other's point of view and modifying one's own point of view. These listener responses have been called *backchanneling* by Duncan and Fiske (1977). They are clear communications to the speaker that the listener is tracking; they can serve to regulate turns; but they are also more than that in the beginning phases of marital conflict resolution. They communicate not agreement with the speaker's point of view or *content,* but that it might make some sense to see things the way the speaker does, (i.e., they communicate agreement with the speaker's *affect*). They thus communicate a great deal. They "grease the wheels" for affective expression.

In the negotiation phase of discussion the agreement codes are very different. They are not assent but agreement with the other's point of view ("yes, you're right," or "I agree with that"), or they involve accepting some modification of one's own point of view for a solution to the problem. The effect of all this is to create a climate of agreement whose presence has profound consequences for the quality of the interaction.

The quality of this interaction is best tapped by the nonverbal codes. Across studies, there was (1) more negative affect in dissatisfied couples; (2) more negative affect reciprocity in dissatisfied couples; and (3) more asymmetry in emotional responsiveness in dissatisfied couples, with the husband less responsive than the wife. These were the three dimensions of the structural model. The overarching construct that emerged is that there was more temporal linkage—that is, interactions among dissatisfied couples were more predictable, or stereotypic than were interaction of satisfied couples. It is worth noting that this was true also for positive affect reciprocity. Each behavior thus provides less information in dissatisfied interaction. Ting-Toomey (1982) replicated this result.

THE UNDERSTANDING OF PATTERN

Three models are discussed for explaining the patterns observed that discriminate satisfied from dissatisfied couples. The first is a model of the couple's perception of their interactions. The second is a response deficit model. The third is an emotional responsiveness model.

Perceptual Models

In a series of studies reported in Gottman (1979) a "talk table" was devised so that as couples interacted each could code the affective impact of messages received from his or her partner, the intended impact of messages received from the partner, and the intended impact of messages sent to the partner. This procedure was used every turn in the conversation. The talk table made it possible to test whether data obtained from the couples' own coding of their interactions on a positive–negative dimension would be veridical with observers' coding of their interactions. Using the intent variable an intent–impact discrepancy model of interaction could also be tested. In addition, the couples' coding of interaction could be tested. Finally, the couples' coding of their interactions could be analyzed sequentially. The results of these studies suggested that negative impact was more likely for dissatisfied than for satisfied couples, as was negative impact reciprocity. Positive impact reciprocity did not discriminate the two groups of couples. Hence the results paralleled the data from other studies in which affect was coded by observers. Subsequent research using a modification of the talk table (Floyd, 1980; Floyd & Markman, 1982) has supported the importance of the impact dimension, particularly for wives' perception of their husbands' messages.

In an important study, Markman (1977) tested the ability of the talk table variable to predict the relationship satisfaction over a $2\frac{1}{2}$-year period among couples planning to marry. Markman found that the impact ratings at Time 1 predicted relationship satisfaction $2\frac{1}{2}$ years later ($r = .88$, $p < .01$ for males; $r = .64$, $p < .01$ for females). These correlations are the highest ever obtained in this literature. Previously obtained measures correlated the same inventory at two time points, so that the earlier correlations shared common method variance. Markman has subsequently found that the strength of these predictions remains high even after $6\frac{1}{2}$ years. These results suggest that even small initial differences in the perception of behavior may eventually lead to large differences in relationship satisfaction.

Further investigation is necessary. We are currently using oral history interviews from 120 randomly selected couples to discover the relationships between couple's philosophy of their marriage and of relationships in general, their interaction patterns, their relationship satisfaction, and social class.

Response Deficit Models

Gottman (1979) reported that when individuals in dissatisfied marriages role-play responding to taped situations in which they pretended to be responding to their spouses, their responses were more negative than were responses by individuals in satisfied marriages. There were no significant interactions on any scale. However, there were main effects for the spouse factor, and these effects had a consistent pattern. Husbands were more positive than wives on the positive scales, whereas wives were more positive than husbands on the negative scales. This crossover effect suggests complementarity of roles: Wives were more likely than their husbands to be agreeable and to express positive affect in response to complaints, even when the complaints were negatively stated. This is consistent with the cognitive editing function of the happily married wife that emerged from sequential analyses of the interaction data—namely, wives were more likely than husbands to deescalate conflict in high-conflict situations.

The results of this study demonstrate that even when individuals *imagine* themselves responding to their spouses, the behavior of low and high marital satisfaction subjects can be discriminated across several content domains of problem situations. This provides support for the individual social competence hypothesis in the marital interaction.

A reanalysis by Gottman of a paper by Birchler *et al.* (1975) showed that people in distressed and nondistressed marriages did not differ in their interactions with strangers; they did, however, differ when interacting with their own spouses. This does not support the notion that response deficits are a cross-relationship trait. Of course, interaction with strangers is not an adequate test of this trait hypothesis; people may replicate interaction patterns only once they develop an intimate relationship.

Gottman (1979), using time-series analysis, reported some evidence to support the notion that in dissatisfied marriages husbands are less emotionally responsive to their wives than wives are to their husbands. This was tested in a recent study (Gottman & Porterfield, 1981) in which spouses sent messages with fixed verbal content to their partners (e.g., "I'm cold, aren't you?"). These messages could have one of three meanings depending on their nonverbal delivery (for example, "Turn up the heat"; "I'm requesting information"; or "I want to snuggle"). By having the messages received by both partners and strangers, it could be determined if there was a deficit in nonverbal communication in dissatisfied couples and, if so, whether it was a listener or a receiver deficit. For example, if a wife could send effectively to a stranger but not to her husband, this was a receiver deficit. The results showed evidence for a deficit as a receiver. Noller (1980) independently conducted a nearly identical study with Australian couples and found exactly the same results. It is possible that the dissatisfied husband's lack of emotional responsiveness to his wife leads to the escalation of negative affect and negative reciprocity in high conflict discussions.

Emotional Responsiveness Model

Gottman (1980) reported that there is a substantially higher cross-situational consistency (from low- to high-conflict tasks) in negative affect reciprocity than in either negative affect, positive affect, or positive affect reciprocity. He speculated that the theoretical basis of the high consistency of negative affect reciprocity is that it creates a temporal physiological linkage between members of the interacting dyad. Support for this notion comes from a study conducted by Kaplan, Burch, and Bloom (1964), who correlated the electrodermal responses of interacting dyads paired on the basis of either mutual like, mutual dislike, or mutual neutrality. Their results indicated that significant predictability of electrodermal response from one member of the dyad to the other occurred only in the dyads that were paired on the basis of mutual dislike. To the extent that dyads paired on the basis of mutual dislike can be expected to reciprocate negative affect, their finding can be seen as supportive of Gottman's speculation. However, Kaplan *et al.*'s study has several statistical problems that must be considered. Because of serial dependency in these kinds of data across time, the significance test of a simple correlation is invalid. In addition, the authors failed to control for autocorrelation in inferring crosscorrelation. More appropriate analyses that are not subject to these problems (such as bivariate time-series analyses) are available for examining the extent of physiological predictability between members of an interacting dyad.

There are also problems with the physiological measure used by Kaplan *et al.* Skin conductance shares a problem with many other autonomic nervous system (ANS) measures, in that they are inherently nonspecific, responding to a wide range of behavioral states including attention, general arousal, activation, stress, and emotion. Skin conductance has unique problems when used as a single measure of ANS activity, in that it is affected only by the sympathetic branch of the ANS and does not reflect parasympathetic branch activity. Equally important, the use of a skin conductance measure by itself allows no sensitivity to the cardiovascular functions of the ANS. Ideally, a physiological measurement battery would be broad enough to reflect the activity of the ANS in the electrodermal (e.g., skin conductance), cardiovascular, and visceral domains. In addition, it should go beyond the ANS to include measures sensitive to skeletal muscle activity, which is closely linked to parasympathetic ANS cardiovascular functions. The case for breadth of physiological measurement is further strengthened by research indicating that certain individuals tend to respond stereotypically across situations with maximal responses in a single physiological response system. Thus limiting physiological measurement to skin conductance will produce problems if the sample includes "cardiovascular responders" or "somatic muscle responders."

Despite these reservations, the results of the Kaplan *et al.* study were sufficiently promising to convince us to design a study that utilized improved statistics and broader physiological measurement to test the hypothesis that negative affect reciprocity creates a temporal physiological linkage between members of the interacting dyad.

This section is a brief report of the design and preliminary data analyses of a study by Levenson and Gottman. The subjects were married couples whose marital satisfaction had been assessed using two self-report measures (Locke & Wallace, 1959; Burgess *et al.*, 1971). Couples came to the laboratory at the end of a day after being separated for at least 8 hours. We obtained videotapes and physiological measures from both the husband and wife during two different kinds of interaction. The first of these was a 15-minute discussion of how their day had gone (preceded by 5 minutes of face-to-face silence).[2]

In our study, discussion of the events of the day was followed by an interview to determine the area of major conflict in the marriage. Then videotapes and physiological measures were obtained during a 15-minute period in which the couple discussed that issue and tried to work toward its resolution (as in the earlier interaction, this was preceded by 5 minutes of face-to-face silence).

In a second session, each spouse returned to the laboratory independently to view the videotape of the original session and provide a continuous rating of his or her recall of affect during the interaction on a positive–negative dimension. Videotapes and physiological measures were obtained during these recall sessions as well.

As indicated earlier, we wanted to obtain a broad set of physiological measures. Difficulties in measuring ANS visceral functions (such as stomach and intestinal responses) and practical limitations of obtaining continuous physiological measurement simultaneously from two subjects led us to select four basic measures from the following domains: somatic (general somatic activity), ANS electrodermal (skin conductance), and ANS car-

---

[2]We chose this topic because it seemed to be typical for American couples. A recent anthropological film by Thomas Gregor of Vanderbilt University provides some indication that this topic might be a cross-culturally universal part of marital interaction in the same way as is gossip, conflict, and decision-making (Strodtbeck, 1951). In this film, the daily life of an Indian tribe, the Mehinaku, in the Amazon region of Brazil (in Xingu Park near Post Leonardo) is explored. The Mehinaku have had very little contact with modern civilization. Theirs is a highly structured society in which men and women have highly specialized traditional roles. Nonetheless, in the evening after supper, husbands and wives are shown lying in their hammocks discussing the events of the day.

diovascular (cardiac interbeat interval and pulse transmission time—PTT—to the finger). Our choice of the two cardiovascular measures was dictated by certain theoretical considerations. Heart rate (measured as heart period or interbeat interval—IBI) is one of the basic ways in which the heart can increase or decrease its output of blood to the body. Unlike skin conductance, which is entirely under sympathetic ANS control, heart rate is usually controlled by the parasympathetic branch of the ANS. Obrist, Webb, Sutterer, and Howard (1970) argued that changes in heart rate under parasympathetic control are closely coupled to the activity of the voluntary (striated) muscles. But heart rate can also be altered by the sympathetic branch of the ANS. This seems to occur under conditions of acute stress when the subject has to do something active to cope with the stress; under these conditions changes in heart rate can become relatively independent of voluntary muscle activity (Obrist, Lawler, Howard, Smithson, Martin, & Manning, 1974). Given that changes in heart rate can be produced by both branches of the ANS, and that sympathetic nervous system activity is an important part of negative emotional states such as anger and fear, as well as playing a crucial role in adaptation to emergency (the so-called fight or flight response), we felt it desirable to have a "purer" sumpathetic cardiovascular measure. Pulse transmission time (PTT) to the finger is such a measure; it measures the interval between an electrical event that signals the heart to begin its contraction (we used the R-wave) and the arrival of the pulse pressure wave at the finger (we detected this with a photoplethysmograph). PTT reflects two sympathetically mediated cardiovascular events: (1) changes in the force of the heart's contraction (the other major method besides changing the rate the heart uses to regulate its output of blood to the body), and (2) changes in the distensibility of the arteries between the heart and the finger. These cardiovascular events are mediated by the beta and alpha subsections of the sympathetic branch of the ANS, with little or no parasympathetic involvement (for a thorough discussion of these cardiovascular measures and their physiological bases, see Newlin & Levenson, 1979). Thus our four measures gave us sensitivity to electrodermal, cardiovascular, and somatic events and within the ANS to the parasympathetic branch and both beta and alpha subsections of the sympathetic branch. In addition to measures of average level, we computed variability measures for (IBI and PTT to provide additional information.

What were our results? First, we briefly refer to some statistical work by Gottman and Ringland (1981) that solved the statistical problems of inferring a relationship between two time-series controlling for autocorrelation in each series. Basically, if two series are X_t and Y_t, we assess the extent to which the past of Y_t accounts for variance in X_t over and above that accounted for by the past of X_t (refer to Figure 4.1). If we find a relationship,

$$x_t = \sum a_i x_{t-i} + \sum b_i y_{t-i} + e_t$$

$\underbrace{\phantom{\sum a_i x_{t-i}}}_{\text{PAST OF X}}$ $\underbrace{\phantom{\sum b_i y_{t-i}}}_{\text{PAST OF Y}}$

A — first sum, B — second sum

$$y_t = \sum c_i y_{t-i} + \sum d_i x_{t-i} + n_t$$

$\underbrace{\phantom{\sum c_i y_{t-i}}}_{\text{PAST OF Y}}$ $\underbrace{\phantom{\sum d_i x_{t-i}}}_{\text{PAST OF X}}$

C — first sum, D — second sum

$X \rightarrow Y$ $Y \nrightarrow X$ ASSYM.	$X \rightarrow Y$ $Y \rightarrow X$ BIDIRECT.
$X \nrightarrow Y$ $Y \nrightarrow X$ NO RELAT.	$X \nrightarrow Y$ $Y \rightarrow X$ ASSYM.

Figure 4.1 Assessing the relationship between two time-series, controlling for autocorrelation in each series.

this implies that Y influences $X(Y \rightarrow X)$. This is similar to a suggestion made by Pierce (1977) for economic time-series. Four patterns are possible: two asymmetrical patterns ($Y \rightarrow X$ but $X \nrightarrow Y$, and $X \rightarrow Y$ but $Y \nrightarrow X$), a bidirectional or feedback pattern ($Y \rightarrow X$ and $X \rightarrow Y$), and no relationship. Also we can assess the strength of these associations statistically.

Our findings supported those of Kaplan *et al.* During the discussion of the events of the day, we found that physiological linkage between the husband and wife across our four measures was related negatively to marital satisfaction using bivariate time-series-analytic techniques. The multiple R during discussion of the events of the day for all physiological predictability measures and marital satisfaction was .44. During discussion of the conflict issue, the patterns of negative affect and negative affect reciprocity increased and a similar pattern of results held except that the relationship was even stronger; the multiple R between the predictability measures and marital satisfaction was .77.

To summarize, we found that (*a*) Kaplan *et al*'s results held, (*b*) with time-series analyses across a broad set of physiological measures the results were strengthened, and (*c*) as the degree of conflict increased, our ability to discriminate between satisfied and dissatisfied marriages also increased. In the same way that earlier studies had identified *behavioral* characteristics of dissatisfied marriages, this new study identified *physiological* characteristics of dissatisfied marriages.

Using multivariate regression techniques, we decided to go a bit further and attempted to determine the amount of variance in marital satisfaction we could account for using only physiological variables. We found that with the physiological linkage variable we discussed earlier and three other categories of physiological measures, we could account for over 84% of the variance in marital satisfaction! These additional three categories were as follows:

1. *Skin conductance before and during conversations.* Skin conductance levels were much higher for satisfied than dissatisfied couples during the 5

minutes of face-to-face silence preceding discussion of the events of the day. Analyzing the content of the discussions, we found the imposed silence to be agony for the satisfied couples and a relief for the dissatisfied couples.

2. *Skin conductance during the video recall session.* Skin conductance responses during the recall session largely paralleled those obtained during the interactions, except that for dissatisfied couples the responses were actually greater in the recall session than in the interaction session. We speculate that for dissatisfied couples, the presence of the partner may inhibit responses and activate avoidance procedures, whereas the partner's absence during the recall session removes these constraints and lowers defenses against experiencing the affect.

3. *Pulse transmission time variability of wife.* In distressed couples the wife showed more variability in this cardiovascular measure of sympathetic ANS response. This single measure was found to be strongly related to how negatively she rated the affect she experienced in the interaction. We speculate that the strong negative emotions experienced by the wife in the dissatisfied couples may be activating the sympathetic ANS response.

As we indicated earlier, these preliminary findings drawn from this study have been largely concerned with the relationship between marital satisfaction and patterns of physiological and affective response that occur between and within members of a couple. We feel that this study will also provide a unique opportunity for exploring basic and long-standing questions pertaining to the nature of emotion per se. The importance of the emotional substrate in close relationships is undeniable, and any progress made in understanding the nature of emotion can only benefit work on relationship processes. With this is mind, we would like to make the case for the desirability of studying emotion in the context of social interaction in an intimate relationship.

Ekman *et al.*'s (1972) extensive review indicates that research on the expression of emotion in the human face has tended to use two methods: (1) using situations and experimental manipulations that are thought to elicit emotions, and (2) using posed expressions by actors. The authors point out that the first method is plagued by the considerable lack of agreement concerning what stimulus elicits a given emotion, by the fact that most stimuli elicit *combinations* of emotions rather than *specific* emotions, and that different individuals respond to a given stimulus with different emotions. They argue that the second method is particularly useful for studying the degree of agreement among judges of the posed expression, and in studying the relationship between observers' judgments of emotions and the subject's phenomenological experience. Of course, legitimate questions can be raised concerning the extent to which emotions associated with posed expressions differ qualitatively and quantitatively from naturally elicited emotions. Still, despite inherent limitations, both methods have proven quite useful in the study of emotion.

There is, however, a third method that has yet to be explored: studying emotion during social interaction. Studying emotions in a social interactive framework has considerable intuitive appeal. In addition, there is good reason to believe that from an evolutionary viewpoint, an important adaptive function of having a rich repertoire of emotional expressions is their social communicative value for conspecifics (see Chevalier-Skolnikoff, 1973, for a comprehensive discussion of this issue).

It has been noted by many investigators that interaction between married couples produces a high level of spontaneous positive and negative affect. The range and variety of this affect can be further broadened by studying couples who vary in their degree of marital satisfaction. Marital interaction would seem to be an ideal paradigm for the study of emotion. Ekman *et al.* (1972) argued that the interactive context provides a unique opportunity to study the consequences of emotional expression, as well as allowing study of concomitant and antecedent events.

> While some investigators of human nonverbal behavior have begun to study interactive sequences, the only studies of the face that utilize this approach have not been concerned with emotion, and have isolated only one aspect of facial behavior for study, looking or not looking at the face of the other person [p. 12].

In part the study of emotion during interactive sequences has awaited the development of appropriate statistical methods for handling the unique kinds of data generated. Now a number of appropriate methods do exist, including Markov models, information theory and lag-sequence analysis, and time-series analysis. Unfortunately, the existence of these analytic techniques does not answer the question, "How should emotion be measured?" Strongman (1978) stated:

> Any theory of emotion or any empirical research on emotion deals only with some part of the broad meaning that the term has acquired. Some theorists stress psychological factors, some behavioral, some subjective. . . . There is no consensus of opinion; at present emotion defies description [p. 102].

We argue that a measurement network adequate for the study of emotion must sample from the physiological, phenomenological, nonverbal behavioral (i.e., facial expressions and other kinesic behaviors), paralinguistic, and linguistic domains. There is a problem inherent in studying emotion of choosing a criterion for determining when emotion and which emotion has occurred. The rules for setting criteria using information from the various domains of emotion are not obvious. We do know that criteria based on a single domain are not very reliable. We have already discussed the problems inherent in the common practice of using the stimulus situation to specify the emotion it produces. Similarly, we would be uncomfortable with criteria based solely on physiological patterns; the evidence for specific physiological patterns for each emotion is inconclusive at best. Linguistic content is so easily manipulated that no researcher would trust it as a single criterion. Similarly, there are problems with using the expressions of the face. For example, most emotional experiences are fleeting and are not accompanied by the classic full-face prototypes of emotion described by Ekman and Friesen (1975) and others. An additional problem pointed to by Ekman *et al.* (1972) is that people sometimes control their faces in ways that mask and distort the signs of emotion. The problem seems at times to be insoluble.

It is our belief that confidence in researchers' ability to identify and classify emotional moments during social interaction requires convergence of information from several domains. For example, if a husband sounds angry (e.g., he is speaking at a high volume with a stacatto rhythm) and the linguistic content of his communication fits a template for anger (e.g., "Will you *stop* interrupting me!), and his face looks angry (e.g., brows down and together, eyelids tensed, lips pushed together), and his gestures suggest anger (e.g., fist clenched), and he is physiologically aroused (e.g., heart contracting forcibly), then we would feel quite confident asserting that he was in fact angry. A convergent approach such as this has been used in the Levenson and Gottman study of marital interaction to identify a corpus of "emotional moments"; our confidence in the accuracy of classification will, of course, vary from emotion to emotion and from moment to moment on the basis of the strength of the convergence and the confidence we have in the mapping of that emotion onto the various domains of measurement. For example, we expect increased cardiovascular activity to accompany many moments of anger, but what kind of cardiovascular changes, if any, will accompany moments of happiness?

We should add that the convergent method of identifying emotional moments provides a means for further studying the relation among domains of emotion. Thus, for example, to answer our question as to whether there is a specific cardiovascular pattern associated with happiness, we would first identify all moments of happiness in our data using information gleaned from measurement domains *other than the physiological,* and then look at the cardiovascular patterns. The same approach can be used to study other patterns in other domains. For example, we have noted that it is rare to find full-face prototypes of emotion during social interaction. However, we believe that consistent patterns of facial movements are associated with the different emotions (of course, not all patterns of facial movement signify emotion). The Facial Action Coding System (FACS) provides a method for describing facial movements adequately, but as its authors (Ekman &

Friesen, 1978) indicate, there is a need for an empirically derived basis for translating facial movement codes into emotions. Using sequential cluster-ing methods to go from discrete FACS codes into larger units of facial action and facial action sequences, we will be able to provide this kind of em-pirically based evidence for assigning emotional labels to certain facial movement sequences, using the emotional moments (defined on bases other than the face) from this study.

SUMMARY

We wish first to underscore the strength of the relationships found in this research program: These relationships are unparalleled in the study of mari-tal satisfaction and suggest that the study of affect will prove promising. The research program began by describing the kinds of interactive sequences that consistently discriminate satisfied and dissatisfied couples during the resolution of conflict. We have found that these sequences generalize from the laboratory to home settings, across a range of issues, and from conflict decision-making to nonconflict tasks. Using information from these studies and from studies of couples' perceptions of their own interactions, we have been able to predict relationship satisfaction in longitudinal studies and have developed methods for intervening effectively to enhance marital satisfaction.

We propose that the underlying mechanism that maintains closeness in marriages is symmetry in emotional responsiveness, particularly in the kind of low-intensity affective interactions captured by sharing the events of the day. It is precisely the absence of this responsiveness, we hypothesize, that leads to high levels of negative affect, which produces emotional withdrawal and bursts of negative affect reciprocity. Using these constructs and mea-sures drawn from the physiological domain, we have been able to account for a large proportion of the variance in marital satisfaction. We believe that with these measures we are tapping the quality of the friendship in the marriage; it is the quality of this friendship that provides the necessary context for the resolution of conflict.

REFERENCES

Ackerman, N. W. The family as a special and emotional unit. *Bulletin of the Kansas Mental Hygiene Society*, 1937, *12*, 1–8.

Ackerman, N. W. The diagnosis of neurotic marital interaction. *Social Casework*, 1954, *35*, 139–147.

Ackerman, N. W., & Sobel, R. Family diagnosis: An approach to the study of the preschool child. *American Journal of Orthopsychiatry*, 1950, *20*, 744–752.

Alexander, F. *Psychosomatic medicine, its principles and applications*. New York: Norton, 1950.

Alexander, J. F. Defensive and supportive communications in family systems. *Journal of Marriage and the Family*, 1973, *35*, 613–617. (a)

Alexander, J. F. Defensive and supportive communication in normal and deviant families. *Consulting and Clinical Psychology*, 1973, *40*, 223–231. (b)

Azrin, N. H., Naster, B. J., & Jones, R. Reciprocity counseling: A rapid learning-based procedure for marital counseling. *Behavior Research and Therapy*, 1973, *11*, 365–382.

Bales, R. F. *Interaction process analysis*. Reading, MA: Addison-Wesley, 1950.

Bateson, C. Critical evaluations. *International Journal of Psychiatry*, 1966, *2*, 415–417.

Bateson, G., Jackson, D. D., Haley, J., & Weakland, J. Toward a theory of schizophrenia. *Behavioral Science*, 1956, *1*, 251–264.

Beels, C., & Ferber, A. Family therapy: A view. *Family Process*, 1969, *8*, 280–317.

Birchler, G. R. *Differential patterns of instrumental affiliative behavior as a function of degree of marital distress and level of intimacy*. Doctoral thesis, Eugene, OR, University of Oregon, 1972.

Birchler, G., Weiss, R., & Vincent, J. Multimethod analysis of social reinforcement exchange between maritally distressed and nondistressed spouse and stranger dyads. *Journal of Personality and Social Psychology*, 1975, *31*, 349–360.

Brannigan, C. R., & Humphries, D. A. Human nonverbal behaviors, a means of communication. In N. B. Jones (Ed.), *Ethological studies of child behaviour*. Cambridge, England: Cambridge University Press, 1978.

Brazelton, T. B., Koslowski, B., & Main, M. The origins of reciprocity: The early mother–infant interaction. In M. Lewis & L. A. Rosenblum (Eds.), *The effect of the infant on its caregiver*. New York: Wiley, 1974.

Bruner, J. S., & Tagiuri, R. The perception of people. In G. Lindzey (Ed.), *Handbook of social psychology* (Vol. 2). Reading MA: Addison-Wesley, 1954.

Burchinal, L. G., Hawkes, G. R., & Gardner, B. Marriage adjustment, personality characteristics of parents and the personality adjustment of their children. *Marriage and Family Living*, 1957, *17*, 366–372.

Burgess, E. W., & Cottrell, L. S. *Predicting success or failure in marriage*. New York: Prentice-Hall, 1939.

Burgess, E. W., Locke, H. J., & Thomes, M. M. *The family*. New York: Van Nostrand Reinhold, 1971.

Burgess, E. W., & Wallin, P. *Engagement and marriage*. Chicago: Lippincott, 1953.

Cannon, W. B. The James-Lange theory of emotions: A critical examination and an alternative theory. *American Journal of Psychology*, 1927, *39*, 106–124.

Caputo, D. V. The parents of schizophrenics. *Family Process*, 1963, *2*, 339–356.

Cheek, F. E. The "schizophrenogenic" mother in word and deed. *Family Process*, 1964, *3*, 155–177.

Chevalier-Skolnikoff, S. Facial expression of emotion in nonhuman primates. In P. Ekman (Ed.), *Darwin and facial expression: A century of research in review*. New York: Academic, 1973.

Corsini, R. J. Understanding and similarity in marriage. *Journal of Abnormal and Social Psychology*, 1956, *52*, 337–342.

Darwin, C. *The expression of the emotions in man and animals*. London: John Murray, 1872.

Dean, D. G. Emotional maturity and marital adjustment. *Journal of Marriage and the Family*, 1966, *28*(4), 454–457.

Duck, S. W. *Personal relationships* (Vol. 4): *Dissolving personal relationships*. London: Academic, 1982.

Duncan, S. D., Jr., & Fiske, D. W. *Face-to-face interaction,* Hillsdale, NJ: Erlbaum, 1977.

Ekman, P. Universals and cultural differences in facial expressions of emotion. *Nebraska Symposium on Motivation,* 1971.

Ekman, P. About brows: Emotional and conversational signals. In M. von Cranach, K. Foppa, W. Lepenies, & D. Ploog (Eds.), *Human ethology*. Cambridge: Cambridge University Press, 1979.

Ekman, P. Methods for measuring facial action. In K. R. Scherer & P. Ekman (Eds.), *Handbook of methods in nonverbal behavior research*. New York: Cambridge University Press, 1982.

Ekman, P. & Friesen, W. V. *Unmasking the face*. Englewood Cliffs, NJ: Prentice-Hall, 1975.

Ekman, P., & Friesen, W. V. *Facial action coding system*. Palo Alto, CA: Consulting Psychologists Press, 1978.

Ekman, P., Friesen, W. V., & Ellsworth, P. *Emotion in the human face*. New York: Pergamon, 1972.

Ekman, P., & Oster, H. Facial expressions of emotion. *Annual Review of Psychology,* 1979, *30,* 527–554.

Floyd, F. *Insiders' and outsiders' perspectives on marital distress*. Unpublished master's thesis, Bowling Green State University, Bowling Green, OH, 1980.

Floyd, F. J., & Markman, H. J. Observational biases in spouse observation: Toward a cognitive/behavioral model of marriage. Unpublished manuscript, University of Denver, Department of Psychology, 1982.

Friesen, W. V. *Cultural differences in facial expressions in a social situation: An experimental test of the concept of display rules*. Doctoral dissertation. University of California, San Francisco, 1972.

Gottman, J. M. *Marital interaction: Experimental investigations*. New York: Academic, 1979.

Gottman, J. M. Consistency of nonverbal affect and affect reciprocity in marital interaction. *Journal of Consulting and Clinical Psychology,* 1980, *48,* 711–717.

Gottman, J. M., Notarius, C., Marman, H., Bank, S., Yoppi, B., & Rubin, M. E. Behavior exchange theory and marital decision making. *Journal of Personality and Social Psychology,* 1976, *34,* 14–23.

Gottman, J. M., & Porterfield, A. L. Communicative dysfunction in the nonverbal behavior of married couples. *Journal of Marriage and the Family,* 1981, *43,* 817–824.

Haley, J. Research on family patterns: An instrument measurement. *Family Process,* 1964, *3,* 41–65.

Haley, J. Speech sequences of normal and abnormal families with two children present. *Family Process,* 1967, *6,* 81–97.

Hall, J., & Williams, M. S. A comparison of decision-making performances in established and ad hoc groups. *Journal of Personality and Social Psychology,* 1966, *3,* 214–222.

Harper, R. G., Wiens, A. N., & Matarazzo, J. D. *Nonverbal communication: The state of the art*. New York: Wiley 1978.

Harvey, J. H., Weber, A., Yarkin, K. L., & Stewart, B. An attributional approach to relationship breakdown and dissolution. In S. Duck (Ed.), *Personal relationships* (Vol. 4): *Dissolving personal relationships*. London: Academic, 1982.

Hetherington, E. M., & Martin, B. Family interaction and psychopathology in children. In H. C. Quay & J. S. Werry (Eds.), *Psychopathological disorders of childhood*. New York: 1972.

Hops, H., Wills, T. A., Patterson, G. R., & Weiss, R. L. The marital interaction coding system (MICS). Unpublished manuscript, Eugene, OR, University of Oregon, 1972.

Izard, C. E. *The face of emotion*. New York: Appleton-Century-Crofts, 1971.

Jackson, D. D. Family rules: Marital quid pro quo. *Archives of General Psychiatry*, 1965, *12*, 1535–1541.

Jacob, T. Family interaction in disturbed and normal families: A methodological and substantive review. *Psychological Bulletin*, 1975, *82*, 33–65.

Jacobson, N. S. Problem solving and contingency contracting in the treatment of marital discord. *Journal of Consulting and Clinical Psychology*, 1977, *45*, 92–100.

Jacobson, N. S., & Martin, B. Behavioral marriage therapy: Current status. *Psychological Bulletin*, 1976, *83*(4), 540–556.

James, W. What is an emotion? *Mind*, 1884, *9*, 188–205.

Kaplan, H. B., Burch, N. R., & Bloom S. W. Physiological covariation in small peer groups. In P. H. Leiderman & D. Shapiro (Eds.), *Psychobiological approaches to social behavior*. Stanford, CA: Stanford University Press, 1964.

Kelley, H. H. An application of attribution theory to reserach methodology for close relationships. In G. Levinger & H. Raush (Eds.), *Close relationships: Perspectives on the meaning of intimacy*. Amherst: University of Massachusetts Press, 1977.

Kelley, H. H. *Personal relationships: Their structure and processes*. Hillsdale, NJ: Erlbaum, 1979.

Laing, R. D., Phillipson, H., & Lee, A. R. *Interpersonal perception*. London: Tavistock, 1966.

Lamb, M. E., Soumi, S. J., & Stephenson, G. R. (Eds.) *Social interaction analysis: Methodological Issues*. Madison: University of Wisconsin Press, 1979.

Landis, C. Studies of emotional reactions: II. General behavior and social expression. *Journal of Comparative Psychology*, 1924, *4*, 447–509.

Landis, C. The interpretation of facial expression in emotion. *Journal of General Psychology*, 1929, *2*, 59–72.

Leary, T. *Multilevel measurement of interpersonal behavior*. Berkeley, CA: Psychological Consultation Service, 1956.

Leary, T. *Interpersonal diagnosis of personality*. New York: Ronald Press, 1957.

Lederer, W. J., & Jackson, D. D. *The mirages of marriage*. New York: Norton, 1968.

Leik, R. K. Instrumentality and emotionality in family interaction. *Sociometry*, 1963, *26*, 131–145.

Levinger, G. A social psychological perspective on marital dissolution. *Journal of Social Issues*, 1976, *32*, 21–47.

Locke, H. J. *Predicting adjustment in marriage: A comparison of a divorced and a happily married group*. New York: Holt, 1951.

Locke, H. J., & Wallace, K. M. Short marital-adjustment and prediction tests: Their reliability and validity. *Marriage and Family Living*, 1959, *21*, 251–255.

Locke, H. J., & Williamson, R. C. Marital adjustment: A factor analysis study. *American Sociological Review*, 1958, *23*, 562–569.

Mahl, G. F. Disturbances and silences in the patient's speech in psychotherapy. *Journal of Abnormal Social Psychology*, 1956, *53*, 1–15.

Margolin, G., & Wampold, B. E. A sequential analysis of conflict and accord in distressed and nondistressed marital partners. *Journal of Consulting and Clinical Psychology*, 1981, *47*, 554–567.

Markman, H. J. *A behavior exchange model applied to the longitudinal study of couples planning to marry*. Unpublished doctoral dissertation. Indiana University, Bloomington, 1977.

Markman, H. J. Application of a behavioral model of marriage in predicting relationship satisfaction of couples planning a marriage. *Journal of Consulting and Clinical Psychology*, 1979, *47*, 743–749.

Markman, H. J. Prediction of marital distress: A 5-year follow-up. *Journal of Consulting and Clinical Psychology*, 1981, *49*, 760–762.

Mathews, V. D., & Milhanovitch, C. S. New orientations on marital maladjustment. *Marriage and Family Living*, 1963, 26(3), 300–304.

Mishler, E. G., & Waxler, N. E. Family interaction processes and schizophrenia: A review of current theories. *International Journal of Psychiatry*, 1966, 2, 375–415.

Mishler, E. G., & Waxler, N. E. *Interaction in families: An experimental study of family process in schizophrenia.* New York: Wiley, 1968.

Murstein, B. I., Cerreto, M., & MacDonald, M. G. A theory and investigation of the effect of exchange-orientation on marriage and friendship. *Journal of Marriage and the Family*, 1977, 39, 543–548.

Navran, L. Communication and adjustment in marriage. *Family Process*, 1967, 6, 173–184.

Newlin, D. B., & Levenson, R. W. Pre-ejection period: Measuring beta-andrenergic influences upon the heart. *Psychophysiology*, 1979, 16, 546–553.

Noller, P. Marital misunderstandings: *A study of couples' nonverbal communication.* Doctoral dissertation. University of Queensland, Australia, 1980.

Obrist, P. A., Lawler, J. E., Howard, J. L., Smithson, K. W., Martin, D. L., & Manning, J. Sympathetic influences on cardiac rate and contractility during acute stress in humans. *Psychophysiology*, 1974, 11, 405–427.

Obrist, P. A., Webb, R. A., Sutterer, J. R., & Howard, J. L. The cardiac somatic relationship: Some reformulations. *Psychophysiology*, 1970, 6, 569–587.

Olson, D. H. Empirically unbinding the double-bind: Review of research and conceptual reformulations. *Family Process*, 1972, 11, 69–94.

Patterson, G. R., Hops, H., & Weiss, R. L. Interpersonal skills training for couples in early stages of conflict. *Journal of Marriage and the Family*, 1975, 37, 295–303.

Patterson, G. R., Ray, R. S., Shaw, D. A., & Cobb, J. A. Manual for coding of family interactions, 1969 revision. Document No. 01234. Order from ASIS/NAPS, Microfiche Publications, 440 Park Avenue South, New York, 10016.

Patterson, G. R., & Reid, J. B. Reciprocity and coercion: Two facets of social systems. In J. Michaels & C. Neuringer (Eds.), *Behavior modification for psychologists.* New York: Appleton, 1970.

Reid, J. B. *Reciprocity and family interaction.* Unpublished doctoral dissertation. University of Oregon, Eugene, OR, 1967.

Riskin, J. & Faunce, E. E. Family interaction scales, III. Discussion of methodology and substantive findings. *Archives of General Psychiatry*, 1970, 22, 527–537.

Rubenstein, L., & Cameron, D. E. Electronic analysis of nonverbal communication. *Comprehensive Psychiatry*, 1968, 9, 200–208.

Ryder, R. G. Husband–wife dyads versus married strangers. *Family Process*, 1968, 7, 233–238.

Schaap, C. *Communication and adjustment in marriages.* The Netherlands: Swets & Zeitlinger, 1982.

Scherer, K. R. Acoustic concomitants of emotional dimensions: Judging affect from synthesized tone sequences. In S. Weitz (Ed.), *Nonverbal communication: Readings with commentary.* New York: Oxford University Press, 1974.

Scherer, K. R. Personality markers in speech. In K. R. Scherer & H. Gilen (Eds.), *Social markers in speech.* Cambridge: Cambridge University Press, 1979.

Scherer, K. R. Methods of research on vocal communication: Paradigms and parameters. In K. R. Scherer & P. Ekman (Eds.), *Handbook of methods in nonverbal behavior research.* New York: Cambridge University Press, 1982.

Scherer, K. R. & Ekman, P. *Handbook of methods in nonverbal behavior research.* New York: Cambridge University Press, 1982.

Shannon, C. E. The mathematical theory of communication. In C. E. Shannon & W. Weaver

(Eds.), *The mathematical theory of communication*. Urbana: University of Illinois Press, 1949.

Spanier, G. B. A new measure for assessing the quality of marriage and similar dyads. *Journal of Marriage and the Family*, 1976, *38*, 15–28.

Strodtbeck, F. L. Husband–wife interaction over revealed differences. *American Sociological Review*, 1951, *16*, 468–473.

Strongman, K. T. *The psychology of emotion*. New York: Wiley, 1978.

Stuart, R. B. Operant–interpersonal treatment for marital discord. *Journal of Consulting and Clinical Psychology*, 1969, *33*, 675–682.

Terman, L. M., Buttenweiser, P., Ferguson, L. W., Johnson, W. B., & Wilson, D. P. *Psychological factors in marital happiness*. New York: McGraw-Hill, 1938.

Terman, L. M., & Wallin, P. The validity of marriage prediction and marital adjustment tests. *American Sociological Review*, 1949, *14*, 497–504.

Tharp, R. G. Psychological patterning in marriage. *Psychological Bulletin*, 1963, *60*(2), 97–117.

Thibaut, J. W., & Kelley, H. H. *The social psychology of groups*. New York: Wiley, 1959.

Tiny-Toomey, S. An analysis of communication patterns in differentially satisfied marital couples. Paper presented at the annual convention of the International Communication Association, Boston, May 1982.

Watzlawick, P., Beavin, J. H., & Jackson, D. D. *Pragmatics of human communication: A study of interactional patterns, pathologies, and paradoxes*. New York: Norton, 1967.

Waxler, N. E., & Mishler, E. G. Sequential patterning in family interaction: A methodological note. *Family Process*, 1970, *9*, 211–220.

Weiss, R., Birchler, G., & Vincent, J. Contractual models for negotiation training in marital dyads. *Journal of Marriage and the Family*, 1974, *36*, 1–11.

Weiss, R. L., Hops, H., & Patterson, G. R. A framework for conceptualizing marital conflict: A technology for altering it, some data for evaluating it. In L. A. Hamerlynch, I. E. Handy, & E. J. Mash (Eds.), *Behavior change: The fourth Banff conference on behavior modification*. Champaign, IL: Research Press, 1973.

Wills, T. A., Weiss, R. L., & Patterson, G. R. A behavior analysis of the determinants of marital satisfaction. *Journal of Consulting and Clinical Psychology*, 1974, *42*, 802–811.

Winter, F., Ferreira, A., & Bowers, N. Decision-making in married and unrelated couples. *Family Process*, 1973, *12*, 83–94.

5

*Social Support Processes**

SHARON S. BREHM

EDITORS' INTRODUCTION

In this chapter, Sharon Brehm presents a theoretical model describing the nature of social support processes in adults. She attempts to provide here a cogent conceptual framework addressing fundamental aspects of social support: its definition, specification of its benefits, and an understanding of the conditions that promote its occurrence. While attribution theory serves as the general theoretical perspective, a number of other social psychological theories are also integrated into the model. Finally, developmental aspects of social support processes are considered in light of the conceptual framework Brehm proposes.

This chapter illustrates an area—social support—that has been of concern in both developmental and social psychology, but in very different ways. It is, therefore, a good example of how researchers often find themselves in distinct areas of a discipline that are also boundary areas but not recognizable as such because of the labels that are used to describe the phenomenon under study. Nurturance and social support are two processes that have typically been studied independently by developmental and social psychologists. However, the processes underlying these phenomena may be quite similar, even though nurturance is usually applied to parent–child interactions and social support is reserved to describe adult relationships. In addition, the work on attribution and its relationship to social

*This chapter was written during the author's term as Fulbright Research Scholar at the École des Hautes Études en Sciences Sociales, Paris, while on sabbatical leave from the University of Kansas. Financial support from the University of Kansas and the Franco-American Commission for Educational Exchange is gratefully acknowledged.

BOUNDARY AREAS IN SOCIAL
AND DEVELOPMENTAL PSYCHOLOGY

support has received some attention in the social psychological literature (e.g., Harvey, Wells, & Alvarez, 1978) but has not been examined by developmental psychologists. Notice how, as the chapter proceeds and the boundary area is encountered (developmental questions regarding attributions and social support), the frequency of reference citations drops precipitously. This is a good illustration of one of the major problems of boundary area research: when specific, integrative issues become of interest, it is difficult—if not impossible—to find relevant empirical research on these issues. Thus, the scholar interested in building an integrative model is thrown back on his or her own speculations. This is not a criticism of the present chapter; it is instead an example of a significant obstacle inherent in the struggle to achieve an interface between established subdisciplines.

INTRODUCTION

It is a virtual truism that social support is good for people. Presumably, children need it from their parents, clients from their psychotherapists, and colleagues, friends, and lovers from one another. For something that is so universally apparent, however, we have surprisingly little understanding of any of the terms of the proposition. What precisely is social support? What are its specific benefits? What are the conditions that promote its occurrence?

I would like to suggest that our understanding of social support processes has been limited by the absence of cogent theoretical models of their characteristics and effects. Perhaps because of the complexity of social support, and perhaps because it is difficult to know precisely what we all know vaguely, the need for prior explicit theorizing appears especially crucial in this area. In the present chapter, I describe a theoretical framework that I hope might assist us in changing social support from a truism into a psychological process that can be recognized and enhanced.

The theoretical perspective presented here has two major metatheoretical characteristics that should be noted. First, the stimuli and responses that are of interest are social in nature. The paradigm to be considered is based on prior social interaction and subsequent social action. While the former focus is, of course, dictated by the topic of *social* support, the latter is more a matter of choice. There are, no doubt, important nonsocial behavioral consequences from receiving social support. However, it is the possibility of continuing social reverberations that seems the most intriguing theoretically and perhaps the most ecologically critical. What others do to us affects what we do to others. This fundamental social psychological principle is reflected throughout the thoughts presented here.

Second, it seems reasonable that if everyone can benefit from social support, a theoretical model of social support processes should be general enough to be applicable across a wide variety of people, relationships, and situations. The articulation of such a general model, while still attempting to maintain sufficient precision to allow the formulation of empirically testable hypotheses, is an extremely difficult task, but should be at least the ideal to which investigators of socially supportive interactions aspire.

In this chapter I offer some preliminary notions about how we might begin to progress in the direction of that ideal. After briefly reviewing some of the relevant literature concerning both adult–child and adult–adult relationships, a theoretical model of social support processes is proposed. Some of the implications of this model for developmental issues are then explored.

ADULT–CHILD RELATIONSHIPS: NURTURANCE

Supportive, accepting, loving behavior by parents toward their children has long been viewed as one of the most critical variables in the socialization process (see Rollins & Thomas [1975] for a review of some of the literature relevant to this proposition). Although the results of correlational work in this area have been termed "very consistent" (Rollins & Thomas, 1975), several major interpretive problems remain. First is the issue of causal direction. It is certainly possible that highly nurturing parents will produce confident, competent children, but it is also possible that "good" children produce nurturant parents. In addition, there may be innumerable third factors (e.g., parental power, physical attractiveness of the child, quality of the relationship between the parents) that influence both socially approved child behavior and parental nurturance or at least moderate the relationship between the two. Second, there is the difficulty of specifying the type of child behavior hypothesized to be affected by parental social support. Sometimes self-reported internal status of the child (e.g., self-esteem) may be considered of prime importance; sometimes relatively nonsocial behavior (e.g., academic achievement); sometimes social behaviors (e.g., conformity or compliance). In general, the literature on child-rearing practices is consistent with the notion that parental nurturance and socially desirable child behavior are associated, but our understanding of the more specific characteristics of this relationship (e.g., causal direction, moderating variables, specificity of effect) is still limited.

Some of these interpretive problems are typical and to some extent unavoidable difficulties of the use of a correlational methodology. Unfortunately, although experimental work on the effects of parental nurturance has allowed greater control and therefore greater specificity, these studies, have usually been restricted to examination of the imitation of a nurturing nonparental adult model (e.g., Bandura, Grusec, & Menlove, 1967; Bandura & Huston, 1961; Mischel & Grusec, 1966) or the imitation of the altruistic behavior of a nurturing adult model (e.g., Grusec, 1971; Grusec &

Skubiski, 1970; Rosenhan & White, 1967; Staub, 1971; Yarrow, Scott, & Waxler, 1973).[1] Moreover, the results of these experiments have been highly variable, finding that nurturance enhances imitation, has no effect on imitation, or may even decrease imitation.

It is quite possible that one major problem with both the correctional and experimental research on nurturance toward children has been the lack of an adequate conceptual definition of nurturance. For example, Yarrow et al. (1973) define nurturance as encompassing "a wide range of behaviors: providing, helping, comforting, giving attention, showing affection" (p. 242). Although such breadth in behavioral form is not necessarily inappropriate—in terms of either the phenomenon or heuristic potency—it needs to be supplemented by other defining characteristics. Rollins and Thomas (1975) offer a more specific conceptualization of nurturance, defining it in terms of intrapsychic effects:

> *Parental* nurturance is defined as behavior manifested by a parent toward a child that makes the child feel comfortable in the presence of the parent and confirms in the child's mind that he or she is basically accepted and approved as a person by the parent [p. 39].

This definition, however, leaves unspecified the conditions under which these effects are likely to occur.

The theoretical model of social support processes to be presented in this chapter bears some resemblance to the work on nurturance briefly reviewed in this section. A wide variety of specific prosocial behaviors are viewed as possible in order to provide social support; internal states of the individual receiving social support are assumed to be affected; and subsequent social behaviors are hypothesized to be influenced. In contrast, however, the present model will emphasize the conditions under which prosocial actions by others toward us affect our internal states as well as overt social behaviors.

ADULT–ADULT RELATIONSHIPS: SOCIAL SUPPORT

Although the presumed importance of social support processes for adults has received the attention of many major theorists in clinical psychology and psychiatry (e.g., Horney, Rogers, Sullivan), empirical research on adults' responses to social support processes available in everyday life (i.e., outside of therapy[2]) is of relatively recent vintage (see, e.g., reviews by Cobb, 1976; Heller, 1979; House, 1981). Moreover, much of this research

---

[1]Both Staub (1971) and Yarrow, *et al.* (1973) also investigated the *direct* effect of nurturance on helping. Staub found that nurturance increased helping, independent of whether or not a helpful adult model had been observed. Yarrow *et al.*, however, obtained no such direct effect.

[2]See also Maslach's work (e.g., 1978) on the importance of social support processes for those providing therapeutic and other services to others.

is correlational, and in linking desirable social situations with desirable feelings and/or behavior by the person, it suffers from the causal direction ambiguity discussed previously.

However, some research, though correlational in approach, has obtained a more differentiated pattern of results that offers somewhat more compelling evidence for the benefits of social support. For example, Nuckolls, Cassell, and Kaplan (1972) found an interaction between a general measure of "psychosocial assets" and reported levels of life change. At low levels of life change, level of psychosocial assets had no effect on complications during pregnancy (as measured through medical records). For those women reporting high levels of life change, however, low psychosocial assets were associated with higher complication rates. De Araujo, van Arsdel, Holmes, and Dudley (1973) obtained a similar pattern of results, finding that only when levels of life change were high did low levels of psychosocial assets increase the average daily dose of steroid medication prescribed for control of chronic intrinsic asthma. Unfortunately, in both these studies, the assessment of "psychosocial assets" was quite general, and variables in addition to social support were probably also being measured (see Brehm, 1983, for a discussion of methodological problems in the social support literature). In their thorough and sophisticated study of depression in women, Brown and Harris (1978) provide a more specific indication of the importance of social support. These investigators found that the most powerful predictor of depression involved a combination of high levels of acute stress and more general "vulnerability factors." By far the single most powerful vulnerability factor was the absence of an intimate, confiding relationship with the woman's husband or boyfriend.

These studies are quite important in suggesting the kinds of major physical and emotional states that may be affected by social support or the lack thereof. However, they were not intended to, and cannot, generate an adequate *conceptual* model of social support. In the following pages I describe one possible approach to the development of this more general, conceptual level of analysis.

SOCIAL SUPPORT PROCESSES

In terms of the present model, social support occurs whenever a positive, prosocial action[3] by one person (called the *Provider*) toward another person

---

[3]In the course of discussions during the conference, Kenneth Walston suggested the intriguing idea that social support could also be provided by what the Receiver perceives, at least initially, to be negative actions (i.e., actions unpleasant for the Receiver). This may well be the case, but theoretical analysis of this proposition is exceedingly complex and has not been attempted in the present chapter.

(called the *Receiver*) implies to the Receiver that he or she possesses attributes that will facilitate his or her obtaining positive benefit from others (i.e., people other than the Provider). This inference is postulated to increase the Receiver's self-confidence and thereby lead to increased self-confident social behavior. Such behavior may, then, actually produce increased benefit from others, but this is not a necessary postulate of the model. Table 5.1 provides a schematic summary of the overall model.

The Attributional Matrix

It is hypothesized that whether or not the Receiver makes the inference that he or she possesses attributes that will positively influence the behavior of others toward him or her depends on the motives the Receiver perceives as having generated Provider's behavior. The importance of perceived motives has been widely discussed in social psychological theories of attribution (e.g., Bem, 1972; Heider, 1958; Jones & Davis, 1965; Kelley, 1967), as well as in considerations of interpersonal processes such as altruism (Krebs, 1970), ingratiation (Jones, 1964; Jones & Wortman, 1973), interpersonal attraction (Tedeschi, 1974), and close relationships (Harvey *et al.*, 1978; Kelley, 1979). Typically, however, the focus of this literature has been on the effects of one's attributions about another's behavior on one's liking for, perception of, and/or interactions with that person. The present model takes a different perspective and will stress the role attributions about one person's behavior toward us can play in affecting our subsequent behavior with other people.

First, it is proposed that perceiving another's positive, prosocial behavior toward us as motivated primarily by *external constraints* (e.g., situational requirements, role requirements, normative expectations such as strict reciprocity) will reduce or prevent the inference that the Provider's behavior was elicited by the Receiver's personal attributes and, therefore, will not produce the social support sequences described here (see, however, Brehm, 1982, 1983, for a discussion of communal social support processes based on normatively required prosocial actions). In addition, actions that are attributed to the uniformly operative *dispositional characteristics of the Provider* also fail to draw the Receiver's attention to his or her own attributes and, thus, cannot serve as a source of social support for the Receiver. This distinction between, on the one hand, normatively-required and/or provider-characteristic actions versus those that are more voluntary and, presumably, more responsive to characteristics of the Receiver is borne out by previous research on interpersonal attraction. We tend to like others who help us deliberately and voluntarily more than those who help accidently or

TABLE 5.1

Social Support Processes

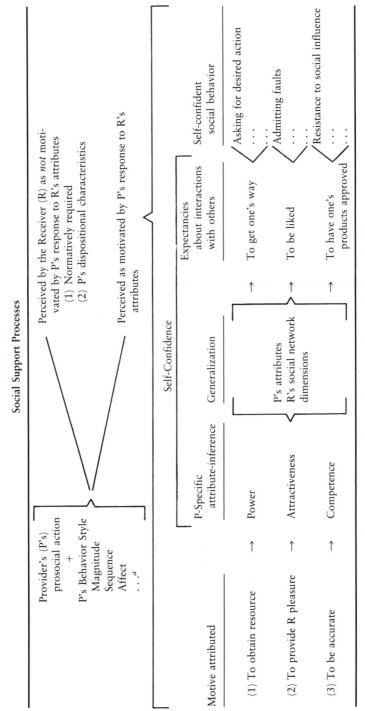

Provider's (P's)
prosocial action
+
P's Behavior Style
Magnitude
Sequence
Affect
. . .[a]

Perceived by the Receiver (R) as *not* motivated by P's response to R's attributes
(1) Normatively required
(2) P's dispositional characteristics

Perceived as motivated by P's response to R's attributes

Self-Confidence

Motive attributed	P-Specific attribute-inference	Generalization	Expectancies about interactions with others	Self-confident social behavior
		P's attributes R's social network dimensions		
(1) To obtain resource	→ Power	→	To get one's way	Asking for desired action . . .
(2) To provide R pleasure	→ Attractiveness	→	To be liked	Admitting faults . . .
(3) To be accurate	→ Competence	→	To have one's products approved	Resistance to social influence . . .

[a] Provision of . . . indicates unspecified but probable additional factors or effects within a specified class.

because it is required (Greenberg & Frisch, 1972; Gross & Latane, 1974; Nemeth, 1970), and prefer discriminating others more than people who seem to like everyone indiscriminately (Walster, Walster, Piliavin, & Schmidt, 1973). We are also more likely to reciprocate voluntary assistance (Goranson & Berkowitz, 1966; Greenberg & Frisch, 1972; Gross & Latané, 1974; Leventhal, Weiss, & Long, 1969).[4]

If the Provider's behavior is *not* perceived as motivated primarily by adherence to extrinsic or dispositional constraints, it is proposed that the Receiver will infer that the Provider's behavior was elicited by the Receiver's personal attributes. Three types of attribute attributions are identified by the present model. First, the Receiver may attribute the Provider's positive behavior to the Provider's desire to obtain *access to resources* controlled by the Receiver. Sometimes the Provider may relatively directly indicate that his/her positive action is intended to obtain access to the specified resources. At other times, the Provider's action may be perceived by the Receiver as ingratiation (Jones, 1964; Jones & Wortman, 1973), where the Provider does something positive for the Receiver in order to obtain a benefit that is not specified as the reason for the initial positive behavior. The empirical literature is reasonably consistent in indicating that ingratiators—once perceived as such—are liked less (Jones, Jones, & Gergen, 1963; Jones, Stires, Shaver, & Harris, 1968; Lowe & Goldstein, 1970) and receive less gratitude (Tesser, Gatewood, & Driver, 1968) than individuals who behave prosocially without apparent strong egoistic motives. Given less attention is the fact that ingratiation, as well as acknowledged quid-pro-quo initiations, imply a positive attribute of the receiver: that he or she has control over resources; that he or she is *powerful*.

A second type of attribute attribution by the Receiver involves the Receiver's perception that the Provider was primarily motivated by the desire *to provide pleasure*. The present model assumes that others' characteristics can be rewarding to us in and of themselves (Lott & Lott, 1974), that others'

---

[4]The study by Goranson and Berkowitz (1966) also examined the effect of receiving freely given, as compared to required, assistance on receiver-subjects' helping of *someone other than the initial Provider;* no effect of the conditions under which prior help had been received was found. On the other hand, a study by Gross and Latane (1974) obtained some evidence that both helping and liking of a third party were increased for subjects who had received voluntary rather than required prior assistance. These data, in combination with the findings from the previously cited work on nurturance, suggest that the relationship between receiving a prosocial action and subsequently helping someone else is likely to be quite complex and may depend to a large extent on the Receiver's interpretation of the meaning of receiving assistance (e.g., Fisher, DePaulo, & Nadler, 1981). Given that the Receiver's perception of the motive of the Provider should be an important factor in any such interpretations, the model presented in this paper is generally consistent with the perspective taken by Fisher *et al.* on recipients' responses to receiving aid.

pleasure can also be rewarding, and that the rewards of providing pleasure to another are enhanced by prior attractiveness. Moreover, it is assumed that people generally hold this view of the relationship between providing pleasure and attraction to others. Thus the perception by the Receiver that the Provider was motivated primarily to provide pleasure does not require the Receiver to view the Provider as acting altruistically in the classic sense of having no egoistical involvement. Rather, it is proposed that the Receiver may more simply infer that the Provider takes pleasure in the Receiver's pleasure and that this signifies the Receiver's *personal attractiveness.*

As a third class of attribute attributions, let us consider a somewhat more delimited set of prosocial behaviors. Up to this point it has been assumed that any type of positive, pleasurable outcome provided by the Provider to the Receiver should serve to initiate the attributive process: the receipt of gifts or compliments, or attention, praise, or consolation. The third class of attributions, however, is restricted to the Provider's positive response to some *product* generated by the Receiver. For example, the Provider may compliment the Receiver's appearance, praise his or her cooking, admire his or her ideas, agree with his or her opinions. It is proposed that if the Receiver perceives the Provider's positive response to have been motivated primarily by the Provider's desire to render *accurate judgments,* the Receiver can make inferences about his or her own *competency.*

Although it is proposed that inferences about one's power, attractiveness, and competency are theoretically distinct and, as will be described later, that there is heuristic value in so distinguishing among them, these three variables are also obviously interrelated. For example, attractiveness can be considered a resource base for interpersonal power. Someone viewed by others as highly attractive can reward those observers with his or her presence, attention, and liking or punish them with withdrawal and rejection. It is important to note, however, that attraction-based power differs in one major respect from power based on control of more tangible resources. With tangible resources, the ultimate source of power rests in the "dependent's" desire for the resource. With attraction-based power, the ultimate source of power is the dependent's desire for the "superior." Power based on tangible resources can withstand the vicissitudes of personal affection; power based on personal attractiveness is itself dependent on the dependent's affection. It is therefore deemed more theoretically useful to describe self-confident feelings of being powerful as different from self-confident feelings of being attractive, though it is recognized that in some situations the two feelings of self-confidence may affect behavior similarly.

Another interrelationship among feelings of power, attractiveness, and competence is more consistent with their separation by the present model. That is, it is proposed that there is a *negative* relationship between inferences of power and attractiveness on the one hand and, on the other, inferences of competency. The more a Receiver attributes the motive for the Provider's statement of positive judgment to the Provider's desire for a resource controlled by the Receiver or the desire to provide pleasure to the Receiver, the less competent the Receiver should feel. When we really do want objective evaluation of our efforts, people who like us or who need our goodwill are not usually considered the best judges.

Generalization

The foregoing attributional processes are believed necessary for social support to occur, but they are not sufficient. These processes allow the Receiver to make inferences about the Provider's view of the Receiver; they do not, however, necessarily allow the Receiver to infer the likely views of others. It is this process of generalization from inferences made on the basis of one person's behavior to expectancies about other people's behavior that is crucial for the present theoretical model. Some of the factors that should facilitate generalization are as follows.

Characteristics of the Provider

It is proposed that the Receiver is likely to feel more generally powerful, the more the ingratiating Provider is perceived as possessing resources; more generally attractive, the more the pleasure-giving Provider is perceived as attractive; and more generally competent, the more the accuracy-motivated Provider is perceived as competent. In other words, it is hypothesized that the more other people themselves possess the attribute in question, the more they will be seen as accurate and representative judges of our attributes.[5]

---

[5]This proposition, then, suggests that people use a form of the representative heuristic (Kahneman & Tversky, 1972; Nisbett & Ross, 1980) in assessing whether to expect that one individual's judgment of an attribute should serve to indicate similar judgments by others. That is, it hypothesizes that a person is seen as a good judge (i.e., predictive of other people's opinions) of whether another person belongs in class X (e.g., highly interpersonally attractive people) to the extent that the person making the judgment is himself/herself a member of this class. While the use of the representative heuristic would appear appropriate for judges of competence, it may or may not be appropriate for assessing judges of power and/or interpersonal attractiveness. Perhaps, for instance, people low in interpersonal attractiveness are the best judges of whether other people will think a given target person is interpersonally attractive. In any event, the present consideration focuses on a generalization rule that people are hypothesized to use; the underlying normative appropriateness of this rule is not a directly relevant issue for the model described here.

Characteristics of the Receiver's Social Network

Dyadic interactions, of course, do not usually occur in isolation. The Provider has relationships with others, and the Receiver's perceptions of these relationships provide important information about the Provider's characteristics that, in turn, affect generalization as described previously. The Receiver, too, has relationships with others, and the character of these relationships also may facilitate or reduce generalization. The greater the number of other people perceived by the Receiver to share the motive attributed to the specific Provider, the more general should be the inference that is made by the Receiver. It is also proposed (though more tentatively) that the more the Receiver regards other people sharing the Provider's motive as differing *in nonattribute-related characteristics,* the more general the Receiver's inference should be. For example, then, I should be more likely to expect more people to evaluate my ideas on social support favorably, the more competent I perceive a person who favorably evaluates them, the greater the number of competent individuals who favorably evaluate them, and—holding perceived competence constant—the more these people vary in such characteristics as theoretical orientation, methodological preference, and cultural background.

Dimensions

For inferences about attractiveness, it is theoretically useful at this point in the development of the model to regard attractiveness as a single dimension—or, at least, as experienced by the Receiver as a single dimension. Such parsimony cannot prevail, however, when we consider inferences about power and competence. For example, one could control access to professional advancement for others but have very limited financial resources. In such a case, it is likely that inferences about one's power are restricted to others who desire professional advancement in one's field, and do not entail the expectancy of having power over individuals interested in obtaining large sums of money. Similarly, inferences about competence should typically be limited to specific areas of endeavor.

Effects

It is hypothesized that based on the motive attributed to the Provider of the positive action, and assuming a reasonable degree of generalization as a function of the variables described earlier, the Receiver will experience an increase in *self-confident expectations* about the behavior of others. These expectations are posited to be specifically related to the specific motive attributed and to have specific effects on the Receiver's *social behavior with others*. Although it is probably the case that a number of specific social behaviors will be affected by each attribute-relevant motive attributed (and the diagram of the model in Table 5.1 suggests this possibility), at present the model predicts only one relatively simple, relatively easily measured exemplar behavior for each motive. In describing the behavioral effects that are predicted, let us examine first each designated attribution–behavior relationship and then consider the possibility that more than one attributed motive may affect each social behavior.

The Receiver of a resource-based prosocial action, the implications of which have been sufficiently generalized, should feel increased confidence about being powerful in relation to others and, thereby, should expect to get his or her way with others who are perceived as also desiring the resource. This self-confident expectation should make it easier for the individual to ask others to behave as he or she desires. Receivers who feel powerful should not expect their requests to be refused. Moreover, the power-based self-confident Receiver should believe that possession of valued resources facilitates the process of and defines the "coin" of "paying" others back for their beneficial actions. Thus the powerful Receiver does not need to be concerned about possible undesirable, unanticipated obligations that receiving a favor can generate (e.g., Brehm & Brehm, 1981; Fisher, De Paulo, & Nadler, 1981). In other words, the Receiver who feels powerful should feel able to compel the favor *and* control the terms of gratitude.

It should be noted that one could make a similar prediction in the absence of receiving a prior prosocial action. That is, the person who perceives himself or herself to control a resource desired by others should be more likely to ask those others to comply with his or her desires. However, there may be times when the person does not recognize his or her power—or, at least, the implications of that power for controlling others' behavior—until he or she receives a direct quid pro quo or an indirect, ingratiating positive action from another. In any event, such actions should increase the Receiver's self-perception of power and augment the proclivity to ask others to behave as he or she wishes.

In contrast, the Receiver of a pleasure-based prosocial action, the implications of which have been sufficiently generalized, should feel increased confidence about being attractive to others and thereby should expect to be liked by others. This self-confident expectation should make it easier for the Receiver to acknowledge undesirable aspects of self to others. Receivers who feel generally attractive should not expect that the admission of any specific deficit(s) should appreciably reduce others' liking for them—or, at least, should expect less reduction than would a person who did not feel so attractive. Moreover, expecting to be liked by a variety of others should reduce perceived dependency on any other single individual as well as perceived importance of rejection by any other single individual. Thus, relative to someone who does not feel very attractive, the person who feels highly attractive should feel more able to get away with admitting faults and should care less if he or she does not.

As with the effects of feeling powerful on asking for compliance by another, the relationship between feeling attractive and being able to admit undesirable aspects of self should hold with or without a prior prosocial behavior. However, unlike the possession of tangible resources where possession can be obtained through essentially nonsocial means (e.g., your Great-uncle Ben, whom you've never met, can always die and leave you several million dollars), feelings of attractiveness must originate in the responses of other people. Once such feelings are established, whenever the person perceives others to act so as to provide him or her with pleasure, his or her feelings of attractiveness should increase, as should a willingness to disclose negative aspects of the self in situations where such disclosures play an instrumental role in attaining desired goals (e.g., sympathy from, intimacy with others).

Finally, it is proposed that the Receiver of an accuracy-based prosocial action, the implications of which have been sufficiently generalized, should feel increased confidence about being competent and thereby should expect that his or her products will be evaluated favorably by others. This self-confident expectation should make it more likely that the individual will resist social influence by others on any topic perceived as related to his or her area of competency. The Receiver who feels competent should feel "right" about the issue at hand and regard others who hold a divergent position as "wrong."

Although the relationship between feelings of competence and resistance to social influence has been reasonably well documented (e.g., Brehm & Brehm, 1981; Sistrunk & McDavid, 1971), the proposed relationship between feelings of competence and expecting others to evaluate one's products favorably may be more debatable. We are all familiar with accounts of individuals, convinced of the worth of their products, who persevere despite receiving little, if any, social approval for their work. However, two questions may be asked about such individuals. How did they come to believe in their work? What sustained this belief? My own hunch is that, in fact, they initially did receive social approval for at least the precursors of their later work and that this approval generated their initial feelings of competence. Moreover, I suspect that even in the total absence of social approval in their actual environment (a supposition, by the way, that seriously underestimates the extent of social support that a good many such "lonely geniuses" actually receive), these people expected eventually that a wiser and better-informed posterity would accord them their just acclaim. In short, I believe feeling competent and expecting favorable evaluations from others are necessarily and directly related, but that the "others" who sustain feelings of competency may become a select and/or hypothesized group.

These predicted relationships can be stated more formally as follows.

1. The more a Receiver attributes the motive for a prosocial act to the Provider's desire to gain access to a resource controlled by a Receiver, the more likely the Receiver should be to ask others (perceived as desiring the resource) to act in accordance with his or her wishes.

2. The more a Receiver attributes the motive for a prosocial act to the Provider's desire to provide pleasure to the Receiver, the more likely the Receiver should be to tell others about his or her perceived undesirable characteristics, failures, embarrassing experiences, and the like, when these disclosures are perceived as facilitating goal-attainment.

3. The more a Receiver attributes the motive for an evaluative prosocial act to the Provider's desire to be accurate, the more likely the Receiver should be to resist social influence on a topic perceived by the Receiver as related to his or her area of competence.

In specifying these attribution—behavior relationships, the present model operates on a "best fit" principle. It cannot claim that these relationships offer the only fit. For instance, receiving what are perceived as pleasure-based prosocial actions may, through increasing feelings of attractiveness, increase the likelihood of expecting compliance by others and therefore of asking others to behave as one wishes. However, such requests are potentially more troublesome interpersonally than those based on feelings of being powerful, since the coin of reciprocity is not so readily apparent (e.g., must the attractive Receiver exchange affection for compliance; what will be the appropriate expression and level of this affection?). Such potential difficulties in reciprocity should reduce the impact of pleasure-based attributions on asking for compliance with one's wishes.

On the other hand, it is the availability of just this coin of reciprocity that should reduce the likelihood that increased feelings of power will increase tendencies to negatively self-disclose. When people acknowledge negative aspects of the self in the service of some desirable goal such as intimacy with another person, consolation from that person, or social comparison information, they usually want to receive a reasonably genuine response in return. The powerful person who discloses to a less powerful person has a difficult time ascertaining whether such responses are, indeed, genuine or are only further attempts to ingratiate.

It is likely that increased feelings of competence, derived from receiving what are perceived to be accuracy-motivated positive evaluations, may lead to increases in asking others to do as one wishes as well as in willingness to acknowledge faults or inadequacies. Indeed, recent work by Wicklund and Gollwitzer (1981; Gollwitzer, Wicklund, & Hilton, 1982) on symbolic self-completion provides evidence for the latter relationship between security about one's competence in an important area of endeavor and negative self-disclosure. However, feelings of competence should affect only behaviors that are relevant to the specific area of one's competency: disclosing faults only in that area, directing others only when their behavior is relevant to that area. In contrast, feelings of power should generalize across areas of behavior (though be limited to people over whom one expects to have power), and feelings of interpersonal attractiveness should produce a generally increased willingness to disclose faults over a variety of aspects of the self.

In terms of resistance to social influence, it is important to note that both increased feelings of power and of interpersonal attractiveness should decrease the perceived social risk entailed by any nonconforming action and, thus, should decrease the anticipated costs of resistance to social influence. However, resistance to any specific influence attempt should only occur if there is some reason for the individual to feel competent on the specific issue.

These considerations suggest that in dealing with complex human behavior, one's heuristic compartments may be useful, though less than impermeable. I believe that the designated attribution–behavior relationships are more direct and stronger than the other possible crossover relationships considered here. Hopefully, this belief will prove both theoretically useful and empirically demonstrable.

The Importance of Style

Although it is not a necessary task for the present model, the process by which the attributional interpretation of prosocial acts takes place should be briefly considered. People do not come equipped (outside the laboratory, at least) with placards displaying their motives. How, then, do we know why someone did something nice for us?

Behavioral style (Moscovici, 1976) may well play a major role. For example, the perfunctory birthday gift probably has little effect on the Receiver's self-confidence, but the extraordinary gift delivered with a flourish may have considerable effect. More generally, one could suppose that whenever people *exceed the requirements*—as perceived by the Receiver—of the situation, roles, and/or norms, this creates the opportunity for the attribution of other, attribute-induced motives.

Other aspects of behavioral style should also be important in determining the type of motive that is attributed. For instance, consider the following two alternative behavior *sequences*. Person A prepares a meal for Person B. In one case, Person A puts the food on the table, sits down, and begins to eat. In another, Person A puts the food on the table, sits down, watches Person B taste and react to the food, smiles when Person B expresses enjoyment of the food, and *then* begins to eat. It seems apparent that in the second case one can more confidently attribute to Person A the motive to provide pleasure to Person B.

The *affect* of the Provider will also provide cues to the Provider's motives. In general, prosocial acts motivated by the desire to provide pleasure to the Receiver should resemble stylistically more traditional descriptions of social support processes such as nurturance. Pleasure-motivated behavior typically should be accompanied by warmth, attentiveness, and emotional involvement on the part of the Provider. In contrast, accuracy-based socially supportive behavior should have a very different affectual style. Here the Provider may have maximum positive effect when he or she appears aloof, cold even, and most of all, issue-oriented.

Most complex of all are the stylistic elements of behavior implying resource control on the part of the Receiver. If an ingratiator is really skillful, his or her prosocial behavior will not be perceived as ingratiating by the Receiver and may well be attributed to the ingratiator's desire to provide pleasure or be accurate. It is likely that we usually perceive ingratiation as a function of the context—that is, as a function of already knowing that we control resources desired by the Receiver—though here too behavioral style may be important. Obsequious, excessive positivity by the Provider, for example, may alert us to the possibility of ingratiation and may, in the absence of previous knowledge, induce us to begin to consider whether we control something the Provider might want.

These remarks sketch out some of the possible elements of behavioral style (e.g., magnitude of the act, sequence, accompanying affect) that may influence the attributional processes described in this chapter. It is hoped that future elaboration of the model will both refine and amplify this consideration.

The Problem with Love

The conceptual model presented here bears some general resemblance to more traditional views of social support: A prosocial act begins the process; the Receiver becomes more self-confident; subsequent social behaviors are all socially desirable (at least, in moderation). Through prior interactions with some people, the receiver becomes more directly assertive about his or her wishes, more able to acknowledge personal inadequacies, and more independent in his or her beliefs during subsequent interactions with other people. Social support has produced an individual less vulnerable to the vicissitudes of social interaction.

In many ways, however, the present model differs considerably from these previous formulations. The importance of cognitive mediation (i.e., the attributional process) is certainly articulated more explicitly here, and the most effective style in providing social support is not assumed always to be one of warmth and emotional involvement. Moreover, any suggestion about the efficacy of love as a (perceived) motive has been studiously and perhaps conspicuously avoided. The reasons for this avoidance will be described briefly.

The problem with love from the point of view of the present conceptual model is that love is, to paraphrase the song title, a very complicated thing. Love can be the product of many situations and personal characteristics. Parents love their children, but would they love them if they were not their children? Married couples love each other, but how large a role is played by services rendered and resources desired? When are people in love with you as opposed to being in love with love or in love with being loved? To say, then, that someone "did it for love" can imply many possible, more specific motives and is not necessarily the same as saying someone "did it because he or she finds me attractive." In addition, I have strong doubts that phenomenologically we first attribute a prosocial act to the Provider's love for us and then feel more personally attractive. Instead, I think it more likely that having attributed the Provider's prosocial act to his or her desire to provide us with pleasure, we then feel more attractive *and* more loved.

These comments may or may not be particularly persuasive to the reader. They should, however, be sufficient to suggest considerable complexity and ambiguity in attributing the motive for a prosocial act to the Provider's love for the Receiver—enough complexity and ambiguity that there is good reason not to emphasize this type of attributed motive in an initial theoretical formulation of social support processes.

Social Support and Stress

One other theoretical issue should be considered. Earlier in this chapter, three studies were mentioned in which social support appeared to protect the person from the otherwise deleterious effects of life stress. I believe that the current model is perfectly consistent with these findings. If one assumes that one of the central effects of life stress is to reduce self-confidence, then it is in times of stress that countervailing actions by others that will offset such reductions are most needed. In addition, however, the present model allows for greater specificity about the types of self-confidence that can be affected by both stress and social support. It may be that there are specific stress × social support interactions, such that a certain type of stress is likely to reduce a certain type of self-confidence and therefore a certain type of social support will be most beneficial. In the following section on developmental aspects of social support processes, I speculate a bit further on this possibility.

DEVELOPMENTAL ASPECTS
OF SOCIAL SUPPORT PROCESSES

For very young children, it is unlikely that the kinds of attribution–behavior relationships proposed here offer a cogent way to conceptualize the effects of the social support they receive. With infants and toddlers, social support is presumably more diffuse, more tied to care for the child's physical well-being, and less cognitively mediated. At this age, the traditional variables of warmth, attentiveness, and helpfulness—generated for whatever reason—probably have a general positive impact on the child's feelings and social behavior.

Rather early in development, however, I think it likely that rudimentary forms of the processes described here come into play as mediators of the relationship between prosocial action received and subsequent social behavior. For instance, as early as preschool age, children should be able to recognize relatively pure pleasure-providing when they see it and to distinguish this from perfunctory prosocial behavior. This distinction, however, may not be as fine-grained as that by an adult. Young children may, for instance, frequently underestimate the effects of role and/or situational constraints in what is, after all, a relatively complex social situation, and may fail therefore to "discount" (Kelley, 1971) an attribute-relevant motive the way an adult would (see discussion by Kassin [1981] of children's use of the discounting principle). Even a preschooler, however, should be able to tell the difference between a joyful response to his or her pleasure and a dutiful smile. Moreover, this perceived difference should affect the child's general good feeling about self and quite possibly the child's willingness to acknowledge what he or she considers "bad things" about himself or herself.

Young children may also make inferences about their power. Consider, in this regard, the implications of an adult's offering a benefit to the child in order to induce the child to behave in a certain way (see Lepper & Gilovich [1981] for a discussion of children's recognition of and responses to adults' uses of social control techniques). Given that adults do not always offer benefits in order to obtain compliance—frequently they simply require compliance and punish noncompliance—the child may well infer that offering the benefit is an implicit recognition of the child's power. That is, the adult ingratiates in order to gain access to the desired resource of a certain behavior by the child, a resource that the child controls (see Edwards & Brauburger, 1973, and Richter, 1968, for a similar notion of child compliance as a resource for child power). Furthermore, feelings of power in children may have at least some effects similar to those for adults, and it is quite possible that the more powerful the child feels, the more likely he or she is to ask others (adults as well as peers) to behave in accordance with his or her wishes.

Young children's inferences about their competence may well be least similar to the processes described in the present model. Their conceptualization of areas of competence is likely to be relatively undifferentiated; the importance of *specific* competencies may be less; their ability to assess the other person's level of expertise is likely to be less; and their discounting of judgments because of extrinsic constraints and/or other nonattribute-based motives may be much less frequent and/or sophisticated. This is not to say, however, that some kind of generalized notion of being competent is not important to a young child. Indeed, as indicated earlier when discussing the general relationship between social approval and feelings of competence, one's earliest and most basic feelings of competency must be based on receiving positive evaluation of one's products by others. What is suggested here is simply that young children are unlikely to be very discriminating about the conditions under which they accept and are made more self-confident by positive evaluations.

Let me now attempt to summarize some general ways in which social support processes as conceptualized by the present model are likely to differ between young children and adults. First, young children should underestimate the role of normative and dispositional constraints. Consistent with a more egocentric perspective and less cognitive differentiation, they should be more likely to see more prosocial acts as motivated by the Provider's response to their attributes. Second, young children should also be strongly influenced by the behavioral style (e.g., the affect expressed by the Provider) accompanying the prosocial act, though they may fail to respond to relatively subtle stylistic cues. Third, young children are likely to overgeneralize inferences they make about themselves as a function of the prosocial acts they receive. That is, they should tend to assume that the adults with whom they interact are representative of at least other adults and are good sources of information about the child's attributes. Finally, I believe that prosocial actions are, in general, more important to and influence children more than adults. Children are more dependent on their immediate interactions with other people than are adults who have memories of past interactions, hopes for future ones, and idealized or hypothesized social support sources from books, movies, and their own thought processes. Furthermore, as described, children should be more likely than adults to perceive a given prosocial act as saying something good about them.

As children develop more differentiated perceptions of themselves and other people, more recognition of the part played by extrinsic constraints in influencing behavior, and more skill at detecting relatively subtle aspects of behavioral style, the present model should become an increasingly appropriate way to conceptualize the ways in which they receive and respond to social support. Moreover, it is possible that developmental context always plays an important role in determining the type of social support that is most beneficial, as developmental context may be associated with specific types of life stress and specific types of threatened reductions in self-confidence. One could, for instance, view adolescence as a time of life for most people when they are intensely concerned about their personal attractiveness, young adulthood as a time when competence concerns become paramount, and retirement as a life event signaling a potential drastic reduction in power. By identifying an individual's specific type of concern about self, we presumably should be able to predict the types of other people whom the individual would value most and probably seek to be with. Perhaps more important, we may be able to increase our understanding of how to modulate our own behavior in order to provide more effective social support to a person in need.

SUMMARY

It was suggested that previous considerations of social support processes have not provided an adequate conceptual model that would allow more precise investigation of the conditions that affect the occurrence of social support and its effects on subsequent social behavior. Accordingly, the present theoretical model was developed.

This model emphasizes the role of our attributed motives for the prosocial behavior of others toward us. If we perceive anothers' action to be motivated by the desire to conform to extrinsic requirements (roles, situations, norms) or by uniform dispositional tendencies of the Provider, it will be less likely that we will infer that the provider's action was in response to our desirable personal characteristics. If, however, we perceive the Provider to have acted so as to (a) obtain access to resources we control, (b) provide us with pleasure, or (c) be accurate in his or her judgments, our self-confidence about our power, attractiveness, or competence (respectively) should be increased. Whether our increased feeling of self-confidence in regard to the Provider will generalize to expectations concerning the behavior of others should be a function of our perceptions of the Provider's characteristics, the characteristics of our own social network, and the dimensions of power and competency that were involved in the Provider's action. Assuming adequate generalization, we should experience (respectively) increased confidence about (a) getting our own way with others, (b) being liked by others, and (c) having our products approved by others. This increase in self-confident expectations should lead, in turn, to (respectively) increases in (a) asking others to behave in accordance with our wishes, (b) admitting perceived faults, and (c) resistence to social influences. In sum, then, attributions of specific attribute-based motives for another's prosocial act are predicted to increase specific types of self-confidence that generate increases in specific types of self-confident social behavior.

A number of issues related to this conceptual model were discussed: the role of the Provider's behavioral style in affecting type of motive attributed, the theoretical difficulties with emphasizing love as a perceived motive for prosocial acts, and possible interactions between life stress and social support processes. Finally, developmental aspects of social support processes were considered in light of the present model.

REFERENCES

Bandura, A., Grusec, J. C., & Menlove, F. L. Some social determinants of self-monitoring reinforcement systems. *Journal of Personality and Social Psychology,* 1967, *5,* 449–455.

Bandura, A., & Huston, A. C. Identification as a process of incidental learning. *Journal of Abnormal and Social Psychology,* 1961, *63,* 311–318.

Bem, D. J. Self-perception theory. In L. Berkowitz (Ed.), *Advances in experimental social psychology* (Vol. 6). New York: Academic Press, 1972.

Brehm, S. S. Social support processes: Theoretical and methodological issues. *Recherches de psychologie sociale,* 1982, *4,* 25–34.

Brehm, S. S. Social support: Problems and perspectives. Manuscript in preparation, University of Kansas, 1983.

Brehm, S. S., & Brehm, J. W. *Psychological reactance: A theory of freedom and control.* New York: Academic Press, 1981.

Brown, G. W., & Harris, T. *Social origins of depression: A study of psychiatric disorder in women.* New York: Free Press, 1978.

Cobb, S. Social support as a moderator of life-stress. *Psychosomatic Medicine,* 1976, *38,* 300–314.

de Araujo, G., van Arsdel, P. P., Holmes, J. H., & Dudley, D. L. Life change, coping ability, and chronic intrinsic asthma. *Journal of Psychosomatic Research,* 1973, *17,* 359–363.

Edwards, J. N., & Brauburger, M. B. Exchange and parent–youth conflict. *Journal of Marriage and the Family,* 1973, *35,* 101–107.

Fisher, J. D., De Paulo, B. M., & Nadler, A. Extending altruism beyond the altruistic act: The mixed effects of aid on the help receipient. In J. P. Rushton & R. M. Sorrentino (Eds.), *Altruism and helping behavior.* Hillsdale, NJ: Erlbaum, 1981.

Gollwitzer, P. M., Wicklund, R. A., & Hilton, J. L. Admission of failure and symbolic self-completion: Extending Lewinean theory. *Journal of Personality and Social Psychology,* 1982, *43,* 358–371.

Goranson, R. E., & Berkowitz, L. Reciprocity and responsibility reactions to prior help. *Journal of Personality and Social Psychology,* 1966, *3,* 227–232.

Greenberg, M. S., & Frisch, D. M. Effects of intentionality on willingness to reciprocate a favor. *Journal of Experimental Social Psychology,* 1972, *8,* 99–111.

Gross, A. E., & Latané, J. G. Receiving help, giving help, and interpersonal attraction. *Journal of Applied Social Psychology,* 1974, *4,* 210–223.

Grusec, J. C. Power and internalization of self-denial. *Child Development,* 1971, *42,* 93–105.

Grusec, J. C., & Skubiski, S. L. Model nurturance, demand characteristics of the modeling experiment, and altruism. *Journal of Personality and Social Psychology,* 1970, *14,* 352–359.

Harvey, J. H., Wells, G. L., & Alvarez, M. D. Attribution in the context of conflict and separation in close relationships. In J. H. Harvey, W. J. Ickes, & R. F. Kidd (Eds.), *New directions in attribution research* (Vol. 2). Hillsdale, NJ: Erlbaum, 1978.

Heider, F. *The psychology of interpersonal relations.* New York: Wiley, 1958.

Heller, K. The effects of social support: Prevention and treatment implications. In A. P. Goldstein & F. H. Kanfer (Eds.), *Maximizing treatment gains: Transfer enhancement in psychotherapy.* New York: Academic, 1979.

House, J. S. *Work stress and social support.* Reading, MA: Addison-Wesley, 1981.

Jones, E. E. *Ingratiation.* New York: Appleton, 1964.

Jones, E. E., & Davis, K. E. From acts to dispositions: The attribution process in person perception. In L. Berkowitz (Ed.), *Advances in experimental social psychology* (Vol. 2). New York: Academic, 1965.

Jones, E. E., Jones, R. G., & Gergen, K. J. Some conditions affecting the evaluation of a conformist. *Journal of Personality,* 1963, *31,* 270–288.

Jones, E. E., Stires, L. K., Shaver, K. G., & Harris, V. A. Evaluation of an ingratiator by target persons and bystanders. *Journal of Personality,* 1968, *36,* 349–385.

Jones, E. E.,& Wortman, C. *Ingratiation: An attributional approach.* Morristown, NJ: General Learning Press, 1973.

Kahneman, D., & Tversky, A. Subjective probability: A judgement of representativeness. *Cognitive Psychology,* 1972, *3,* 430–454.

Kassin, S. M. From laychild to "layman": Developmental causal attribution. In S. S. Brehm, S. M. Kassin, & F. X. Gibbons (Eds.), *Developmental social psychology: Theory and research.* New York: Oxford University Press, 1981.

Kelley, H. H. Attribution theory in social psychology. In D. Levine (Ed.), *Nebraska symposium on motivation* (Vol. 15). Lincoln: University of Nebraska Press, 1967.

Kelley, H. H. *Attribution in social interaction.* Morristown, NJ: General Learning Press, 1971.

Kelley, H. H. *Personal relationships: Their structures and processes.* Hillsdale, NJ: Erlbaum, 1979.

Krebs, D. L. Altruism—An examination of the concept and a review of the literature. *Psychological Bulletin,* 1970, *73,* 258–303.

Lepper, M. R., & Gilovich, T. J. The multiple functions of reward: A social developmental perspective. In S. S. Brehm, S. M. Kassin, & F. X. Gibbons (Eds.), *Developmental social psychology: Theory and research.* New York: Oxford University Press, 1981.

Leventhal, G. S., Weiss, T., & Long, G. Equity, reciprocity, and reallocating the rewards in the dyad. *Journal of Personality and Social Psychology,* 1969, *13,* 300–305.

Lott, A. J., & Lott, B. E. The role of reward in the formation of positive interpersonal attitudes. In T. Huston (Ed.), *Foundations of interpersonal attraction*. New York: Academic, 1974.

Lowe, E. A., & Goldstein, J. W. Reciprocal liking and attributions of ability: Mediating effects of perceived intent and personal involvement. *Journal of Personality and Social Psychology*, 1970, *16*, 291–298.

Maslach, C. The client role in staff burn-out. *Journal of Social Issues*, 1978, *34*, 111–124.

Mischel, W., & Grusec, J. C. Determinants of the rehearsal and transmission of neutral and aversive behaviors. *Journal of Personality and Social Psychology*, 1966, *3*, 197–205.

Moscovici, S. *Social influence and social change*. New York: Academic, 1976.

Nemeth, C. Effects of free versus constrained behavior on attraction between people. *Journal of Personality and Social Psychology*, 1970, *15*, 302–311.

Nisbett, R., & Ross, L. *Human inference: Strategies and shortcomings of social judgment*. Englewood Cliffs, NJ: Prentice-Hall, 1980.

Nuckolls, K. B., Cassel, J., & Kaplan, B. H. Psychosocial assets, life crisis, and the prognosis of pregnancy. *American Journal of Epidemiology*, 1972, *95*, 431–441.

Richter, S. The economics of child-rearing. *Journal of Marriage and the Family*, 1968, *30*, 462–466.

Rollins, B. C., & Thomas, D. L. A theory of parental power and child compliance. In R. E. Cromwell & D. H. Olson (Eds.), *Power in families*. New York: Wiley, 1975.

Rosenhan, D., & White, G. M. Observation and rehearsal as determinants of prosocial behavior. *Journal of Personality and Social Psychology*, 1967, *5*, 424–431.

Sistrunk, F., & McDavid, J. W. Sex difference in conforming behavior. *Journal of Personality and Social Psychology*, 1971, *17*, 200–207.

Staub, E. A child in distress: The influence of nurturance and modeling on children's attempts to help. *Developmental Psychology*, 1971, *5*, 124–132.

Tedeschi, J. T. Attributions, liking, and power. In T. Huston (Ed.), *Foundations of interpersonal attraction*. New York: Academic, 1974.

Tesser, A., Gatewood, R., & Driver, M. Some determinants of gratitude. *Journal of Personality and Social Psychology*, 1968, *9*, 233–236.

Walster, E., Walster, G. W., Piliavin, J., & Schmidt, L. "Playing hard to get": Understanding an elusive phenomenon. *Journal of Personality and Social Psychology*, 1973, *26*, 113–121.

Wicklund, R. A., & Gollwitzer, P. M. Symbolic self-completion, attempted influence, and self-deprecation. *Basic and Applied Social Psychology*, 1981, *2*, 89–114.

Yarrow, M. R., Scott, P. M., & Waxler, C. Z. Learning concern for others. *Developmental Psychology*, 1973, *8*, 240–260.

6

Children's Peer Relationships:
An Examination of Social Processes

SHERRI ODEN
SHARON D. HERZBERGER
PETER L. MANGIONE
VALERIE A. WHEELER

EDITORS' INTRODUCTION

In the following pages Sherri Oden and her colleagues present an examination of the social processes inherent in children's peer relationships, raising questions about the degree to which the complexity of these relationships has been appreciated adequately in theory or research. Then they present an original study that focuses on how children get to know one another. The major concern is with the mechanisms by which children develop the skills for becoming acquainted and becoming friends, and for the various kinds of interactions that are entailed in friendship, acquaintanceship, or getting to know someone. Attention is also given to the social conditions that may influence the process of forming relationships. The conceptual and empirical elements of this chapter involve an examination of the influence of both social and developmental processes on peer relationships. For example, consideration is given to the social and cognitive processes that underlie relationships among peers (e.g., Carroll & Payne, 1976). Oden et al. also argue that it is important to consider the progression of peer relationships from a developmental perspective. That is, in what sense do children maintain, change, or enhance their relationships over time? Methods that may be used to address relational issues with children are analogous to the sociometric and observational

BOUNDARY AREAS IN SOCIAL
AND DEVELOPMENTAL PSYCHOLOGY

techniques that have been used to assess adults' close relationships (e.g., Kelley, 1979), and the present chapter indicates the importance of considering both the social and developmental literatures in understanding the processes underlying the character and development of peer relationships in children.

INTRODUCTION

In the last decade of research on children's social development, a growing appreciation of the contributions of children's peer relationships has emerged. Whereas previously it was generally assumed that the parent–child relationship was the major source of children's social development, researchers began to examine the role of a child's peers toward the development of social, cognitive, and language competence. The peer context has increasingly been considered a source of unique experiences for children's overall development as well as their development of relationship skills and competencies. In peer interaction, in contrast to adult–child interaction, a child experiences social interaction with another child who is generally at a similar level of experience, competence, and authority status. The peer context may also constitute the most independent sphere of a child's experience, in that the adult's role appears to become increasingly limited to that of a referee, guide, and occasional consultant. The child's peers are also a source of diversity and enrichment and may present challenges to ideas and values grounded in the child's family experience.

Peer interactions were first proposed to be major resources for children's overall cognitive development by Piaget (1932). In more recent studies, specific attention has been given to growth in children's perspective-taking or ability to take the role of the other (e.g., Selman, 1981) and their conceptions of friendships and fairness (e.g., Berndt, 1982; Damon, 1979). Sullivan (1953) and Youniss (1980) pointed out that close friendships, in particular, contribute to the development of children's interpersonal sensitivity. Hartup (1978) also emphasized the particular contributions of mixed-age peer relationships in children's social and cognitive development. Studies have also found correlations between children's social, behavioral, and cognitive skills and their peer acceptance or social adjustment (Asher, Oden, & Gottman, 1977; Oden, 1980; Spivack & Shure, 1974).

Much of the empirical research on peer interactions and relationships in childhood has focused on social cognitive processes in reference to hypothetical relationships and situations and assessment of levels or types of social skills—for example, cooperation and helpfulness at school or on the playground. However, insufficient attention has been given to the fact that as children progress in their development, they gain their social experiences in the context of actual peer relationships they establish limit, maintain, or enhance. Many investigators have taken this social reality partly into account by employing sociometric instruments and observational assessments to determine the degree to which children relate to each other in school settings (e.g., Asher, Markell, & Hymel, 1981; Coie, Dodge, & Coppotelli, 1982).

A few studies have focused on actual peer relationships and have examined the formation and maintenance processes of the relationships (e.g., Gottman & Parkhurst, 1979; Putallaz & Gottman, 1981), and more empirical work will certainly develop in this direction. However, in conceptual discussions of children's peer interactions and relationships, the relationships that are found to be positive and have some continuity are most often considered to be friendships. We propose that this is an oversimplification of the peer context that includes a diversity in the types of relationships. For example, Cooper, Ayers-Lopez, and Marquis (1982) and Mangione (1981) conducted research with peers in school situations and demonstrated that children often act as collaborators in activities in providing information, instruction, and evaluation to each other. Furthermore, in approximately one-fourth to one-half of peer relationships in a given setting, there is likely to be only a modest degree of liking or attraction. Hallinan and Tuma (1978), for example, employed a sociometric questionnaire in 19 upper elementary school classrooms. The instrument was designed so that children could indicate their "best friends," "friends," and "nonfriends" in the classroom. The friend category represented 49% of the children's choices; the other half of the choices were divided between best friends and nonfriends. It would be inappropriate to conclude that nonfriends are disliked. In a study of preadolescent boys, for example, Fine (1981) found that 18% of all the possible relationships in Little League baseball were rated as close friends, 31% as friends, only 2% were disliked, and 47% were neither disliked nor considered friends. The extent to which children actually interact regularly with nonfriends and the nature and purpose of these relationships should certainly be examined in future research.

In the course of this chapter we first present a conceptual scheme for generating future research and then present a study we conducted in which we observed children becoming acquainted. The study is relevant to many of the issues discussed in the proposed conceptual scheme. Finally, future research directions are discussed.

A CONCEPTUAL APPROACH
TO CHILDREN'S PEER RELATIONSHIPS

From a study of the child development research on peer interaction and relationships and the social psychology literature primarily on adult relationships, we developed a conceptual approach that we think can be applicable for developing research questions to examine peer relationship processes in children. This conceptual scheme is presented not as a theoretical model of peer relationships but rather as an approach for generating research questions toward that goal. The proposed conceptual framework was developed primarily for research on children's dyadic relationships, although the basic approach may be useful in formulating research questions regarding triads and small groups (e.g., Hallinan, 1981; Putallaz & Gottman, 1981). Various combinations of close friendships, activity partners, social friends, and acquaintances—including adversaries—could be assessed with small groups or social networks.

First, we propose some broad definitions. A *relationship* can range from an intimate relationship to an acquaintance. Relationships, defined broadly, are associations between two or more persons that are somehow connected with each other (see Figure 6.1). Two major types of relationship factors are proposed to be distinct from one another: *friendship* and *partnership*. For

	Partnership	No Partnership
Friendship	Close Friends High degree of mutual liking. Unique personal characteristics of each valued. Personal information and secrets exchanged. Problems and activities shared, help exchanged. May contribute to mutual goals and projects.	Social Friends Minimal to high degrees of liking. Enjoyment of social activities together. Personal information and secrets may be exchanged. Problems and activities may sometimes be shared, help exchanged. May sometimes contribute to mutual activity goals and projects.
No Friendship	Activity Partners Minimal to high degrees of liking and attraction. Sharing of activity, materials and provide task-related help and instruction. Unique personal characteristics valued as pertain to task-related skills or knowledge. Personal information infrequently exchanged and/or not intimate. Contribute to mutual activity goals and projects.	Acquaintances No or minimal to high degrees of attraction. No or minimal to high degrees of friendliness. Persons know each other usually in particular setting (e.g., classroom or neighborhood). Minimal or no attention to unique personal characteristics. Minimal or no interdependence for problems or projects.

Figure 6.1 A conceptual scheme for categorizing children's peer relationships.

friendship, we think of features such as personal sharing, emotional closeness, and mutuality of liking, whereas in a partnership we think of participating with someone in a venture, occupation, or task. Friendships may
also be partnerships. We propose that for children, these latter friendships
are most likely to be close friendships. This is supported by relevant empirical data from developmental and social psychology research. For example,
Bigelow's (1977) study of children's expectations of friendships found that
ego reinforcement and sharing appear to occur throughout childhood. More
developmental research is needed that examines shifts in the bases of children's actual peer relationships. Youniss's interview studies with children
found that primary-school-age children stressed kindness, sharing, and
helping within their best friendships, whereas older children included sharing secrets and feelings and knowing each other well. According to Huston
and Burgess's (1979) accounting of exchange theory regarding adult relationships, close relationships involve high degrees of interdependency or
mutual dependency in which persons are likely to share much about themselves and contribute to each other's endeavors or pursue joint endeavors.

In contrast, *social friends* are here proposed to include a range from
casual friendships in which there is infrequent contact and/or a low degree
of attraction, liking and/or sharing and helping to friendships in which there
is more frequent contact and/or moderate to high degrees of mutual attraction, liking, and personal sharing and helping. In the social friend relationship, the friends are not interdependent of or integral to each other's lives
and endeavors, as in the close friendship. According to Huston and Burgess
(1979), close relationships differ from other types because the commitment
is related to the discovery that the participants have an uncommon ability to
reward one another. The close friendship is not expected to be easily repeatable or duplicated, whereas the social friendship has more repeatable characteristics in that many persons may serve the same functions. Social friends
thus are not partners in any real sense and are not likely to seek opportunities and endeavors deliberately to aid, care for, or support one another's
well-being and livelihood. Certainly the character of a particular close or
social friendship, activity partner, or acquaintance may shift with time and
circumstances. Some peer relationships may develop from one type of relationship to another, thus moving along with the vertical or horizontal lines
in Figure 6.1 that may function as continua. Relationships may also shift
across quadrants (e.g., from activity partner to social friend). Also, some
relationships may be difficult to categorize. It would be important to determine the extent to which these distinctions can be made with reference to
young children who often report that their best friends are children with
whom they play and share things (e.g., Berndt, 1982).

There are also *activity partnerships* in which there is no friendship. For children, for example, these relationships would include working on a project with another, performing a joint task, or participating in some curriculum activity with a peer where each child contributes in some way to the other child's activity. These relationships are analogous to adult work relationships or task-oriented relationships in which the purpose of the interaction is not to enjoy one another's company or to learn about the other person. Rather, the main purpose is to work out ways to contribute to one another's work or to perform mutual tasks. The social skills involved here are important to adjustment in childhood as well as in adulthood. Although such partnerships may involve feelings of liking and socializing, as occurs among social friends, the basis of the relationship centers more on mutual activity concerns. As indicated previously, activity partnerships that involve friendship are likely to be close friendships. Unfortunately, investigations of partnerships are rare. Research by Cooper *et al.* (1982) are indicative, however, of the need for such research even with children.

Some relationships, however, are neither friendships nor partnerships, and we propose that these are *acquaintances*. This category does represent a type of relationship, in that persons have some connection with each other. In childhood and adult relationships, acquaintances include neighbors and classmates or people at the workplace or club with whom there is no friendship or partnership. Acquaintanceship may thus be largely a function of some proximity factor. These relationships may also include persons with whom there is frequent contact, but when there is no participation in activities, as in friendships and partnerships, we would expect acquaintances to engage in more superficial greetings and conversations. Acquaintance relationships may range from unfriendly to friendly in affective quality. Friendly acquaintances serve some social function in adult relationships, such as establishing feelings of emotional security, physical safety, and social variety and stimulation in the neighborhood, workplace, and public places. Such relationships also constitute an ever-present pool of potential friends and activity partners. Except to provide a contrast to friendships, the functions of acquaintances has been largely overlooked in child development, with a few exceptions (e.g., Furman & Willems, 1982).

Examining Peer Relationships

In developing research directed toward a greater understanding of the bases and operations of diverse peer relationships in children and the range of qualitative differences within each of the proposed four types of peer relations, several major factors or variables should be addressed. For a given type of peer relationship, these include (1) the children's perception or definition of the interactional context, (2) the interactional structure or organization that children construct, and (3) the range of social behaviors that constitute the content of the relationship. These major variables are discussed in reference to relevant existing research in developmental and social psychology.

Peer Interactional Context

There is a growing interest in factors that define the peer interaction context at the outset. Research in which children were interviewed about making friends (e.g., Youniss & Volpe, 1978) or being friendly (Stein & Goldman, 1981) indicates that children's ideas for relevant responses differ according to their perception regarding the purpose of a given peer interactional situation or context. More research is needed that examines the definitions, expectations, and goals of each member of the peer relationship at the outset for the situation or context under investigation. Is the situation defined by the children's perception as a friendship-making one, or to accomplish a task?

Additional factors that members of a relationship bring to the relationship at its outset require consideration. The status and role characteristics of members of the relationship (e.g., age, gender, race, physical size or appearance) are what may be considered part of the perceived social context. Numerous studies conducted by sociologists and psychologists in elementary school classrooms (e.g., Hallinan, 1981; Singleton & Asher, 1979) indicate that same-gender and same-race characteristics correlate positively with sociometric ratings and friendship nominations. According to attribution theory, such characteristics are used by persons to provide an efficient basis for making predictions and interpreting the social actions of others (Heider, 1958; Berscheid & Graziano, 1979). Research on adult relationships indicates that persons are attracted by a high degree of similarity between themselves and others, and that close relationships in adults and children are characterized by similarity in these status factors (Tesch, 1983). Persons who are of similar cultural background or socialization may experience greater ease in relationship development and maintenance because they may share similar values, goals, and communication styles.

Newcomb's (1961) conceptualization of relationships, which focused on complementarity factors, is relevant here. Children and adults may be attracted to characteristics that differ from their own when they represent potential sources of reinforcement. However, in adult and child contexts where persons of diverse status and role characteristics have little contact and few opportunities to get to know each other, potential relationships based on both similarity and complementarity of personality and social behavioral characteristics are less likely to occur. Furthermore, when persons expect to find no compatibility, it may be less likely to develop. Participation in relationships with persons whose characteristics are considered by one's own social group to be of lower social status may also bring disapproval and other negative consequences. According to exchange theory conceptualizations of relationship maintenance (e.g., Levinger, 1979), sufficient degrees of mutual reward or benefit would be difficult to maintain in such relationships. Overall, we expect that the definitions and expectations of the interactional context, including status and role expectations, will affect the nature and course of the interaction.

Structure or Organization

A second major consideration in studying relationships is the type of structure or organization of the actions of the members. Among the necessary and sufficient conditions for relationships—particularly for friends and partners—a structure is necessary that allows each member of the relationship to participate. Social psychologists have focused on equity in exchange processes as a factor that facilitates the development and maintenance of a relationship, but there is considerable debate on what constitutes equity or balance. Child developmentalists have focused on children's growing ability to engage in various forms of reciprocity—to coordinate as a dyad in their conversations and activities, to cooperate in activities (e.g., by sharing and taking turns), and to provide mutual emotional support and help.

Three basic types of organization have received attention in social psychological studies of adult relationships and more recently in child development research. For the purpose of discussion, these are categorized here as (1) complementarity–reciprocity, (2) direct reciprocity and mutuality, and (3) developmental process. All relationships are likely to involve each process to some extent, although some may be characterized most strongly by only one or two.

Complementarity–Reciprocity In this type of interactional pattern, each member acts to facilitate, to support, or *not* to constrain or interfere with the *different* interests, goals, and concerns of the other. The exchange process for relationships involves a focus on the differences between the individuals. For example, one child likes art and the other likes sewing; each takes an interest or participates by assisting in the other's projects. According to Youniss's (1980) interpretations of Piaget (1932) and Sullivan (1953), children develop cooperative procedures that keep differences from disordering the relationship. Discussion, debates, arguments, negotiation, and compromise are used to establish patterns of dominance and balance. Among the items in Huston and Burgess's (1979) composite list of exchange theorists' research, partners "begin to increasingly feel that their separate interests are inextricably tied to the well-being of their relationships" (p. 8).

Direct Reciprocity and Mutuality A second type of structure is one in which each member acts to facilitate, support, or not interfere with the goals, interests, and concerns *both hold in common.* There appear to be two types of dyadic reciprocity structures here.

In *direct reciprocity,* both members share the same goal or interest, their exchange is of the same nature (e.g., both children like art and provide one another with resources for their individual projects). Reciprocal exchange is a category mentioned frequently in regard to friendship processes in even young children (e.g., Bigelow, 1977; Youniss, 1980). As indicated previously, in the social psychology literature, researchers have often focused on the degree of equity in social exchanges in a relationship. Ridley and Avery (1979) and Burns (1973) also presented a range of types of exchange patterns that included both negative and positive orientations of each member to the other. In general, social reciprocity in adult relationship research has focused on the exchange of love, affection, rewards, goods and services, and social and personality gratifications.

Mutuality is the pattern where members of the relationship must coordinate to accomplish a joint goal. For example, two children work on a joint art project, or two friends or partners jointly cook a meal or start a business. Some social psychologists have focused more on mutuality as a major feature of many relationships in which the individual and common concerns begin to converge (Pruitt & Kimmel, 1977). Piaget (1932) pointed to the critical task in peer relationships of arriving at mutual understanding. Youniss (1980) found that children 9 years and older defined friendship as involving learning about another person with whom similarity and common interests are examined and each person is understood by the other. Whereas older children focused on mutuality of emotional experience and sharing interests, younger children focused on joint activity, as in playing together. In reciprocity, exchange processes between individuals is the pattern. Mutuality is indicated by the coordination of two persons working as a joint unit. Relationships would seem to involve both of these patterns to varying degrees.

Developmental Processes A third type of structural process is found in relationships in which each member acts to facilitate and support those goals, interests, and concerns that directly help to maintain and promote the well-being of the relationship. Little research has been conducted in child development with this focus. Research has been conducted—especially on married partners—by social psychologists and sociologists to examine the processes that contribute to longevity of close relationships. Among the operations studied (see Huston & Burgess, 1979), the most critical for researchers of child development appear to be the following:

1. *Proximity.* The members of the relationship make arrangements to provide opportunities to interact.

2. *Frequency of interaction.* The members of the relationship must interact frequently enough to construct and maintain the relationship.

3. *Positive affect.* The members of the relationship maintain a sufficient degree of positive affect and develop strategies to manage and limit negative affect.

4. *Communication system.* Each member of the relationship must communicate with sufficient skill and appropriateness with one another in order not to impede the construction and maintenance of the relationship.

5. *Social-cognitive processes.* Each member of the relationship requires sufficient and appropriate social-cognitive ability (e.g., role-taking, person or social perception, information-processing) to gain knowledge of one another and to coordinate problem-solving.

Although some of these processes have been studied in child development research, including communication, social cognition, and conflict resolution (e.g., Selman, 1981), the methods employed have been hypothetical and have not typically involved studies of actual relationships. Future investigations of various types of peer relationships in child development research may differ, in part, according to three major types of social structure discussed previously—direct reciprocity, complementarity—reciprocity and mutuality, and the developmental processes. As indicated, it may be that although close friendships, social friendships, activity partnerships, and acquaintanceships may involve each of these structures to some extent, some structures may tend to be more characteristic of one type of relationship than another. Structures may also differ with the age of the children and their social or cultural experiences.

Social Behavioral Content

The third major variable for focus in research on relationships is the social behavioral content of the relationship. Given that relationships have a social interactional context and structure, the content constitutes the more observable behavioral actions and themes (e.g., helping, sharing) found in a variety of social interactions and relationships. The social content also constitutes the behavioral form of the developmental processes discussed previously that facilitate the development of a relationship (also see Levinger, 1979). According to Sullivan (1953), close friendships provide children with unique experiences in which they develop interpersonal sensitivity, kindness, and empathy. Research on older children and adults indicates the importance of self-disclosure in friendship relationships (Tesch, 1983). In reciprocity and mutuality processes, children's social content thus should include gaining knowledge and information about each other, participating in activities and interests, providing instruction and help, and sharing feelings and ideas.

In summary, in research on the types of children's relationships at various ages, evaluations should include a focus on the social context, structure, or organization of the interactions and the social behavioral content. Such research data would allow the identification of the range of variations for each type of relationship, the developmental phases of the relationships, the critical differences between the major types of relationships, and the quality and effectiveness of a particular relationship.

A STUDY OF CHILDREN BECOMING ACQUAINTED

Overview of the Study

The study presented here is an examination of the social processes enacted by 5-, 6-, and 7-year-old, same-age, same-gender dyads as they became acquainted. Thus the study begins with one type of peer relationship: new acquaintances. It was of interest to examine the extent to which these previously unacquainted children would get to know each other as persons and as activity partners.

The study included five 10-minute sessions that took place over a 5-day period. The sessions were videotaped from behind a two-way mirror. The children were informed that we were interested in learning how children play together and make friends. Each day, some new art materials were provided in addition to a good supply of paper, crayons, and felt-tip markers. These new materials included clay, tracing materials, coloring papers, and other materials typically found in classrooms and homes. It was thought that these materials would allow children to elect to interact and share materials or to play on their own. However, we wanted to have one session that provided a more structured art activity that would require more planning and problem-solving by a dyad. A battery-operated art toy (Spin Art) was thus provided in the third or fourth session. This toy was constructed so that a small sheet of paper would rotate as marking pens were used to make interesting designs. We had employed this toy in previous research and knew that it was usually one that required children to take turns or share a picture.

In the play sessions, children were expected to exchange information about each other and their family, friends, and activities. In addition, we expected that they would set up activity and interaction goals and rules and help and instruct each other about the materials and activities. It was expected that the children's interactions would vary from infrequent to frequent and include a range from infrequent cooperative play to joint or cooperative play. To examine the possible friendship beginnings that might evolve, we assessed the extent to which the children made statements about their relationship in terms of its continuity. In actuality, statements of this kind were rare, although some dyads appeared to have the potential to develop into social or close friends if given the opportunity for more interaction. However, the situation was considered analogous to many school activities that are also structured by time constraints and oriented toward developing projects.

The specific coding scheme employed in this study was a modification of some codes used in previous research by Gottman and Parkhurst (1979) and codes developed in light of research findings obtained by Peevers and Secord (1973) and Livesley and Bromley (1973). The latter two studies indicated the types of information that children of these ages process about their peers. The general issues of the scheme also reflect those typically examined in the social psychology research on adult relationships. The results for the codes are presented first, followed by a discussion of how they relate to various features of the proposed conceptual approach to studying children's peer relationships presented in the first section of the chapter.

Subject Selection and Procedure

Selected to participate from a pool of approximately 100 children were 40 subjects. Letters of invitation to participate in a study of how children become acquainted were sent to a large group of parents and children with the cooperation of elementary schools in two middle-socioeconomic status (SES) areas. Children were blocked by age and gender in order to achieve same-gender pairs of subjects who were closest in age and did not attend the same school. Each of the 20 dyads selected differed in age by no more than 6 months. The ages ranged from 5 years, 3 months to 7 years, 5 months, with a mean dyad age of 76 months (or 6 years, 4 months). One dyad did not talk during the sessions, and as we were mainly taking account of the verbal interactions, this dyad was not included in analyses, resulting in 38 subjects and 19 dyads (9 male and 10 female).

The study took place in a playroom in a university setting, where the children played alone while the experimenter waited outside the room. Parents waited in a separate waiting area. The room contained a small table with two pillows set up next to each other on one side of the table, which faced a two-way mirror. A knee-high barrier was placed between the table and mirror. On the first day, each child was introduced to his or her partner by a male experimenter for the boys and a female experimenter for the girls, and they were told that each day they could talk and play with the art materials for 10 minutes.

Coding System

The coding system (see Table 6.1) was oriented largely toward an examination of the children's conversations in terms of the communication processes employed and the social behavioral content and interactional structure. The study resulted in nearly 19 hours of videotapes (50 minutes per dyad) that were transcribed and coded, message by message, for three code levels. Coding was conducted by reading transcripts and viewing the videotapes. Each message (defined as a meaningful message, phrase, or sentence) was coded at three levels.

1. *Communication codes* (e.g., questions, demands). These codes focused on the type of communicated message that would facilitate or constrain the interaction and lead to or maintain an interaction.

2. *Social behavior codes* (e.g., exchanging information about each other, conversing about topics, structuring and directing activities and interactions). These behaviors included the type of content in the interactions that constitute the focus of the interaction and, at the same time, depending on the type and extent of the content exchanged, may serve to facilitate and maintain the interaction and enhance the construction of a relationship. The codes included a range from those that would indicate antagonism to those that would indicate noninvolvement, to simply conversing, to working and playing together, and finally to forming an activity partnership and a friendship.

3. *Social structure codes* included the direction of the verbal messages— that is, references to *self* (I, me, mine), to *peer* (you, yours), and to *dyad* (us, our, we) or *other* (activity, setting, or other factors). Dyads should differ in the distributions of messages that concern self, peer, and dyad. Reciprocity may be indicated by a balanced focus on self and peer, and mutuality should be indicated by joint concerns.

Positive affect was implied by prosocial and antisocial codes that were included as part of the social behavioral content codes. Children exhibited few antisocial codes in this context. Social-cognitive codes were also included to determine the level of information exchanged. The information

TABLE 6.1

Major Dyad Interaction Codes[a]

Variable	Definition or examples	Overall frequency (%)
Communication		
Statements	"This is a nice color." "Blue is best."	47.0
Questions	"How old are you?" (Also, tag question—e.g., "Okay?")	12.5
Requests–Suggests	"Can I have a turn?" "Let's do this first."	4.6 (NR)
Demand–Command	"Stop that now!" "Give me that pen."	4.6
Agree–Comply	"Okay." "Yes, it's your turn." (Provides pen).	10.4
Negate or Refuse	"No, you can't!"	2.9
Requests Clarification	"How big?" "Which pen?"	3.5
Clarify	"The *purple* pen."	3.8 (NR)
		89.3
Social behavior		
Personal Information	Information provided or requested about self (or partner), family, friends, school, including feelings, activities, interests, and physical characteristics.	11.5
Structuring Activity or Interaction	Making rules, goals; setting an agenda; general structuring or activity or ways of interacting.	24.3
Prosocial Behavior	Praise, help, instruction, empathy.	6.2
Conversing	General discussion of knowledge, facts, types of materials and activities.	52.0
Narrating	Talking or commenting to oneself, usually while doing an activity.	2.1
		96.1
Social structure		
Self	References to oneself or one's activity: "I like this color." "This is mine."	38.3
Partner	References to the partner or partner's activity: "What grade are you in?" "Is this your pen?"	26.3
Dyad	References to the dyad or dyad's activity: "We should do two pictures." "This is our best one."	6.5
		71.1

[a]NR indicates code was not reliable. Each meaningful message or speech unit was coded for all three categories, according to appropriate code in each category. Additional subcodes were also indicated to determine more specificity (not listed here).

exchanged was found to focus largely on concrete characteristics (e.g., physical appearances) and behavioral actions or events (e.g., describing behaviors rather than intentions), a tendency that has also been found in other studies of children of these ages (e.g., Peevers & Secord, 1973; Livesley & Bromley, 1973).

Two undergraduate students (one male and one female) and two graduate students (one male and one female) coded the data. The coders were previously unfamiliar with the study. A separate reliability study was conducted by having each coder also code randomly selected 3-minute segments of videotape using the transcripts and tapes from three of the five sessions for three or four dyads they had not previously coded. Correlations between coders were considered to indicate sufficient reliability if the significance level was at least $p < .001$. The average significant correlations between coders for codes within three major levels or categories was as follows: communication, $r = .77$; social behavioral content, $r = .67$ and social structure, $r = .79$. Borderline significant correlations were found for demand, negate, conversing, and dyad references. Codes that included activity references were also collapsed so that activity could be used as a separate variable ($r = .88$, $p < .001$). The overall patterns of the major codes indicated that low frequencies of variables, occurring 1% or 2% percent or less, tended to be of insufficient reliability. Given that the reliability study employed a selection procedure that interrupted the flow of the dialogue, some codes were more difficult to discriminate. Reliability coding for the Spin-Art session in which Spin-Art was employed was thus conducted by comparing continuous coding, and correlations for the codes ranged from .70 to .94.

General Patterns of Social Interaction

Overall, the codes showed that children increased in their levels of activity-focused comments across sessions, resulting in 55% of all messages coded. The social content codes showed that children's messages were more activity-focused than any other single type of content. The children appeared to have conceptualized the situation as one in which they were to play or work well together. Given the constraints of the contrived situation, had the children viewed the relationship potential as strictly making an acquaintance, then we would not have expected them to work out ways to contribute to each other's activity or to share much beyond minimal introductory information. Instead, we observed, from both the quantitative data and the transcripts, that the children appeared to operate more as activity partners. Note in the following excerpt from a transcript of a first-session dyad the extent to which the children were constructing their own art activity, while they were also contributing to each other's activity, defining mutual interests and sharing personal information.

Child A	Child B
I like spaceships.	
	I'm gonna try one of them.
Now which spaceship are you—oh I'm gonna make one of those things.	
	What is this?
	I'm gonna try and make a different kind of spaceship
You mean your own kind of spaceship?	
	Yeah. It's gonna have all these different kinds of shapes. No, this is the wrong kind.
Oh, I'm gonna stop on mine. I'm gonna use the back.	
Hey, you make a fing . . . finger print, it looked like.	
	I know, I'm not (inaudible) to do it. Watch this I colored my finger, right?
Oh, I know what you're doing.	
	There it is, and here it is.
I'm gonna try it. I'm gonna try it.	
	It's really hard. But ya have to squish yourself . . . .
	Well . . . just put 'em in any color. Doesn't matter what color you put 'em in.
I'm makin . . . somethin'. I'm makin' a design.	
	Oh . . . that looks like . . . .
Oh, it didn't work!	
	What . . . what are you tryin' to do?
I'm gonna make one of these kind of spaceships.	
	I'm not gonna use that. I'm gonna try to make a bird spaceship.
Why don't you make one? That cricket spaceship in the comic book?	
	Cricket?
Yeah, it's like a cricket spaceship, and it's alive.	
	I wanna see it first. I don't see any comics.
Well . . . I . . . my brother . . . me and my brother have a comic book.	

(continued)

Child A	Child B
	I got "Credible Hulk." I do. That's the only comic I have. I wanna try some . . . some of my . . . special stuff. There. Always poke holes. Oh, why did I take that? This isn't gonna be a sun.
There's a spaceman.	
	This isn't a house. How do you . . . start up on a spaceship?
Here's a spaceman. And then here's a little space capsule.	
	Hey, that's neat!

In the next excerpt, another dyad in a fourth session strives to provide instruction and help as they attempt to trace with spirographs.

Child C	Child D
Ya trace it. Hey! This doesn't do anything. Watch this, it just makes . . .	
	I know how to use that. It's *real easy.*
How?	
	I'll show you. Well, you take one of these . . . Let me put in the kind you like. You need one of *these.* Oooh, that's a little . . . Oh, okay? Hold it, this is too small. . . . Now . . . ya put your pen and rub these holes and then ya hold this down, and ya move this around the circle, and it makes a flower of some sort. Some sort of flower.
Paper. Nice paper. Nice paper. Very, very nice paper.	
	I can hardly *do* this! I can do it. It's easy for me.
Yeah, look. Neat!	
	I know. Cool.
I'm gonna use a different one. This is gonna be (inaudible) there, put that. . . . Put this there. I'll take the big one. The big one! I need good ones . . . wait . . . do it up here. A different color. It's very slow. (Mumbling to self) I'm just making a	

(*continued*)

Child C	Child D
scribble. I like that one. I don't know how I did that one. I'm gonna do one *all* different colors. But I don't know which ones. Who wants me to do the smallest one?	
	Me.
Oh . . .	
	Hold it. You only . . .
Oh . . .	
	You only need the smallest one. 'Cause this—hold it, let me see. Let me see which is smaller. I think this one. It's smaller.
I'll try blue.	
	Oh, I see what your problem is . . . you're not going around the outside, you're just scribbling in the middle. Okay, now, look!

In the present study, children quickly became acquainted. Nearly every dyad had the inclination and social competence to interact positively and to coordinate their activity planning and participation. In this sense, they appeared to be forming a relationship more similar to an activity partnership. Though limited, it is analogous to relationships that children and adults experience in work or school or similar, more structured settings.

Major Results

We have treated the dyad as the basic unit of analysis rather than individual subjects. A mean score for the dyad for each variable was thus calculated for use in the statistical analyses. To examine age differences, subjects were divided into younger versus older groups of males and females (determined by the mean age of dyad partners) according to a median split at 77 months, resulting in 9 younger dyads (4 male and 5 female dyads) and 10 older dyads (5 male and 5 female). Although the cell size was small for an examination of higher-order interactions, analyses of variance were conducted to determine patterns of significant differences for gender, age, and session. For all major variables, gender (2) × age (2) × session (5) analyses of variance were conducted. In general, few significant two-way or three-way interactions were found. Significant findings ($p < .05$) and trends ($p < .10$) for all major variables are reported. Where no significant findings or trends were found, only descriptive data are reported.

Communication Skills

The approximate average of statements per session was 77 messages, or 47% of all messages, with a tendency for an increase in both overall verbal messages and statements from the first to the second session; however, no significant differences were found across sessions. There was a trend for gender differences; females made more statements and overall communications than did males.

We expected that early verbal messages would be largely in the form of questions as the children got to know each other. Questions represented 12.5% of the information exchange process. There was a trend for age differences, with older dyads asking more questions than younger dyads.

There are very few studies of children's language development after the age of 5 years. The assumption has been that not much language development goes on after age 5 or so, yet the research that does exist indicates that this is not really the case (see deVilliers & deVilliers [1978] for a review). Older children do continue to develop competence in the production of complex sentences and conversational techniques. We had expected that many children might have difficulty communicating basic information and conversing with a new acquaintance, although we expected the form of their conversation to be similar to that of adults. However, we found that children tended to talk in complete sentences with less than 1% Interruptions and Incomplete messages, both common features in adult conversation.

Children requested clarification throughout the sessions. However, Request Clarification amounted to only 3.5% of all verbal messages, and clarifications were provided in 3.8% of all messages. We expected that children might provide maintenance feedback much as adults frequently do, such as "hmmm," "aha," "yes," and the like. We found less than 2% of these techniques, and the transcript was strict in the accurate recording of these utterances. Children often made use of various language forms that facilitate the communication of structuring, directing, and instructing in interactions. These included forms of Requests, Suggests, and Demands as initiations of structuring the interaction, and Provide-Comply, Agree, and Negate-Resist as responses. Requests and Suggests messages combined comprised nearly 5% of the total verbal messages. Demand-Command messages, which are more direct and assertive forms, comprised nearly 5% of the total. Alternately, Comply and Agree together comprised approximately 10%, whereas Negate was less frequent at nearly 3%. In general, the children's communication skills at these ages indicated considerable competence and facility.

Social Behavior Content

For the initial session, we also expected that initially children would focus primarily on routines for gaining basic information about each other (e.g., "What school do you go to?"). Such routines are typical of adults in initial encounters (see Table 6.2). Personal Information did tend to be somewhat more frequent in the first two sessions. Overall, personal information comprised 11.5% of all communications, and no significant increase was obtained across the five sessions. A study of the transcripts indicated that children tended to exchange personal information as relevant or as it might occur to them throughout the sessions.

Conversing included social content not included under the other content codes. Conversing comprised 52% ($\bar{X} = 39$ per dyad) of all coded messages. The subcodes indicated that conversing mainly included discussion of various topics such as general Knowledge (e.g., regarding motor boats, airplanes, geographical locations, and definitions and spelling of words), which comprised 2%, and Language Play (rhyming words and other types of word

TABLE 6.2

Means for Social Content of Interactions[a]

Dyads	N	Information self–partner	Rule–agenda, making	Prosocial behavior	General conversation
Dyad means across sessions					
Younger males	4	6.88	17.45	4.85	33.75
Older males	5	8.30	16.40	3.78	45.24
Younger females	5	9.76	20.98	4.64	35.42
Older females	5	10.38	22.96	6.36	40.06
Younger	9	8.32	19.22	4.75	34.59
Older	10	9.34	19.68	5.07	42.65
Males	9	7.59	16.93	4.32	39.50
Females	10	10.07	21.97	5.50	37.74
All dyads	19	8.93	19.55	4.91	38.87
Dyad means across gender and age					
Session					
1		11.89	12.63	4.21	35.55
2		7.53	20.00	5.26	43.50
3		6.32	27.24	6.61	41.11
4		8.71	20.79	5.37	35.37
5		10.21	17.11	3.11	38.84

[a]Means are based on the averages of total scores for children in each dyad.

play)—often found to a larger extent with preschool children—which comprised 2.3%. Most of the conversing messages were related to the immediate activity, including comments on the nature and function of the materials and references to the child's immediate ideas and reacting about the activity. Conversing, in contrast to Narration, consisted only of messages exchanged between dyad partners. Older children tended to converse more than did younger children.

Narration referred to comments an individual made to himself or herself, usually while doing an activity. Narration comprised 2% of the messages.

Structuring and Directing comments to the partner regarding one's own or the partner's activity and/or interaction comprised over 24% of the messages coded. It is interesting that there was a significant increase in these messages across sessions. This would seem to indicate that the children became increasingly involved with each other as they interacted.

Prosocial Behaviors (e.g., praise, help, instruct, and empathy) comprised about 6% of the total messages; the most frequent of these was Instructing and Helping which accounted for 4% of all prosocial behaviors. Prosocial behaviors tended to increase across sessions. Negative or Antisocial Behaviors (e.g., criticize, name-call, push) occurred less than 1% of the time.

All codes that included references to activity-related content were collapsed to determine the extent of children's activity focus. Activity was indicated in 59.2% of all children's communications. References to activity-related content also increased significantly across sessions.

Social Interaction Structure

The codes for social structure showed that the children's references to self accounted for over 38% of the total messages and tended to increase across the sessions. Female dyads made significantly more Self references than did males. References to Partner comprised over 26% of the total messages, with a significant increase across sessions. Older dyads increased significantly more in Partner references than did younger dyads. References to the Dyad (we, ours) accounted for 6.5% of all verbalized messages. There was a trend for increases in references to the dyad across sessions for females and younger dyads. Other messages consisted of third-person references or the activity, materials, or setting. The Other references tended to decrease across sessions. Activity-referenced comments that included references to the Self, Partner, or Dyad were *not* coded in the other category (e.g., "My turn." or "Is this your pen?" or "We should do a picture now."). Over 70% of the total messages thus included personal and social references, indicating that children's verbal messages indicated social exchange. Children made substantially fewer references to the Dyad while increasing in references to

Partner across session. This may be an indication of a reciprocity rather than mutuality orientation in the dyadic interactions.

Overall, few significant age and gender differences or trends were found. As indicated, significant increases across sessions were obtained for Activity, Prosocial, Structuring Activity–Interaction, and Partner. In addition, some significant changes across session were clearly nonlinear, including Demand and Agreement. Increases for these codes were observed in the third or fourth sessions when dyads played with the Spin-Art toy. Additional analyses were thus conducted on children's interactions during the Spin-Art sessions and are discussed in the next section.

Spin-Art Session

As indicated previously, the role of situational influence was examined in this study by the inclusion of the aforementioned Spin-Art activity. In this activity, children could take turns using the machine and designing pictures of their own, or they could forego doing their own pictures and design joint pictures and then divide them. Only one dyad elected the latter strategy, and one dyad did not take turns. The other dyads took turns. One-half of the dyads had been randomly selected to be given this activity in the third session and one-half in the fourth session. By comparing the third and fourth sessions for dyads with Spin-Art versus dyads with some other art materials, the effects of Spin-Art activity per se indicated substantial increases for Requests, Demands, Negate, Structuring, Directing, and Instructing.

Since the Spin-Art session involves inherent conflicts of interest and problem-solving challenges, an additional coding scheme was developed for this session. The codes focused on the extent to which children employed various social strategies to avoid, deflect, or attenuate disputes (see Oden, Wheeler, & Herzberger, in press). The children's behavior during the aforementioned Spin-Art session was organized around task roles in which each child would enact one of three roles: *primary role*—that is, using the Spin-Art toy by designing a picture; *secondary role*—that is, observing, commenting, or assisting the peer in the primary role; and *nonparticipating*—that is, the child may glance but does not observe the child in the primary role and instead does a different activity until his or her turn. The secondary and nonparticipant roles could vary considerably across children.

Assessments relating to these roles—primary, secondary, and nonparticipant—were conducted. These analyses allow for further assessment of the dyadic structure or organization. For example, discrepancy scores within dyads were created that consisted of the discrepancy between children in total time in the primary role. The median (*Mdn*) primary role discrepancy between partners in the 18 dyads that were assessed was nearly 1 minute (*Mdn* = 56 seconds). Nearly equal numbers of male and female younger and older dyads fell above and below the median. In this analysis, most children appeared to be aware of equity issues in the situation in reference to both the time constraint (i.e., the 10-minute session) and the number of turns. Eight dyads had *no* discrepancy in the total number of turns taken by each child in the 10 minutes, and for those with a turn-taking discrepancy, an average discrepancy of 1.1 turns was found.

In addition, *dispute episodes* were also counted. The disputes most frequently concerned when the child in the primary role was going to relinquish the toy for the other child's turn. Disputes also occurred over picture style, color, quality, or techniques. Overall, 7 dyads had no disputes. Of those who did have disputes, the average number was 2.4, with an average duration of 74.5 seconds (1 minute, 15 seconds). In one dyad, one child played exclusively with the toy; in another, the children played jointly. These two dyads were not included in the analyses in which low and high discrepancy (turn duration discrepancy) dyads were compared. When compared to high-duration discrepancy dyads, the low-duration discrepancy dyads had significantly fewer disputes and their disputes were of significantly shorter duration. Children thus appeared to be quite aware of a lack of equity in the amount of time in turn-taking.

It was then of interest to assess how newly acquainted peers might differ from other types of peer relationships in the aforementioned Spin-Art activity. The 6- and 7-year-old newly acquainted dyads ($N = 12$) in this data base were then compared with first-grade friendly dyads ($N = 24$) who were also paired for the Spin-Art activity in another study (Wheeler, 1981). In the Wheeler study, dyads were paired according to the results of sociometric analyses conducted several weeks prior to the Spin-Art session. These dyads were paired according to high degrees of mutual liking and/or friendship.

On a number of variables, Friendly Classmate dyads were found to differ from the Newly Acquainted dyads. Classmate dyads employed 21% demand communications compared to 12% for newly acquainted dyads. For classmate dyads, 59% of their messages were comments about their partners' or their own Spin-Art activity, compared to 24% for acquainted dyads. Classmate dyads, compared to acquainted dyads, also switched turns significantly more often ($\bar{X} = 4.33$ versus $\bar{X} = 2.04$) and their disputes, which did not differ in number, were of shorter duration ($\bar{X} = 11$ versus $\bar{X} = 45$ seconds). These data further illustrate the need for comparing different types of peer relationships.

DISCUSSION

The major finding of the present research pertained to increases in several major variables over the five sessions. Overall, increases were found for dyads in Demand–Command, Structuring–Directing, Prosocial Behavior, references to Self and Partner, and all activity-related messages. Nearly 60% of all messages were activity-related. At the same time, the activity focus of the dyads in this research was highly social. Analysis of the social structure codes indicated that the majority of all messages included references to Self, Partner, or Dyad. Only 2% of activity-related comments included references children made to themselves about their own activity. Furthermore, in this interactional context, the majority of their prosocial behavior consisted of instruction or help. As dyads interacted across the sessions, they became increasingly more direct in their communications, as indicated by increases in the Demand–Command and Structuring–Directing codes. Thus children related socially, but largely in the context of the activity. In this research, children appeared to move readily from acquaintances toward a type of peer relationship more similar to that of activity partner.

Age and gender differences were not often obtained. This may be due partly to the small number of subjects per cell. Compared to male dyads, female dyads made more statements and more references to self and increasing references to the dyad across sessions. Comparison of same- and opposite-gender dyadic interactions would be an especially interesting direction for future studies. In contrast to the social psychology literature, this is a fairly neglected area in child development research. Older dyads asked more questions than did younger dyads. It may be that the activity-oriented situation per se did not reveal age or gender differences that may exist in peer interaction in children in this age range. Alternatively, children of 5 to 7 years of age may simply be highly similar in their peer interaction.

Social Interaction Context, Structure, and Social Content

As indicated in the first section of this chapter, three major variables may be applicable to an analysis of children's peer relationships. The present research relates to these variables to some extent.

Social Interactional Context

The study reported here was initially designed with the expectation that children would reveal typical patterns of acquaintanceship. Indeed, children's personal information exchanges was both an initial and consistent part of the dyads' interactions. Children appeared, however, quickly and increasingly to behave like activity partners. This is likely to be partly a function of the situation per se. Children's perception of the interactional context appeared to be realistic, in that although an opportunity was constructed for each child to get to know another child, there was no plan to create future opportunities. The situation's limitations do appear to be analogous to other situations where children are simply put together for an activity. Future studies should consider that some experimental situations may tend to encourage particular types of peer relationships.

Structure or Organization

Three types of structure were identified in the proposed conceptual model: complementarity–reciprocity, direct reciprocity and mutuality, and developmental processes. For complementarity–reciprocity, additional codes, other than those employed in the present research, would be needed to assess the extent to which children contributed to each other's different interests and activities. The Instruct–Help code (under prosocial), for example, is relevant, in that children provided help for partners who did not know how to trace a picture, use the spirograph, and so forth. The Instruct–Help code in the present research was not constructed to differentiate between asking for and giving instruction or help, since the dyad was considered the focus. This and other codes could be constructed to detect the extent to which each partner contributed to the other's interest and activity. Discrepancy scores for a given code could be calculated for dyads to assess balance and imbalance on variables of interest. It would be useful for future studies to examine the interactions of peers in longer-standing relationships where the self-selected diverse interests of the peers would then be the focus.

For direct reciprocity and mutuality, the Spin-Art toy is the most relevant test case in the present research. Dyads had a goal in common (the aforementioned use of the Spin-Art toy), and in those dyads where partners did not constrain or interfere with the participation, of one another, there were fewer or no disputes, and the disputes that did occur were of shorter duration. Only one dyad played with the toy with a mutual goal—that is, joint pictures. Again, it would be interesting for future studies to set up situations that relate to actual interests of children (e.g., hobbies, self-selected projects) to evaluate the patterns of direct reciprocity and mutuality.

The developmental processes of proximity and frequency of interaction were set by the experimental situation in this study. An attempt was made to assess the degree of positive, negative, and neutral affect, but reliability for the ratings was not sufficient. It appeared that more specification of the kinds of vocal tones and facial and postural expressions corresponding to positive, negative, and neutral need to be developed. The communication system employed by the children appeared to be sufficient. Assessment of the extent to which each partner's comments were connected meaningfully to the other appears to be an interesting research direction (see Gottman & Parkhurst, 1979). Sequential analyses would be aided by a set of rules about what constitutes a related response to a partner's initiations. The extent to which partners and dyads differ in initiation of topics and shifting topics might provide one basis for determining the extent of peer interaction that is connected. Analysis of the disputes in the aforementioned Spin-Art session per se, however, appeared to reveal not lack of clarity of communication but perceptions and misperceptions about the motives of the partners (e.g., to deprive a partner's use of the Spin-Art).

Social-cognitive processes included assessment of the children's information exchange about each other and constituted nearly 12% of their communications. Information as coded could be calculated to detect discrepancies within dyads on the amount of information asked for versus information provided. Prosocial behavior codes, particularly Instruct–Help, could also be revised to detect similarity or discrepancy. It may be that some partners are more interested or supportive of partners and that some partners are more effective in eliciting these behaviors. Dyads may differ in similarity and discrepancy on these and other variables that would appear to be important to the relationship's development. Future studies might also look at additional variables to assess in relation to interactional variables (e.g., perspective-taking and problem-solving). It would be interesting to evaluate children's problem-solving in more real-life conflict-of-interest situations to determine patterns such as avoidance, confrontation, dominance, and submission for particular peer relationships. Another approach would be to assess children's peer relationships in part by taking inventories of partners' cumulative knowledge of each other.

Social Content

As indicated throughout this chapter, the major focus of the social content was on dyads' exchange of personal and activity-related information. Personal information included discussion of personal interests, characteristics, family, friends, home, school, and special events (e.g., vacations and class play). Activity information included comments and instruction on types and use of materials, activity planning, goals, evaluation, and ways of interacting in the activity (e.g., taking turns). Many content codes were used infrequently, including codes referring to the establishment and continuity of a future peer relationship. Future studies could build coding schemes with more consideration of the type of peer interaction most likely to develop in a given context.

Diverse Types of Peer Relationships

Although the present research had little to say about social or close friends, comparison of the newly acquainted dyads with the friendly classmate dyads in the aforementioned Spin-Art session is particularly interesting. Compared to the newly acquainted dyads, classmate dyads were more direct, made more comments about their own and their partner's Spin-Art activity, switched turns more frequently, and had disputes of shorter duration. It appeared that children did interact somewhat differently in these two types of relationships. It would be interesting to observe classmates who do not know each other very well—that is, actual ongoing acquaintances—with those who have more developed relationships.

It may be that the organization or structure (i.e., complementarity– reciprocity, direct reciprocity and mutuality, and developmental processes) of different types of peer relationships shifts according to status variables such as age, gender, and cultural group. Some types of peer relationships, such as close friendships and partnerships, may tend to be more effective with certain types of structure or organization and developmental process. The descriptors presented in Figure 6.1 thus require further examination; they were suggested on the basis of previous research but may be inappropriately placed or may not be relevant at certain ages. Descriptors not mentioned may be more relevant.

The dyads in the present study interacted more like activity partners, as depicted in Figure 6.1. However, it seems unlikely that they formed a well-developed activity partnership in the course of the time provided. The dyads, however, did appear to show a full range of strategies and skills relevant to this type of peer relationship. In this sense, the dyads simply may have interacted in an activity partner mode, thus showing how they usually interact with partners for activities and projects. It would be interesting to develop studies that would require children to enact or role-play friendship peer relationships or change a peer relationship from that of acquaintance to activity partner or friend. This strategy might be especially useful for investigating peer relationships with older children, who are likely to be more conscious of observers and may consider such interest distracting, if not detrimental. Investigations of actual peer relationships with older children may also use self-reports or reports from parents and teachers. It would also be interesting to evaluate settings such as the classroom to determine the range of diverse types of relationships that appear to be feasible to develop. Many classrooms may be structured such that activity partnerships are the most likely to develop (see Oden, 1982).

In summary, we presented a conceptual model that may be useful for generating research questions that attempt to consider the extent to which children exhibit a range of peer relationships. This research direction considers that children's relationships may have greater complexity than we had anticipated or than children report. Adults often refer to children who are playing together as friends. The limited terminology or conception that we communicate to children may limit their own conceptions or reports, but it may not affect the nature and structure of their peer relationships.

REFERENCES

Asher, S. R., Markell, R. A., & Hymel, S. Identifying children at risk in peer relations: a critique of the rate-of-interaction approach to assessment. *Child Development*, 1981, *52*, 1239–1345.

Asher, S. R., Oden, S. L., & Gottman, J. M. Children's friendships in school settings, In L. G. Katz (Ed.), *Current topics in early childhood education* (Vol. 1). Norwood, NJ: Ablex, 1977.

Berndt, T. J. Fairness and friendship. In K. H. Rubin & H. S. Ross (Eds.), *Peer relationships and social skills in childhood*. New York: Springer-Verlag, 1982.

Berscheid, E., & Graziano, W. The initiation of social relationships and interpersonal attraction. In R. L. Burgess & T. L. Huston (Eds.), *Social exchange in developing relationships*. New York: Academic, 1979.

Bigelow, B. J. Children's friendship expectations: A cognitive–developmental study. *Child Development*, 1977, *48*, 246–253.

Burns, T. A structural theory of social exchange. *Acta Sociologica*, 1973, 16, 183–208.

Carroll, T. S., & Payne, J. W. (Eds.). *Cognition and social behavior*. Hillsdale, NJ: Erlbaum, 1976.

Coie, J. D., Dodge, K. A., & Coppotelli, H. Dimensions and types of social status: A cross-age perspective. *Developmental Psychology*, 1982, *18*, 557–570.

Cooper, C. R., Ayers-Lopez, S., & Marquis, A. Children's discourse during peer learning in experimental and naturalistic situations. *Discourse Processes, 1982, 5,* 177–191.

Damon, W. *The social world of the child*. San Francisco: Jossey-Bass, 1979.

deVilliers, J. G., & deVilliers, P. A. *Language acquisition*. Cambridge, MA: Harvard University Press, 1978.

Fine, G. A. Friends, impression management, and preadolescent behavior. In S. R. Asher & J. M. Gottman (Eds.), *The development of children's friendships*. New York: Cambridge University Press, 1981.

Furman, W., & Willems, T. *The acquaintanceship process in middle childhood*. Paper presented at the International Conference on Personal Relationships, Madison, Wisconsin, 1982.

Gottman, J. M., & Parkhurst, J. T. A developmental theory of friendship and acquaintanceship processes. In W. A. Collins (Ed.), *Minnesota symposium on child psychology* (Vol. 13). Hillsdale, NJ: Erlbaum, 1979.

Hallinan, M. T. Recent advances in sociometry. In S. R. Asher & J. M. Gottman (Eds.), *The development of children's friendships*. New York: Cambridge University Press, 1981.

Hallinan, M. T. & Tuma, N. B. Classroom effects on change in children's friendships. *Sociology of Education*, 1978, *51*, 270–282.

Hartup, W. W. Children and their friends. In H. McGurk (Ed.), *Issues in childhood social development*. London: Methuen, 1978.

Heider, F. The psychology of interpersonal relations. New York: Wiley, 1958.

Huston, T. L., & Burgess, R. L. Social exchange in developing relationships: An overview. In R. L. Burgess & T. L. Huston (Eds.), *Social exchange in developing relationships*. New York: Academic, 1979.

Kelley, H. H. *Personal relationships: Their structure and processes*. Hillsdale, NJ: Erlbaum, 1979.

Levinger, E. A social exchange view on the dissolution of pair relationships. In R. L. Burgess & T. L. Huston (Eds.), *Social exchange in developing relationships*. New York: Academic, 1979.

Livesley, W. J., & Bromley, D. B. *Person perception in childhood and adolescence*. London: Wiley, 1973.

Mangione, P. L. *Children's mixed- and same-age dyadic interaction*. Paper presented at the biennial meeting of the Society for Research in Child Development, Boston, April 1981.

Newcomb, T. *The acquaintance process*. New York: Holt, 1961.

Oden, S. The child's social isolation: Origins, prevention, intervention. In G. Cartledge & J. Milburn (Eds.), *Teaching social skills to children: Innovative approaches*. Elmsford, NY: Pergamon, 1980.

Oden, S. Peer relationship development in childhood. In L. G. Katz (Ed.), *Current topics in early childhood education* (Vol. 4). Norwood, NJ: Ablex, 1982.

Oden, S., Wheeler, V. A., & Herzberger, S. D. An analysis of children's conversations within a conflict-of-interest situation. In H. E. Sypher & J. L. Applegate (Eds.), *Understanding interpersonal communication: Social cognitive and strategic processes in children and adults*. Beverly Hills, CA: Sage, in press.

Peevers, H., & Secord, P. F. Developmental change in attribution of descriptive concepts to persons. *Journal of Personality and Social Psychology*, 1973, *26*, 120–128.

Piaget, J. *The moral judgment of the child*. London: Routledge & Kegan Paul, 1932.

Pruitt, D. G., & Kimmel, M. J. Twenty years of experimental gaming: Critique, synthesis and suggestions for the future. In M. R. Rosensveig & L. Porter (Eds.), *Annual Review of Psychology*, 1977, *28*, 363–392.

Putallaz, M., & Gottman, J. Social skills and group acceptance. In S. R. Asher & J. M. Gottman (Eds.), *The development of children's friendships*. New York: Cambridge University Press, 1981.

Ridley, C. A., & Avery, A. W. Social network influence on the dyadic relationship. In R. L. Burgess & T. L. Huston (Eds.), *Social exchange in developing relationships*. New York: Academic, 1979.

Selman, R. L. The child as a friendship philosopher. In S. R. Asher & J. M. Gottman (Eds.), *The development of children's friendships*. New York: Cambridge University Press, 1981.

Singleton, L. C., & Asher, S. R. Social integration and children's peer preferences: An investigation of developmental and cohort differences. *Child Development*, 1979, *50*, 936–941.

Spivack, G., & Shure, M. B. *Social adjustment of young children*. San Francisco: Jossey-Bass, 1974.

Stein, N. L., & Goldman, S. R. Children's knowledge about social situations: From causes to consequences. In S. R. Asher & J. M. Gottman (Eds.), *The development of children's friendships*. New York: Cambridge University Press, 1981.

Sullivan, H. S. *The interpersonal theory of psychiatry*. New York: Norton, 1953.

Tesch, S. A. Review of friendship development across the life span. *Human Development* 1983, 26, 266–276.

Wheeler, V. A. *Reciprocity between first-grade friend and non-friend classmates in a conflict of interest situation.* Unpublished doctoral dissertation, University of Rochester, Rochester, NY 1981.

Youniss, J. *Parents and peers in social development.* Chicago: University of Chicago Press, 1980.

Youniss, J., & Volpe, J. A relational analysis of children's friendship. In W. Damon (Ed.), *New directions for child development (No. 1): Social cognition* San Francisco: Jossey-Bass, 1978.

7

A Developmental Approach
to Social Exchange Processes

WILLIAM G. GRAZIANO

EDITORS' INTRODUCTION

In this chapter, William Graziano clearly reveals his persistent interest in molar, abstract theoretical propositions and their integration with one another and with empirical data. On a broad conceptual level, he discusses the complementary natures of two major theories, one proposed by Kurt Lewin and the other by Heinz Werner. Mindful of the separate social and developmental roots of these theories, Graziano brings them to bear on questions regarding social exchange processes and their role in social relationships from infancy to adulthood. The multifaceted way in which developmental perspectives may be integrated into both theory and research about social behavior is clearly illustrated as the chapter considers both the development of social exchange processes per se and the differences in their operation for individuals at different levels of development during childhood and adolescence. In addition to a discussion of the application of social exchange processes to children's social behavior, theoretical and methodological issues are raised concerning the obstacles faced by developmental and social psychologists who find themselves in a boundary area by dint of their interest in social exchange. Graziano further provides some suggestions for ways in which these obstacles may be overcome, such as building research at a boundary on a base of strong specialization rather than of universal scholarship.

INTRODUCTION

The purpose of this chapter is to discuss the development of social exchange processes. Both social psychology and developmental psychology

BOUNDARY AREAS IN SOCIAL
AND DEVELOPMENTAL PSYCHOLOGY

claim variants on the topic, and it is fair to describe it as an important boundary issue. Both branches of psychology address exchange phenomena, but each approaches these phenomena with different theoretical perspectives. In the first section of the chapter I discuss critically some theoretical accounts of the development of exchange processes from the perspectives of social and developmental psychology. In the second section I attempt to relate some of these theoretical ideas to empirical research on the development of exchange processes in infants and young children. The focus of the second section is on the development of standards of fairness or deservingness in exchange.

IDENTIFYING COMPLEMENTARY THEORETICAL APPROACHES

Two Historically Important Themes

In the introductory chapter of the present volume, Masters, Yarkin-Levin, and Graziano propose that research in boundary areas between disciplines can lead to profitable outcomes when researchers seek to identify complementary theoretical formulations. Such guidelines are easier to propose than to follow. Actually identifying such complementary themes from social and developmental psychology as they apply to exchange processes is quite difficult. Nonetheless, some complementary themes relevant to interpersonal relationships in general can be extracted. Here I consider two historically important themes that helped to shape modern social and developmental psychology: those presented by Kurt Lewin and Heinz Werner. These two themes are then compared with a third theme presented by contemporary exchange theorists.

Lewin had a considerable affect on contemporary social psychological theory and research (e.g., Brehm, Kassin, & Gibbons, 1981, pp. vi–ix; Festinger, 1980; Hendrick, 1977), and it is not necessary to recapitulate his well-known ideas here other than to note that Lewin does offer some valuable insights on the nature of groups and of relationships. Groups and relationships are seen as emergent units that are more than simply the sum of the individuals involved (e.g., Lewin, 1943, 1944); rather, they derive their characteristics from the functional interdependence of the individual components making up the system (e.g., Lewin, 1940). Because Lewin stressed the "principle of contemporaneous causes," he had relatively little to say about developmental processes per se (for an exception, see Lewin, 1951).

Werner offers a valuable complement to Lewin's ideas, in that Werner has relatively little to say about social processes per se, but he does offer some valuable insights on the ways developmental processes may influence social interactions. Because some of Werner's more important ideas are not as well known as Lewin's, they are presented in some detail here. For Werner, development is seen as a dialectical synthesis of two antithetical processes: (1) the tendency to conserve one's integrity as an individual, to maintain a sense of continuity across time, and (2) the tendency to undergo transformations, to become more differentiated and hierarchically integrated (e.g., Werner, 1948, 1957). From Werner's perspective this dialectical synthesis of development, called the *orthogenetic principle,* is a progression from simple, undifferentiated states to more complex, hierarchically integrated states (cf. Lewin, 1936, p. 155; 1951). Complex differentiated states are not merely simple accretions; they are transformations of simpler undifferentiated states (e.g., Werner, 1957; Werner & Kaplan, 1963).

Beyond this basic orthogenetic principle are other notions from the Wernerian approach that are relevant to the social processes of relationships. First, in complement to the Lewinian focus on efficient causation, Werner expresses strong interest in material causation. Unlike the Lewinians (and many contemporary social psychologists), Werner was concerned with self-regulatory processes inherent in the organism's original functional structures that contribute to developmental transformations (Werner, 1948). Part of the "genetic principle of spirality" (Werner & Kaplan, 1963), for example, is the notion of analogous functioning in which advanced stages and systems are transformed from the raw materials of more primitive systems. Second, the Wernerians emphasize the parallel activities not only within different levels of a particular line of development (e.g., the development of mathematical reasoning) but also between different lines of development (e.g., the parallel processes in the development of mathematical reasoning and the development of social cognition). This notion is phrased succinctly by Flavell: "Just remember that the head that thinks about the social world is the selfsame head that thinks about the nonsocial world" (1977, p. 122).

The third and fourth relevant characteristics of the Wernerian approach follow from the two previous characteristics. For Werner, the developing organism is involved in active interaction with the environment. Although organisms are strongly influenced by environmental events, the nature of the influence is determined by the level of functioning at which the organism is operating at the time of the event. The notion of "scene-to-actor shift" (Werner & Kaplan, 1963), for example, implies that at more primitive levels of functioning, the organism is relatively passive, and the psychological environment (scene) is the primary instigator of interaction. At more sophisticated levels of functioning, however, the organism itself becomes a primary instigator (actor) of organism–environment interactions (compare the more recent notion of "reactive" versus "active" genotype–environment correlation presented by Plomin, DeFries, & Loehlin [1977]). According to Werner, the equilibration between an organism's functional structures and the organism–environment interaction is the key to understanding processes of development (Langer, 1970; Werner, 1948). The fourth relevant characteristic of the Wernerian approach is the emphasis on the cognitive schema, a general rule or formula that guides mental activity. Although the notion of cognitive schemata has wide currency in contemporary social psychology (e.g., Abelson, 1981; Fiske & Linville, 1980; Isen & Hastorf, 1982; Tesser, 1978), the Wernerian approach may be considered complementary due to its developmental emphases (e.g., scene-to-actor shifts, progressive differentiation).

The final characteristic of the Wernerian approach deserves some attention. For Werner, there is an important distinction between the *form* of an act and the *content* of an act. The organism's functional structures (i.e., cognitive schemata) determine the form an act will take, whereas experiences from the physical and social environment determine the specific content of the act.

In sum, the approach of Werner represents a valuable complement to the formulations of Lewin. Werner emphasized progressive differentiation induced by the transformation of primitive systems into more complex systems. Transformations occur as a result of active organism–environment interactions. Organisms exhibit continuity and stability in the form of acts, but they also exhibit elaborated discontinuity in the content of acts across time due to the nature of processes within the organism.

A Third Complementary Theme:
A General Exchange Perspective

In addition to the general themes provided by Lewin and by Werner, there is a third general theoretical approach that has its origins in sociology and social psychology. For present purposes we refer to this approach as "exchange theory." There are important differences among the varieties of exchange theories (e.g., Adams, 1965; Burgess & Huston, 1979; Foa & Foa, 1974; Gergen, 1980; Homans, 1974; Thibault & Kelley, 1959; Walster, Walster, & Berscheid, 1978), and where necessary these differences will be discussed. Nonetheless, the various exchange theories also share some important commonalities as an approach to social behavior. Like the Lewinian approach, this approach emphasizes the mutual interdependence of social behaviors, the importance of the social context of relationships, and does not emphasize developmental aspects of social phenomena. Despite the nondevelopmental emphasis, exchange theories may offer special insights to persons interested in several important social development phenomena (Lerner, 1979).

Probably the most basic proposition common to exchange theories is the idea that people join together in relationships only insofar as it is in their mutual interest to do so (e.g., Burgess & Huston, 1979; Burgess & Nielsen, 1974). Relationships develop because people have needs they cannot meet on their own; theoretically, an entirely self-sufficient person has no need of relationships. For exchange theorists, an intrinsic part of relationships involves the establishment of a mutually contingent response system and the bartering of the rewards and costs of interactions.

There is an appealing quality to such an apparently parsimonious account of the initiation and maintenance of relationships, but a number of ambiguities remain. First, in order to evaluate the adequacy of the outcomes they are receiving in a relationship, persons must have some kind of criterion for such a judgment. How these evaluations occur is not clear. The simplest possibility is that persons know what they need and what they are receiving from others; outcomes are evaluated against some internalized standard within an individual. That is, if Jan needs love and security, she can evaluate the outcomes in her relationship with Tim directly by seeing whether she is, or is not, receiving love and security in return for what she gives to Tim.

The possibility of direct evaluation of outcomes against an internalized standard raises a host of complex questions. Exactly how do people acquire internalized evaluative standards, and how invariant are they? People's evaluation of the adequacy of their current outcomes is likely to be influenced by past outcomes, both from other relationships and from the present relationship. Furthermore, the judged adequacy of an outcome is likely to be influenced by expectations about outcomes that could be obtained in other relationships. Finally, even if we assumed that persons had stable internalized evaluative standards of which they were fully aware, we would still have to assume that they could be very accurate in relating these standards to the external events of the exchange. There is evidence that people have considerable difficulty in performing such tasks accurately (Nisbett & Wilson, 1977).

In their version of exchange theory, Thibaut and Kelley (1959) deal with the problem of evaluation standards by the introduction of two constructs: *comparison level* (CL) and *comparison level for alternatives* (CL$_{alt}$). According to these authors, the CL is "a standard by which the person evaluates the rewards and costs of a given relationship in terms of what he feels he 'deserves'" (p. 21). When outcomes in a relationship rise above the CL, the relationship is judged relatively satisfying. (The equity version of exchange theory does not accept this assumption. See Walster *et al.* [1978, footnote 31].) The CL is influenced by all outcomes known to the person, either directly or indirectly, weighted by *salience*. Salience is influenced at least partially by the recency of the experienced outcomes.

According to Thibaut and Kelley (1959),

> the comparison level depends in general upon the outcomes which are salient (actively stimulating or vividly recalled) at any given time. If we assume that all the recently experienced outcomes are salient, then the better they have been, the higher the CL and the less satisfaction with any given level. Thus the CL tends to move to the level of outcomes currently being obtained. In other words, the person adapts to the presently experienced levels: after shifting upward to a new level, the once longed for outcomes gradually lose their attractiveness; after a downward shift to a new lower level, the disappointment gradually wears off and the once dreaded outcomes become accepted [pp. 97–98].

The CL_{alt} is defined "informally" by Thibaut and Kelley as

> the lowest level of outcomes a member will accept in light of the available alternative opportunities. It follows from this definition that as soon as the outcomes drop below the CL_{alt} the member will leave the relationship. The height of the CL_{alt} will depend mainly on the quality of the best of the members, available alternatives, that is, the reward–cost positions experienced or believed to exist in the most satisfactory of the other available relationships [pp. 21–22].

The notions of CL and CL_{alt} are superior to the notion of direct evaluation against an internalized standard, but a number of ambiguities still remain for the researcher interested in the development of exchange processes. Both constructs of CL and CL_{alt} assume a person has experienced a range of relationships, can recall outcomes from these relationships, and can engage in meaningful social comparison with other persons in other relationships. At least in the case of younger children, there is reason to believe that these assumptions are arguable (Feldman & Ruble, 1977; Masters, 1971; Ruble, Feldman, & Boggiano, 1976; Ruble, Boggiano, Feldman, & Loebl, 1980).

Another problem is that even if younger children had the social experience and cognitive capacities called for in this theory, young children usually do not have the option to leave many relationships, whether unsatisfactory or not. That is, younger children may be more likely to find themselves in "closed-field encounters" (Murstein, 1970) with others than are older children and adults. In the case of adults, there is reason to believe that the open versus closed nature of the encounter influenced evaluations (e.g., Graziano & Musser, 1982), and similar processes may operate in younger children as well.

A second set of ambiguities revolves around the terms used in exchange theories. It is not clear which terms in exchange theory are merely metaphors for complex processes that are poorly understood. Terms like "barter" or "negotiate" imply conscious, covert, strategic activities in each participant in an exchange. Are these terms just metaphors? It is not clear from most exchange theory accounts whether exchange processes are primarily the result of conscious strategic choices or are primarily responses to contingency systems outside the participants' awareness. (See, for example, the discussion of the Kula ring in Walster *et al.* [1978, pp. 96–98].)

If exchange theory terms are more than metaphors, then it would be profitable to focus on covert processes among individual participants in an exchange in an attempt to identify each participant's goals, strategies, and the perception of resources involved in the exchange. From this perspective, at least some of the variability in exchange processes could be attributable to individual differences in covert cognitive and motivational processes in individual participants (Danheiser & Graziano, 1982). For example, females may approach an exchange with the strategy of minimizing status differences between participants, whereas males may seek to enhance status differences between participants (Reis & Jackson, 1981). On the other hand, if exchange theory terms are merely convenient metaphors for describing contingency systems outside the participants' awareness, or are noncausally related to the participants' cognitive activity, then relatively little can be gained from focusing on covert cognitive events. At best, such a focus would produce retrospective rationalizations that are largely epiphenomenal to the prior exchange (Nisbett & Wilson, 1977).

A third ambiguity is related to the second. It is not clear how important it is for partners to be aware of what commodities are being exchanged, or even that an exchange is occurring. Most exchange theorists argue that exchange contingency systems do *not* require participants' knowledge or awareness of what is being exchanged (Burgess & Huston, 1979; Homans, 1961; Kelley & Thibaut, 1978; Walster *et al.*, 1978). In fact, many exchange theorists share with the psychological behaviorists an abhorrence for assigning causal status to covert mental events. In the words of one exchange theorist, "we will not presume to know the needs and motives of men" (Emerson, 1972, p. 45). Such an orientation stands in marked contrast to the highly cognitive approaches of Lewin and Werner and seems to imply that exchanges must involve, at some level of analysis, objectively observable commodities.

Despite the apparent consensus, it is extraordinarily difficult to find an exchange theorist who will commit himself or herself to a list of objectively observable commodities or rewards and costs associated with individual persons (for an exception, see Walster [1977], cited in Walster *et al.* [1978, p. 178]). Commodities apparently arise primarily out of the interpersonal exchange itself, not from individual participants' store of resources. Blau

(1964) suggests that "it is not what lovers do together but their doing it *together* that is the distinctive source of their special satisfaction—not seeing the play but sharing the experience of seeing it" (p. 15). The examples of rewards and costs discussed in the classic Thibaut and Kelley (1959) volume are similarly emergent. As a consequence of these conceptions of exchange, most exchange theorists and researchers focus on processes of exchange, not on the actual commodities, resources, or rewards that change hands during the process (see, for example, Homans [1974, p. 250; 1976, p. 237]).

These ambiguities create problems for the researcher interested in the development of exchange processes. First, although it is likely that relationships as well as individual persons show developmental patterns (Graziano & Musser, 1982), it is plausible that at least some of the variability in the development of such processes must be attributable to individuals' changing conceptualizations of commodities and rewards. These changes may be due to objectively observable learning experiences, but they may be due to more covert processes of cognitive and emotional development as well.

Second, Emerson's (1972) comment notwithstanding, it is necessary to know precisely what commodities are being exchanged and when if we are to avoid the kind of tautology and circularity that plagued early psychological behaviorists in their theorizing on the law of effect (e.g., Meehl, 1950). If resources, commodities, or reinforcements cannot be established independently and empirically, then exchange theories will remain mere heuristics, capable of retrospective explanation but incapable of reliable prediction. Furthermore, if we can specify exactly what commodities are being exchanged in what kind of relationships, we may be able to learn a great deal more about the exchange process itself. Finally, the specification of commodities being exchanged may help us understand how the exchange process itself develops. Until relatively recently little attention has been paid to the development of exchange processes, or even to time frames for exchanges, other than to offer some ad hoc speculation about so-called unfair exchanges leading to the termination of a particular relationship.

Kelley and Thibaut (1978) have acknowledged implicitly some of the foregoing ambiguities in the revision of their earlier conceptualization of exchanges in relationships. Thibaut and Kelley (1959) proposed that interpersonal relationships can be conceptualized as a matrix of interdependent choices. For example, a husband or wife can choose either to cooperate or not to cooperate with his or her spouse's choice for a joint weekend recreational activity. This yields a 2×2 decision matrix. The outcome of each partner is influenced by the pattern of joint choices. Kelley and Thibaut (1978) note that in their earlier work, at certain times this decision matrix was interpreted objectively, whereas at other times it was interpreted subjectively.

To develop a more coherent, systematic account of interdependent exchanges, Kelley and Thibaut (1978) draw a distinction between the *given matrix* and the *effective matrix*. Behavioral choices in the given matrix are strongly influenced by such objective factors as the institutional structure within which a relationship occurs, tbe physical environment, and relevant attributes of the individual persons involved in the exchange. The matrix is given because choices are influenced by factors external to the interdependent relationship itself.

Through the operation of covert social motives and the evaluation of patterns in the given matrix, choices are redefined, evaluative criteria are shifted, and the given matrix is transformed into the effective matrix. The effective matrix allows a person to evaluate outcomes beyond the immediate consequences and to introduce other considerations, such as past outcomes or expected future outcomes. According to Kelley and Thibaut, it is the effective matrix, not the given matrix, that is the most immediate determinant of behavior.

Such a revision has at least two major consequences. First, several theoretical ambiguities may be resolved by placing transformation processes at the core of an explication of interdependent relationships. We may speculate, for example, that persons may be more likely to attempt to engage in negotiation or strategic behavior within the context of the given matrix. Similarly, persons may be more aware of resources or commodities and patterns of exchange in the context of the effective matrix than in the context of the given matrix.

Second, developmental processes of one kind or another become central to an exchange theory account of relationships. Whether we regard the transformation as a microdevelopmental process occurring over a few hours or days, or a macrodevelopmental process occurring over years, a sequence of change involving both structure and function is proposed. Such transformations and sequences of change are the very essence of developmental psychology (Overton & Reese, 1973; Overton, 1981). The link between Kelley and Thibaut (1978) and Werner (1948) is particularly clear: Werner conceptualized development as a tendency for systems to undergo a definite sequence of transformations.

Similarly, the transformation processes of Kelley and Thibaut can be linked to Lewinian social psychology. There are clear differences, but there are also remarkable resemblances between aspects of the effective matrix and Lewin's phenomenologically interpreted life space. Lewin (1944, 1951) repeatedly emphasized that it was the subjectively interpreted "psychological environment," not the so-called objective environment, that was the immediate determinant of behavior.

Though some of these potential theoretical links have been recognized, other links have been overlooked due to a unidisciplinary focus. According to Kelley and Thibaut (1978), further resolution of the transformation problem is the business of social psychology:

> The problems involved in identifying the antecedents of the *effective* matrix are essentially social-psychological in nature and have to do with analyzing products of social learning—the acquisition of social values and the development of beliefs about social structures and causes of social behavior. Although some of these phenomena have been studied outside social psychology (especially in developmental psychology), their systematic delineation and analysis would seem to be the responsibility of social psychology and not likely to present themselves as problems to other areas of psychology [p. 15].

In the present chapter I argue that our understanding of social exchanges can be enhanced by considering such exchanges not only as social phenomena but also as developmental phenomena. First, I consider three theoretical accounts of the development of exchange processes, with particular attention to the way commodities, resources, or rewards associated with individual persons are involved in the exchange. Second, I consider how well the empirical data from infants and young children corroborate these theories. Finally, I consider some future directions for research on the development of exchange processes.

THREE THEORETICAL ACCOUNTS OF THE DEVELOPMENT OF EXCHANGE PROCESSES

Not all theorists have ignored developmental issues in the study of exchange processes. Here I consider three conceptualizations that have at least attempted to add a developmental dimension to the exchange process. All three use several of the preceeding themes.

The Foa & Foa Model of Cognitive Development and Resource Differentiation

Foa and Foa (1974) suggest that cognitive development has a powerful influence on exchange processes, primarily through its impact on the differentiation of categories of responses to social events. At the beginning of life, an infant has very few categories of social behavior, and reactions are largely undifferentiated. Development occurs in a series of three binary divisions, with the differentiation of a new category from an earlier category. Differentiation produces boundaries between categories, but partitions are not tight; events in one category can influence events in a neighboring category. The weaker the differentiation, the more permeable the boundary (cf. Lewin, 1936; Werner & Kaplan, 1963).

At birth, there is at least one differentiation: Events are either pleasant or unpleasant. Consequently, the first differentiation made by the infant is in terms of *mode*. Events are interpreted in terms of either acceptance or rejection of an event. Acceptance of an infant by caretakers is expressed as giving affection and care, whereas rejection is expressed as deprivation or taking away of affection and care. The first social resources encountered by the infant are love and services. The second dimension of differentiation to occur is in terms of *actor*. Here a distinction is made between self and nonself as agents of action. At this level of development, there are four categories of social events: self as agent giving, other as agent giving, self as agent taking away, and other as agent taking away. The third dimension of differentiation to occur is in terms of *object* or *target* of behavior. The target of behavior can be either the self or other. Thus the three successive binary differentiations produce eight classes of social events: self giving to self, self giving to other, other giving to self, other giving to other, self taking from self, and so on. This system conceptualizes social action as behavior through which an actor increases or decreases the amount of something possessed by an object by giving or taking it away from the object.

Just as actions are differentiated through a series of three binary divisions, resource classes are also differentiated. In the initial relatively undifferentiated period of infancy, the major category of resources involves warmth, softness, food, and care. As the child acquires psychomotor skills and a conception of self as agent, differentiation occurs between love and services. At this developmental level, a mother can provide love but not services by asking the child to serve himself or herself (e.g., feeding, washing hands). The next differentiation to occur is the separation of goods from services and status from love. Notice the permeability between the neighboring categories of goods and services. For example, food, which is a good, is usually delivered prepared, which is a service.

In the final stage of resource differentiation, money is differentiated from goods, and information is differentiated from status. Thus at the final level of differentiation, there are six classes of resources: love, status, information, money, goods, and services. These six resource classes can themselves be ordered along two dimensions: *concreteness* and *particularism*. On the concreteness dimension, goods and services are more concrete than love and money, which are more concrete than status and information. On the particularism dimension, love, status, and services are more particular than are information, goods, and money (but see Brinberg & Castell, 1982).

Most children's earliest exchanges occur in a family context. According to Foa and Foa, the family provides the child with the opportunity to engage in three successive role differentiations. The major mechanism responsible for these differentiations is social comparisons with other family members.

First, the child differentiates actor from nonactor. This differentiation was noted earlier in the discussion of the differentiation of social events and is basic to the other differentiations. Second, the child differentiates same-gender from different-gender interactions. Father–son interaction is different from mother–son interaction. Finally, the child differentiates roles based on same power with those based on different power. For example, parent–child interactions involve different levels of power, whereas interaction with siblings involves similar levels of power. Thus eight roles are differentiated within the family and lay the groundwork for later exchanges.

According to Foa and Foa (1974), these distinctions have important implications for exchange processes. First, the unit of exchange is defined by any given combination of an actor, an object, a mode, and a resource class. Second, the optimum condition for an exchange occurs whenever one person who needs a resource, A, and has accumulated an amount of resource B beyond his or her need encounters another person needful of B with an overabundance of resource A. Foa and Foa hypothesize that people are attracted to persons who need a particular resource; those who need money are attracted to the rich, and those who need status are attracted to important persons. Given that boundaries between neighboring resource classes are permeable, however, certain resources can be substituted for others in an exchange. A person who seeks love in a particular exchange but cannot obtain it will prefer status to money as a substitute resource. Overall, exchanges with the same or proximal resources should be more frequent than transactions involving distal resources (cf. Foa & Foa, 1980; p. 88).

When an actual exchange is considered for initiation, a person estimates the probability of the success of the exchange, knowing that a satisfactory relationship involves some balance of giving and receiving. Foa and Foa note that most formulations of exchange theory (e.g., equity theory) assume that a partner in an exchange must incur certain costs to obtain rewards. Hence deservingness or fairness of exchange, the relationship between costs and rewards, is a central issue. These authors suggest, however, that the nature of the resource being exchanged is related to the cost of giving it. Foa and Foa hypothesize that the more particularistic the resource, the less negative the cost of giving it. In summary, Foa and Foa suggest that at least three interrelated processes influence the ontogeny of social exchanges: cognitive development, differentiation of resource classes, and social comparison within the family.

The Lerner, Miller, and Holmes Contractual Model

A second conceptualization relevant to the development of exchange processes comes from Lerner, Miller, and Holmes (1976). This conceptualization is distinctly psychological, in that it focuses primarily on an individual's intrapsychic events. The key note is *deservingness,* which for these theorists is essentially the relationship between a person and that person's outcomes. A person is said to deserve an outcome if the person has met the appropriate conditions for meeting the outcomes.

For Lerner *et al.,* the notion of deservingness develops as the child recognizes that it is in his or her long-term interest to postpone immediate gratification. By delaying gratification, the child makes a "personal contract" with himself or herself to orient toward the world on the basis of what is earned or deserved from prior investments, rather than on the basis of what can be obtained at any given moment. There are two major threats to the personal contract: the child's continuing impulses for immediate gratification, and the apparent violation of the contract by environmental events or even the planned acts of others. For the former threat to be controlled, the child must believe he or she lives in an orderly, predictable just world.

Lerner *et al.* (1976) argue that these notions have important implications for social exchanges. When persons observe an innocent victim suffering harm and are incapable of helping, they should at first be upset and distressed. To reduce this distress and to maintain their belief in a just world, they may try to persuade themselves that the apparently innocent victim was in fact deserving of the outcome that befell him or her (e.g., Lerner, 1965). On the other hand, when children are led to believe they were overpaid for performing a task, they were more willing to reduce their own outcomes by donating more to a supposed poor orphan than were children who thought they were properly paid (Long & Lerner, 1974). Thus both apparently heartless derogation of victims and altruism to the needy are social exchanges mediated by the individual's personal contract with a just world.

Lerner *et al.* (1976) recognize that deservingness depends on more than intrapsychic manipulations within one individual. These theorists propose two presumably independent social psychological factors that influence exchanges. The first of these is the perceived relationship between two persons. In an *identity* relationship, only a minimal distinction is seen between one person and the other. In essence, what happens to one person is perceived empathetically as happening to the other. In a *unit* relationship, there is no sense of identity, but there is a sense of similarity and of belonging together. In a *non-unit* relationship, persons are bound together, but as competitors or contestants. The second social psychological factor, cross-cutting the relationship factor, is the object of the relationship in terms of roles. The object of a relationship is seen as either a *person* or as a *position.* For example, a child can relate to an adult either as a friendly man who plays a guitar or as a father.

According to Lerner *et al.* (1976), these two factors produce a 3 × 2 matrix of six cells, each of which corresponds to a distinct kind of exchange relationship. For example, when a person believes he or she has a unit relationship with a person, exchanges are based on parity—individuals receive equal outcomes regardless of inputs. When a person believes he or she has a unit relationship with a position, however, exchanges are based on equity—individuals receive outcomes proportional to inputs (cf. Blau, 1964, p. 100).

There are several important implications of the Lerner *et al.* (1976) conceptualization. First, exchange processes are deeply embedded within individual persons' notions of deservingness and a personal contract with a just world. Second, exchange processes are strongly influenced by a person's perception of the relationship within which he or she is operating, and the nature of the entity who is the object of the relationship. In certain cases, exchanges may occur without regard to the inputs of the partner, but they are exchanges nonetheless (cf. Mills & Clark, 1982).

The Walster and Walster Power Model

Walster and Walster (1975) offer a more sociological conceptualization of the development of exchange processes, relative to the preceding two conceptualizations. Rather than focusing on the classification of commodities or kinds of relationships, these theorists focus on the social evolution of the notion of an exchange attribute. At least since the time of Aristotle, theorists have noted that individuals or groups can define the same attribute as a valuable asset, a debilitating liability, or not an attribute at all, for an exchange. For example, a worker who contributes 80% of the total amount of work may receive 80% of the available rewards even if he is, say, shorter or does not come from a so-called better family, relative to the worker who contributes only 20% of the total work. In this case, physical size and family background are not relevant attributes to the exchange, but it is not difficult to imagine contexts in which they might be seen as relevant. For another example, being a Francophone in England after the Norman invasion may have been a valuable asset, but it probably was a debilitating liability in Canada following the British subjugation of Quebec.

Walster and Walster suggest, however, that there is a pattern underlying this apparent indeterminancy. In any society, attributes associated with power come to be perceived as inputs relevant to any exchange by both the powerful and the powerless. There are several reasons for this. First, powerful persons come to possess resources others desire because the powerful have the ability to take and retain these resources. Second, powerful people may attempt to persuade others that this distribution of resources is reasonable. These persuasive attempts are aided by people's need to believe this is a just world in which people get what they deserve (Lerner, 1965; Lerner *et al.*, 1976). Over time, status attributes associated with powerful persons in a particular society come to be seen as relevant inputs, justifying the present distribution of resources.

Walster and Walster (1975) frame their propositions in terms of the evolution of societal rules over time. But one should not conclude that the associations among power, status, and exchange norms occurred only in the barbarous and primitive past. There are several reasons why children in contemporary society should be particularly responsive to cues associated with power. First, powerful persons have the ability to mediate rewards for children. Attributes associated with powerful persons may become discriminative stimuli for reward and may become particularly salient. Nunnally, Duchnowski, and Parker (1965), for example, found that children directed more attention to visual cues associated with reward than to neutral stimuli. Yussen (1974) found that children direct more attention to models who were associated with reward than they do to neutral models.

Second, cues associated with power and status (e.g., size, age, race, gender) may be salient because they are relatively easy to assess. Younger children in particular may be especially responsive to such cues because they are obvious external attributes that can be assessed with relatively little cognitive sophistication. In fact, younger children are more likely than older children to describe others in terms of obvious external attributes (Flavell, 1977; Peevers & Secord, 1973; Shantz, 1975).

Third, an intrinsic part of the socialization process is the explicit training of children to comply with the requests of such authority figures as parents, teachers, religious leaders, police, and temporary caretakers. These authority figures have resources to bring to bear (e.g., physical size) when compliance is not forthcoming, and these resources may come to be associated with authority. In essence, children are being implicitly trained to comply with power when they are being explicitly trained to comply with authority.

EMPIRICAL DATA RELEVANT
TO THE DEVELOPMENT OF EXCHANGE PROCESSES

Exchange Processes in Infant–Caretaker Interactions

If we attempt to apply the principles just outlined directly to the development of exchange processes, we encounter some problems. First, the foregoing analysis is dynamic, but it assumes that in some sense the relationship has already been established, and that each partner has well-developed expectations about the likely behavior of the other partner. In the case of the earliest exchanges between adults and children, this is not a reasonable assumption.

Three interrelated theoretical possibilities are relevant to this assumption. First, though it is clear that parents incur enormous costs in having children (see Walster *et al.,* 1978, pp. 184–197) the rewards and costs *most* salient to caretakers in early caretaker–infant interchanges may not be those coming from the infant, but those coming from other adults. That is, most societies assign to caretakers responsibility for their infants and young children. If caretakers do not provide adequate care for their charges, approbations and sanctions are brought to bear (Hamilton, 1978). Such a situation would be advantageous to an infant, who has no experience with social exchanges, relatively limited cognitive capacities, and a relatively limited set of resources to bring into the exchange. It is not inconceivable that most societies have evolved norms for care of infants for precisely such reasons. In the terms of Kelley and Thibaut (1978), caretaker–infant exchanges may be influenced more strongly by the given matrix than are other kinds of relationships.

Second, adults in asymmetrical caretaker–infant interchanges may move rapidly from the given to the effective matrix and incorporate a larger time frame into the interchange. Many studies have documented caretakers' beliefs that children are investments in *future* economic, social, and even religious security (e.g., McBride, 1973; Pohlman, 1969). Infants may have relatively few commodities to bring to the relationship in the first few months of life, but as children grow older their value increases considerably.

The third theoretical possibility is related to the two outlined earlier. If norms dictate that inherently asymmetrical caretaker–infant interchanges are unique kinds of exchanges involving long-range investments, then caretakers may have a special responsibility to train the infant on exchange rules. In essence, the high resource caretaker first may have to "hook" the lower-resource infant on the benefits to be obtained, and the rules for obtaining them, prior to any subsequent exchange (cf. Werner's notion of scene-to-actor shift).

Research by Bell and his colleagues on caretaker–infant interaction is instructive here. Bell (1974) reports that in the infant's first few weeks of life caretakers often learn to anticipate the infant's crying and engage in caretaking before the crying actually occurs (see also Wolff, 1966). For their part, infants apparently learn that certain looking behaviors elicit maternal vocalizations, touching, and so on. The evidence suggests an evolving system of exchange and a kind of mutual accommodation, not merely a unilateral responsiveness of caretaker to infant (Lerner, 1979).

At least three factors determine how satisfying these early exchanges are for each partner. First, the capacities and developmental level of the infant influence reactions to the caretaker. For example, younger and older infants differ in their responses to signs that a caretaker is about to depart (cf. Cairns, 1979, pp. 104–108). Bell (1974) reports a developmental pattern for infants' fussing and crying: 3-month-olds show higher rates of wakeful attentiveness, and lower rates of fussing and crying, than do younger infants. Mothers of infants who show no decrease in rates of fussing and crying by 3 months report less attachment to their infants than do mother of more typical infants (Robson & Moss, 1970).

Second, a caretaker's interpretation of an infant's response determines the level of satisfaction in caretaker–infant exchanges. An infant's fussing and crying are especially aversive if the behavior is interpreted as evidence that the caretaker is incompetent (Bell, 1974; Lerner, 1979; Sameroff, 1975). Sameroff (1975) argues that some abnormal behavior in children may arise from the caretaker's inability to understand patterns and to make sense of children's development. These early unsatisfying transactions may help establish and maintain an abnormal exchange and the unusual behaviors in the child.

A third factor is the apparent predictability or contingency that emerges in each partner's behavior. We noted earlier that exchanges depend on expectations that a particular behavior will lead to a particular outcome. If no contingencies can be seen, or if a partner's behavior is seen as unpredictable, exchanges will be difficult and unsatisfying. This theme has been echoed in the literature on both children and adults. Work by Davis and her colleagues suggests that contingent responsiveness to one's partner is one mechanism that helps to maintain relationships (Davis, 1982; Davis & Perkowitz, 1979). Davis (1982) hypothesizes that four factors affect contingent responsiveness in interactions: (1) attention, (2) accuracy in understanding others' communications, (3) a response repertoire that makes adequate response possible, and (4) motivation to be responsive. According to Davis, contingent responsiveness affects both the process and the outcome of people's interactions. In terms of process, contingent responsiveness to a partner helps to maintain the interaction and to allow an initiator some control over an interaction. In terms of outcome, contingent responsiveness increases the partner's attraction to the initiator and makes the partner appear to be more attracted to the initiator.

Within the child development literature, several researchers have also noted the importance of contingent responsiveness in the establishment and maintenance of relationships (e.g., Condon & Sanders, 1974; Konner, 1975; Osofsky & Danzger, 1974). Konner (1975) suggests that part of the reason adults and older children are attractive to younger children is their greater contingent responsiveness, predictability, and lack of egocentrism, relative to the younger child's agemates. In his thoughtful paper on exchange processes, Lerner (1979) notes that the establishment of mutually satisfying, contingently responsive, predictable behavior exchanges is far from automatic in caretaker–infant interactions. For example, some of the developmental differences found by Thomas, Chess, and Birch (1968) between so-called easy and difficult children may be due to the different levels of energy caretakers have to expend to maintain a relationship with these two types of children. That is, diffficult children exhibit less regularity and rhythm in their behaviors, and their behaviors are more difficult to predict. Consequently, caregiver–infant interactions in this case may be less contingently responsive and less mutually satisfying.

In another example, Bell and Ainsworth (1972) analyzed maternal responsiveness to infant crying in the infant's four quarters of life. They found that the more an infant cried in any one quarter, the more the mother ignored the crying in the subsequent quarter. Apparently, after the caretaker's behavior failed to lead to a decrease in crying, the mother began to withdraw the more the infant cried. Taken together, these results suggest that contingent responsiveness and predictability are important for the establishment of a mutually satisfying exchange, that these processes are far from automatic, and that certain kinds of noncontingent responding may tax a relationship and even lead to subsequent developmental problems. With time, however, most adult–child relationships become more symmetrical—or at least the child gains more resources to bring to the exchange.

In summary, early social exchanges involving adult caretakers and children may be asymmetrical due to the greater resources, capacities, and power of adults, but there is a bidirectional flow of influence and a genuine exchange. Both partners appear to be involved actively in the exchange, and both partners appear to desire predictability and contingent responsiveness for a mutually satisfying relationship.

Exchange Processes in Young Children

Early Empirical Studies of Children's Notions of Equity

One problem in applying exchange theories to children's social behavior is that children's conceptions of exchanges may be considerably different from those of adults. According to the equity version of exchange theory, for example, a relationship between two persons is considered a "fair" exchange if each person's outcomes are proportional to his or her inputs. Those studies that have attempted to corroborate this proposition with children have met only limited success (see Hook & Cook, 1979). A limitation here is that most researchers working in this area have attempted to define inputs solely in terms of relative task performance. Although relative task performance may be a highly salient input in adult judgments, it is apparently less salient to children or is easily "swamped" when presented simultaneously with other information.

Given that children's earliest relationships appear to have the qualities of at least a primitive exchange, an important task facing the developmental researcher is uncovering ways in which early exchange processes are transformed into the more sophisticated exchanges exhibited by adults. Here Werner's *form versus content* distinction might be useful. Werner suggested that children exhibit continuity and stability in the forms of acts, but they also exhibit elaborated discontinuities in the contents of acts across time. This suggestion has several different implications for the researcher interested in the development of exchange process. First, some basic exchange processes may occur at all developmental levels, but the processes and contents of the exchange may become progressively differentiated and hierarchically integrated with development. For example, children's earliest exchanges with adult caretakers may influence their general ideas about exchange processes and influence their later exchanges with other children. A second related possibility is that the processes of exchange remain invariant, but the content of resources exchanged shows a developmental change. In either case, it becomes important to uncover ways in which children's exchanges differ from adults' exchanges. One way to attack this problem is to examine children's exchanges to see how the concepts of resources, deservingness, and the exchange process in general develop.

The first two empirical studies designed to investigate exchanges in children in the context of deservingness came to remarkably similar conclusions despite their slightly different theoretical orientations. Masters (1968) found in three converging studies that 4-year-old children do not respond in ways predicted by Adams's (1963) inequity version of exchange theory. Masters suggested that children this young may lack the cognitive sophistication to compare themselves with others in terms of input–outcome ratios. He does note, however, that social comparison and equity notions gradually develop in the context of variables other than task performance, such as "Johnny deserves more than you because he worked harder" or "because he is older" (Masters, 1968, p. 400).

Leventhal and Anderson (1970) found that preschool children respond in ways only roughly consistent with Adams's (1963) version of inequity theory. Relative task performance of the child and the partner did influence allocations of rewards, but the children always allocated more rewards to themselves than to the partner. Furthermore, children did not cognitively distort their own or their partner's performance to justify the particular allocations they made. The picture that emerges from these two studies is that younger children's exchanges are not equitable (in the adult sense). These children are seen as basically self-centered, due at least in part to their limited cognitive capacity to weight outcomes in terms of inputs.

An Alternative Approach to Children's Notions of Equity

Both the Masters (1968) and the Leventhal and Anderson (1970) studies are exemplars of high quality, methodologically rigorous, social psychological laboratory research. Yet, two aspects of these studies are worthy of further attention. First, exchanges are operationally defined narrowly and nonempirically, in terms of commodities. Only two commodities are considered part of the exchange: relative task performance and reward chips. Rather than concluding that young children do not behave equitably, could it not be argued in Wernerian terms that the *form* of the children's and adult's exchanges are similar, but that the *contents* differ? In equity theory terms, is it not possible that children may use different inputs than those used by adults? Second, the relationship within which the exchange occurred is defined narrowly in terms of an ad-hoc pairing of unacquainted same-age children. There is no prospect of continuing interaction; nor is it likely that the children perceive themselves as having a relationship with the partner or as being part of a common unit. In terms of the Kelley and Thibaut (1978) model, a given matrix has been constructed, but no attempt has been made to assess any resulting effective matrix.

Graziano (1978) investigated exchange rules in children using procedures similar to those used by Masters (1968) and by Leventhal and Anderson (1970). First- and third-grade children were given prize tokens to allocate to two other children whose task performance had been manipulated. Unlike the previous studies, however, the children's task performance was presented simultaneously with some supposedly irrelevant information about power: the relative physical size and relative age of the other children. The key idea here is that children may indeed be equitable, but their most important inputs are attributes associated with power, not relative task performance (Walster & Walster, 1975). That is, when players are the same size and age, rewards are allocated equally because players are equivalent on the most important input; task performance is not a relevant input.

Results indicated that younger children did allocate rewards on the basis of task performance, but only when the players were the same age and size. When one of the players was older and larger, however, the use of a task-based allocation rule almost disappeared. A most striking finding was that even when the older, larger player performed less well than the younger, smaller partner, the former was reliably allocated more than half of the rewards. Apparently, even though younger children were capable of recognizing task performance as an input, they also considered age and size more important resources warranting greater reward. Older children, however, ignored age and size and consistently used a task-based allocation rule. We may speculate that the older children used their more sophisticated cognitive skills to form a general abstract rule and to transform the given matrix into an effective matrix that was quite different from that of the younger children.

There are two potentially interesting aspects of this study. First, from the perspective of Walster and Walster (1975), as young children leave their homes and the power of their parents to participate in other social institutions under the power of other adults and other caretakers, notions of a link between power and age or size may be functional for a smooth transition between these two stations in life. Increased social experience and cognitive sophistication in dealing with power may render the size–power link less functional as the child grows older (cf. Damon, 1975). From the perspective of Werner's form versus content issue, younger children's experiences with the relatively straightforward contingencies among power, age, size, and deservingness may provide the simpler training ground for more complex notions of deservingness.

In their treatment of the development of social cognition, both Shantz (1975) and Flavell (1977) suggest that young children are likely to describe other people in terms of obvious external attributes. By contrast, older children frequently make reference to other, more abstract, often covert qualities in others. Is it possible that children's exchanges are mediated by their conceptions of resources, which in turn are mediated by their ability to assess the dimensions of other persons? (Is it possible that the therapeutic effects of mixed-age interaction [e.g., Furman, Rahe, & Hartup, 1979] are due to different rates of behavior exchange that occur in same-age and mixed-age groups?) That is, the socially withdrawn but older partner receives more rewards from his or her younger partner than his or her behavior justifies, and this kind of exchange increases the older child's rate of social participation. In this sense, therapy is defined as receiving more rewards than a person is entitled to receive. (Furman *et al.* [1979, p. 920] discount this explanation, but their data are not unequivocal on this point.)

Factors Influencing Young Children's Exchange

Although there is evidence that children's exchanges and conceptions of resources do differ systematically from those of adults, it is still not clear what factors are responsible for such differences. Here I consider three possible developmental factors: differences in social cognition and cognitive–intellectual abilities, differential treatment by adults, and differential experiences with peers.

The development of social cognition and exchange processes. As noted earlier, several theorists have hypothesized that there is a developmental pattern in the way children perceive and conceptualize others: younger children are more likely to describe others in terms of concrete, external attributes than are older children (e.g., Peevers & Secord, 1973; Scarlett, Press, & Crockett, 1971). If this developmental pattern in social cognition reflects a more general pattern in cognitive and intellectual development, then we would expect children's conceptions of social resources and exchanges to be related to levels of cognitive and intellectual development (cf. Enright, Enright, & Lapsley, 1981; Heller & Berndt, 1981). That is, younger children and children at lower levels of intellectual development may be more likely to find a peer's concrete, external attributes salient, and to base decisions on these attributes, than will older children and children at higher levels of intellectual development (Damon, 1975; Hook & Cook, 1979). Furthermore, those external attributes associated with power and status may receive special attention as resources, entitling the bearer to special treatment (Walster & Walster, 1975).

Graziano, Musser, Rosen, and Shaffer (1982) investigated this hypothesis in a series of three studies. In the interest of generality, two different external attributes associated with status were independently manipulated: relative size and race. There is evidence that children's social judgments, both about themselves and others, are influenced by age and size (e.g., Graziano, 1978) and race (e.g., Clark & Clark, 1947; Cohen, 1972; Katz, Sohn, & Zalk, 1975; Stephan, 1977; Turner & Forehand, 1976). For children, apparently superior social status is associated with being older and larger and white rather than black. Most of these studies of social status, however, have not been concerned explicitly with the ways in which these social judgments might influence judgments of deservingness. Furthermore, it is not clear how several status-related attributes are combined to produce a final judgment when presented concretely and simultaneously.

Implicit in the *Brown* v. *Board of Education* decision (1954) mandating desegregation in United States schools is the notion that children in desegregated schools learn to discount race as a resource relevant to exchanges. One problem overlooked in the Brown decision is that although objectively black and white children may have similar "qualifications," subjectively, black and white children may not readily perceive such a similarity. Suppose, for example, a black child outperforms a white child on a task. It is not clear that race will be discounted here. In fact, according to status generalization theory (Berger, Cohen, & Zelditch, 1966; Webster & Driskell, 1978), a "burden of proof" is placed on the lower-status child to demonstrate that a pervasive status characteristic such as race is *not* relevant. There is a substantial body of literature suggesting that black children may find such countervailing evidence hard to come by (e.g., Cohen, 1972; Cohen & Roper, 1972).

From the perspective just outlined, these apparently invidious acts of racial discrimination in younger children may merely reflect limited abilities in social cognition, which in turn influence children's conceptions of resources. Specifically, if the hypothesis about developmental patterns in social cognition is correct, then older children will be less likely than will younger children to base their reward allocations on the concrete, external attribute of a peer's race. An alternative hypothesis is that racial discrimination is gradually learned and is more likely to characterize older children than younger children. In one study, first- and third-grade children were shown pictures of two towers of wooden blocks, each supposedly built by two same-age but unfamiliar peers. Relative size of the players' towers was manipulated so that one player's performance was either inferior, equal, or superior to that of the other player. In addition, children were shown pictures of the two players, both of whom were either white or black. The children were to decide how many prize chips each of the two players should receive. A second study followed similar procedures, except that one player was black, the other white, and one player was physically taller than the other. In the third study, children were assessed longitudinally across a four-year period.

Several results from this series of studies are noteworthy. First, in all cases, older children based their allocations on task performance to a greater extent than did younger children. Second, although younger children were less likely to use a task-based allocation rule than were older children, there was no systematic evidence that they were more likely to use a race-based rule. Third, given equal task performance, both older and younger children allocated more rewards to the taller of the two players. Fourth, use of a task-based allocation rule was related to both age and to measures of cognitive–intellectual development. That is, younger children, children with lower scores on the Metropolitan Achievement Tests, and children who had been retained in grade based their reward allocations less on task performance than did the other children.

Taken together, these results provide only mixed support for the development of social cognition hypothesis as it applies to exchanges. Use of a task-based allocation rule was related to age and to indexes of cognitive–intellectual development, but children's use of concrete, external attributes of peers as inputs or resources is less clear. The fact that children consistently used size but not race in making allocations suggests that generalizations about all concrete, external attributes of persons is at best hazardous. Of course, I am not arguing that notions of resources and exchange are unrelated to the development of social cognition; rather, I argue that the developmental level of social cognition is far from the sole factor in children's conceptions of resources and exchanges (cf. Damon, 1975; Hook, 1982; Hook & Cook, 1979).

Differential adult treatment and exchange processes in children. Another factor that may influence children's conception of resources and exchanges is their differential treatment by adults. As noted earlier, several theorists have argued that persons are motivated to believe that the world is a just place in which people get what they deserve (Lerner et al., 1976; Walster & Walster, 1975). In light of the fact that children are generally dependent on adults for many of their outcomes, one input that may receive special attention from children is the child's perception of how deserving an adult believes the child to be. If a child's relative task performance and an adult's judgment of deservingness do not match, the child may alter his or her evaluation of his or her task performance to correspond to the adult's judgment. That is, when a child sees an equivalently performing peer receive more rewards than him- or herself from an adult, the child may distort his or her perception of each persons' task performance. The peer *must* have performed better, the child reasons, or the adult would not have given the peer more rewards.

To explore this hypothesis, Bernstein and Graziano (1981) conducted a study in which an adult gave black preschool children and their partners either equal or unequal social reinforcement for equivalent performances on a tower-building task. After the first adult experimenter departed, a second adult experimenter appeared and asked the children to play a completely different kind of game—star-pasting (cf. Masters & Santrock, 1982). The partners were separated; the adult allowed the child to paste eight stars and then announced when time was up. After getting the partners's star sheet, the experimenter counted stars and pointed out that *both* partners had pasted eight stars. The star sheets were then removed and each child was asked to report how many stars each partner had pasted. Finally, the child allocated prize chips both to himself or herself and to the partner.

As expected, children receiving social reinforcement in the first task reported that they had pasted more stars on the second task than did the partner. The ignored child reported that he or she had pasted fewer stars than the partner had pasted. The reward allocation results were parallel to the recall results. Apparently actual, concrete task performance was a less salient input than the adults' less tangible social evaluation. Actual, concrete task performance was misreported to make it more congruent with the adult evaluation and to make an otherwise inequitable exchange appear equitable. These results suggest that children's evaluations of inputs in social exchanges are strongly influenced by adult evaluations of their previous task performances. Furthermore, it suggests that adult discrimination against certain children may have a prolonged and invidious effect on those children's self-evaluation.

Prior experience with peers and exchange processes in children. The foregoing evidence suggests that children's exchanges are influenced not only by relative task performance and levels of cognitive–intellectual development but also by certain social experiences that may arise in adult–child interactions. Another possible source of systematic influence is children's experiences in peer groups, and the definition of their relationship with a particular peer. For example, attributes that are regarded as inputs or resources in non-unit relationships may become less salient or even irrelevant when the relationship is redefined as a unit relationship (Lerner *et al.*, 1976). In addition, children may learn that defining certain peer attributes as inputs in certain relationship contexts can have unpleasant consequences.

One peer-context variable that may influence children's exchanges is the prospect of future interaction. Equity research has demonstrated that adults adhere less strictly to a task-based allocation rule when they anticipate future interaction with a partner than when they do not. When future interaction is anticipated, there is an increased tendency to follow an equality rule and to weight relative task performance less heavily (Greenberg, 1978; Shapiro, 1975). One explanation for this pattern can be derived from the central hypotheses of equity theory: When people expect continuing interaction with others, they can maximize their future outcomes by using the potential rewarding or punishing power of the partner as an input in their equity equation. That is, there may be longer-range payoffs for generous allocation when a partner has the capacity to retaliate sometime in the future (cf. Danheiser & Graziano, 1982). Another explanation is that the prospect of future interaction induces a person to perceive a unit relationship between himself or herself and the partner (e.g., Darley & Berscheid, 1967; Tyler & Sears, 1977). A third explanation is that when future interaction is anticipated, imbalances in equity will be expected to even out (e.g., Greenberg, 1978).

A second peer-context variable that may influence children's exchanges is the perceived motivation of the partner. Research by Berndt and Berndt (1975), for example, has shown that even preschool children understand the concept of motive, but the ability to make accurate inferences about motives follows a developmental pattern. These researchers also found that preschool, second-, and fifth-grade children all used motivation information when evaluating the behavior of an actor. Given these findings, it is not unreasonable to assume that perceived or inferred information about a partner's motives could function as an input for young children.

Consider the following scenario. A child must allocate prizes to two peers who have just finished playing a tower-building game. The goal of the game was to build the tallest tower possible with blocks. The tower of one player is noticeably shorter than the tower of the other player. Would a child's allocations be different if the child were told that the reason for the shorter tower was that the shorter-tower player (a) spent most of his or her time trying to knock the other player's tower over versus (b) tried to help the tall-tower player when that player's tower fell over? How would the prospect of future interaction with such a previously aggressive player influence a child's allocations? Would younger and older children be influenced in the same way by the social context information?

The preceeding scenario also allows an assessment of the relative merits of the two explanations for generosity when there is a prospect of future interaction. If generosity is due to the definition of a unit relationship, children should be equally generous to an altruistic and aggressive peer when there is a prospect of future interaction. If generosity is due to fear of some future aggressive retaliation, children should be more generous to an aggressive peer than to an altruistic peer when there is a prospect of future interaction.

Graziano, Brody, and Bernstein (1980) explored these questions with first- and third-grade children. To acquaint them with the materials, children were asked first to play a tower-building game with wooden blocks. Children were then shown photographs of towers built by two same-age but unfamiliar peers. One player's tower was shorter than the other player's tower. A third of the children were told the player's tower was shorter because (a) he or she had helped to pick up the other player's tower when it fell over (*altruistic motive*), or (b) he or she had tried to knock over the other player's tower (*aggressive motive*), or (c) no reason was provided for the difference in task performance. Crossed with the motive information was a prospect of future interaction manipulation. Half of the children were led to expect that they themselves would play the tower game again with these two players but that next time the other players would decide how the prizes should be divided. For the other half of the children, there was no mention of any future interaction.

Results were interesting. As in previous studies, reward allocation was related both to the player's relative task performance and to the allocator's age. Given equivalent task performance, however, more rewards were allocated to an altruistic player than to an aggressive player. Apparently, past performances with peers (or "motives") can function as inputs and influence children's exchanges. More interesting, however, is the finding that older children were much more generous toward a previously aggressive peer, and less generous to a previously altruistic peer, when there was a prospect of future interaction than when there was no such prospect. (One of our colleagues calls this the "Neville Chamberlain Effect.") The prospect of future interaction had no effect on younger children's allocation to the peers.

These results are interesting for another reason. In the preceding research, it was found that older children consistently were more likely to follow a task-based allocation rule than were younger children. This pattern of results lends itself to facile discussions of socialization into an achievement-oriented Calvinistic work ethic, or of children's growing awareness of motives to try, and so on. In this case, however, *younger* children's allocations were tied more closely to peers' motives and relative task performance. Such results remind us not only of the influence of subtle social situational cues but also that at least part of social development involves learning how to "read" social situations. For example, one interpretation of these results is that older children have had more experience with peer interaction and have learned that retaliation can occur when future interaction takes place. Furthermore, previously aggressive peers may be more likely to retaliate for an unfavorable exchange than would previously altruistic peers.

SUMMARY AND CONCLUSIONS

Researchers working in the boundary area between the established disciplines of social and developmental psychology face many obstacles. The two different disciplines have different metatheoretical, theoretical, and methodological preferences. These preferences may make research easier for researchers working near the core of either discipline, but they may also create problems for the researcher working near the edge of a discipline. Furthermore, boundary researchers often handicap themselves by seeking to become universal scholars who have mastered both disciplines completely.

Some guidelines are proposed for overcoming these obstacles. Boundary researchers should strive for intense specialization, not universal scholarship. Universalist impulses should be directed at the identification of a recurrent substantive process or phenomenon of common interest to several different disciplines. Ideally, such a process or phenomenon is explained by several different complementary theoretical formulations or approaches.

In this chapter social exchanges were identified as one recurrent kind of process of common interest to both social and developmental psychology.

Until relatively recently most social exchange theories paid little attention to how developmental processes operating among individuals might influence the content and structure of social exchanges. It was commonly assumed that social exchanges were emergent relationships between people or groups that are more than the simple sum of the individuals involved. Exchanges derive their characteristics from the functional interdependence of the separate components making up the system. Covert cognitive and motivational processes in individuals are of secondary theoretical interest.

These assumptions may be useful for the investigation of established relationships among adults, but they are less useful to the researcher interested in the development of social exchange processes. By focusing on attributes of individual persons, including covert cognitive and motivational processes, we may be able to uncover ways in which social exchanges, like individuals, exhibit differentiation and hierarchical integration. The development of certain aspects of these processes are addressed by complementary theoretical formulations proposed by Lewin and by Werner.

These assertions are examined within the context of three related exchange theories. Foa and Foa (1974) propose that social exchanges develop through a process of differentiating exchange resources or commodities. Lerner et al. (1976) propose that social exchanges emerge from a child's belief in a contingently responsive just world in which people get what they deserve. Deservingness, a notion central to exchange processes, is determined by the kind of relationship in which a person believes he or she is operating. In some types of relationships, a person is regarded as deserving an outcome even if that person does not have relevant resources to exchange. Walster and Walster (1975) propose that notions of resources and deservingness develop as a result of people's recognition of differences in social power. Attributes associated with the socially powerful come to be seen as resources entitling the bearer to greater outcomes in social exchange.

Empirical research on exchange processes in infants and young children is limited, but results from several different literatures are generally consistent with exchange notions. Infant–caretaker interchanges appear to be evolving exchanges in which each partner learns to anticipate the behavior of the other and to adjust behavior accordingly. These early exchanges may lay the groundwork for the more complex exchanges seen among young children and adults.

A central issue in the exchanges of young children is deservingness. The earliest empirical research on exchange processes in children was derived from equity theory. The outcomes of these early studies were interpreted to mean that young children did not engage in equitable exchanges, due in part to limited cognitive capacities. Although some subsequent research has corroborated this interpretation, other research suggests that young children's notions of deservingness and exchanges do not involve the same commodities as do adult exchanges. Children's exchanges and notions of deservingness are related not only to cognitive–intellectual development but also to certain exchange experiences with adults and peers.

It is apparent, even in this brief review, that a considerable amount of research needs to be conducted before any firm conclusions can be reached about the development of exchange processes. There is only a limited literature that addresses this topic directly and there are all too many plausible alternative explanations for the studies that have been completed. This chapter will have served its function, however, if it reminds researchers that there are discoveries yet to be made in the boundary area between social and developmental psychology.

ACKNOWLEDGMENTS

The author expresses his appreciation to Wyndol Furman, Clyde Hendrick, Robert Pollack, Harry Reis, and Abraham Tesser for their comments on an earlier version of this manuscript. Special appreciation is expressed to Sidney Rosen for his detailed and useful critique.

REFERENCES

Abelson, R. P. Psychological status of the script concept. *American Psychologist,* 1981, *36,* 715–729.

Adams, J. S. Toward an understanding of inequity. *Journal of Abnormal and Social Psychology,* 1963, *67,* 422–436.

Adams, J. S. Inequity in social exchange. In L. Berkowitz (Ed.), *Advances in experimental social psychology* (Vol. 2). New York: Academic, 1965.

Bell, S. M., & Ainsworth, M. D. S. Infant crying and maternal responsiveness. *Child Development,* 1972, *43,* 1173–1190.

Bell, R. Q. Contribution of human infants to caregiving and social interaction. In M. Lewis & L. Rosenblum (Eds.), *The effect of the infant on its caregiver.* New York: Wiley, 1974.

Berger, J., Cohen, B. P., & Zelditch, M. Status characteristics and expectation states. In J. Berger, M. Zelditch, & B. Anderson (Eds.), *Sociological theories in progress* (Vol. 1). Boston: Houghton Mifflin, 1966.

Berndt, T. J., & Berndt, E. G. Children's use of motives and intentionality in person perception and moral judgment. *Child Development,* 1975, *46,* 904–912.

Bernstein, S., & Graziano, W. G. *Effects of inequitable treatment by an adult on perception of deservingness and peer reward allocation in black preschoolers.* Paper presented at the biennial meetings of the Society for Research in Child Development. Boston, MA, April, 1981.

Blau, P. M. *Exchange and power in social life.* New York: Wiley, 1964.

Brehm, S. S., Kassin, S. M., & Gibbons, F. X. (Eds.). *Developmental social psychology.* Oxford: Oxford University Press, 1981.

Brinberg, D., & Castell, P. A resource exchange theory approach to interpersonal interactions: A test of Foa's theory. *Journal of Personality and Social Psychology, 1982, 43,* 260–269.

Brown v. *Board of Education Topeka,* 98F. Supp. 797 (1951), 347 U.S. 483 (1954), 349 U.S. 294 (1955).

Burgess, R. L., & Huston, R. L. (Eds.). *Social exchange in developing relationships.* New York: Academic, 1979.

Burgess, R. L., & Nielsen, J. An experimental analysis of some structural determinants of equitable and inequitable exchange relations. *American Sociological Review, 1974, 39,* 427–443.

Cairns, R. B. *Social development: The origins and plasticity of interchanges.* San Francisco: Freeman, 1979.

Clark, K. B., & Clark, M. P. Racial identification and preference in Negro children. In T. M. Newcomb & E. L. Hartley (Eds.), *Readings in social psychology.* New York: Holt, 1947.

Cohen, E. Interracial interaction disability. *Human Relations, 1972, 25,* 9–24.

Cohen, E., & Roper, S. Modification of interracial interaction disability: An application of status characteristics theory. *American Sociological Review, 1972, 6,* 643–657.

Condon, W. S., & Sanders, L. W. Synchrony demonstrated between movements of the neonate, and adult speech. *Child Development, 1974, 45,* 456–462.

Damon, W. Early conceptions of positive justice related to the development of logical operations. *Child Development, 1975, 46,* 301–312.

Danheiser, P. R., & Graziano, W. G. Self-monitoring and cooperation as a self-presentational strategy. *Journal of Personality and Social Psychology, 1982, 42,* 497–505.

Darley, J. M., & Berscheid, E. Increased liking as a result of the anticipation of personal contact. *Human Relations, 1967, 20,* 29–40.

Davis, D. Situational and dispositional determinants of responsiveness in dyadic interaction. In W. Ickes & E. Knowles (Eds.), *Personality roles and social behavior.* New York: Springer-Verlag, 1982.

Davis, D., & Perkowitz, W. J. Consequences of dyadic responsiveness in dyadic interaction: Effects of probability of response and proportion of content related responses to interpersonal attraction. *Journal of Personality and Social Psychology, 1979, 37,* 534–550.

Emerson, R. M. Exchange theory. In J. Berger, M. Zelditch, & B. Anderson (Eds.), *Sociological theories in progress* (Vol. 2). Boston: Houghton Mifflin, 1972.

Enright, R. D., Enright, W. F., & Lapsley, D. K. Distributive justice development and social class: A replication. *Developmental Psychology, 1981, 17,* 826–832.

Feldman, N. S., & Ruble, D. N. Awareness of social comparison interest and motivations: A developmental study. *Journal of Educational Psychology, 1977, 69,* 579–585.

Festinger, L. Looking backward. In L. Festinger (Ed.), *Retrospections on social psychology.* New York: Oxford University Press, 1980.

Fiske, S. T., & Linville, P. W. What does the schema concept buy us? *Personality and Social Psychology Bulletin, 1980, 6,* 543–557.

Flavell, J. H. *Cognitive development.* Englewood Cliffs, NJ: Prentice-Hall, 1977.

Foa, E. B., & Foa, U. G. Resource theory: Interpersonal behavior as exchange. In K. J. Gergen, M. S. Greenberg, & R. H. Willis (Eds.), *Social exchange: Advances in theory and research.* New York: Plenum, 1980.

Foa, U. G., & Foa, E. B. *Societal structures of the mind.* Springfield, IL: Thomas, 1974.

Furman, W., Rahe, D. F., & Hartup, W. W. Rehabilitation of socially withdrawn preschool children through mixed-age and same-age socialization. *Child Development, 1979, 50,* 915–922.

Gergen, K. J. Exchange theory: The transient and the enduring. In K. J. Gergen, M. S. Greenberg, & R. H. Willis (Eds.), *Social exchange: Advances in theory and research*. New York: Plenum, 1980.

Graziano, W. G. Standards of fair play in same-age and mixed-age groups of children. *Developmental Psychology*, 1978, *14*, 524–530.

Graziano, W. G., Brody, G. H., & Bernstein, S. Effects of information about future interaction and peer's motivation on peer reward allocations. *Developmental Psychology*, 1980, *16*, 475–482.

Graziano, W. G., & Musser, L. M. The joining and parting of the ways. In S. Duck (Ed.), *Personal relationships 4: Dissolving personal relationships*. London: Academic, 1982.

Graziano, W. G., Musser, L. M., Rosen, S., & Shaffer, D. The development of fair-play standards in same- and mixed-race situations: Three converging studies. *Child Development*, 1982, *53*, 938–947.

Greenberg, T. Effects of reward value and retaliative power on allocation decisions: Justice, generosity, or greed? *Journal of Personality and Social Psychology*, 1978, *36*, 367–379.

Hamilton, V. L. Who is responsible? Toward a *social* psychology of responsibility attribution. *Social Psychology*, 1978, *41*, 316–328.

Hartup, W. W. The peer system. In P. H. Mussen & E. M. Hetherington (Eds.), *Carmichael's manual of child psychology* (4th ed., Vol. 4). New York: Wiley, 1983.

Heller, K. A., & Berndt, T. J. Developmental changes in the formation and organization of personality attributions. *Child Development*, 1981, *52*, 683–691.

Hendrick, C. Social psychology as an experimental science. In C. Hendrick (Ed.), *Perspectives on social psychology*. Hillsdale, NJ: Erlbaum, 1977.

Homans, G. C. *Social behavior: Its elementary forms*. New York: Harcourt, 1961.

Homans, G. C. *Social behavior: Its elementary forms* (rev. ed.). New York: Harcourt Brace Jovanovich, 1974.

Homans, G. C. Commentary. In L. Berkowitz & E. Walster (Eds.), *Equity theory: Toward a general theory of social interaction. Advances in experimental social psychology* (Vol. 9). New York: Academic, 1976.

Hook, J. G. Development of equity and altruism in judgments of reward and damage allocation. *Developmental Psychology*, 1982, *18*, 825–834.

Hook, J. G., & Cook, T. D. Equity theory and the cognitive ability of children. *Psychological Bulletin*, 1979, *86*, 429–445.

Isen, A. M., & Hastorf, A. H. Some perspectives on cognitive social psychology. In A. H. Hastorf & A. M. Isen (Eds.), *Cognitive social psychology*. New York: Elsevier, 1982.

Katz, P. A., Sohn, M., & Zalk, S. R. Perceptual concomitants of racial attitudes in urban grade-school children. *Developmental Psychology*, 1975, *11*, 135–144.

Kelley, H. H., & Thibaut, J. W. *Interpersonal relations: A theory of interdependence*. New York: Wiley, 1978.

Konner, M. Relations among infants and juveniles in comparative perspective. In M. Lewis & L. Rosenblum (Eds.), *Friendship and peer relations*. New York: Wiley, 1975.

Langer, J. Werner's theory of development. In P. H. Mussen (Ed.), *Carmichael's manual of child development* (3rd ed., Vol. 1). New York: Wiley, 1970.

Lerner, M. J. Evaluation of performance as a function of performer's reward and attractiveness. *Journal of Personality and Social Psychology*, 1965, *1*, 355–360.

Lerner, M. J., Miller, D. T., & Holmes, J. G. Deserving and the emergence of forms of justice. In L. Berkowitz & E. Walster (Eds.), *Equity theory: Toward a general theory of social interaction. Advances in experimental social psychology* (Vol. 9). New York: Academic Press, 1976.

Lerner, R. M. A dynamic interactional concept of individual and social relationship development. In R. L. Burgess & T. L. Huston (Eds.), *Social exchange in developing relationships*. New York: Academic, 1979.

Leventhal, G. S., & Anderson, D. Self-interest and the maintenance of equity. *Journal of Personality and Social Psychology*, 1970, *15*, 57–62.

Lewin, K. *Principles of topological psychology*. New York: McGraw-Hill, 1936.

Lewin, K. Formalization and progress in psychology. *University of Iowa Studies in Child Welfare*, 1940, *16*, 9–42.

Lewin, K. Defining the "field at a given time." *Psychological Review*, 1943, *50*, 292–310.

Lewin, K. Constructs in psychology and psychological ecology. *University of Iowa Studies in Child Welfare*, 1944, *20*, 1–29.

Lewin, K. Regression, retrogression, and development. In D. Cartwright (Ed.), *Field theory in social science*. Chicago: University of Chicago Press, 1951.

Long, G. T., & Lerner, M. J. Deserving the "personal contract" and altruistic behavior by children. *Journal of Personality and Social Psychology*, 1974, *29*, 551–556.

Masters, J. C. Effects of social comparison upon subsequent self-reinforcement behavior in children. *Journal of Personality and Social Psychology*, 1968, *10*, 391–401.

Masters, J. C. Social comparison by young children. *Young Children*, 1971, *27*, 37–60.

Masters, J. C., & Santrock, J. W. Social reinforcement and self-gratification: Effects of absolute and socially compared levels of nurturance. *Journal of Genetic Psychology*, 1982, *140*, 59–69.

McBride, A. B. *The growth and development of mothers*.New York: Harper & Row, 1973.

McGuire, W. J. The yin and yang of progress in social psychology: Seven koans. *Journal of Personality and Social Psychology*, 1973, *26*, 446–456.

Meehl, P. E. On the circularity of the law of effect. *Psychological Bulletin*, 1950, *47*, 52–75.

Mills, J., & Clark, M. S. Exchange and communal relationships. In L. Wheeler (Ed.), *Review of personality and social psychology* (Vol. 3). Beverly Hills, CA: Sage, 1982.

Murstein, B. Stimulus–value–role: A theory of marital choice. *Journal of Marriage and the Family*, 1970, *32*, 465–481.

Nisbett, R. E., & Wilson, T. D. Telling more than we can know: Verbal reports on mental processes. *Psychological Review*, 1977, *84*, 231–259.

Nunnally, J. C., Duchnowski, A., & Parker, A. Association of neutral objects with reward: Effects on verbal evaluation, reward expectancy, and selective attention. *Journal of Personality and Social Psychology*, 1965, *1*, 270–274.

Osofsky, J. D., & Danzger, B. Relationships between neonatal characteristics and mother–infant interaction. *Developmental Psychology*, 1974, *10*, 124–130.

Overton, W. F. *Historical and contemporary perspectives on development*. Paper presented at the Southeastern Conference on Human Development, Baltimore, MD, 1981.

Overton, W. F., & Reese, H. W. Models of development: Methodological implications. In J. R. Nesselroade & H. W. Reese (Eds.), *Life-span developmental psychology: Methodological issues*. New York: Academic, 1973.

Peevers, B. H., & Secord, P. F. Developmental changes in attribution of descriptive concepts to persons. *Journal of Personality and Social Psychology*, 1973, *27*, 120–128.

Plomin, R., DeFries, J. C., & Loehlin, J. C. Genotype–environment interaction and correlation in the analysis of human behavior. *Psychological Bulletin*, 1977, *84*, 309–322.

Pohlman, E. *The psychology of birth planning*. Cambridge, MA: Schenkman, 1969.

Popper, K. R. *Objective knowledge*. Oxford: Oxford University Press, 1972.

Reis, H. T., & Jackson, L. A. Sex differences in reward allocation: Subjects, partners, and tasks. *Journal of Personality and Social Psychology*, 1981, *40*, 465–478.

Robson, K. S., & Moss, H. A. Patterns and determinants of maternal attachment. *Journal of Pediatrics*, 1970, *77*, 976–985.

Ruble, D. N., Boggiano, A. K., Feldman, N. S., & Loebl, J. H. Developmental analysis of the role of social comparison in self-evaluation. *Developmental Psychology,* 1980, *16,* 105–115.

Ruble, D. N., Feldman, N. S., & Boggiano, A. G. Social comparison between young children in achievement situations. *Developmental Psychology,* 1976, *12,* 192–197.

Sameroff, A. Transactional models in early social relations. *Human Development,* 1975, *18,* 65–79.

Scarlett, H. H., Press, A. N., & Crockett, W. H. Children's description of peers: A Wernerian developmental analysis. *Child Development,* 1971, *42,* 439–453.

Shantz, C. U. The development of social cognition. In E. M. Hetherington (Ed.), *Review of child development research* (Vol. 5). Chicago: University of Chicago Press, 1975.

Shapiro, E. G. Effects of expectation of future interaction on reward allocations in dyads: Equity or equality. *Journal of Personality and Social Psychology,* 1975, *31,* 873–880.

Stephan, W. G. Cognitive differentiation in intergroup perception. *Sociometry,* 1977, *40,* 50–58.

Tesser, A. Self-generated attitude change. In L. Berkowitz (Ed.), *Advances in experimental social psychology* (Vol. 11). New York: Academic, 1978.

Thibaut, J. W., & Kelley, H. H. *The social psychology of groups.* New York: Wiley, 1959.

Thomas, A., Chess, S., & Birch, H. G. *Temperament and behavior disorders in children.* New York: New York University Press, 1968.

Turner, S. M., & Forehand, R. Imitative behavior as a function of success–failure and racial–socioeconomic factors. *Journal of Applied Social Psychology,* 1976, *6,* 40–47.

Tyler, T. R., & Sears, D. O. Coming to like obnoxious people when we must live with them. *Journal of Personality and Social Psychology,* 1977, *35,* 200–211.

Walster, E., & Walster, G. W. Equity and social justice: An essay. *Journal of Social Issues,* 1975, *31,* 21–43.

Walster, E., Walster, G. W., & Berscheid, E. *Equity: Theory and research.* Boston: Allyn & Bacon, 1978.

Webster, M. J., & Driskell, J. E. Status generalization. *American Sociological Review,* 1978, *43,* 220–236.

Werner, H. *Comparative psychology of mental development.* New York: International Universities Press, 1948.

Werner, H. The concept of development from a comparative and organismic point of view. In D. B. Harris (Ed.), *The concept of development.* Minneapolis: University of Minnesota Press, 1957.

Werner, H., & Kaplan, B. *Symbol formation.* New York: Wiley, 1963.

Wolff, P. H. *The Causes, Controls, and Organization of Behavior in the Neonate.* New York: International Universities Press, 1966.

Yussen, S. Determinants of visual attention and recall in observational learning by preschoolers and second graders. *Developmental Psychology,* 1974, *10,* 93–100.

8

The Influence of Group Discussions
on Children's Moral Decisions*

THOMAS J. BERNDT

EDITORS' INTRODUCTION

Thomas Berndt's interest in cognitive and social aspects of children's group interaction has led him to consider the relevance of both social and developmental psychology in this important area. Indeed, both the processes and the outcomes of group influence are of interest to social and developmental psychologists, and individuals in each subdiscipline have relied increasingly on a common method to examine the phenomenon of group influence, observations of group discussions, and an assessment of their effects on individual decisions and behavior. They do so, however, from theoretical perspectives that differ in important ways. Berndt points out how both groups of psychologists assume that concerns with social approval lead to changes in individuals' responses after a discussion; but developmental psychologists have usually emphasized an individual's desire to conform to the group, whereas social psychologists have emphasized an individual's desire to be different from the rest of the group in a way that makes him or her better than average.

The developmental perspective on the consequence of exposure to new information and different viewpoints during a discussion is that it will lead to improvements in an individual's own decisions and behavior, following an abstract no-

*The research reported in this chapter was conducted in collaboration with Kathleen Mc-Cartney, Barbara Caparulo, and Allison Moore at Yale University. They contributed to the design of the study, the collection of the data, and the interpretation of the results.

BOUNDARY AREAS IN SOCIAL
AND DEVELOPMENTAL PSYCHOLOGY

tion of the inherent character of maturation or development. On the other hand, social psychologists anticipate that such exposure would lead to change, but an outside observer might not regard this change as advancement or improvement. This nexus of similarities and contrasts between the perspectives of developmental and social psychology defines a very exciting boundary area with respect to the character and processes of group influence in peer relations.

INTRODUCTION

For a long time there have been two conflicting views regarding the outcomes of group influence. Several writers have argued that the influence of groups on the decisions and behavior of individuals is predominantly negative, encouraging irrational decisions or undesirable behavior. LeBon's (1896) book on mob psychology is an early example of this perspective on group functioning. In more recent writings social psychologists have described flaws in decision-making and failures of social control in adults' groups (Janis, 1972; Zimbardo, 1969). Developmental psychologists have also drawn attention to the effects of participation in peer groups on children's antisocial behavior (e.g., Devereux, 1970). Moreover, there is a sizable literature on urban gangs—mostly contributed by sociologists—which vividly portrays the delinquent behavior of some adolescent groups (see Johnson, 1979). The following anecdote from one of the first systematic studies of gangs (Thrasher, 1927) describes a prototypical example of the negative effects of group interaction on children's behavior. The example was provided by a former member of the group.

> A gang of about eight fellows with a cabin under a big rock in the Appalachian woods originated from the boys' driving [their families'] cattle back and forth every morning and evening. Each family had a big pasture about a mile from town.

> This particular day we went frog-hunting with a gun. Later we arrived at the cattle pen and the boys got the cows about halfway up the hill, when they happened to start shooting with the gun.

> "I dare you to shoot one of those cows off the hill," someone ventured. The others took the dare and started shooting at the cattle. There was some hesitancy at first, but before long five of the eleven boys were participating. Each boy would shoot at the other fellow's cow if possible. One cow was shot in the neck. Another one was killed. The boy whose cow dropped told his folks that she was sick and they had better come up to see about her. Four of the gang had to pay for her; it cost them $20 a piece [p. 304].

The negative view of group influence that is stressed in the preceding example is matched by an equally long tradition of theory and research on the positive outcomes of group interaction. For example, in social psychology, hundreds of studies have been done over nearly a century to answer the question of whether problem-solving by groups is superior to that by individuals (Dashiell, 1935; Hackman & Morris, 1975). As in most cases where a large body of research has accumulated, no simple answer to the question is possible. Nevertheless, there are many instances in which performance by groups is not only better than the average performance of individuals but is also better than that of the most capable member of the group when working on his or her own. In developmental psychology, the most forceful statement of the positive influence of children's peer groups was presented by Piaget (1932/1965). He argued that discussions with peers promote increases in children's abilities to think logically, to understand other people's points of view, and to make mature moral judgments. Kohlberg (1969) advanced a similar hypothesis, although he assumed that group discussions can facilitate moral development even if the groups are not composed exclusively of children and their peers.

I suspect many people would attempt to resolve the conflict between the positive and negative views of group influence by arguing that both views are correct: They simply refer to different types of outcomes. For example, the effects of group influence on actual behavior might be contrasted with its effects on moral reasoning. The conflict could not be resolved completely in this way, but its bounds might be narrowed.

In contrast, a direct focus on the conflict could be heuristically valuable. It could lead to a better understanding of the processes of group influence, because the conflict between the two views regarding the outcomes of group influence is based partly on different assumptions about these processes. Two general types of processes can be distinguished (see Jones & Gerard, 1965; Lamm & Myers, 1978). One type focuses on an individual's concern with the approval of the group. In theories of this type, group influence depends on the power of other group members to reward and punish or praise and blame an individual. The individual's response is chosen so as to increase the others' acceptance and approval of him or her. The negative effects of group interaction are generally explained by an individual's concern with social approval. In Thrasher's (1927) example, the boys apparently went along with the initial suggestion to shoot at the cows because they expected to be teased or labeled cowards if they did not.

The second type of influence process focuses on the facts and reasons that are exchanged during a group's interactions. Theories of this type assume that individuals are influenced by participation in groups primarily because they are exposed to information they had not previously known or understood. Each individual responds to the messages he or she receives during the group's interactions, rather than to the people who sent them. The positive effects of group interaction typically are explained by some form of informational influence. For example, Piaget assumed that discussions among peers contribute to moral development because children refine their own moral positions after hearing other children's judgments and reasoning.

Direct tests of the conflicting perspectives on the processes and outcomes of group influence are rare, particularly in developmental psychology. To a large degree, each theory has generated its own research literature; few attempts to compare different theories have been made (but see Devereux, 1970). The main purpose of this chapter is to illustrate and contrast different ways in which group influence has been conceptualized and measured. The chapter begins with a brief review of the methods used most commonly for examining peer group influence in childhood and adolescence. Then one example from the developmental literature on the effects of group discussion is presented. In the third section, one paradigm for research on decision-making in adult groups—that on the choice shift, or group polarization, phenomenon—is considered. A recent study on the processes and outcomes of moral discussions in children's groups is then presented. Finally, important limitations in the current research are discussed. Throughout the chapter, contrasts between theories and research methods in social psychology and in developmental psychology are emphasized. Each subfield possesses a rich set of concepts for understanding group influence and a great variety of measures and procedures for investigating this topic. A secondary purpose of this chapter is to encourage greater integration of the work on children's and adults' groups.

MEASUREMENT OF PEER INFLUENCE: THREE RESEARCH TRADITIONS

Three methods for studying peer group influence have been used in most of the previous developmental research. By far the largest amount of research has been done with the Asch (1951) paradigm, or some variant of it. Children have been asked to make some judgment—usually a perceptual one—after hearing several of their peers make the same, obviously incorrect, response. The degree to which children go along with the peer majority, even when the peers are clearly wrong, serves as the measure of peer influence or peer conformity. Conformity is traditionally regarded as a reflection of a child's concern with his or her peers' approval or disapproval.

The central question in previous research was how conformity to peers changes with age. Unfortunately, studies over the last two decades have not provided a clear answer to the question. Age trends during childhood and adolescence differ dramatically across studies. Some investigators report an increase in conformity with age; others report a decrease; still others report curvilinear trends with peaks at widely different ages (see Allen & Newtson,

1972; Berndt, 1979). Apparently there is no general trend for peer conformity in Asch-type situations. The age changes that are obtained in any specific study seem to be affected greatly by details of the stimuli, instructions, and procedures. Moreover, the Asch paradigm now seems a poor analogue to the process of peer influence in natural settings, in part because it eliminates all face-to-face interaction and discussion among group members.

A second method for measuring peer influence was devised by Brittain (1966) and Bronfenbrenner (1970). Children respond to hypothetical situations in which their peers are said to urge them to choose a particular alternative. Occasionally parents and peers are said to support different alternatives; often responses for different types of behavior or different types of situations are compared with one another. Peers' influence on choices of friends may be compared with their influence on educational plans. Peers' influence on responses to situations involving antisocial behavior may be compared to their influence on situations involving prosocial or neutral behavior (Berndt, 1979; Larson, 1972).

Results obtained with this method seem more reliable and more valid than those obtained with the Asch paradigm. For situations involving antisocial or delinquent behavior, increases in conformity to peers are found between 9 and 15 years of age. There is a small drop in antisocial conformity to peers after age 15. This trend matches data from other self-report measures and from official statistics on arrests for similar types of behavior (see Berndt, 1979). In cross-cultural research, responses to the situations have been used to test hypotheses about cultural differences in socialization (e.g., Bronfenbrenner, 1970). The cross-cultural data have also served as the basis for a classification of different types of moral orientations, and a theory of the developmental sequence for these types (Garbarino & Bronfenbrenner, 1976).

The major drawback to the use of hypothetical situations is lack of information about the process of peer influence. Children who choose the alternative supported by peers are usually regarded as bowing to social pressure, but there are other possible interpretations. Children may accept the peer-supported alternative willingly rather than under pressure. They may *want* to do what the peers are doing, rather than feel compelled to do so. Moreover, hypothetical situations inevitably are indirect measures of peer influence. It would be desirable to assess the actual process of influence as it operates in a group's interactions.

Naturalistic observation of interactions between children and their peers is a third method for exploring the processes and outcomes of peer influence. Because it is not always easy to gain access to children's and adolescents' groups, or easy to schedule observations at times convenient for researchers, few studies using this method have been done. Some outstanding examples include the Sherifs' investigations of group formation and intergroup relations in a special summer camp for preadolescent boys (Sherif, Harvey, Shite, Hood, & Sherif, 1961) and their later investigations of high school boys' groups in completely natural settings (Sherif & Sherif, 1964). In addition, several investigators of gangs and delinquent behavior have employed the technique of participant observation (e.g., Suttles, 1968).

Unfortunately, most of these studies had small samples of children and often the sample was restricted to boys. Precise comparisons between groups differing in age, gender, social class, or other variables are seldom possible because different groups were not observed under the same conditions. Most important, the studies have not focused on the phenomenon of group influence. Either they described group functioning in a general way or they placed special emphasis on another issue, such as the factors that promote cooperation between groups (Sherif *et al.,* 1961).

Nevertheless, several of the reports contain interesting and provocative comments about the process of decision-making in groups. One investigator suggested that few decisions in adolescent boys' groups result from pressure by a majority on the rest of the group. In the groups he studied there was

> an avoidance of explicit decision making and a good deal of byplay to achieve consensus or a common direction. Banter, joking, and uproarious fantasy introduced possible choices as a way of seeking agreement. Boys would privately "feel one another out" before "showing their hand"; and sometimes, when they were all together, each member seemed to be waiting for the other "to make a move." A rumored fight or a street argument might weld them all together and produce immediate consensus. Otherwise each group could spend days simply "hanging," joking, gossiping, and waiting for something to happen [Suttles, 1968, p. 194].

The statement is based on only one observer's impressions, but it might serve as a starting point for more systematic research.

In summary, the three methods used in most previous research do not seem to be ideal for examining the processes and outcomes of group influence in childhood and adolescence. New methods are needed that are closer to actual group interaction than to laboratory or questionnaire measures but that are more standardized than completely naturalistic observation. I suggest that observation of discussions by groups of peers under standard conditions falls in this middle ground.

Before turning to studies of group discussion, one additional comment about the previous research should be made. At a quick glance, most of the earlier studies suggest a negative view of group influence: A group majority leads children to make incorrect judgments even when they know the right answer; encouragement by peers leads children to endorse antisocial or delinquent behaviors; and in naturalistic observations most groups perform illegal or socially undesirable behaviors on one or more occasions. A closer look at these research paradigms suggests a more complex conclusion. Conformity to peers might promote correct judgments and socially desirable behaviors, if most of the peers favor those judgments and behaviors (Berndt, 1979). In observation of adolescent gangs, there are some reports of organized efforts by gang members to achieve socially desirable goals (Horowitz & Schwartz, 1974). Nonetheless, the emphasis in these research traditions is on the negative consequences of group influence. The opposite emphasis prevails in research on discussions among peers.

GROUP DISCUSSION AND DEVELOPMENTAL THEORY: AN EXAMPLE

The literature on children's group discussions is not extensive. A large number of topics have been explored, but in most cases only a few studies have been done on each topic (see Hartup, 1970). The greatest attention has been paid to the effects of group discussion on two types of responses: children's performance on cognitive tasks and their reasoning about moral dilemmas. There is substantial overlap in the themes and major conclusions of research on group influence in the cognitive domain and the moral domain. Consequently, the general research paradigm can be illustrated with a single example, an experiment by Berkowitz, Gibbs, and Broughton (1980) on the effects of moral discussion between pairs of college students.

As mentioned earlier, both Piaget and Kohlberg proposed that moral discussions are an important factor in the development of moral reasoning. Through discussions, individuals hear other points of view and become aware of problems or inconsistencies in their own moral reasoning. As they attempt to eliminate these problems or inconsistencies, they increase the maturity of their moral reasoning. Most of the previous research on this hypothesis has explored the effects of moral discussions led by adults. Research in laboratory settings and in classrooms has indicated that discussions in which an adult presents reasoning at a stage higher than a subject's own stage lead to increases in moral reasoning (Rest, 1979). Berkowitz and his colleagues did not deny the value of this research, but they argued that a study of discussions not led by an adult experimenter would have greater ecological validity and provide more definitive evidence on Piaget's original hypothesis that discussions between peers play a major role in the development of moral reasoning.

The design for their study was relatively complex. The college students first were pretested on Kohlberg's standard moral dilemmas interview. Then pairs were formed that included either two students at the same stage of moral reasoning, two students whose reasoning differed by roughly a full stage, or two students who had the same major or modal stage but had a different minor stage. The usual scoring convention is that a difference in minor stage score corresponds to one-third of a stage. By including pairs whose reasoning showed a relatively low disparity and pairs with a disparity of a full stage, the researchers hoped to determine the optimum disparity for developmentally effective moral discussions. In addition, the students' decisions on the pretest dilemmas were considered when pairing subjects. In order to provoke serious and extended discussions, the pairs were composed of students who disagreed about what the main character should do on 50% or more of the pretest moral dilemmas. Finally, the study included a fourth group of subjects who served as controls and did not participate in any discussions.

Each of the pairs of students met on five occasions 1 to 2 weeks apart. They discussed one moral dilemma for approximately 1 hour on each occasion. Two weeks after the discussions ended, they were again given the Kohlberg interview as a posttest.

Two different analyses of the data have been reported. Berkowitz *et al.* (1980) described data on changes in moral reasoning from pretest to posttest. As expected, significant changes were found only for pairs in which subjects differed in their initial levels of moral reasoning. However, the amount of change was not equal in pairs with low and high disparities in pretest scores. Larger gains were found for pairs in which differences in reasoning were one-third of a stage rather than a full stage. Berkowitz and his colleagues pointed out that the results do not contradict those from previous studies, because earlier studies did not include a group in which disparities were less than one full stage. The researchers explained the effectiveness of the low-disparity condition in terms of the lower-stage subject's ability to assimilate the reasoning of his or her partner. Assimilation was probably facilitated, Berkowitz *et al.* (1980) argue, by the overlap in the reasoning structures of the two subjects in the pairs where the initial disparity in reasoning was low.

The moral discussions did not affect significantly the reasoning of students who initially were at a higher moral stage than their partner. In addition, no effects were found for pairs of students who initially reasoned at the same stage. These findings suggest that discussions of conflicting opinions on moral dilemmas are not sufficient by themselves to lead to improvements in moral reasoning. A model of higher-stage reasoning also is necessary. If these conclusions are correct, the results might be explained equally well by a theory of observational learning. More research on this question is clearly required, because the theoretical issue is both significant and unresolved (see Bandura & McDonald, 1963; Cowan, Langer, Heavenrich, & Nathanson, 1969).

A second report on the experiment, which presented a different explanation for the results, included an analysis of the discussions themselves (Berkowitz & Gibbs, 1981). A coding system for the discussions was derived from cognitive-developmental theories and earlier hypotheses by Dewey regarding the conditions that promote development. The key construct in the coding system is transactive dialogue, which is defined as "verbal interaction in which the speaker is actively analyzing and transforming the reasoning of another in relation to, or in the context of, his/her own reasoning" (p. 2). Instances in which one person constructs examples or analogies based on another person's statements qualify as transactive dialogues. Verbal interactions in which individuals merely present their own opinions on the issue, agreeing or disagreeing with one another without trying to understand the other person's perspective, do not qualify.

Berkowitz and Gibbs (1981) reported that the frequency of transactive interchanges in discussions of one dilemma (the only one coded as yet) distinguished between pairs that did and did not show improvements in moral reasoning from pretest to posttest. Moreover, the frequency of transactive dialogues accounted for more of the variance in pre-post change than the disparity between subjects in their present stages of moral reasoning. Berkowitz and Gibbs concluded that the presence of transactive dialogue accounts for the effects of moral discussions on adults' stages of moral reasoning. They caution, however, that their system for coding moral discussions may need substantial modifications before it can be used in research with children. In addition, they refer to recent work by Damon (Damon & Killen, 1982), which suggests that the processes responsible for the positive effects of discussions on children's moral reasoning may be different from the processes that operate in adults' discussions.

Nevertheless, in this research tradition there is little disagreement about the expected outcome of group discussions or the processes responsible for these effects. There is clear consensus that group discussions can and often do have a positive effect on the cognition and moral reasoning of children and adults. The positive effects are attributed to processes that have been given several different names but that all assume that group influence is basically a consequence of information exchange. In addition, change typically is measured by structural development, particularly in research on the moral domain. Emphasis is placed on structures of moral reasoning rather than actual moral decisions. This general perspective contrasts sharply with that in the older research traditions on peer influence. It also contrasts with social psychological research on group functioning.

SOCIAL INFLUENCE IN ADULT GROUPS:
THE CHOICE SHIFT

There is a vast literature on group dynamics and group functioning in social psychology (see Lindzey & Aronson, 1969), but much of the research on group influence has focused on a phenomenon known as the *choice shift,* or *group polarization* (Lamm & Myers, 1978). After discussing a decision in a group, adults typically make individual choices that are more extreme than their choices before the discussion. The shift in choices usually is in the direction of the initial choices—that is, it magnifies the initial bias in responses. Stated another way, choices after a discussion are more polarized than were initial choices. The choice shift was observed first with hypothetical situations that focused on risky or cautious responses, but many other dimensions of choice were subsequently investigated. Choices after a discussion may be more altruistic, more aggressive, more lenient to a transgressor, or more liberal than responses before the discussion, provided the initial choices show a tendency in those directions.

Many explanations for the choice shift have been offered over the years, but only two theories have been emphasized since the 1960s (see Myers & Lamm, 1976; Lamm & Myers, 1978). First, the choice shift has been attributed to a process of social comparison (Sanders & Baron, 1977). The central assumption in social comparison theory is that people believe they are not just average; they are and want to be different from the average in desirable ways. As Brown (1974) put it, "To be virtuous, in any of an indefinite number of dimensions, is to be different from the norm—in the right direction and to the right degree" (p. 470). People's assumption that they are different from the average is likely to be disconfirmed during a group discussion, because they will learn that other people hold opinions similar to their own. In order to maintain the desirable difference between themselves and the rest of the group, they shift toward a more extreme choice. The net effect of each individual's shifts is the choice shift for the group.

Second, the choice shift has been attributed to the exchange of persuasive arguments during a discussion (Burnstein & Vinokur, 1977). According to persuasive arguments theory, decisions by individuals or by groups depend on the balance of the arguments for each alternative. Responses before the discussion indicate the bias in the pool of arguments relevant to the situation under consideration. In other words, they indicate which alternative is supported by the greatest number of persuasive arguments. The same bias is expected to apply to the arguments expressed during the discussion, but through discussion people also hear arguments they failed to think of themselves. As they reflect on the novel arguments, they develop an even stronger preference for the initially favored alternative, producing the choice shift.

Various attempts to test these two competing explanations have been made. Unfortunately, many of the tests are based on experimental manipulations that limit the applicability of the conclusions to discussions in natural settings. For example, because exposure to other people's opinions is a critical factor in social comparison theory and hearing other people's arguments is not, individuals may be required to state their opinions without stating the reasons for them (Goethals & Zanna, 1979). Because reasons for opinions are more important in persuasive arguments theory than who states the reasons, subjects may be asked to argue for positions opposite to the ones they actually hold (Burnstein & Vinokur, 1973). In a few cases the theories have been tested with data obtained from content analyses of unmanipulated discussions (e.g., Vinokur, Trope, & Burnstein, 1975), but the analyses often focus on a specific aspect of the discussion rather than on all the conversation that occurs.

Despite these problems, theories and research on the choice shift provide an unusual perspective from which to examine the two strands of developmental literature on group influence. The hypothesis in social comparison theory that individuals want to be distinctively different from their peers stands in sharp contrast to the prevailing notion in developmental research that children feel obliged to conform to the pressure of a majority. Persuasive arguments theory seems analogous to cognitive-developmental theories of group influence, because they both focus on the comprehension of new information exchanged during a discussion. In persuasive arguments theory, however, group discussion is not viewed as crucially important for a choice shift. Changes in responses are expected even if individuals reconsider a choice or decision on their own, without group discussion (Tesser, 1978; Vinokur & Burnstein, 1974). These differences in theoretical orientation might be regarded as limiting the relevance of the choice shift literature to developmental research. From another perspective, the differences may be a source of questions and methods for the study of children's and adolescents' groups.

CHOICE SHIFTS AND CHILDREN'S MORAL DECISIONS

Along with three graduate students, I conducted a study of shifts in children's moral decisions after a group discussion (Berndt, McCartney, Caparulo, & Moore, 1982). The study included 108 children fairly evenly divided between third and sixth graders and between boys and girls. The children first were given a sociometric questionnaire on which they indicated their best friends, the classmates they liked, and the classmates with whom they played outside of school. Responses to the questionnaire were used to form same-gender groups of four classmates who had a fairly high degree of mutual attraction. Not all groups were composed of close friends, but groups were created that were as cohesive as possible. By forming groups in this way, we could observe discussions among children who normally associated with one another at school and at home.

In the second session, the groups were taken one at a time to an empty room in their school. Each child in the group first was asked to respond independently to four moral dilemmas. Two of the dilemmas presented a choice between honest and dishonest behavior. The other two dilemmas presented a choice between altruistic and self-interested behavior. The dilemmas were different from those used in previous research on moral development. Each dilemma included details that could be used to justify either alternative to the dilemma. For example, information that could be used to justify a choice of the dishonest alternative was provided. However, the dilemmas were always written so that the socially desirable response was clear. Therefore, if there was a shift in children's responses after a group discussion, we could judge whether the shift was toward or away from the socially desirable alternatives—honesty and altruism.

The following is an example of an honesty dilemma:

> Joe went to the drugstore after school to buy some candy. The store was crowded, and the saleslady was very grouchy. She told the kids not to touch anything they weren't going to buy. She also waited on all the adults first, instead of giving everyone their turn in order. Finally it was Joe's turn. He paid for his candy quickly and left. On the way home Joe noticed that the saleslady had given him too much change—50¢ more than he was supposed to have.

> What do you think Joe should do, go back to the store and return the change, or keep the change and forget about it?

Responses to the dilemmas were made on an 11-point scale with 0 for a certain choice of the socially desirable alternative, 10 for a certain choice of the socially undesirable alternative, and 5 for "not sure."

After they had responded to the dilemmas on their own, children in two-thirds of the groups discussed nonmoral topics such as a trip to the beach or a scary movie. Before the moral discussions, children were told to talk about the dilemmas one at a time. They were told to start each discussion by giving each child a turn to state his or her opinion, and then to continue the discussion until they reached an agreement on the decision or until 7 minutes had passed. Nearly all groups reached an agreement in 7 minutes. Most discussions lasted between 3 and 4 minutes. The discussions were videotaped with the children's knowledge, but the experimenter was absent from the room. Following the discussions, children in all groups again were asked to respond to the dilemmas on their own.

After the data were collected and a preliminary scan of the videotapes was made, a coding system for the discussions was devised that included three major sets of categories. The first set consisted of statements in favor of the socially desirable alternatives (honesty and altruism), statements in favor of the socially undesirable alternatives (dishonesty and the nonaltruistic response), and statements in favor of a response of not sure. For example, a child who said, "I think he should keep the money," would be coded as making a statement in support of the socially undesirable alternative. This set of categories is particularly relevant to social comparison theory because the statements indicate the opinions of other group members.

The second set of categories consisted of reasons or arguments for each of the alternatives. One reason frequently given for keeping the money was that "the saleslady was grouchy." This set of categories is relevant to persuasive arguments theory and other theories that focus on information exchange during discussions.

The third set of categories referred to various aspects of group dynamics. It included verbal aggression by one child toward another (e.g., "You're cheap."), commands ("Stop fooling around."), comments about the proper procedure for the discussion ("We're supposed to take turns."), and comments about group functioning ("We can't agree. This is hard"). A final category for off-task periods referred to occasions in which the group began talking about topics unrelated to the dilemmas or laughing and joking around. These aspects of group functioning have not been considered in the major theories of the choice shift, but they were an important part of the children's discussions. Coding of the frequencies of responses in each category for each discussion was done by two persons independently. Correlations between the two observers' scores for 25% of the discussions ranged from .89 to .99.

The first analysis of the data was on individual children's responses. Significant shifts in responses between the pretest and the posttest were found after moral discussions but not after discussions of nonmoral topics (Table 8.1). The pattern of shifts varied, however, for the honesty and altruism dilemmas. Mean scores after the discussions were higher than before them on the honesty dilemmas, indicating that the discussions produced a shift toward the dishonest alternative. Mean scores after the discussions were lower than before them on the altruism dilemmas, indicating that the discussions produced a shift toward the altruistic alternative.

The pattern of shifts is surprising, given that pretest means were on the socially desirable end of the response scale for both types of dilemmas. If group polarization had occurred in both cases, shifts toward the altruistic

TABLE 8.1

Mean Pretest and Posttest Scores for Each Condition on Each Type of Dilemma[a]

	Condition			
	Moral discussion		Control	
Type of dilemma	Pretest	Posttest	Pretest	Posttest
Altruism	2.14	1.20*	1.76	1.46
Honesty	3.31	4.35**	1.14	1.22

[a]On the response scale, 0 corresponds to the altruistic or honest choice, 10 corresponds to the nonaltruistic or dishonest choice, and 5 is "not sure."

*$p < .05$ for pretest–posttest difference. **$p < .01$ for pretest–posttest difference.

alternative and toward the honest alternative would have been found. There are a few exceptions to polarization in the literature on adult groups, particularly when one alternative is socially undesirable (e.g., an aggressive respones), so the results for the children's discussions are not entirely novel. The most important question is whether or not an explanation for the shifts on both types of dilemmas can be found in the discussions themselves.

In the first analysis of the discussion variables, the frequencies of reasons for the specific categories coded from discussions were compared for the two types of dilemmas. A significant difference was found in only one case. Children gave more reasons for the socially undesirable alternatives—dishonesty and a nonaltruistic response—on the honesty dilemmas than on the altruism dilemmas. Reasons for the socially desirable alternatives did not vary for the two types of dilemmas. Consequently, the proportion of reasons in favor of the socially undesirable alternatives was greater for the honesty dilemmas than for the altruism dilemmas (44% for the honesty dilemmas versus 24% for the altruism dilemmas). The difference in proportions is consistent with the difference in the direction of shifts for the honesty and altruism dilemmas. Apparently children shifted toward a dishonest response but not toward a nonaltruistic response because they heard more arguments in favor of the dishonest response. Thus the results can be explained partly by persuasive arguments theory, though persuasive arguments theory is not a complete explanation because it does not say why children expressed more reasons for the dishonest response than the nonaltruistic response. It therefore needs to be supplemented by other hypotheses.

Initially social comparison theory does not seem to provide an adequate explanation for the choice shifts, because the statements favoring each alternative that provided information about other children's opinions did not vary for the two types of dilemmas. However, social comparison theory might be better tested if data were available on children's perceptions of their peers' opinions before the discussion. As mentioned earlier, the fundamental assumption of social comparison theory is that people change their responses because they realize they are not as different from their peers as they thought they were. Previous research indicates that children believe they prefer socially desirable behaviors, including altruism, more than their peers do (Emmerich, Goldman, & Shore, 1971). During the discussions each child could have discovered that his or her peers were actually quite favorable toward the altruistic alternatives. Children could have shifted toward the altruistic responses so that they could maintain their belief that they had a stronger preference for altruism than did their peers.

Social comparison theory also has been used in previous research to explain shifts toward less socially desirable responses after adults' discussions (Pruitt, 1971). Adults who secretly favor the less socially desirable alternative in a particular situation initially may be unwilling to indicate this preference to an experimenter, but they may be more willing to do so after hearing other people advocate this response. Similarly, children apparently were unwilling to choose the dishonest alternative on the pretest when the experimenter was present, but after hearing their peers suggest this alternative during the discussion, they were more likely to support it on the posttest, even though the experimenter again was present.

In two major reviews of the research on adult groups, Myers and Lamm (1976; Lamm & Myers, 1978) argued that both persuasive arguments and social comparison must be considered in any complete explanation of the choice shift. Reviews suggest that evidence for persuasive arguments theory is clearer and more consistent than evidence for social comparison theory, just as in our study. The difference might be reduced, however, if greater attention was given to the measurement of the process of social comparison in a discussion.

In a second analysis of the discussion variables, we attempted to predict the mean score for each group on the posttest from the features of that group's discussions. Mean posttest scores were used as the criterion in multiple regression equations with the variables coded from the discussion as predictors. Because of the relatively large number of coding categories, the analyses were performed for each set of categories separately. In all analyses, the mean pretest score for each group was entered first, so that the effects of the discussion would not be confounded with the consistency in responses from pretest to posttest.

The results of the analyses are summarized in Tables 8.2 and 8.3. Because the number of groups was fairly small, significant effects were not always obtained, even when a variable accounted for a sizable proportion of the

TABLE 8.2

Contributions of Discussion Variables to Mean Posttest Scores for Each Group on the Honesty
Dilemmas

Variable[a]	R^2	ΔR^2	Beta at point of entry	F value for beta[b]
Pretest	.605	.605	.778	24.52***
Statements				
Not sure	.663	.058	−.246	2.57
Socially undesirable	.728	.065	.311	3.34*
Socially desirable	.781	.053	−.251	3.15*
Reasons				
Socially desirable	.639	.034	−.195	1.42
Socially undesirable	.688	.049	.260	2.19
Not sure	.690	.002	−.044	<1
Group dynamics				
Verbal aggression	.732	.127	.357	7.11**
Group process	.813	.081	−.491	6.10**
Procedure	.816	.003	.051	<1
Off-task	.820	.004	−.141	<1
Commands	.820	.000	.001	<1

[a]Mean pretest scores were entered first in all equations. For each set of discussion variables, the listing is by order of entry into the equation.

[b]For the F-ratios, dfs range from (1, 16) to (1, 11), depending on the number of variables already in the equation.

*$p < .10$. **$p < .05$. ***$p < .01$.

variance in posttest scores. Nevertheless, the overall pattern is both clear and interpretable. The findings for statements supporting each alternative and reasons for these statements can be considered first. In all cases a positive beta weight for a category indicates that the category was associated with shifts toward the socially undesirable alternatives, because these alternatives were scored at the high point on the response scale. Conversely, a negative beta weight for a category indicates that the category was associated with shifts toward the socially desirable alternatives. As expected, statements and reasons for the socially undesirable alternatives were associated with shifts toward those alternatives; statements and reasons for the socially desirable alternatives were associated with shifts toward those alternatives.

The beta weights for the not sure alternatives differ for the two types of dilemmas. In both cases the not sure response seems to be related to the choice that was least preferred after the discussions. That is, comments supporting the not sure response were related to shifts toward the honest alter-

TABLE 8.3

Contributions of Discussion Variables to Mean Posttest Scores for Each Group on the Altruism Dilemma

Variable[a]	R^2	ΔR^2	Beta at point of entry	F value for beta[b]
Mean pretest score	.218	.218	.467	4.45*
Statements				
Socially undesirable	.326	.108	.337	2.41
Not sure	.364	.038	.211	<1
Socially desirable	.425	.061	−.425	1.39
Reasons				
Socially undesirable	.369	.151	.393	3.58*
Socially desirable	.471	.102	−.379	2.71
Not sure	.519	.048	.298	1.31
Group Dynamics				
Commands	.473	.255	.627	7.28**
Procedure	.564	.091	−.402	2.91
Group process	.595	.031	.270	1.00
Off-task	.635	.040	.466	1.31
Verbal aggression	.636	.001	.038	<1

[a]Mean pretest scores were entered first in all equations. For each set of discussion variables, the listing is by order of entry into the equation.

[b]For the F-ratios, dfs range from (1, 16) to (1, 11), depending on the number of variables already in the equation.

*$p < .10$. **$p < .05$.

native and shifts toward the nonaltruistic alternative. Apparently children were most likely to say they were uncertain when they opposed the general trend for the groups.

The analyses of statements and reasons do not demonstrate clearly that persuasive arguments are a better explanation for the choice shifts than is exposure to other children's opinions. Instead, the importance of the two sets of categories seems to differ for the honesty and altruism dilemmas. When the three types of statements were considered as a set, they had a significant effect on pre-post shifts for the honesty dilemmas, $F(3, 13) = 3.48$, $p < .05$, but not for the altruism dilemmas, $F(3, 13) = 1.56$, $p > .20$. Conversely, when the three categories of reasons were considered as a set, they had a marginally significant effect on pre-post shifts for the altruism dilemmas, $F(3, 13) = 2.71$, $p < .10$, but they had a nonsignificant effect on shifts for the honesty dilemmas, $F(3, 13) = 1.19$, $p > .25$.

One could conclude that the shift toward dishonest responses was due more to social comparison (the sheer exchange of opinions) and less to persuasive arguments than the shift toward altruism. This conclusion would certainly be consistent with the stereotype that bad decisions are unlikely to be based on a careful consideration of relevant reasons and arguments. In contrast, the conclusion is not consistent with that derived from the first analysis of the coding categories, which suggested that children shifted toward the dishonest alternative because they heard more reasons for that alternative. It is safest and probably wisest to suggest again that persuasive arguments and social comparison must both be considered when attempting to account for choice shifts. The results of the multiple regression analyses further imply that the relative importance of others' opinions and their reasons may vary for different types of decisions.

The choice shifts after the discussions were also related to the set of variables concerned with aspects of group dynamics. Because of the inter-correlations among these variables, the significance levels for single variables need to be interpreted cautiously. For example, although commands had a significant effect on choice shifts for the altruism dilemmas and off-task comments did not, these two variables were strongly correlated ($r = .89$). Commands were more strongly related to choice shifts, so they were entered first in the equation, leaving off-task comments as a nonsignificant predictor. The beta weights for each variable are less subject to this problem, because they indicate the relative contribution of a variable without regard to its order of entry into the equation.

The signs for variables having large beta weights form an intriguing pattern. For the honesty dilemmas, the beta weight for verbal aggression is positive and that for comments about the group process is negative. These weights indicate that shifts toward the dishonest alternative were more common for groups in which verbal aggression was expressed frequently; they were less common for groups in which comments about how the group was functioning were frequent. For the altruism dilemmas, the beta weights for commands and off-task comments are positive and the beta weight for comments about procedures for the discussion is negative. These weights indicate that shifts toward the altruistic alternative were less common for groups in which children ordered one another around or did not focus on a discussion of the moral dilemma; they were common for groups in which children stressed following the proper procedure (e.g., taking turns).

The relations of group dynamics to choice shifts imply that the character of a discussion partly determines its outcome, regardless of the content of the discussion. The relations might be summarized by referring to an orderliness dimension for group interactions. Interactions that are more orderly—ones in which children explicitly discuss what is happening in the group and whether they are following the proper procedure—seem to facilitate socially desirable group outcomes. Less orderly interactions—ones in which children frequently engage in laughing, joking, teasing, and yelling at one another—seem to promote less desirable outcomes. These features of group dynamics may have been overlooked in research with adults because adult groups that are observed in laboratory settings rarely show these types of behaviors (Argyris, 1969).

Finally, boys selected the dishonest and nonaltruistic alternatives on the dilemmas more than did girls. During their discussions, boys gave more reasons for the dishonest and nonaltruistic alternatives than did girls; boys gave fewer reasons for the honest and altruistic alternatives. These differences are consistent with a large body of previous research (see Berndt, 1979). Sixth graders stated more reasons for their choices than did third graders, but age differences for other discussion variables and for individual children's pretest and posttest responses were nonsignificant. The multiple regression analyses could not be done for each age separately because of the small number of groups in the study. Obviously, age changes in the processes and outcomes of group influence could be explored more fully if there were a larger number of groups at each age and a larger age range, perhaps comparing third and eighth graders.

CONCLUSIONS

One important conclusion can be drawn from this survey of theory and research on group influence: Both desirable and undesirable outcomes of group influence can occur. After discussing moral dilemmas together, children may be more willing to say that another child should behave altruistically and may be more willing to say that another child should behave dishonestly. After a series of discussions of more complex moral dilemmas, college students may or may not have developed greater sophistication in judging moral issues. Concerns with the approval of one's peers and responsiveness to the social pressure of peers may lead to actions consistent or inconsistent with social norms, depending on the position supported by peers.

The conclusion that peer influence is neither entirely positive nor entirely negative seems consistent with common sense as well as the research literature, but I think most people will regard it as unsatisfying. People want to know in what conditions positive outcomes of peer group interaction will occur and in what conditions negative outcomes will occur. In both our study (Berndt et al., 1982) and that of Berkowitz and his colleagues, attempts were made to explain why group discussion had variable effects on children's decisions and behavior. In both cases, however, the specific pattern of effects was not predicted in advance. To predict the effects of group interaction, a more precise and comprehensive theory of the processes of group influence is necessary.

At the beginning of the chapter, two general types of influence processes were described. Children and adults may alter their decisions and behavior after a group discussion either because they want to gain the approval of other group members or because they have obtained new information about the topic under discussion. The distinction between these two types still seems valuable, but it needs to be refined in several respects.

First, distinctions within each general type need to be made. For example, the desire for social approval is an important construct in theories that attribute group influence to social pressure and theories that attribute group influence to social comparison. The theories differ, however, in their assumptions about how individuals will try to gain social approval. Social pressure theories assume that individuals try to be like the rest of the group; social comparison theories assume that individuals try to be desirably different.

The apparent conflict might be resolved by suggesting that these two theories refer to different phenomena. Social pressure may explain the process by which individuals come to a consensus, as a group, on an issue. Social comparison may explain why the group consensus is different from the average position of group members before a group discussion—that is, the shift in responses due to discussion. In our study of moral decisions (Berndt et al., 1982) we focused on choice shifts and not on the processes that led to the group consensus during the discussion. One reason for this focus was that the group consensus disappeared when individuals responded to the posttest on their own. The variability of posttest scores within each group of four subjects was as great after the discussions as before, and as great for groups who discussed the dilemmas as for those who did not.

One could argue that social pressure is not an important factor in discussions of hypothetical moral dilemmas but is important in other situations. After all, a moral discussion is exactly the context in which Piaget (1932/1965) expected children to show mutual respect and tolerance of disagreements. Observations of adolescent groups in natural settings suggest that social pressure is exerted frequently when groups are planning illegal or dangerous activities (Sherif & Sherif, 1964; Suttles, 1968). A group member who hesitates to participate in these activities may not only jeopardize their success but may also be more likely to inform on the rest of the group if questioned by the authorities.

On the other hand, the difference between social pressure and social comparison theories should not be dismissed easily. Formulation of a theory that integrates these two processes of influence should be possible. Recall that Brown (1974) stated the central proposition of social comparison theory in terms of an individual's desire to be different "to the right degree." In trying to gain the approval of others, individuals in groups try to choose a position that is close enough to everyone else's position to make them acceptable but different enough to make them special. This balancing process is what requires explanation.

Distinctions also can be made among theories of informational influence. The effects of hearing other people's reasons for their opinions have been explained in terms of active assimilation (Berkowitz *et al.*, 1980), transactive dialogue (Berkowitz & Gibbs, 1981), observational learning (Bandura & McDonald, 1963), and comprehension of novel and persuasive arguments (Burnstein & Vinokur, 1977). Even these examples do not exhaust the possibilities. Other writers have explained the effects of group discussions of cognitive tasks in terms of a reorganization in thinking after the experience of social cognitive conflicts (e.g., Mugny & Doise, 1978; Perret-Clermont, 1980).

One source of differences between these theories is the emphasis placed on a basic process of acquisition of new information rather than a process of restructuring in the cognitive system after reflection on the information exchanged. Although this difference has often been emphasized by cognitive-developmental theorists, it is of questionable importance for the theories under consideration. For example, although persuasive arguments theory focuses mainly on an individual's exposure to new information during discussion, it says little about the effect of the new information on the individual's existing cognitive structures. It certainly does not rule out the possibility that access to new information might lead to changes in other, more general features of an individual's thinking.

Another difference between the theories concerns the relative emphasis placed on changes in decisions and changes in the reasoning behind those decisions. Again cognitive-developmental theory stands out because it focuses on changes in cognitive structures utilized in reasoning about an issue, rather than on the judgments that result from reasoning. Yet this difference can be exaggerated as well. Previous research has shown relations between stages of moral reasoning and concrete decisions or behaviors, even in young children (Blasi, 1980; Eisenberg-Berg & Hand, 1979). The relations also were apparent in our study of moral decisions. For example, on the drugstore dilemma children often justified a choice of the dishonest alternative by saying that the saleslady was grouchy. The saleslady's grouchiness and the child's decision to keep excess change are reciprocal in a crude way; similar examples of crude or inexact reciprocity are described by Damon (1977) as marking a fairly low stage of moral reasoning.

One difference among theories of informational influence that does seem significant concerns the expected direction of change due to discussion. Cognitive-developmental theories assume that group discussions normally will lead to decisions based on more mature moral reasoning, if any change is observed. Persuasive arguments theory does not contain a comparable hypothesis. The direction of change depends on the pool of persuasive arguments relevant to the topic discussed, and it seems intuitively plausible that some of these arguments might be persuasive without being based on high levels of moral reasoning. For example, an argument might be persuasive because it illustrates convincingly the benefits of an alternative to the child or adult involved. Of course, there may be circumstances in which each of these hypotheses is correct. It would be valuable to know when the exchange of information during a discussion leads not only to more informed decisions but also to decisions based on more mature reasoning.

A second problem with many theories of group influence is lack of clarity about how the hypothesized process of influence can be measured. The research on peer conformity with the Asch paradigm is an outstanding example of a methodological tradition in which attention was directed almost exclusively at the outcomes of social influence. The process responsible for these outcomes was neither directly nor indirectly assessed. In research with adult groups, influence processes often have been measured indirectly through experimental manipulations that are presumed to affect the operation of these processes. Several examples of this strategy were described in the review of the choice shift literature. Berkowitz and his colleagues (1980) used the same strategy when they manipulated the disparity of moral reasoning stages in their pairs of college students.

The most direct method for assessing influence processes, with measures of actual group discussions, often has been used to examine the effects of information exchange on individuals' decisions. The research on persuasive arguments theory provides several examples (e.g., Vinokur *et al.*, 1975), as does the study I described earlier (Berndt, *et al.*, 1982). Fewer attempts have been made to devise measures of social pressure or social comparison in acutal group interactions. Consequently, one potential source of evidence for these theories is unavailable.

Still another strategy for assessing processes of group influence depends on the coordination of data from analyses of group discussions and responses of individual subjects. The possibility of testing social comparison theory with data on children's perceptions of their peers' opinions was mentioned earlier. The same strategy could be used to examine the relations between the outcomes of a discussion and the moral maturity of the reasons expressed during it. The reasons actually given in one group's discussions could be rated for their moral maturity by psychologists knowledgeable about current descriptions of moral reasoning, by a sample of college students, and by children the same age as those who participated in the discussion. In the near future we plan to try this approach with the data we have already collected.

A third problem with the distinction between two general types of group influence is that it ignores the effects of the affective quality of a discussion on its outcomes. To reiterate briefly, we found that discussions characterized by comments about the proper procedure for a discussion and comments about how the group was functioning led to shifts toward more socially desirable alternatives. Discussions characterized by verbal aggression, periods of laughing or joking about irrelevant topics, and frequent instances in which children gave commands to one another led to shifts toward socially undesirable alternatives. The less orderly discussions seem to be much like those described in the naturalistic observation quoted from Suttles (1968) near the beginning of this chapter. However, these effects would have been overlooked completely if the coding system had been tied strictly to previously described processes of influence.

The preceding comments are intended less as criticisms of earlier research than as an indication of how much needs to be done before the outcomes of group interaction can be understood. My last comment refers to the least studied and most open question of all—how group influence changes with age. Almost no research has explored the developing influence of groups on children's decisions and behavior. Our study of moral decisions included children at two different ages, but age changes in the relations of group discussions to individuals' decisions could not be examined fully with the size of the sample at each age. Previous literature suggests that there are age changes in the effectiveness of information exchange (Flavell, 1977), in the weight placed on peers' approval or disapproval (Berndt, 1979), and in the affective features of group discussions (Smith, 1973). The direct assessment of these changes should be a high priority in the future.

REFERENCES

Allen, V. L., & Newtson, D. Development of conformity and independence. *Journal of Personality and Social Psychology,* 1972, 22, 18–30.

Argyris, C. The incompleteness of social psychological theory: Examples from small group, cognitive consistency, and attribution research. *American Psychologist,* 1969, 24, 893–908.

Asch, S. Effects of group pressure upon the modification and distortion of judgment. In M. H. Guetzow (Ed.), *Groups, leadership, and men.* Pittsburgh: Carnegie Press, 1951.

Bandura, A., & McDonald, F. J. Influence of social reinforcement and the behavior of models in shaping children's moral judgments. *Journal of Abnormal and Social Psychology,* 1963, 67, 274–281.

Berkowitz, M. W., & Gibbs, J. C. *Transactive communication as a condition for moral development.* Paper presented at the biennial meetings of the Society for Research in Child Development, Boston, MA, April 1981.

Berkowitz, M. W., Gibbs, J. C., & Broughton, J. M. The relation of moral judgment stage disparity to developmental effects of peer dialogues. *Merrill-Palmer Quarterly,* 1980, *26,* 341–358.

Berndt, T. J. Developmental changes in conformity to peers and parents. *Developmental Psychology,* 1979, *15,* 608–616.

Berndt, T. J., McCartney, K. A., Caparulo, B. K., & Moore, A. M. Processes and outcomes of social influence in children's peer groups. Submitted for publication, 1982.

Blasi, A. Bridging moral cognition and moral action: A critical review of the literature. *Psychological Bulletin,* 1980, *88,* 1–45.

Brittain, C. V. Age and sex of siblings and conformity toward parents versus peers in adolescence. *Child Development,* 1966, *37,* 709–714.

Bronfenbrenner, U. Reaction to social pressure from adults versus peers among Soviet day school and boarding school pupils in the perspective of an American sample. *Journal of Personality and Social Psychology,* 1970, *15,* 179–189.

Brown, R. Further comment on the risky shift. *American Psychologist,* 1974, *29,* 468–470.

Burnstein, E., & Vinokur, A. Testing two classes of theories about group-induced shifts in individual choice. *Journal of Experimental Social Psychology,* 1973, *9,* 123–137.

Burnstein, E., & Vinokur, A. Persuasive argumentation and social comparison as determinants of attitude polarization. *Journal of Experimental Social Psychology,* 1977, *13,* 315–332.

Cowan, P. A., Langer, J., Heavenrich, J., & Nathanson, M. Social learning and Piaget's theory of moral development. *Journal of Personality and Social Psychology,* 1969, *11,* 261–274.

Damon, W. *The social world of the child.* San Francisco: Jossey-Bass, 1977.

Damon, W., & Killen, M. Peer interaction and the process of change in children's moral reasoning. *Merrill-Palmer Quarterly,* 1982, *28,* 347–368.

Dashiell, J. F. Experimental studies of the influence of social situations on the behavior of individual human adults. In C. Murchison (Ed.), *Handbook of social psychology.* Worcester, MA: Clark University Press, 1935.

Devereux, E. C. The role of the peer group experience in moral development. In J. P. Hill (Ed.), *Minnesota symposium on child psychology* (Vol. 4). Minneapolis: University of Minnesota Press, 1970.

Eisenberg-Berg, N., & Hand, M. The relationship of preschoolers' reasoning about prosocial moral conflicts to prosocial behavior. *Child Development,* 1979, *50,* 356–363.

Emmerich, W., Goldman, K. S., & Shore, R. E. Differentiation and development of social norms. *Journal of Personality and Social Psychology,* 1971, *18,* 323–353.

Flavell, J. H. *Cognitive development.* Englewood Cliffs, NJ: Prentice-Hall, 1977.

Garbarino, J., & Bronfenbrenner, U. The socialization of moral judgment and behavior in cross-cultural perspective. In T. Lickona (Ed.), *Moral development and behavior: Theory, research, and social issues.* New York: Holt, Rinehart & Winston, 1976.

Goethals, G. R., & Zanna, M. P. The role of social comparison in choice shifts. *Journal of Personality and Social Psychology,* 1979, *37,* 1469–1476.

Hackman, J. R., & Morris, C. G. Group tasks, group interaction process, and group performance effectiveness: A review and proposed integration. In L. Berkowitz (Ed.), *Advances in experimental social psychology* (Vol. 8). New York: Academic, 1975.

Hartup, W. W. Peer interaction and social organization. In P. H. Mussen (Ed.), *Carmichael's manual of child psychology* (Vol. 2). New York: Wiley, 1970.

Horowitz, R., & Schwartz, G. Honor, normative ambiguity, and gang violence. *American Sociological Review,* 1974, *39,* 238–251.

Janis, I. L. *Victims of groupthink.* Boston: Houghton Mifflin, 1972.

Johnson, R. *Juvenile delinquency and its origins.* New York: Cambridge University Press, 1979.

Jones, E. E., & Gerard, H. B. *Foundations of social psychology.* New York: Wiley, 1965.

Kohlberg, L. Stage and sequence: The cognitive-developmental approach to socialization. In D. A. Goslin (Ed.), *Handbook of socialization theory and research.* New York: Rand McNally, 1969.

Lamm, H., & Myers, D. G. Group-induced polarization of attitudes and behavior. In L. Berkowitz (Ed.), *Advances in experimental social psychology* (Vol. 11). New York: Academic, 1978.

Larson, L. E. The influence of parents and peers during adolescence: The situation hypothesis revisited. *Journal of Marriage and the Family,* 1972, *34,* 67–74.

LeBon, G. [*The crowd.*] London: Unwin, 1896.

Lindzey, G., & Aronson, E. (Eds.) *The handbook of social psychology* (2nd ed., 5 vols.). Reading, MA: Addison-Wesley, 1969.

Mugny, G., & Doise, W. Socio-cognitive conflict and structure of individual and collective performance. *European Journal of Social Psychology,* 1978, *8,* 181–192.

Muers, D. G., & Lamm, H. The group polarization phenomenon. *Psychological Bulletin,* 1976, *83,* 602–627.

Perret-Clermont, A. N. *Social interaction and cognitive development in children.* New York: Academic, 1980.

Piaget, J. *The moral judgment of the child.* New York: Free Press, 1965. (Originally published, 1932.)

Pruitt, D. G. Choice shifts in group discussion: An introductory review. *Journal of Personality and Social Psychology,* 1971, *20,* 339–360.

Rest, J. R. *Development in judging moral issues.* Minneapolis: University of Minnesota Press, 1979.

Sanders, G., & Baron, R. S. Is social comparison irrelevant for producing choice shifts? *Journal of Experimental Social Psychology,* 1977, *13,* 303–314.

Sherif, M., Harvey, O. J., Shite, B. J., Hood, W. R., & Sherif, C. W. *Inter-group conflict & cooperation: The robbers' cave experiment.* Norman: Institute of Group Relations, University of Oklahoma Press, 1961.

Sherif, M., & Sherif, C. *Reference groups: Exploration into conformity and deviance of adolescents.* New York: Harper & Row, 1964.

Smith, H. W. Some developmental interpersonal dynamics through childhood, *American Sociological Review,* 1973, *38,* 543–552.

Suttles, G. P. *The social order of the slum.* Chicago: University of Chicago Press, 1968.

Tesser, A. Self-generated attitude change. In L. Berkowitz (Ed.), *Advances in experimental social psychology* (Vol. 11). New York: Academic, 1978.

Thrasher, F. M. *The gang.* Chicago: University of Chicago Press, 1927.

Vinokur, A., & Burnstein, E. Effects of partially shared persuasive arguments of group-induced shifts: A group problem-solving approach. *Journal of Personality and Social Psychology,* 1974, *29,* 305–315.

Vinokur, A., Trope, Y., & Burnstein, E. A decision-making analysis of persuasive argumentation and the choice shift. *Journal of Experimental Social Psychology,* 1975, *11,* 127–148.

Zimbardo, P. G. The human choice: Individuation, reason, and order versus deindividuation, impulse, and chaos. In W. J. Arnold & D. Levine (Eds.), *Nebraska symposium on motivation.* Lincoln: University of Nebraska Press, 1969.

9

Inferences about the Actions of Others: Developmental and Individual Differences in Using Social Knowledge*

W. ANDREW COLLINS

EDITORS' INTRODUCTION

The work of W. Andrew Collins on children's processing of media content has consistently provided an excellent example of work at the interface of social and developmental psychology. Individuals' social inference processes have been a continuing area of substantive research endeavors in social psychology (Harvey, Ickes, & Kidd, 1978, 1980; Harvey, Weber, Yarkin-Levin, & Stewart, 1982; Heider, 1958, Jones & Davis, 1965; Kelley, 1967, 1973). Nevertheless, for all practical purposes this literature has ignored how these processes might be affected by age-related factors of developing cognitive ability or accrued knowledge. In this chapter, Collins provides empirical information regarding age-related and individual differences in the formation of inferences about social actions and interaction as they are presented in the media (e.g., commercial television programs). Variation in children's understanding of the motives and actions of others can be interpreted meaningfully in terms of individual and age differences in knowledge, or in the use of knowledge for the retention of content and the generation of inferences regarding motives and other causal factors related to the actions of others.

*Preparation of this chapter was facilitated by PHS grant no. 24197 from the National Institute of Mental Health.

BOUNDARY AREAS IN SOCIAL
AND DEVELOPMENTAL PSYCHOLOGY

INTRODUCTION

The focus of this chapter is age-related and individual differences in making inferences about the actions of others. The particular problem of interest is the analysis of social inference processes when the stimuli are complex, quasi-natural events and persons. Simon (1976) characterized such stimuli as "ill-structured problems" because they involve multiple attentional, selective, encoding, and retrieval demands that ordinarily are carefully controlled in laboratory analogs of social inference-making. In much of the research I describe, the ill-structured task is making inferences about characters in commercial television programs. Such programs are produced with an adult audience in mind, but they attract large numbers of viewers of all ages; consequently, the characters portrayed in them are readily available social influences for children of widely varying capabilities and experience. Making inferences about these characters and their actions brings into confluence issues of socialization, social influence, and social-cognitive processes that have long existed on the boundary of social and developmental psychology. I examine the potential contributions of both developmental and social psychological analyses of these common social inferences in an attempt to understand more fully the nature and development of inferences about others and their impact on social behavior.

Social psychological and developmental considerations heretofore have largely remained separate in studies of the social role of television. Questions of socialization and social influence have dominated the literature (Collins, 1983), with little recognition that viewers of different ages, capabilities, and propensities might respond differently to content. Until recently no consideration was given to children's or adults' understanding of potentially influential televised models, despite the fact that television portrayals are considerably more complex and more subject to vagaries in comprehension than the laboratory analogues used in most research on basic social influence processes (e.g., Bandura, 1969). Although TV portrayals are somewhat better defined and more limited to specific times and places than most real-life behavior, comprehension of much televised behavior requires attentional, organizational, and inferential skills that are formidable, especially for young children.

Our research program at the University of Minnesota concerns how, within the demanding processing tasks represented by television dramatic plots, viewers of different ages make inferences about others and their actions. One tenet of our approach is that the social effects of the information conveyed by television are a function not only of what appears on the screen but of the perceptions of actors and events by viewers who differ in age-related cognitive skills and in individual and age-related experiences and knowledge for comprehending shows.

An example illustrates this point. A commonly portrayed character in many typical television dramatic programs is the double-dealer, who superficially appears benevolent but is subtly and gradually revealed to be malevolent. Preschool and young grade-school viewers may fail to comprehend the duplicity in such a portrayal. At these ages children tend to focus on isolated salient cues and in many instances may evaluate a duplicitous character's behavior more positively than the portrayal warrants. Of course, some children may be especially familiar with the types of an ambiguous character's social actions and the settings of the portrayal; and these children may be better able than others of their age to comprehend subtleties, infer causes and dispositions, and weigh apparently conflicting cues.

In this chapter I first describe some recent findings about how social inferences from complex events vary across age groups and across individuals. The variations involve differences in both *skills* and implicit strategies for processing information and in *knowledge* relevant to particular social inference tasks. Generally in developmental, cognitive, and social psychology, the emphasis has been on the former. One of my goals is to indicate a shift in current research by describing some findings in which the role of social knowledge is evident. I also suggest how the study of this aspect of processing social information might be elaborated in the study of social inferences more generally.

INFERENCES ABOUT TELEVISION CHARACTERS

My conclusions about developmental aspects of processing are based on studies of understanding dramatic plots in programs produced for adults but heavily viewed by children (e.g., action-adventure programs, family dramas, situation comedies). These programs are narratives made complicated enough to keep adult viewers interested; the particulars of the plots are often subtle, inexplicit, and interspersed with extraneous or tangentially relevant material. We focused on the extent to which children of different ages remember two kinds of information from these complex television plots: (1) *explicit events* that occur in single scenes of the shows, particularly those that are essential to the sense of the plot, in that without them the story cannot be comprehensively retold; and (2) *implicit information* that is not explicitly mentioned or depicted but is implied by the relations between the scenes. An example is the causal or enabling relation between the events portrayed in separate scenes. We were especially interested in the process of *temporal integration,* in which viewers infer the relations among discretely presented units that often occur at temporally distant points in the program.

The task of analyzing comprehension and inferences from plots begins with careful specification of the content and structure of programs. Content items and relations between them are identified in *event analyses* of program plots (Omanson, 1981; Warren, Nicholas, & Trabasso, 1979). These analyses are similar to story structure analyses in studies of prose comprehension. In contrast to analyses developed for prose narratives, however, this analysis is designed for deriving the structure of narratives, rather than fitting narrative content to predetermined idealized story structures. A list of all events from the program is then given to groups of adults, usually volunteers from community groups or undergraduate classes. They are asked to select those events without which the plot of the program could not be understandably retold. Interrater agreement on these central events ranged from .76 to .94.

A variety of procedures is used to assess children's understanding. The primary measurement technique consists of multiple-choice recognition items developed in extensive pretesting with adults and children. To make the items readily understandable by children, the wording for stems and for correct and incorrect alternatives comes from children's responses in the pretest interviews. Other techniques, such as open-ended interviews and reconstructions of sequences of still pictures taken from the program, are used when appropriate to the research question.

Developmental Patterns of Inferences and Evaluation

A number of studies of children's comprehension have now been completed using different types of television dramatic programs. In a representative study (Purdie, Collins, & Westby, 1979), we examined factors in children's understanding of cues relevant to the evaluations of the character's actions—namely, his motives for an antisocial act and the causal relations between motives and aggression. The program was an edited version of commercial network action-adventure drama. The plot involved a man searching for his former wife to prevent her from presenting damaging testimony against him in a kidnapping case. He finds the house where she is hiding and attacks with an automatic weapon, but his goal is thwarted when law officers arrest him. The main events of the plot were retained, but some extraneous material and all commercials were deleted. Two versions containing exactly the same material were created. In the *distal-motive version*, the protagonist's motives and aggression were separated from each other by a period of about 3 minutes. In the *proximal-motive version*, the motive and aggression information were presented contiguously. We then showed one of the two versions to 200 second- and fifth-grade boys and girls.

Second graders answered correctly an average of only 65% of the recognition measure items about explicit content judged by adults to be essential to understanding the plot. This proportion is significantly less than the 85% remembered by fifth graders. Furthermore, even when the younger children knew the explicit scenes required to infer implicit content, they were less likely to infer the relation between them than were fifth graders. That is, inferences about the actions of others were not an artifact of poor comprehension. These findings replicated the results of other studies of age-related patterns of comprehension (e.g., Collins, Wellman, Keniston, & Westby, 1978; Newcomb & Collins, 1979).

The manipulation of proximity of motive and aggression scenes affected children's success at inferring the relation between these cues. Both second and fifth graders in the proximal-motive condition understood the implicit motive–aggression relationship better than did children in the distal-motive condition. To determine whether the manipulation had actually facilitated inferences, we computed conditional probabilities for correct inferences, given that children answered both explicit scenes correctly, or only one, or neither one. The conditional probabilities replicate age differences we have observed in studies with a number of other types of television programs (Collins, et al., 1978; Newcomb & Collins, 1979). As in these other studies, both second and fifth graders performed at chance level when only one or neither explicit premise was known. However, the way in which cues are presented can facilitate comprehension. As Figure 9.1 shows, when children knew both requisite scenes, the probability for the second graders in the proximal-motive group was .52, while distal-motive condition second graders made correct inferences only at chance level (.29). Fifth graders' probabilities were higher and essentially equal in both viewing conditions. Thus the proximal-motive manipulations dramatically improved inference-making by younger groups whose comprehension tends to be poor under ordinary circumstances. Still, even with the advantage of a well-structured presentation, age differences persist.

How do these comprehension differences affect evaluations of the goodness or badness of the aggressor? We measured children's evaluations when they were interrupted and at the end of the program. The measurement technique was the graduated squares measure invented by Costanzo, Coie, Grumet, and Farnill (1973). It is a variation of the Likert scale, in which six size-graduated squares are labeled from "very bad" to "very good"; children point to the square that shows how good or how bad the character is. Children who answered all three motive–aggression inference questions correctly were significantly more negative in their evaluations of the aggressor than were children who understood two or fewer inferences. Whether motives and aggression were proximally or distally portrayed also affected evaluation. At both grades, distal-motive viewers evaluated the

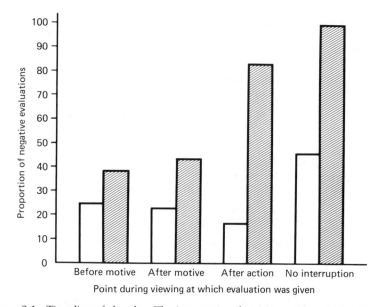

Point during viewing at which evaluation was given

Figure 9.1 Time line of the plot. The interruption design: points at which initial comprehension and evaluation measures are taken. Asterisks denote points of interruption.

characters *less* negatively than did proximal-motive viewers, particularly following portrayal of the aggressive action. Thus children's inferences about central links were correlated with evaluative responses, which in turn potentially affect adoption of observed behaviors.

In these complex stimuli, inferences about others' behavior and evaluations of the actors apparently were constrained by viewers' abilities to process the content of programs. One factor in young viewers' understanding is the structure of the social stimulus, but marked age differences also appeared in apparent benefits from the organizational characteristics of the program used in the study. Indeed, the most salient finding of research to date on children's comprehension of televised social behavior is pronounced age differences in retention of important information and inferences of the implicit content that often underlie social evaluation processes.

KNOWLEDGE AND INFERENCES

In recent years we have taken a somewhat different perspective on the problem of children's comprehension and inferences about television content. Given that younger viewers understand less than older children, we have turned our attention to what young viewers retain from viewing typical shows and how their representations of social stimuli are constructed. The gist of our findings is that besides age-related differences, representations of others' social behavior reflect differences in children's knowledge of persons, settings, and events. The question still to be answered is how prior knowledge is invoked and how it affects understanding of newly encountered persons and events.

Several leads have emerged. For example, Collins and Wellman (1982) reported analyses of data gathered to complement recognition item measures of plot comprehension. These analyses focused on what children included in their representations of the program, particularly those children whose understanding of the show was poor. In the study we interrupted two-thirds of the second-, fifth-, and eighth-grade participants at one of two points during viewing. These points had previously been agreed upon by adult raters as suspense points, or scenes after which something noteworthy was obviously going to happen. We then asked the children to predict what was going to happen next, and we coded their predictions according to whether or not they mentioned previous events from the program in explaining their answers. (We were not interested in the accuracy of their predictions.)

The majority of the fifth and eighth graders (78% and 68%, respectively) predicted events that invoked or followed from the sequence of plot events prior to interruption. Second graders rarely (28% of the cases) predicted events that followed logically from the preinterruption scenes; instead, their answers were stereotypes based on the immediately preceding scene alone and did not invoke the relation of that scene to others in the continuing narrative.

How do predictable action sequences enter into comprehension of social action? At this point we can only speculate. In constructing a representation, mature viewers may use increasingly more specialized action sequences. At one level, comprehension may be based on various standard sequences that are evoked by details of the portrayal. For example, from seeing police in uniforms even a young child may understand that the plot is a police story and could infer that police are chasing someone who is guilty of some transgression, and so forth. Thus certain types of *common knowledge* content are likely to be represented in children's understanding of portrayals at every age. On the other hand, certain variations or embellishments on these simple sequences constitute *program-specific knowledge,* or more specialized understanding that probably would occur only among older children.

Instances of these categories of content were examined in interview protocols from children who had been asked to retell the narrative "so that someone would be able to tell what happened in the show." Collins and

Wellman (1982) first had adults code content propositions into either the program-elicited common knowledge or the program-specific knowledge category (proportion of agreement was .98). We then noted the frequency with which children mentioned content from these categories in their narratives. As Table 9.1 shows, among second graders the mean proportion of children who mentioned the content that fit knowledge scripts readily known by all age groups was 81%, but the mean proportion of these younger children who mentioned the more specialized knowledge was only 16%. Fifth and eighth graders were just as likely as the younger children to mention common knowledge items, but many more fifth and eighth graders than second graders mentioned the program-specific knowledge—55% and 98% were the relevant mean proportions in fifth and eighth grades, respectively, compared to 16% for second graders. Thus generally familiar sequences of events dominated the representations of the younger viewers. These common expectations are probably the bases for children's retention of much television program material. For the participants in our study, expectations intruded on inferences about information implied in the plot and served as a basis for predictions about future behavior of the characters, even when the children had immediate information that would have been a better basis for prediction.

Developmental differences in understanding typical portrayals, then, appear to reflect an interplay between age-related skills for processing audiovisually presented social information and the nature and extent of antecedent social experiences from which different degrees and kinds of knowledge result. We did not find, as developmentalists might have expected to, evidence of different but systematic organization for younger children as compared to older children. Rather, we found evidence that children of all ages use extra program information within the limits of their familiarity with aspects of the presentation and the age-related skills with which they can employ the knowledge available to them.

TABLE 9.1

Proportions of Children who Mentioned Common Knowledge and Program Specific Contents in Retelling the Televised Narrative

Grade	Common-knowledge content				Program-specific content		
	Police	Murder	Bad guy caught	Buying groceries	Show premise	Villian's crime	Forgery
Second	9:17	12:17	15:15	16:17	2:17	3:17	1:17
Fifth	10:19	14:19	19:19	19:19	7:19	12:19	12:19
Eighth	3:14	12:14	12:14	14:14	13:14	14:14	14:14

This interaction of knowledge and processing skills is often manifested in interesting variations in comprehension *within* as well as *between* age groups. Within-group differences are particularly likely among younger viewers, whose comprehension of the narrative sense of programs is often poor. For example, Newcomb & Collins (1979) reported individual differences in second graders' understanding of persons, events, and causes in narratives as a function of differential familiarity with the types of persons and settings portrayed. The experiments involved equal numbers of children from both lower-socioeconomic and middle-socioeconomic status (SES) samples at Grades 2, 5, and 8. Half of the children—including all of these subgroups—viewed an edited version of a commercial network show featuring middle-class characters. The other half saw a show with a similar plot line featuring lower-class characters. The children were tested for understanding of the events, the inferred causes of action, and the emotion of the characters.

The children performed best when the social group milieu portrayed in the show was the same level as their own social group background. Middle-SES second-graders who viewed the middle-class show inferred more about the causes of actions and feelings and emotions of the characters than did lower-SES youngsters who watched middle-class shows; and lower-SES youngsters who watched the lower-class-character show inferred more of the same kind of information from that show than did the middle-SES children who watched the lower-class show. Fifth- and eighth-grade viewers did not show social group differences. Younger children's general comprehension difficulty, which may be partly attributed to developmental factors, was most evident when they did not have the advantage of familiarity with characters and settings. Despite the salutary effects of pertinent social experience, however, even the best-performing second graders were still significantly poorer than fifth and eighth graders.

Both age-related cognitive skills and the social experiences in which general and specific knowledge is accumulated are thus important to children's social inferences in television-viewing. Their predictive value results not just from their correlations with behavioral tendencies and motivations, however. Skills and social experiences are also pertinent because they determine the bases of knowledge that affect the processing of newly encountered social stimuli.

KNOWLEDGE AND ITS USE

At present we have few leads on how and under what conditions preexisting knowledge enters into inferences about complex observed behavior.

Several possibilities occur readily, of course. Perhaps young viewers' relatively lower level of knowledge simply impairs all aspects of processing new instances for which the knowledge is relevant. This *knowledge-deficiency view* is a simple but unparsimonious account of young viewers' age-related comprehension difficulties. An alternative, but compatible, *application-deficiency view* implies that even when young children have information that should facilitate comprehension, they may apply it less flexibly than do older children. Once information has been instantiated by salient cues (for example, the label "police" for seeing uniformed characters), younger children may behave as though the program simply follows a standard, preset sequence of events that is familiar to them. As a result, they may fail to notice—or may ignore—ways in which the program varies from familiar sequences. Consequently, explicit and implicit details of observed events may be short-circuited by rigid expectations about actors and actions. More mature, more knowledgeable viewers may be more likely to recognize the significance of departures from expected sequences and to process them as significant aspects of stories.

This hypothesis has received suggestive support in a study of children's moral judgments of television characters (Collins & Westby, 1981). Most studies of moral judgment involve laboratory studies of reactions to brief stories. The basic assumption behind this research is that moral judgments about characters depend on comprehension and weighting of information about motives and consequences of their action. Television dramas, however, include numerous evaluation-relevant cues presented less explicitly and in a more complex content than the simple stories used in most moral judgment research. In the study cited, we used an interruption procedure to trace evaluations over the course of viewing a program. We then examined the emerging evaluations in relation to comprehension of evaluation-relevant cues. This strategy involved interrupting subgroups of children at different points in the course of viewing to test their understanding. A diagram of the procedure appears in Figure 9.1. In one group children were interrupted before the scenes in which motive for the aggression action was portrayed (before-motive group); in the second group interruption was immediately after the motive scene but before the aggression (after-motive group); and in the third group viewing was halted just after the aggressive action (after-action group). All of these children were tested on the content of the program up to the point of interruption and then were tested on the remainder of the program when it was over. A fourth group saw the program without interruption.

The stimulus was the program described earlier in which a kidnapping suspect searches for his wife to prevent her from testifying against him. We interrupted 88 second- and fifth-grade boys and girls at one of the four interruption points and asked them to evaluate the goodness or badness of the character. We also tested their comprehension of the program up to that point using a recognition item measure similar to the one described earlier.

We found the usual age differences in comprehension between second and fifth graders and similar grade-level differences in the degree to which children evaluated the antisocial character as bad. Especially pertinent are the patterns of evaluation that emerged from the beginning to the end of the program. As Figure 9.2 shows, second graders typically gave negative evaluations only after seeing consequences, whereas fifth graders' evaluations were generally negative at earlier points in the program. At the first two interruption points, second and fifth graders' evaluations did not differ significantly from each other and were generally positive. Only 25% of the second graders and 40% of the fifth graders gave negative evaluations after these early scenes. Later, following the aggressive action, fifth graders' evaluations wre overwhelmingly negative (83%), whereas the proportion of second graders giving negative evaluations did not change. Only at the end of the program, after the protagonist had been arrested by the police, did the proportion of second graders evaluating him negatively increase significantly, and then only to 46%.

Why did some second graders eventually change from positive to negative evaluations of the protagonist when others did not? Because final evaluations were not contaminated by the comprehension and evaluation questions earlier in the program, we examined this question in a within-subject analysis. Second graders whose evaluations were positive both during and after the program (nonchangers) were compared to those whose evaluations were initially positive but became negative at the end (changers). Changers and nonchangers were not different in comprehension of the motive scene or of aggressive action alone, but changers did understand the implicit causal links among motives, actions, and consequences scenes better than did nonchangers. Thus evaluation differences among second graders were associated with differences in understanding the aggressive action in terms

Condition			
I. Before-motive group:	°Motive portrayal	Aggressive action	Consequences
II. Before-action group:	Motive portrayal	°Aggressive action	Consequences
III. After-action group:	Motive portrayal	Aggressive action	°Consequences
IV. No interruption group:	Motive portrayal	Aggressive action	Consequences°

Figure 9.2 Proportion of second and fifth graders who evaluated antisocial character as negative at different points in viewing of an action-adventure program. Open bar represents second graders; hatched bar represents fifth graders.

of the motive scenes. These differences among second graders in comprehension of the important later scenes in the show are not attributable to differences in verbal ability, which we had controlled in covariance analyses. Nor was there a tendency for nonchangers to pick up less information from the program generally; nonchangers actually scored higher than changers on recognition of content that was presented early in the program but that was unrelated to the character's motives.

Although this study was not designed to yield a definitive explanation for the changer–nonchanger differences, one possibility may lie in changers' and nonchangers' contrasting formation and application of knowledge about the character's behavior. For example, changers and nonchangers gave markedly different reasons for their initial evaluations (coded as either positive or negative; interrater agreement = 0.94). Although participants interrupted before the motive scene gave uniformly positive evaluations, 75% of those who *remained* positive explicitly justified their initial judgments with detailed, but incorrect, positive interpretations of ambiguous events occurring early in the program (i.e., "He is trying to help the girl." or "He is trying to find her so she won't be scared."). By contrast, children who eventually changed their evaluations typically gave initially noncommittal answers (80%), often indicating that they did not have a reason for their evaluations. After the program, nonchangers continued to explain evaluations in terms of the positive interpretation of early cues (83%), whereas changers focused the negative motives or action (73%).

Thus although both changers' and nonchangers' evaluations were initially positive, the two groups may have differed in selection and retention of plot information as a function of the explicitness of their early-instantiated expectations about the actor. Nonchangers' initial positive perceptions may have facilitated their retention of plot events, much as social prototypes or schemata have been found to affect memory for social information (e.g., Hastie, 1981; Schneider, Hastorf, & Ellsworth, 1980); but detailed initial expectations may well have interfered with their recognition of the negative implications of the consequences. By contrast, changers' less explicit initial expectations probably did not facilitate overall comprehension but may have permitted assimilation of later negative cues.

Differences among children in response to sequences of cues about an actor's behavior point to the need for closer analyses of what viewers *do* when they encounter new instances of others' behavior. This need can be met partly by careful analyses of social stimuli under conditions in which the knowledge and motivations that underlie particular responses are controlled. However, we also need to understand better the motivations and knowledge that are likely to be elicited in social perception tasks outside the laboratory, and we need to know more about how such motivations and knowledge then guide subsequent responses. For example, the moral judgment findings described earlier would be illuminated by information about children's usual expectations about "good guys" in shows and their predictions about event sequences that begin as do the instances in the program. Perhaps the differences between changers and nonchangers depend on the extent to which such expectations are initially well formed or the extent to which only one (as compared to several) alternative sequence or event chain is envisioned. These possibilities cannot be examined adequately without methods for specifying pre-viewing knowledge.

ASSESSING KNOWLEDGE

Assessing what children—or adults—*know* or *expect* relevant to a stimulus presents a set of methodological problems and issues that by and large have not been addressed in developmental, cognitive, and social psychology. Knowledge and its use has been of less interest than use per se. Although social cognition has interested developmental psychologists for at least 15 years, the extant research mostly addresses issues suggested by cognitive-developmental theories, rather than social–behavioral analyses of children in context. To be sure, the topics of interest have concerned persons—what they perceive, how they feel, what they know, whether they are good or bad or naughty or nice. However, tasks have typically been selected for their analogy to the tasks used by cognitive-developmental researchers to study objects other than social ones. Consequently, the research has been pertinent theoretically, but with few exceptions it has concerned a restricted set of social inference tasks that give a limited view of the skills that may be required of children in social life.

An important set of psychological problems in analyzing social inferences that are more typical of children's common experiences involves the knowledge that is likely to be elicited in a situation, and how it is used once elicited. In terms of television research, several questions emerge about children's understanding of a particular program: What knowledge is relevant? How is it brought into play during viewing? What effects do different levels and forms of knowledge have on such socially pertinent outcomes as attributions, evaluations, predictions about future behavior, and judgments about self-relevance? The answers to these questions are likely to depend not only on skills and strategies available to children but on what individuals know, expect, and feel as a function of age, individual experiences, or the demographic characteristics that constitute their "social addresses" (Bronfenbrenner, 1981).

Typically, however, knowledge has been treated either as error variance or as a variable to be manipulated (e.g., Bransford & Nitsch, 1978). For example, Trabasso (Trabasso, 1975), in well-known research on transitivity, controlled knowledge levels relevant to their tasks by carefully training subjects on the elements involved in order to reduce the sources of error that masked logical competence. Their long train of successors in developmental studies have similarly focused on procedural competence rather than performance (including knowledge relevant to solving ordinarily complex problems). What one does with regard to the factor of knowledge depends on one's research goals, of course; that is why Bryant and Trabasso's experiment—like the efforts of other experimentalists interested in the use of knowledge—earns our admiration. The problem remains: How can we independently assess the states and expectations in the viewer that are relevant to comprehension and/or responses to new instances of social information? At this point, we can only raise some pragmatic considerations about how this might be accomplished.

First, it is clear that a range of types of knowledge will need to be assessed. The knowledge category of particular interest will, of course, depend on the goals of a study. But at least for the present, it is important to sample knowledge relevant to a particular social stimulus as broadly as possible— knowledge about persons, situations, interaction, events, and so forth—in order to be able to examine different possible ways in which knowledge enters into understanding.

Next, in deciding how to assess knowledge relevant to a given stimulus, we can take some leads from the precedent literature, particularly the literature of cognitive social psychology. It is possible to propose several categories of knowledge that have been implied or assumed in studies of specific memory and inference phenomena and that may be considered potential factors in inferences about others' behavior. Obviously, when applied to complex actions and situations, these categories may often be overlapping and interrelated, rather than distinct, as they are in typical experimental analyses. At this point, however, problems of overlap are outweighed by the need to begin to assess independently the implicit knowledge viewers bring to their perceptions of social situations and behavior.

The following list shows several general categories of knowledge as a starting point.

1. Task-specific knowledge
   a. Familiarity with elements or attributes
   b. Behavioral norms
   c. Usual contingencies, constraints, sequences
2. General knowledge
   a. About sequences of events or actions
   b. About attributes of persons and their relationships, etc.

      i. Interpersonal relations
     ii. Intrapersonal correlations among traits
    iii. Common goals or purposes
  c. About causal and other relational rules

It is helpful to make a fundamental distinction between *general knowledge,* or "world" knowledge, and *task-specific knowledge* pertinent to particular domains of behavior or particular sets of circumstances. For example, when assessing knowledge relevant to a particular social stimulus, it makes sense to assess the following: (1) awareness of, or familiarity with, the elements or attributes of particular situations; (2) behavioral norms that may apply to such situations or to particular actors; and (3) *usual* consequences, contingencies, or constraints that are assumed to operate for an actor or for a situation. Many of these task-specific knowledge considerations have been used in previous research primarily to control for sources of variance that are not of particular interest—for example, in the Trabasso (Trabasso, 1975) study, in which familiarity with elements or attributes was a major concern. Task-specific knowledge is interesting in its own right, however. In their classic work on human information-processing, Newell and Simon (1973) investigated the role of knowledge of chess and other topics in processing information in new instances. Chi (1978) attempted similar analyses with children. Their work is a good example of what can be gained from carefully specifying links between the structure of knowledge and the nature of cognitive tasks.

It is possible that domain or task-specific influences are so great that more *general knowledge* should also be assessed in terms of the domain of behavior or settings in question. However, by general social knowledge I do not mean peculiarities or particulars of behavior patterns within given frames or settings. In all cases, general knowledge relevant to particular topics is much more abstract, nonspecific, and asituational than is the knowledge of particular domains. Furthermore, general social knowledge in the categories referred to here is not necessarily veridical; rather, general knowledge includes viewers' subjectively held beliefs or expectations about persons, behavior, and events.

A reasonable approach to characterizing knowledge relevant to particular instances of behavior is to draw from three categories of knowledge that are being examined extensively:

1. Knowledge about sequences of events or action—what Schank and Abelson (1977) and Bower (Bower, Black, & Turner, 1979) call *scripts.*
2. Knowledge about attributes of persons and their relationships. In this category we include (*a*) schemas of *interpersonal relations,* in the sense that Kuethe (1962) used the term; (*b*) assumptions about *intrapersonal correla-*

tions among traits, as naive personality theorists (Schneider, 1973) have described them (this subcategory also includes stereotypes and personality "types," as described by prototype theorists like Cantor and Mischel [1979; Cantor, Mischel, & Schwartz, 1982]); and (*c*) assessing knowledge of *common goals* of others (Sedlak, 1979), which is important in many instances. A number of theorists (e.g., Schmidt, 1976) have argued that comprehension of action depends on some recognition of an actor's goals and plans for achieving them. In many cases, it is reasonable to assess the extent to which subjects know generally about goals of the types represented in stimuli and can apply their knowledge to instances like the ones depicted. Like the other types of general knowledge, knowledge of generic goals can probably be assessed most usefully in terms of the particular type situation or scenario associated with a stimulus.

3.Knowledge of causal and other relational rules for inferring connections among actors and settings. Examples are Kelley's (1973) causal schemata or Jones and Davis's (1965) rules of correspondence. This type of knowledge involves the conditions under which causation or behavioral dispositions are to be inferred. This latter category especially raises the distinction between "declarative" and "procedural" knowledge suggested by Winograd (1979). Although causal and other relational rules tell us more about knowing *how* than knowing *what*, they nevertheless function as knowledge in the sense that they constitute tendencies that seem to be applied fairly automatically in perceiving newly encountered instances of behavior.

Although this list is neither exhaustive nor conceptually novel, it does cover a range of intuitively important types of knowledge. Furthermore, at least some information has been accumulated about how to assess the categories and what relationships to expect between them, characteristics of the stimulus and the particular outcomes of interest in a particular study. One way to think about *assessing* knowledge is to consider variants of the tasks currently being used in laboratory experiments to assess the *effects* of particular types of social knowledge or social structure on processing of new information. For example, the false recognition paradigm (see Collins *et al.*, 1978; Hastie, 1981) can be used in connection with "skeleton," or brief, related scenarios prior to exposure to a particular stimulus to assess common expectations about persons or events. Assumptions about traits, given minimal information about a person, are another indicator of preexisting knowledge. Similarly, getting predictions of behavior or event sequences, given an initial event or a very general descriptor term, is a useful technique, as work on assessing knowledge of scripts has indicated (Bower, Black, & Turner, 1979). Although these strategies must be considered idiographic approaches to assessment, they represent a reasonable first step toward a more careful examination of the nature and role of knowledge in social perception and inferences.

Some Pitfalls in Knowledge Assessment

In adopting these strategies, however, there are certain pitfalls to be considered. The first is how the knowledge pertinent to a stimulus can be assessed independent of the content of that stimulus and of the outcomes of exposure to it. Unless we can achieve this independence of measurement, of course, we risk tautology. The extent to which studies are vulnerable to this charge depends on the extent of similarity between preexposure and dependent assessments of knowledge. It will be important to consider the array of assessment methods available and to minimize artifactual or confounded results.

In addition, techniques must be chosen that assure that the knowledge being assessed is pertinent to the social inference task under study. The most prudent strategy is probably to work backwards to preexposure assessment of knowledge from careful analysis of the stimulus and also from the choice of outcome measures to which one wants to predict. Given the variety of tasks already being used in the literature, it should be possible to make judicious links among the preexposure assessment, the characteristics of stimuli and outcomes—whether cognitive, evaluative, or behavioral.

CONCLUDING REMARKS

A complete view of the perceiver's role in inferences about others' behavior requires a more detailed process model than I have attempted here. At best, I have suggested a set of considerations for assessing the knowledge that observers bring to the observation of others' behavior. These considerations may serve as precursors of a badly needed model that would eventually allow us to make judicious predictions about the effects of different types or categories of knowledge on inferences and judgments about particular types of observed behavior. Several attempts have been made to formulate a model of the use of social knowledge; for example, both Hastie and Carlston (1980) and Wyer and Srull (1980) proposed processing models that acknowledge the role of more or less specific knowledge. At present, however, the most pressing issue is how knowledge will be specified and addressed. The developmental and individual differences observed in children's understanding and inferences about television characters and their action suggest that further analyses of the role of knowledge is a worthwhile and potentially fruitful endeavor to be undertaken at the boundary of developmental and social psychology.

REFERENCES

Bandura, A. Social-learning theory of identificatory processes. In D. Goslin (Ed.), *Handbook of socialization theory and research*. Chicago: Rand McNally, 1969.

Bower, G. H., Black, J. B., & Turner, T. J. Scripts in memory for text. *Cognitive Psychology, 1979, 11,* 117–220.

Bransford, J., & Nitsch, K. Coming to understand things we could not previously understand. In J. Kavanaugh & W. Strange (Eds.), *Speech and language in the laboratory, school, and clinic*. Cambridge, MA: MIT Press, 1978.

Bronfenbrenner, U. *Developmental processes in social context: Research perspectives*. Paper presented at a conference on Boundary Areas in Psychology: Developmental and Social Psychology. Nashville, TN: Vanderbilt University, June 1981.

Cantor, N., & Mischel, W. Prototypes in person perception. In L. Berkowitz (Ed.), *Advances in experimental social psychology* (Vol. 12). New York: Academic, 1979.

Cantor, N., Mischel, W., & Schwartz, J. Social knowledge: Structure, content, use, and abuse. In A. Hastorf & A. Isen (Eds.), *Cognitive social psychology*. New York: Elsevier, 1982.

Chi, M. Knowledge structures and memory development. In R. Siegler (Ed.), *Children's thinking: What develops?* Hillsdale, NJ: Erlbaum, 1978.

Collins, W. A. Social antecedents, cognitive processing, and comprehension of social portrayals on television. In E. T. Higgins, D. Ruble, & W. Hartup (Eds.), *Developmental social cognition: A sociocultural perspective*. New York: Cambridge University Press, 1983.

Collins, W. A., & Wellman, H. Social scripts and developmental changes in representations of televised narratives. *Communication Research, 1982, 9,* 380–398.

Collins, W. A., Wellman, H., Keniston, A., & Westby, S. Age-related aspects of comprehension of televised social content. *Child Development, 1978, 49,* 389–399.

Collins, W. A., & Westby, S. *Moral judgments of TV characters as a function of program comprehension*. Paper presented at the biennial meeting of the Society for Research in Child Development, Boston, April 1981.

Costanzo, P. R., Coie, J. D., Grumet, J. F., & Farnill, D. A reexamination of the effects of intent and consequence on children's moral judgments. *Child Development, 1973, 44,* 154–161.

Harvey, J. H., Ickes, W. J., & Kidd, R. F. (Eds.). *New directions in attribution research* (Vol. 2). Hillsdale, NJ: Erlbaum, 1978.

Harvex, J. H., Weber, A., Yarkin-Levin, K., & Stewart, B. An Attributional approach to relationship breakdown and dissolution. In S. Duck (Ed.), *Personal relationshps* (Vol. 4): *Dissolving personal relationships*. London Academic, 1982.

Hastie, R. Schematic principles in human memory. In E. T. Higgins, C. Sherman, & M. Zanna (Eds.), *The Ontario symposium on personality and social psychology: Social cognition*. Hillsdale, NJ: Erlbaum, 1981.

Hastie, R., & Carlston, D. Theoretical issues in person memory. In R. Hastie, T. Ostrom, E. Ebbesen, R. Wyer, D. Hamilton, & D. Carlston (Eds.), *Person memory: The cognitive basis of social perception*. Hillsdale, NJ: Erlbaum, 1980.

Heider, F. *The psychology of interpersonal relationships*. New York: Wiley, 1958.

Jones, E. E., & Davis, K. From acts to dispositions: The attribution process in person perception. In L. Berkowitz (Ed.), *Advances in experimental social psychology* (Vol. 2). New York: Academic, 1965.

Kelley, H. Attribution theory in social psychology. In D. Levine (Ed.), *Nebraska symposium on Motivation*. Lincoln: University of Nebraska Press, 1967, 192–238.

Kelley, H. The process of causal attribution. *American Psychologist*, 1973, *28*, 107–128.

Kuethe, J. Social schemas. *Journal of Abnormal and Social Psychology*, 1962, *64*, 31–38.

Newcomb, A. F., & Collins, W. A. Children's comprehension of family role portrayals in televised dramas: Effects of socioeconomic status, ethnicity, and age. *Developmental Psychology*, 1979, *15*(4), 417–423.

Newell, A., & Simon, H. *Human problem solving*. Englewood Cliffs, NJ: Prentice-Hall, 1973.

Omanson, R. An analysis of narratives: Identifying central, supportive, and distracting content. *Discourse Processes*, 1981.

Purdie, S., Collins, W. A., & Westby, S. *Children's processing of motive information in a televised portrayal*. Unpublished manuscript, Institute of Child Development, University of Minnesota, 1979.

Schank, R., & Abelson, R. *Scripts, plans, goals, and understanding*. Hillsdale, NJ: Erlbaum, 1977.

Schmidt, C. Understanding human action: Recognizing the plans and motives of other persons. In J. Carroll & J. Payne (Eds.), *Cognition and social behavior*. Hillsdale, NJ: Erlbaum, 1976.

Schneider, D. Implicit personality theory: A review. *Psychological Bulletin*, 1973, *79*, 294–309.

Schneider, D., Hastorf, A., & Ellsworth, P. *Person perception* (2nd ed.). Reading, MA: Addison-Wesley, 1980.

Sedlak, A. Developmental differences in understanding plans and evaluating actors. *Child Development*, 1979, *50*, 536–560.

Simon, H. Cognition and social behavior. In J. Carroll & J. Payne (Eds.), *Cognition and social behavior*. Hillsdale, NJ: Erlbaum, 1976.

Trabasso, T. Representation, memory and reasoning: How do we make transitive inferences? In A. Pick (Ed.), *Minnesota symposia on child psychology* (Vol. 9). Minneapolis: University of Minnesota Press, 1975.

Warren, W., Nicholas, D., & Trabasso, T. Event chains and inferences in understanding narratives. In R. Freedle (Ed.), *Advances in discourse processes* (Vol. 2). Hillsdale, NJ: Erlbaum, 1979.

Winograd, T. Computer memories: A metaphor for memory organization. In C. N. Cofer (Ed.), *The structure of human memory*. San Francisco: Freeman, 1979.

Wyer, R., & Srull, T. The processing of social stimulus information: A conceptual integration. In R. Hastie, T. Ostrom, E. Ebbesen, R. Wyer, D. Hamilton, & D. Carlston (Eds.), *Person memory: The cognitive basis of social perception*. Hillsdale, NJ: Erlbaum, 1980. 227–294.

10

A Distinction between Two Types of Relationships and Its Implications for Development*

MARGARET S. CLARK

EDITORS' INTRODUCTION

In this chapter Margaret Clark draws an important distinction between two types of social relationships—communal (in which members feel a special obligation to be responsive to one another) and exchange (in which members do not feel an obligation to be mutually responsive). A point made by other chapters in this volume (e.g., Gottman & Levenson, Chapter 4) but especially strongly here is that relationships have their own developmental history, and in this case it is argued that different types of relationships may develop in different ways. More important, however, Clark discusses how different types of relationships may involve different norms for what constitutes fair treatment, something that may allow sensible interpretation of what otherwise appear to be incompatible findings, but that has not been taken into account in developmental studies of children's interpersonal relationships. The research presented by Clark also illustrates new variables that may be crucial to the understanding of how norms develop that govern relationships. Finally, she suggests some new methodologies for studying children's conceptions of fairness and considers some limitations in

*Preparation of this chapter and a portion of the research reviewed was supported by National Institute of Mental Health grant no. R-03 MH35844-01. I thank Tom Berndt for his helpful comments on an earlier version of this chapter.

BOUNDARY AREAS IN SOCIAL
AND DEVELOPMENTAL PSYCHOLOGY

*generalizability for findings that have been reported in the developmental litera-
ture. Overall, this chapter presents a strong argument for the necessity of integrating social and developmental theory and method in the study of interpersonal
relationships among children or adults.*

INTRODUCTION

This chapter focuses on social relationships and the norms governing
behavior in those relationships. Investigations of norms governing behavior
in social relationships have long been of interest to researchers in both social
and developmental psychology. However, this chapter differs from most
previous work on fairness in both fields in focusing on *distinguishing* the
norms that apply to different types of relationships.

To be more specific, a distinction between two types of relationships—
communal and exchange—and the norms that apply to each is drawn. Then
a program of research supporting the distinction is reviewed. This research
was done entirely with adults.

Following the description of existing work on communal and exchange
relationships, I make a case that such research can make a contribution to
understanding the development of children's concepts of fairness and thus is
quite relevant to this volume on the interface between developmental and
social psychology. It can make a contribution for two reasons. First, it
suggests some potentially fruitful new areas for research on the development
of fairness concepts. To date, developmental researchers interested in standards of fairness have tended to focus on just one standard of fairness and to
look for just one sequence of stages through which children's understanding
of fairness progresses (e.g., Hook & Cook, 1979). In the present chapter I
suggest that there is probably not just one sequence of stages through which
children's judgments of fairness pass. Rather, children must learn to distinguish between types of relationships and must acquire the appropriate
standards that apply to each. Thus it may prove fruitful to study how
children make such distinctions and how they acquire communal and exchange norms. Second, this distinction may make a contribution to developmental psychology because it suggests that conflicting claims developmental
researchers have made as to the standards of fairness children will use at
different ages may simply be due to different researchers having chosen to
study different types of relationships.

I am, however, getting ahead of myself. I turn now to a review of the
distinction between communal and exchange relationships and to research
supporting that distinction. This review comprises the bulk of the chapter.
Following the review I return to my argument that the distinction has

important implications for developmental research on children's understanding of fairness.

A DISTINCTION BETWEEN TWO TYPES
OF RELATIONSHIPS

Recently I, along with Mills, drew a distinction between communal and exchange relationships (Clark & Mills, 1979; Clark, 1981; Mills & Clark, 1982).[1] These relationships differ from one another in many ways. Perhaps the most important and basic difference is that in communal relationships, members feel a special obligation to be responsive to one another's needs, whereas in exchange relationships they do not. On the other hand, in exchange but not in communal relationships, members are responsible for benefiting the others in response to specific benefits received from the others, and they benefit one another with the expectation of receiving a comparable benefit in return. The relationships between kin, romantic partners, and friends often exemplify communal relations. The relationships between people in business or between two acquaintances often exemplify exchange relationships.

DETERMINANTS OF A DESIRE FOR A COMMUNAL
OR AN EXCHANGE RELATIONSHIP

When will a person apply communal norms to a relationship, and when will a person apply exchange norms? Consider communal norms first. Our culture dictates that people should apply communal norms to relationships with members of their family. Whether or not they apply communal norms to their other relationships seems to depend on several factors: the general attractiveness of the other and oneself, the availability of the person and of the other for a communal relationship, and whether the person and other can fulfill each other's needs—especially needs left unmet by other communal relationships.

[1]In virtually all relationships, benefits are exchanged in a broad sense—that is, members give one another benefits (see Graziano, Chapter 7, this volume.) However, the term *exchange* is used in a narrower sense here to refer to a type of relationship in which the giving of a benefit creates a specific obligation on the part of the recipient to return a comparable benefit. At this point it should also be noted that throughout the paper the term benefit is used to refer to something of value that one person in a relationship intentionally gives to the other. This excludes many rewards which a person may derive from a relationship such as pride in the existence of the relationship itself which the person's partner did not intentionally give to the person.

First, consider the attractiveness of the other. Forming a relationship in which each person expects to be responsive to the other's needs involves an expectation that the relationship will endure for some time (Mills & Clark, 1982). Furthermore, at least to some extent, it involves letting another respond to your needs *and* attending to that other's needs. Finally, people in a communal relationship are likely to be perceived as a unit by outsiders, and one person's attributes may reflect on the other (see, for example, Sigall & Landy, 1973). Consequently, it should come as no surprise that the more generally attractive the other is—whether physically, in terms of personality, intelligence, or whatever—the more willing people seem to be to form a communal relationship with that other. In addition, a person's *own* attractiveness relative to that of the other may affect whether or not the person expects the other to pursue a communal relationship and consequently whether the person will attempt to form such a relationship with that other. The latter idea has been expressed before by Berscheid, Dion, Walster, and Walster (1971), who noted that people choose others for romantic relationships who "match" themselves in terms of physical attractiveness (although here I would include other types of attractiveness—for example, of personality—and other types of communal relationships, such as friends).

Next, consider the availability of the person for a communal relationship. The number of communal relationships a person will be comfortable having has an upper limit. Although communal relationships provide people with a sense of security, given that the other has an implicit responsibility for the person's needs, they also carry an obligation for one to be responsive to the other's needs. Thus having too many of these relationships will seem burdensome. Further, given a certain number of communal relationships, adding more will not increase the person's sense of security by much. Thus if all else is equal, the more communal relationships a person already has, the less likely that person will be to desire a communal relationship with a new person. For example, if a person had five friends, that person should be less interested in forming a friendship with a sixth person than should a person who is new in town and has no local friends. Similarly, the availability of the *other* for a communal relationship will affect the probability of a person attempting to form a communal relationship. The more communal relationships the other has, the less likely that other will be to desire a communal relationship.

Finally, holding constant attractiveness and the number of communal relationships a person and other already have, the better able two people are to fulfill one another's needs, the more likely they may be to form a communal relationship. Furthermore, people may be especially anxious to form communal relationships with each other when they can fulfill needs left unfilled by other communal relations. Imagine, for example, a writer who has many friends and kin but who knows no other writers who could understand and be sympathetic to his or her frustrations with writing. Such a person might be especially anxious to form a communal relation with a new writer in town, because that writer could fulfill needs left unfulfilled by other communal relationships. This may be one reason why similarity is associated with friendship formation.

Next, consider when people form exchange relationships with one another. Cultural factors dictate that people apply exchange norms to relationships with people with whom they do business. Furthermore, as was the case with communal norms, they may choose to apply exchange norms to other relationships as well. There are many benefits of value to us that our communal relations either cannot provide at all or cannot provide as easily or as expertly as others. There are other times when we perceive that if people with whom we have communal relationships provided for our needs, that would interfere with their *own* needs (Clark, 1983). Under such circumstances, we turn to others who have the resources we need and with whom we can establish implicit or explicit agreements to exchange comparable benefits. Thus one may call a plasterer to fix one's wall for pay, or one may accept help from an acquaintance with the expectation of repaying him or her with a comparable benefit. These are exchange relationships.

Now that some of the conditions affecting when people will form communal and exchange relationships with others have been specified, consider several characteristics that seem to differentiate communal from exchange relationships.

When Benefits Are Given

As already noted, in communal relationships a norm exists to give benefits when the other has a need for them. Benefits are also appropriately given when something can be provided that would be particularly pleasing to the other. Such behavior conveys one's special concern for the other. Parents, for instance, often do such things as help their children with their homework, comfort them when they are feeling down, or surprise them with gifts that suit the children's preferences. People with whom we have communal relationships expect to be benefited in response to their needs. They react positively when they receive such benefits and negatively when the benefits are not forthcoming.

The general obligation members of communal relationships have to benefit one another when needs arise is not altered by receipt of a specific benefit (Mills & Clark, 1982). In other words, when one member of a communal relationship provides another with a benefit, the two people's general obligation to be responsive to one another's needs is not altered.

In contrast to communal relationships, in exchange relationships benefits are given when one person owes the other for a benefit received, or they are given with the expectation of receiving a comparable benefit in return. Recipients of benefits in exchange relationships expect to repay the other for specific benefits and know the other expects to be repaid for benefits as well. If benefits are not repaid, negative feelings result on the part of both the person owed and the debtor.

Members of exchange relationships do not have a special obligation to fulfill the other's needs.[2] They presumably keep track of the benefits given and received to ensure that the norms for this type of relationship are being followed (Clark, 1981; Mills & Clark, 1982).

Comparability and Timing of Benefits Given and Received

Members of exchange relationships should tend to give and receive comparable benefits. Returning a benefit that is comparable to a benefit received makes it clear that the debt created by that prior benefit has been eliminated. Members of exchange relationships should also tend to return benefits (or promise to return benefits) very soon after having received a benefit. The sooner a debt is eliminated, the better. In contrast, members of communal relationships may often give and receive *noncomparable* benefits. This should happen in part because they need not be concerned with fulfilling specific debts, and in part because two people's needs and preferences are rarely the same. In addition, members of communal relationships may actually *avoid* giving a benefit soon after receiving a benefit if the other has no need for the benefit or if a suitable occasion has not arisen. To do so may imply a preference for an exchange relationship (Clark & Mills, 1979; Mills & Clark, 1982).

Variability in Strength of Relationships

Communal relationships may vary in strength (Mills & Clark, 1982). A communal relationship with one's child may be stronger than a communal relationship with a friend. Therefore the needs of the child may take precedence over the needs of the friend. In a case in which the friend's needs are being neglected because the person has to attend to the needs of the child, the friend should understand and no negative feelings should result toward

[2]However, as Schwartz (1975) noted, people tend to have some feelings of social concern for any other person, and I do not disagree. As Mills and Clark (1982) noted, people have very weak communal relations with most other people.

the person. In other words, one could specify a hierarchy in terms of strengths, for any one person's communal relationships. There may, of course, be instances in which a person and another with whom he or she has a communal relationship disagree about what the person's hierarchy of communal relationships *should* be. Such disagreements may lead to conflict. For instance, a woman might consider her parents' needs to be more important than those of her spouse, whereas her husband believes his needs come first. When the parents and husband have needs that arise at the same time and the woman responds to the parents, arguments may arise.

Unlike communal relationships, exchange relationships do not vary in strength. If we have debts to six people, we cannot excuse those debts by saying that we have sufficient resources to fulfill only one. This is not to say that people never find themselves in a position in which they must fulfill debts to one person with whom they have an exchange relationship and leave others hanging. Rather, it means that doing so is not condoned by anyone involved. Those people who are not repaid will be resentful and the person who has not repaid them will probably feel guilty. This follows from equity theory (e.g., Walster, Walster, & Berscheid, 1978).

Certainty about Relationships

People's certainty about having either a communal or an exchange relationship with another may also vary (Mills & Clark, 1982). For instance, after meeting a new roommate in college for the first time, a person may desire a communal relationship with that person. However, the person may be uncertain about whether the roommate desires the same kind of relationship and therefore uncertain about whether to characterize their relationship as communal or exchange. Later, after both people have followed communal norms in their relationship for a month, certainty should be much higher.

Certainty about exchange relationships may also vary. A man might ask a neighborhood child to shovel the snow from his walk while he is away for a month. The child may agree, thinking at the time that he or she will be paid. However, after the man leaves without having mentioned payment, the child may wonder whether the relationship really is an exchange relationship. Will the man actually give him or her something in exchange for the snow shoveling? Perhaps the man thinks they have a communal relationship and simply expects the service because he needs it. Or perhaps the man is thinking in neither communal nor exchange terms and intends to exploit the child. In such a case uncertainty is high. If, on the other hand, the child had shoveled the man's walk many times in the past and had always been paid, certainty about the exchange nature of the relationship would be much higher.

Do People *Always* Follow Either Communal or Exchange Norms with a Given Other?

What has been said thus far might be taken to imply that our relationship with any given other is either a communal or an exchange relationship and that we always follow communal or exchange norms when interacting with that other. I do not mean to imply this. Relationships that are neither communal nor exchange exist (Mills & Clark, 1982). Furthermore, it is possible to have both a communal and an exchange relationship with the same other depending on the situation (Mills & Clark, 1982). Finally, there are situations in which, even in our predominantly communal or exchange relationships, neither communal nor exchange rules apply.

Consider first the point that types of relationships other than communal and exchange relationships exist. One example of another type of relationship is an exploitive relationship (Mills & Clark, 1982). In an exploitive relationship, the person in power is not concerned with the other's needs, as would be the case in communal relations, nor is he or she concerned with repaying the other for benefits received from that other, as would be the case in an exchange relationship. Instead, the person in power is concerned with maximizing his or her benefits and the other is concerned with avoiding the potential negative consequences of the person's power.

Next, consider the point that one may have both a communal and an exchange relationship with a given other depending on the situation (Mills & Clark, 1982). A person involved in a family business, for example, may apply exchange norms to all business-related interactions with family members but communal norms to all other interactions with the same people.

Finally, consider the point that there are some situations in which neither communal nor exchange norms are applied to our predominantly communal or exchange relationships. For instance, when involved in a competitive game, two people are supposed to maximize their gains at the other's expense regardless of the type of relationship they ordinarily have with one another. They are *not* supposed to be responsible for the other's need to win, nor are they supposed to repay the other when they are benefited at the other's expense. Indeed, such concerns, unless effectively disguised, would lead to behavior the other would perceive as ruining the game.

EVIDENCE SUPPORTING A DISTINCTION BETWEEN COMMUNAL AND EXCHANGE RELATIONSHIPS

A number of studies based on the foregoing distinction between communal and exchange relationships have now been completed. Although these studies do not support every point made earlier, taken together they do provide good support for the distinction. These studies are described briefly in the following section.

Studies on Attraction

The first studies designed to test predictions derived from the communal—exchange distinction were performed by Clark and Mills (1979). In our first study (Clark & Mills, 1979, study 1) we reasoned that if, in exchange relationships, people benefit others with the expectation of receiving benefits in return, then a person who expects an exchange relationship with another should like that other better if the other repays him or her for the benefit than if the other does not. However, because in communal relationships, people presumably benefit others in response to their needs rather than with the expectation of specific repayment, they should *not* expect the other to repay with a benefit soon afterwards. Such a benefit is not called for, and indeed may decrease attraction since it may be taken as a sign that the other prefers an exchange to a communal relationship.

To test these hypotheses, we set up a situation in which our subjects would benefit another. We manipulated both the type of relationship our subjects expected with another as well as whether or not the other responded to the subject's benefit by giving the subject a benefit. Then we measured attraction.

The study went as follows. Unmarried, male subjects were recruited for a study on task performance. On arrival the subject was seated where he could see an attractive female on a TV monitor. The woman, he was told, was the other subject, who was in an adjacent room. They would be in separate rooms at first but later would have an opportunity to meet. The first task for both subjects was a vocabulary task. They were to form ten words each using letter tiles. They could not talk but were allowed to send notes and letter tiles back and forth via the experimenter if they wished. Both subjects would receive points toward an extra credit if they finished quickly. The subject was told he had an easier task than the other and could earn one point toward an extra credit point for finishing quickly. The other had the more difficult task and therefore could earn up to four points.

All subjects worked on their task, finished before the other, and received one extra point for finishing quickly. Then, in response to the experimenter asking if they wished to send any letters to the other who was still working, all subjects sent letter tiles to the attractive woman. She could be seen on the monitor receiving the letters, finishing her task, receiving a credit form from the experimenter, and writing a note. The experimenter then came into the subject's room, said the other had earned four points, and gave the subject a note, supposedly from the other. The note thanked the subject or thanked him and gave him one of her points.

At this point the type of relationship subjects expected with the other was varied. The experimenter made it clear that the other was anxious to get on to the next part of the experiment (in which the two would meet) either because her husband would be picking her up afterwards (exchange conditions) or because she was new at the university and was looking forward to meeting people (communal conditions). The idea behind this manipulation was that because the other was attractive and most of the young male college students were presumably available for a communal relationship, a communal relationship would be desired and expected if the woman was available. However, an exchange relationship should be desired if she was not available. Therefore, in our communal conditions she was clearly available; in our exchange conditions she was clearly not.

Finally, following the relationship manipulation, we measured the subjects' attraction for the other by having them rate her on a "first impressions" form presented as a premeasure for the next task. Results on this measure were as expected. In the communal conditions subjects liked the other better when she did not benefit them following their aid than when she did benefit them. In contrast, in the exchange conditions, subjects liked the other better when she did benefit them than when she did not benefit them after having received a benefit from them.

In a second study also designed to test predictions regarding attraction derived from the communal–exchange distinction, we examined people's reactions to a request for a benefit after they had either received or not received aid from the other (Clark & Mills, 1979, Study 2). We predicted that when a person expects an exchange relationship with another who has just aided the person, the person will like the other better if the other requests a benefit than if he or she does not. In an exchange relationship, the receipt of a benefit presumably creates an obligation to return a comparable benefit, and a request for a benefit provides an opportunity to repay the debt. Supporting this idea is the fact that in previous studies involving pairs of strangers, having an opportunity to repay another for a benefit has been shown to increase attraction (Castro, 1974; Gergen, Ellsworth, Maslach, & Seipel, 1975). We also predicted that a request for a benefit in the absence of prior aid should *decrease* attraction in exchange relationships. To grant such a request would create a debt.

In contrast to our predictions for exchange relationships, we predicted that when a person expects a communal relationship with another who has just aided the person, the other will be liked better if she does not request a benefit than if she does. Requesting a benefit after aiding someone in a communal relationship is inappropriate. It calls into question the assumption that the original aid was given to fulfill the person's needs and, indeed, the assumption that the other *desires* a communal relationship at all. Finally, we predicted that a request for a benefit in the absence of prior aid might increase attraction because it might signal the other's interest in a communal relationship. Indeed, asking for a benefit is a technique that Jones and Wortman (1973) have suggested as a means to get others to like us, and Gottman, Gonso, and Rasmussen (1975) reported that third and fourth graders will suggest asking another for information or help as a technique for making friends.

In this study female college students served as subjects and, again, an attractive female served as the confederate. Relationship expectations were manipulated when subjects arrived. As in the first study, when subjects arrived they were seated in one room and could see the other on a monitor. In the communal conditions subjects were told that the other was anxious to begin because she was new at the university and was interested in meeting people. They were also told that they would have an opportunity to discuss common interests with her later and that in the past people who had done so had sometimes gotten to know one another quite well. In the exchange conditions subjects were told that the other was anxious to begin soon because her husband was coming to pick her up and then they had to pick up a child. They were also told that they would be discussing differences in interests later. (Again, we were manipulating expectations for a communal or exchange relationship with the other by altering perceptions of an attractive other's availability for a communal relationship. We assumed that young female college students would be interested in and would expect a communal relationship—in this case a friendship—with an available, attractive female who wished to meet new people. In addition we thought this interest and expectation would be reinforced by anticipating a discussion of common interests with the other. In contrast, we assumed that young female college students would *not* be interested in nor expect a friendship with a busy, married woman who had a child. In addition we thought this lack of interest and expectation would be reinforced by anticipating a discussion of differences in interests with the other.)

As in the first study, the subject and the other performed a vocabulary task involving word formation and could earn points toward an additional credit by finishing quickly. However, this time the subject had the more difficult task and could earn up to four points, whereas the confederate had the easier task and could earn only one. The confederate finished first and either did or did not send letters to the subject. Receipt of this aid allowed the subjects to complete their tasks and to earn four points. (Actually, even subjects who did not receive aid did receive four points.) Then the confederate sent a note which either requested a point from the subject or explicitly stated she did not want any points. Finally, a measure of attraction for the other was taken under the guise of a pretest for a second task.

Results on the attraction measure confirmed three of our four hypotheses. In the exchange conditions a request for a benefit following prior aid *increased* attraction, whereas a request for a benefit in the absence of prior aid *decreased* attraction. In contrast, in the communal conditions, a request for a benefit following prior aid *decreased* attraction relative to receiving no request. The only hypothesis not supported was the hypothesis that a request for a benefit, in the absence of prior aid, would *increase* attraction in relationships expected to be communal ones. A request for a benefit under these circumstances had no effect on attraction relative to receiving no request. This may be due to such a request producing ambivalent feelings in the subjects. The request may have indicated that the other desired a communal relationship, but it may also have reminded the subjects that the other did not aid them earlier when help was needed (Clark & Mills, 1979).

A Study on Decision Making in Groups

Another area for which the distinction between communal and exchange relationships has implications is the area of group decision-making. Specifically, the distinction has implications for the perceived appropriateness of group decision-making by consensus or majority rule. In decision-making by consensus members discuss the available options, take everyone's opinions into account, and settle on one. The option chosen should be one to which no member has strong objections. In contrast, when deciding by majority rule, group members simply vote for their preferred option and the option receiving the most votes is chosen.

Our distinction implies that consensus should be considered more appropriate than majority rule by members of communal groups. Decision-making by consensus allows all members to take into account each other's needs and feelings easily, something dictated by communal norms. Use of majority rule, on the other hand, may lead to some members becoming committed (by the action of the group) to an option to which they have strong objections. In other words, their needs would have been neglected.

In contrast, given little knowledge about other group members' opinions, majority rule and consensus may be considered equally appropriate by members of exchange groups. Members of exchange relationships have no special obligation to be responsive to one another's needs, yet there is no clear prohibition against taking other's needs into account.

William Sholar and I recently tested these ideas in a laboratory study (Sholar & Clark, 1982). In this study we assumed that friendships are communal relationships.[3] Half of our subjects were led to expect to become friends with members of their group; half simply expected to participate in a group with people whom they were unlikely to have met before. Members of all groups found themselves faced with a decision. Half were told to make that decision by consensus and half were told to make it by majority rule. Finally, all subjects judged the appropriateness of their assigned decision-making rule.

We accomplished this in the following manner. Subjects were recruited for a study on group problem-solving. On arrival they were seated in a large room along with others scheduled to participate at the same time. All were told they had been assigned to a group of four people based on extensive pretesting done at the beginning of the semester. They would be introduced to the other three members of their group and their group would solve a joint problem shortly, but first, the experimenter said, he wanted to get some preliminary procedures out of the way. The experimenter then described five potential problems to the subjects—solving a block puzzle, creating an elaborate menu, putting together a jigsaw puzzle, writing a poem, or solving math problems. Each group, he said, would choose its own problem after reading and filling out some forms. He then handed each subject a booklet containing these forms.

The first sheet included manipulations of the two independent variables—that is, relationship type (communal or exchange) and decision-making rule (consensus or majority rule). First, relationship expectations were manipulated. In the exchange conditions this sheet informed subjects, "We have carefully selected groups of people who are unlikely to have spent much time with one another." In the communal conditions, the sheet contained this information and more. It said, "We have carefully selected groups of people who are unlikely to have spent much time with one another, but who like to get to know other people and would be likely to become friends. (In fact, past researchers have found that friendships have often resulted among group members who have been selected in the manner we have used.)" Next, the sheet informed half of the subjects in each relationship group that their group was to choose a problem by majority rule and the remainder that they were to choose a problem by consensus. Finally, subjects were asked to fill out premeasures that included the crucial question, which asked how appropriate they considered their assigned decision-making procedure to be.

The results were as expected. In the communal conditions subjects rated consensus as being significantly more appropriate than majority rule. In the exchange conditions subjects rated consensus and majority rule to be equal-

---

[3]A manipulation check supported this assumption.

ly appropriate. Furthermore, exchange subjects' appropriateness ratings of both majority rule and consensus were higher than communal subjects' appropriateness ratings of majority rule. This makes sense from our theoretical perspective—only the communal subjects in the majority rule conditions were assigned to use a rule that might lead them to violate group norms (by neglecting the needs or ignoring the preferences of some group members).

In this particular study the exchange subjects did not know whether their own opinions about which task to do were in the majority or in the minority. If exchange subjects did have this knowledge, the perceived appropriateness of decision-making rules might have been influenced. If they held the majority opinion, they might have preferred majority rule; if they held the minority opinion, they might have preferred consensus.

Studies on Observers' Perceptions of Relationships

The distinction between communal and exchange relationships also has implications for the cues observers use to determine what kind of relationship exists between others. It implies that noncomparability of benefits given and received in a relationship may serve as a cue to the existence of a communal relationship. Why? Noncomparable benefits may be given and received more commonly in communal relationships than in exchange relationships. As previously noted in communal relationships members have an implicit agreement to be responsive to one another's needs. At any given point in time the needs and preferences of members of such a relationship are likely to be different.[4] Thus within a short period, members should be unlikely to give and receive exactly comparable benefits. Further, members of communal relationships may intentionally *avoid* giving exactly comparable benefits because the second benefit may appear to be a repayment for the first, something that is inappropriate in communal relationships.

In contrast, members of exchange relationships have a different kind of implicit agreement. The receipt of a benefit in such relationships results in a specific obligation to return a benefit of comparable value. The easiest way to eliminate that debt is to return a comparable benefit. Consequently the exchanging of comparable benefits should be common in exchange relationships. Thus the giving and receiving of noncomparable benefits may serve as a cue to the existence of a communal relationship, whereas the giving and receiving of comparable benefits may signal the existence of an exchange relationship.

[4]Of course, when needs are equal and repetitive tasks need to be performed, turn-taking may well take place in communal relationships and this may lead to comparable benefits being given and received in communal relationships.

Three studies support these ideas (Clark, 1981). In the first two, subjects simply read paragraphs describing one person giving a benefit to another followed by the other giving the person a benefit. Half of the subjects read paragraphs in which those benefits were noncomparable and half read paragraphs in which the two benefits were exactly comparable. In the comparable conditions of the first study the people described gave *and* received rides or gave *and* received lunches; in the noncomparable conditions the people described gave and received a combination of those two benefits. In the second study, matched pairs of either pens, pads of paper, coffee, or candy were given and received in the comparable conditions, whereas in the noncomparable conditions the pairs of benefits were combinations of these benefits. After reading each paragraph, subjects judged the degree of friendship existing between the two people. As predicted, in both studies the degree of perceived friendship was significantly higher in the noncomparable than in the comparable benefits conditions.

It was assumed that the comparability of benefits given and received in a relationship influenced perceived friendship because it affected perceptions of the reason why the second benefit was given. A third study was conducted to test this idea explicitly. In this study subjects read the same paragraphs that had been used in the second study. However, this time subjects were asked to give a reason why the second benefit was given. As predicted, a second benefit that was comparable to the first was significantly more likely to be perceived as a repayment than was a second benefit that was *not* comparable to the first one. More precisely, subjects in the comparable conditions were more likely to say that the second benefit was given "as a repayment," "out of obligation," or "as a replacement" than were subjects in the noncomparable conditions, whereas subjects in the noncomparable conditions were more likely to say that the second benefit was given "as a thank you," "out of appreciation," "to fulfill a need," "to start a friendship," "to please the other," or "out of kindness" than were subjects in the comparable conditions.

Studies on Feelings of Exploitation

Along with Barbara Waddell, I conducted two studies on feelings of exploitation that also support the distinction between communal and exchange relationships (Waddell & Clark, 1982). In the first study we tested the hypotheses that (1) in an exchange relationship, failure to receive a benefit or a promise of a benefit soon after benefiting another should produce feelings of exploitation, whereas (2) in a communal relationship failure to receive a benefit or a promise of a benefit soon after benefiting another should not produce feelings of exploitation.

To test these hypotheses, female college students were recruited for a study supposedly designed to find out how getting to know another person through a discussion improved one's insight into that other. On the subject's arrival, the experimenter said that the other subject—another woman—had already arrived but had left and would be back soon. Then the experimenter briefly explained the study to the subject, mentioning that it would include, in the communal conditions, a discussion of common interests and, in the exchange conditions, a discussion of differences in interests. She also mentioned she was surprised the other had not yet returned because the other's husband would be picking her up immediately after the study (exchange conditions) or because the other had been looking forward to meeting people (communal conditions).[5] Shortly thereafter, a friendly, attractive female confederate, who was unaware of the relationship manipulation, arrived.

The experimenter explained that they would be filling out measures of insight into one another both before and after having a discussion. The first measure of insight involved filling out a word association form for herself and guessing the other's association to the same words. Both subjects began to fill out this form and the experimenter left the room, supposedly to get some additional materials.

When both had finished, and prior to the experimenter's return, the confederate asked the subject to fill out a lengthy survey and to mail it back for her class project. All subjects agreed. Then the confederate either told the subject she would be paid $2 from class funds for filling out the survey (benefit conditions) or that there had been class funds but they had run out (no benefit conditions). Finally, the experimenter returned and administered a first impressions measure, which was presented as a second pretest of insight into the other but which, in fact, was administered in order to collect the dependent measures. It included questions asking how "exploitive" and "willing to take advantage" of others the confederate was. As predicted, in the *exchange* conditions, failing to provide a benefit after having requested and received a benefit from the other resulted in the other being rated as significantly *more* exploitive than was the case when a return benefit had been provided. Also as predicted, failure to provide a benefit after having requested and received a benefit from the other did not influence feelings of exploitation in the communal conditions.

The results of this first study on feelings of exploitation supported our hypothesis that when an exchange relationship is desired—but not when a communal relationship is desired—failure to repay a benefit will produce feelings of exploitation. These same hypotheses and two additional ones

[5]For this study separate subjects were used to examine the effectiveness of these manipulations for producing expectations of communal and exchange relationships. The results supported the effectiveness of these manipulations.

were supported by the results of a questionnaire handed out to students by Waddell and Clark (1982). The two additional hypotheses concerned the conditions under which a person in a communal relationship would feel exploited. We predicted that (1) in a communal relationship a person will feel more exploited when the other fails to fulfill his or her *need* than when the other does fulfill his or her need; and (2) failure to fulfill a need will not produce feelings of exploitation in an exchange relationship.

The questionnaire asked subjects to imagine themselves in situations with other people with whom they had existing communal or exchange relationships. The communal relationships they imagined included their relationship with a parent and their relationship with a romantic partner. The exchange relationships they imagined included their relationship with a landlord and their relationship with a fellow student or co-worker with whom they were not friends.[6]

Subjects pictured themselves in four situations with each of these people. In two the subject had a particular need about which the other knew. In the other two the subject had just provided the other with aid. After reading about each situation, subjects rated how exploited and hurt they would feel if the other did not fulfill their need or repay them, as well as (for comparison purposes) how exploited and hurt they would feel if the other *did* fulfill their need or repay them.

The results of this questionnaire study fit with our expectations. As in the first study, situations in which the subject benefited the other and was not specifically repaid were associated with reports of greater exploitation and hurt feelings in exchange than in communal relationships. Furthermore, situations in which the subject had a need that was not fulfilled were associated with reports of greater exploitation and hurt feelings in communal than in exchange relationships. Of course, because this study involved only self-reports of what subjects believed they would feel under certain conditions, these results must be interpreted with caution.

Keeping Track of Inputs in Relationships

Finally, I conducted a series of studies in which I tested the hypothesis that when two people perform a joint task for which there is a reward, they will be less likely to keep track of their individual inputs if they have a communal than if they have an exchange relationship. Why? In exchange relationships, benefits are presumably given in response to past debts or with the expectation of future benefits. Therefore it is crucial to keep track

---

[6]Manipulation checks supported our assumptions regarding the nature of these relationships.

of one's inputs into such a relationship in order to determine what outcomes one deserves. In contrast, in a communal relationship, presumably the rule is to be responsive to one another's needs. Thus, keeping track of inputs into a joint task should be unimportant in determining how rewards should be divided.

To test these ideas, I conducted three studies. In the first, male subjects were recruited for a study on perceptual skills. Expectations for communal or exchange relationships were manipulated in much the same manner as used in previous studies. Specifically, subjects participated in the study with an attractive female whom, the subject was led to believe, was either available or not available for a communal relationship. This time, however, the information about the subject was conveyed on a questionnaire rather than by the experimenter so the experimenter could remain unaware of conditions.[7] Specifically, the confederate filled out the top half of a group premeasure indicating in the communal conditions that she was single (in response to a question about marital status) and that she was anxious to meet people (in response to a question about why she had signed up for the study), and in the exchange conditions that she was married and had signed up for the study because it would end at a time convenient for her husband to pick her up. This questionnaire was given to the subject supposedly for him to answer the same questions on the bottom of the page, but actually to give him an opportunity to read the confederate's answers.

After completing his part of the questionnaire, each subject worked on a joint task with this woman. The task consisted of examining a large array of numbers and locating and circling prescribed strings of numbers. The confederate started this task by herself in one room; then the experimenter stopped her and the sheet she had already worked on was turned over to the subject, who had been put in a separate room, for his turn. The subject expected that the pair would receive a small monetary reward for each number sequence correctly located and that they would divide the reward at the end.

When the sheet was turned over to the subject he found that the confederate had circled her numbers with a black or a red pen. The subject always had a choice of pens on his table, including black and red. The measure of the subject's motivation to keep track of benefits was whether he chose to make his circles with a pen of the same color or with a pen of a different color as that which had been used by the other. If subjects chose a different color pen more than 50% of the time, we considered that to be evidence that they were trying to keep track of individual inputs. The results supported

[7]In previous studies in which interactions were predicted and the experimenters were unaware of the second independent variable, this was not considered necessary.

our hypotheses. Of the subjects in the exchange condition, 88%, significantly more than expected by chance, chose a different color pen than that chosen by the confederate. In contrast, only 12% of the subjects in the communal condition chose a different color pen. This 12% was not only significantly lower than 88%, but also significantly lower than what would have been expected by chance. In other words, not only did the exchange subjects intentionally keep track of inputs as we had expected, but the communal subjects actually seemed to avoid keeping track of benefits. We did not predict the latter effect, because communal norms do not require that subjects go out of their way to avoid keeping track of individual inputs into joint tasks. However, perhaps at the beginning of communal relationships people intentionally avoid following exchange norms to demonstrate they are *not* interested in that kind of relationship.

In a second study, the same hypothesis was tested again. This time, however, we began by recruiting pairs of actual friends to participate in a study we billed as involving filling out questionnaires on friendship. Just before the study, we called them and told them our friendship study was over but that we were conducting a new study having nothing to do with friendship but in which we would like to have them participate anyway because it required two people. Once pairs of friends volunteered for this new study, we scheduled them in such a way that they would participate with a friend (communal condition) or with a stranger who was a member of a different pair of friends (exchange conditions). When each pair arrived, the study proceeded much as the first one had, except that subjects were separated right away, there was no manipulation of relationship type, and *both* were led to believe that they would be the second member of their pair to work on the joint task.

The results from this study showed that 94% of the exchange subjects chose a different color pen, whereas only 42% of the communal subjects chose a different color pen. Thus our hypothesis was confirmed again. Exchange subjects are significantly more likely than communal subjects to have chosen a different color pen. Furthermore, once again, exchange subjects chose a different color pen more often than would be expected by chance. However, this time communal subjects seemed to have picked a pen randomly. Perhaps in *established* communal relationships people no longer feel compelled to demonstrate that they are not interested in an exchange relation.

Finally, in a third study we again recruited pairs of friends and again called them before the study to tell them our study on friendship was complete but that we would like them to participate in a different study. Then they were scheduled to participate with a friend or nonfriend. This time, however, when they arrived for the study we simply explained the number-circling task and sent both subjects into a room *together* to work on the task. In the room was the sheet of numbers and a pencil holder with two black pens and two red pens. We examined their sheets at the end of the session to see whether pens of different colors or of the same color had been used. For a third time, the results supported our hypotheses. Of the pairs of nonfriends, 90% used pens of different colors, whereas only 30% of the friends did so. Again, exchange subjects were significantly more likely than communal subjects or chance to have used different color pens, and again as in the second study friends' choice of pens did not differ from what would be expected by chance.

Summary of Existing Studies

In sum, then, several studies have provided evidence that a distinction between communal and exchange relationships is useful for understanding what behaviors are "correct" in those relationships, as well as for understanding how behaviors conforming or failing to conform to these standards influence attraction, decision-making, observers' perceptions of relationships, feelings of exploitation, and keeping track of inputs in relationships. Now I turn to a discussion of some developmental implications of this distinction.

IMPLICATIONS OF THE COMMUNAL–EXCHANGE DISTINCTION FOR DEVELOPMENT

What are some of the implications of the distinction between communal and exchange relationships for development? The evidence just reviewed suggests that assuming there is one developmental sequence for children's conception of correct behavior in relationships, as has often been done in the past (e.g., Damon, 1975, 1977; Piaget, 1965; Hook, 1978; Hook & Cook, 1979), may not be the most fruitful approach to understanding the norms children use to judge behavior in their interpersonal relationships. Rather, it may prove more fruitful to take relationship type into account and to search for evidence of children's acquisition of at least *two* sets of norms for correct behavior in relationships—a set of norms they apply in their communal relationships with such people as parents and friends, and a set of norms they apply in their exchange relationships with such people as store clerks and acquaintances.[8] Such a strategy would involve (1) studying

[8]A few others, it should be noted (e.g., Berndt, 1982a; Montada, 1980), have also suggested taking relationship type into account in order to understand truly children's conceptions of fairness, although not in connection with the communal–exchange distinction.

the development of children's understanding of two distinct sets of norms— sets of norms whose acquisition may depend on quite distinct cognitive abilities and social experiences, and (2) studying the cognitive abilities and experiences necessary to categorizing relationships so that appropriate norms may be applied.

What we know about communal and exchange norms in adults in *combination* with knowledge about development of children's cognitive abilities and changes in their social environments points to (1) the types of developmental changes we might expect to observe in children's understanding of fairness in these two types of relationships, (2) factors that might be expected to facilitate acquisition of these norms, and (3) even methodological techniques that might be adapted for use with children to detect their understanding of different kinds of relationships.

Development of Communal Norms

I now turn to a discussion of the possible courses children's understanding of relationships might take. Consider the course acquisition of the concept of communal relationships might take first. Beginning at birth and continuing through early childhood, children experience rather one-sided communal relationships with their parents or primary caretakers. In other words, parents are responsive to their children's needs without expecting very much in return (but see Graziano, Chapter 7, present volume). Thus communal relationships may be the first type of relationship to which children are exposed, and they may acquire some rudimentary knowledge about such relationships early in life. Specifically, they learn that they can count on others to be responsive to their needs. Soon they will also be exposed to others who are not responsive to their needs, and as this occurs, perhaps the second thing children will begin to understand about communal norms is that they are not universal. Certain people can be counted on to be responsive to their needs, but others cannot.

At this point the child must still learn that communal relationships are not one-sided; that the other person in a communal relationship will expect the child to respond to the other's needs, at least to the best of the child's ability. When will this knowledge that communal relationships are two-sided be acquired? One crucial antecedent certainly should be the child's acquisition of some *ability* to be responsive to the parent's needs (at least when told about those needs). Acquisition of such abilities should spur the parents and others to begin to teach a child explicitly that he or she is expected to be responsive to others' needs. For instance, as a child acquires the ability to control his or her vocalizations, that child might be instructed to keep quiet so that another member of the family can get needed sleep; or as a child begins to understand instructions, he or she may be told to share a toy with an upset sibling, perhaps to "make her feel better." Thus children may begin to acquire the notion that in communal relationships each member is expected to be responsive to the other member's needs.

An even better understanding of communal relationships may occur when the child can infer the other's needs or feelings *on his or her own* and then respond to those needs. Only then can the child understand that communal duties require more than simply responding to requests for aid or to obvious needs. They also require actively inferring the other's needs and responding to them. This may not happen until the child acquires the cognitive ability to take another person's perspective, something children may begin to do with some regularity when they are 6 to 8 years old but at which they are not skilled until at least 10 years of age (Kurdek, 1977; Rubin, 1978; Selman, 1971). Going even further, one might argue that children do not truly understand communal relationships until (1) they not only infer the other's needs but also *expect* the other to infer their needs, (2) they can infer that the other will expect them to be responsive to his or her needs and will be upset if that responsiveness is not forthcoming, and (3) they can infer the other will understand a failure on their part to respond to the other's needs due to conflicting responsibilities in stronger communal relations. Understanding these things requires not only simple perspective-taking but "mutual role-taking" (Selman, 1976a,b). In other words, they require the ability not only to take another's perspective but also to understand that the other can take their perspective—a skill which Selman (1976) argues does not even emerge until 10–12 years of age. These things also require the ability to think abstractly (e.g., about strengths of relationships), providing still another reason to suspect communal norms are not fully understood until at least adolescence.

These speculations about the development of children's understanding of communal norms certainly fit with the frequently reported observation that children develop their first strong and intimate friendships in which members actually define their friendships largely in terms of the fact that they are responsive to one another's needs as they approach adolescence (e.g., Berndt, 1982b; Bigelow, 1977; Mannarino, 1980; Rubin, 1980; Selman, 1976a,b). They also fit well with some recent findings such as those of Diaz and Berndt (1982) and Youniss (1980). Specifically, Diaz and Berndt (1982) found that fourth and eighth graders did not differ in their knowledge of directly observable aspects of people whom they called their friends (e.g., things like their friend's telephone numbers and names of the friend's parents) but that eighth graders did have more intimate knowledge about their friends than did fourth graders (e.g., things that worried their friend, how to make their friend feel better when he or she was upset). (To determine accuracy, friend's reports were compared to those friends' self-reports.) Youniss (1980) found that children's reports of sharing with friends in situations in which one friend had a need or was worse off than the other increase from 6 to 14 years of age.

Development of Exchange Norms

Next, consider how the development of children's understanding of and adherence to *exchange* norms might proceed. During infancy and very early childhood, children's understanding of exchange relationships is probably very limited—more limited than their understanding of communal relationships—for two reasons. First, as noted earlier, the primary relationships for such children are those with their caretakers. In these relationships, the other often *unconditionally* provides benefits to fulfill the child's needs. Even if an infant does provide rewards to its caretaker, the rewards are provided unintentionally. So although resources of value may be given and received early in such a relationship, one is not a formal condition of the other. Second, it seems that even if a very young child *were* regularly exposed to others not especially concerned about his or her welfare, it would still be unlikely that he or she would learn much about exchange relationships because very young children do not have many benefits they can intentionally give to the other.

Children may first learn something about exchange relationships by observing their parents' exchanges with others (Cochran & Brassard, 1979), and knowledge of exchange relationships should increase rapidly as they begin to have extensive interactions with peers, to have goods or services that would be of use to others, and especially when they begin to use money.

Indeed, parents may teach exchange rules to children quite explicitly when they teach children about money. A parent, for instance, may teach the child explicitly that when he or she goes into a store, money must be given to the storekeeper in order to get something in return, and/or that in order to get an allowance, chores must be done.

Because children need not infer others' needs in order to follow exchange norms effectively, nor do they need to order exchange relationships in terms of strength, it may be that exchange norms are followed in a form fairly close to their adult form prior to the time at which communal norms are followed in a form close to their adult form. Of course, what values are placed on goods and services—indeed, what goods and services are considered to be inputs into a relationship—may change considerably over the course of development (Graziano, 1978). In addition, there is very good

evidence indicating that the computational methods children use to calculate when a fair exchange of benefits has taken place will change as children
acquire increasing cognitive skills, as Hook and Cook (1979) have pointed
out.

Development of a Distinction between Communal and Exchange Relationships

A question closely related to that of how children's understanding and use
of communal and exchange norms develop is how children make distinctions between relationships in which communal norms should apply and
those in which exchange norms should apply.

What variables should be important in this regard? It seems that one
crucial factor will be simple exposure to people with whom different types
of relationships are possible and who will follow different norms in their
interactions with the child. As already noted, early on a child is exposed
primarily to one-sided communal relationships. Somewhat later, the child
will be exposed to other adults and peers who will not be as responsive to
his or her needs. Some of these people will give something to the child only if
the child gives something to them (e.g., storekeepers). As such exposure to
new individuals occurs, children should begin to make distinctions between
relationships, although before they acquire the ability to categorize it is
probably not safe to say that they truly understand that communal and
exchange relationships are two broad types of relationships.

Of course, simple exposure to different types of relationships is probably
not the only way children acquire the distinction between communal and
exchange relationships. Adults may teach children explicitly about communal and exchange norms and at the same time about the specific relationships in which each set of norms applies. For example, a parent might say
such things as, "Sam is not a stranger. He is your brother. When he's
unhappy you should let him use your toy." Or, "When we go to the store,
pick out what you want, give the clerk behind the counter your money, and
then she will give it to you." Later, as children acquire the cognitive capacity
to categorize people into groups (such as relatives or store clerks), they may
quite readily fit new people into these categories and utilize the correct
norms.

However, such categories will not determine what norms should be applied to *every* new person one encounters. What if a new person does not fit
into a culturally dictated communal or exchange category? We have assumed that what adults do in such cases is to draw distinctions based on
such things as the ability to fulfill one another's needs, and general attrac-

tiveness (including attractiveness of values, personality, etc.) However, given that, as has already been noted, taking others' values and needs into account requires cognitive skills that do not emerge until early adolescence, children probably do not draw distinctions among people with whom communal and exchange relationships are appropriate (at least nonculturally dictated ones) as adults do until at least that time.

INDIVIDUAL DIFFERENCES THAT MIGHT BE CORRELATED WITH UNDERSTANDING RELATIONSHIP NORMS

Of course, our theorizing about relationships suggests more than just the developmental course children's acquisition of communal and exchange norms might take. As should already be obvious, it also suggests specific environmental variables and cognitive skills that should contribute to the acquisition of such norms and thus, as least in certain age groups, should be correlated with children's understanding of those norms. Consider social factors first. Having extremely nurturant parents, for example, might foster the development of children's earliest conception of communal norms, whereas later development of children's understanding of communal norms might be fostered by having parents who expect children to be responsible to *their* needs. Similarly, being given an allowance to spend or being exposed to many people *outside* kin and friendship networks may foster the development of exchange norms.

Next, consider cognitive skills. As already noted, the ability to categorize should facilitate the ability to apply communal or exchange norms appropriately to new people; the ability to take another's perspective may facilitate applying communal norms appropriately to be responsive to one another's needs.

IMPLICATIONS OF THE COMMUNAL–EXCHANGE DISTINCTION FOR INTERPRETING PREVIOUS DEVELOPMENTAL WORK

As has just been noted, the communal–exchange distinction and research presented in this chapter suggest that the standards by which children judge behavior in interpersonal relationships at any given point in time may depend on the type of relationship existing between the people in question. This suggests not only some guidelines for future research but also at least two things to keep in mind when interpreting previous developmental and, indeed, social psychological work on relationships. First, we must keep in mind that the generalizability of such research may be limited to the particular type of relationship examined in the study. Second, relationship type may turn out to be a variable that will account for apparent discrepancies in previous research (Berndt, 1982a).

These points apply to a considerable body of research in both social and developmental psychology, but I use just a few articles as illustrations here. First consider the suggestion that many research findings on interpersonal relationships in both social and developmental psychology may be limited in generalizability. Most such experimental studies in social psychology and many studies in developmental psychology as well involve relationships between strangers meeting for the first time. We suspect that such relationships tend to be exchange relationships and therefore that the results of such studies may generalize to other exchange but not to other communal relationships. In social psychological studies of relationships with adults, we already have some evidence for this claim.

Consider the study by Gergen *et al.* (1978) done with adults mentioned earlier. In this study subjects received aid from another, who then either told them not to bother returning aid, asked them to return an equal amount of aid, or asked them to return an equal amount of aid and suggested that they do something more as well. Subjects had no previous acquaintance with the confederate and had no reason to expect to interact with the confederate in the future. Given this, we suspect the subject perceived exchange rules to be most appropriate to his or her relationship with the other, and it is not surprising that subjects liked another who asked them to return an equal amount of aid better than another who told them not to repay or to repay and do something more. However, the second Clark and Mills (1979) study described earlier demonstrates that this result has limited generalizability. In the *exchange* conditions of that study we also found that subjects liked another who aided them better if that other asked for a repayment than if he or she did not. However, in our *communal* conditions just the opposite finding was obtained: Subjects liked another better who aided them if that other did not than if the other did ask for repayment.

The same lack of generalizability of laboratory results using pairs of strangers may also apply to much developmental work, although this claim remains to be subjected to a clear empirical test. As one of many possible examples, consider the results of some work by Hook (1978). He was interested in discovering how children allocate rewards they have earned jointly with another child. He included 5-, 9-, and 13-year-old children in his study. They worked on a task, saw another child's completed work on the same task, and then were given a joint reward to divide between themselves and the other child. The subject did 75%, 50%, or 25% of the total work. The results revealed that 5-year olds tended to keep most of the money for themselves regardless of the amount of work done, that 7- to 12-year-olds gave more money to the person who did more work but did not follow a norm of proportional equity, and that 13-year-olds did follow a norm of proportional equity. The author points out that this sequence closely paralleled these children's understanding of proportionality (Hook, 1978; Hook & Cook, 1979) and notes that this ability may underlie the sequence observed.

However, the present research suggests a possible boundary condition for such findings. In the Hook (1978) study, children divided rewards between themselves and "another boy [or girl, referring to the same gender as the subject child] your age who was helping me [the experimenter] with these games just awhile ago." In other words, the other was a stranger to the child. Thus the evolution of reward allocation norms Hook (1978) observed may apply only to exchange relationships. Had the other been the child's friend or sibling, something that is probably more common in actual situations in which rewards are allocated, the results might have differed. In such cases communal norms that are not as dependent on understanding of proportionality as exchange norms may come into play.

As evidence that Hook's (1978) findings indeed may not be as generalizable as one might expect, and as evidence for the point that taking relationship type into account may help to clarify prior seemingly disparate research findings, consider Hook's (1978) findings again and contrast them with some obtained by Damon (1975). Recall that Hook (1978) asked children to make reward allocations between themselves and a child whom they did not know and found that children used self-interest as a standard at about 5 years of age, then ordinal equity at 7–12 years, and finally proportional equity at 13 years. In contrast, Damon (1975) studied justice using techniques in which subjects make judgments about divisions of goods between themselves and their *best friend* or between people who know each other well. He found that his youngest group of subjects used a similar technique in dividing rewards (i.e., self-interest) as that used by Hook's youngest children. He also found, however, that 8-year-olds often considered *both* equality as well as equity. Why did one group of children in middle childhood show at least some tendency to use equality as a standard (those Damon observed) whereas others did not (those Hook observed)? Although it is recognized that the Hook (1978) and Damon (1975) methods differ in many ways in addition to type of relationship studied, here it is suggested that the type of relationship is a very plausible place to start in accounting for such differences in findings. Hook (1978) had children dividing rewards between themselves and a stranger, whereas Damon (1975) had subjects dividing rewards between themselves and a friend. As evidence reported earlier suggests, friends may be less likely to keep track of inputs into joint tasks and may therefore be more likely to divide rewards equally at the end of joint tasks, whereas strangers may keep track of benefits and tend to divide rewards according to inputs. Of course, the usefulness of this suggestion awaits further empirical work with children in which relationship types, and nothing else, are varied.

SUMMARY

In summary, I have presented a distinction between communal and exchange relationships as well as evidence to support this distinction. Specifically, several studies with adults have been presented suggesting that people apply different norms to their behavior in communal and exchange relationships and that this affects such diverse variables as attraction, feelings of exploitation, decision-making, and keeping track of benefits. Then a case was made that this work lies on the boundary between social psychology and developmental psychology for several reasons. First, the work suggests that searching for the development of distinct concepts of justice and correct behavior in close versus more formal relationships, as well as for individual differences among children that correlate with use of communal and exchange norms, may prove fruitful. Second, it suggests some potential boundaries on the generalizability of previous developmental and social psychological studies. Finally, the distinction between communal and exchange relationships may provide a resolution between some previous, seemingly conflicting findings.

As a final note, future work on development of children's understanding and use of norms in interpersonal relationships may not only benefit from theoretical work on relationships done with adults, but may usefully borrow and adapt methodological techniques from that work. For instance, such things as reactions (in terms of attraction) to being repaid for help and whether or not subjects keep track of benefits in joint tasks might be used effectively as indications of whether communal and exchange norms are being followed in children's relationships at different stages of development. Of course, how useful the communal–exchange distinction and existing methodology will prove in understanding the development of children's conceptions and use of relationship norms remains to be put to empirical test.

REFERENCES

Berndt, T. J. Fairness and friendship. In K. H. Rubin & H. S. Ross (Eds.), *Peer relationships and social skills in childhood.* New York: Springer-Verlag, 1982. (a)

Berndt, T. J. The features and effects of friendship in early adolescence. *Child Development,* 1982, *53,* 1447–1460. (b)

Berscheid, E., Dion, K., Walster, E., & Walster, G. W. Physical attractiveness and dating choice: A test of the matching hypothesis. *Journal of Experimental Social Psychology,* 1971, *7,* 173–189.

Bigelow, B. J. Children's friendship expectations: A cognitive-developmental study. *Child Development,* 1977, *48,* 246–253.

Castro, M. A. C. Reactions to receiving and as a function of cost to donor and opportunity to aid. *Journal of Applied Social Psychology,* 1974, *4,* 194–209.

Clark, M. S. Some implications of close social bonds for help seeking. In B. M. DePaulo, A. Nadler, & J. Fisher (Eds.), *New directions in helping: Help seeking.* New York: Academic, 1983.

Clark, M. S. Noncomparability of benefits given and received: A cue to the existence of friendship. *Social Psychology Quarterly,* 1981, *44,* 375–381.

Clark, M. S., & Mills, J. Interpersonal attraction in exchange and communal relationships. *Journal of Personality and Social Psychology,* 1979, *37,* 12–24.

Cochran, M. M., & Brassard, J. A. Child development and personal social networks. *Child Development,* 1979, *50,* 601–616.

Damon, W. Early conceptions of positive justice as related to the development of logical operations. *Child Development,* 1975, *46,* 301–312.

Damon, W. *The social world of the child.* San Francisco: Jossey-Bass, 1977.

Diaz, R. M., & Berndt, T. J. Children's knowledge of a best friend: Fact or fancy? *Developmental Psychology,* 1982, *18,* 787–794.

Gergen, K. J., Ellsworth, P., Maslach, C., & Seipel, M. Obligation, donor resources and reactions to aid in a three-nation study. *Journal of Personality and Social Psychology,* 1975, *31,* 390–400.

Gottman, J., Gonso, J., & Rasmussen, B. Social interaction, social competence, and friendship in children. *Child Development,* 1975, *46,* 709–718.

Graziano, W. G. Standards of fair play in same-age and mixed-age groups of children. *Developmental Psychology,* 1978, *14,* 524–530.

Hook, J. G. The development of equity and logico-mathematical thinking. *Child Development,* 1978, *49,* 1035–1044.

Hook, J. G., & Cook, T. D. Equity theory and the cognitive ability of children. *Psychological Bulletin,* 1979, *86,* 429–445.

Jones, E. E. & Wortman, C. *Ingratiation: An attributional approach.* Morristown, NJ: General Learning Press, 1973.

Kurdek, L. A. Structural components and intellectual correlates of cognitive perspective-taking in first- through fourth-grade children. *Child Development,* 1977, *48,* 1503–1511.

Mannarino, A. P. The development of children's friendships. In H. C. Foot, A. J. Chapman, & J. R. Smith (Eds.), *Friendship and social relations in children,* New York: Wiley, 1980.

Mills, J., & Clark, M. S. Communal and exchange relationships. In L. Wheeler (Ed.), *Review of personality and social psychology* (Vol. 3). Beverly Hills, CA: Sage, 1982.

Montada, L. Developmental changes in concepts of juisice. In G. Mikula (Ed.), *Justice and social interaction: Experimental and theoretical contributions from psychological research.* New York: Springer-Verlag, 1980.

Piaget, J. *The moral judgment of the child.* New York: Free Press, 1965.

Rubin, K. H. Role-taking in childhood: Some methodological considerations. *Child Development,* 1978, *49,* 428–433.

Rubin, Z. *Children's friendships.* Cambridge, MA: Harvard University Press, 1980.

Schwartz, S. The justice of need and the activation of humanitarian norms. *Journal of Social Issues,* 1975, *31,* 111–136.

Selman, R. L. The relation of role-taking to the development of moral judgment in children. *Child Development*, 1971, *42*, 79–91.

Selman, R. L. Social-cognitive understanding: A guide to educational and clinical practice. In T. Lickona (Ed.), *Moral development and behavior*. New York: Holt, Rinehart & Winston, 1976. (a)

Selman, R. L. Toward a structural analysis of developing interpersonal relations concepts: Research with normal and disturbed preadolescent boys. In A. D. Pick (Ed.), *Minnesota symposium on child psychology* (Vol. 10). Minneapolis: University of Minnesota Press, 1976. (b)

Sholar, W., & Clark, M. S. *Deciding in communal and exchange relationships: By consensus or should majority rule?* Paper presented at the annual meetings of the Eastern Psychological Association, Baltimore, MD, 1982.

Sigall, H., & Landy, D. Radiating beauty: The effects of having a physically attractive partner on person perception. *Journal of Personality and Social Psychology*, 1973, *28*, 218–224.

Waddell, B., & Clark, M. S. *Feelings of exploitation in exchange and communal relationships.* Paper presented at the annual meetings of the Eastern Psychological Association, Baltimore, MD, 1982.

Walster, E., Walster, G. W., & Berscheid, E. *Equity: Theory and research*. Boston: Allyn & Bacon, 1978.

Youniss, J. *Parents and peers in social development*. Chicago: University of Chicago Press, 1980.

11

Self-Evaluation Maintenance Processes: Implications for Relationships and for Development*

ABRAHAM TESSER

EDITORS' INTRODUCTION

Over the past several years, Abraham Tesser has developed a self-evaluation model predicated on the tenet that people are motivated to maintain a positive self-evaluation. The specific dynamics of the model revolve around two opposing processes: reflection and comparison. Reflection focuses on how an individual's self-evaluation can be raised by the good performance of others, whereas comparison focuses on how an individual's self-evaluation can be lowered by the good performance of close others. The model assumes that an individual's self-evaluation is determined in large part by how well people close to the individual perform in various activities. In the present chapter, Tesser considers the developmental aspects and implications of the model, essentially moving a theoretical model and domain of empirical research into a boundary area. The fruits of this conceptual move are significant in leading to serious considerations of developmental questions that otherwise would not have been asked. For example, Tesser theorizes that the developing child may serve as a foil in the self-evaluational maintenance processes of others such as siblings, peers, or adults (parents). In addition, self-evaluation maintenance processes deserve developmental consideration them-

* Preparation of this chapter was partially supported by National Science Foundation grant BNS-8003711. I wish to thank Sharon Brehm, Jennifer Campbell, Margaret Clark, Bill Graziano, Lynn Musser, Dave Shaffer, and Jerry Suls for their helpful comments.

selves, in terms of both their origin and increasing sophistication. The present chapter provides, in part, a case study of the movement of both a concept and an investigator into the boundary area between social and developmental psychology.

INTRODUCTION

In this chapter I acquaint you with some of the social psychological research in which I have been involved over the last few years and explore some implications for developmental psychology. First, I sketch a self-evaluation maintenance (SEM) model that serves as the framework guiding the research. Then I spell out some of the hypotheses dealing with interpersonal relations and review some experimental data that were collected to evaluate these hypotheses. The rest of the chapter is devoted to pointing out some of the developmental aspects of the approach.

THE SELF-EVALUATION MAINTENANCE (SEM) MODEL AND ITS OPERATION

The SEM Model

The self-evaluation maintenance model has as its major premise the notion that people are motivated to maintain a positive self-evaluation. *Self-evaluation* refers to the relative goodness an individual attaches to himself or herself or that he or she believes others attach to him or her. The model assumes that persons choose to behave in ways that will lead them to evaluate themselves positively or that will lead others to evaluate them positively: If a situation will inevitably result in a decrease in self-evaluation, people will behave so as to minimize that loss in self-evaluation. The model also assumes that an individual's self-evaluation is determined to a substantial degree by people close to that individual and how well those people perform in various activities.

The specific dynamics of the model depend on two opposing processes. The *reflection process* focuses on how an individual's self-evaluation can be *raised* by the good performance of close others; the *comparison process* focuses on how an individual's self-evaluation can be *lowered* by the good performance of close others. I define each of these processes and their two constituents: closeness and performance. Then I describe how the relevance of another's performance to one's own self-definition determines how important comparison processes are, relative to reflection processes. Finally, I point out the hypothetical nature of the self-evaluation construct and the systemic nature of the model.

Reflection Process

Each of us has had the experience of being confronted by someone who insists on telling about the now-famous person who went to their high school or about their second cousin who was a runner-up in the Miss America contest. In general, they point out their close association to good performers and magnify the accomplishments of persons to whom they are close. They do this despite the fact that they clearly have had no instrumental role in the accomplishments of those others. They do it, I believe, because to do it allows them to raise their self-evaluation by basking in the reflected glory of those accomplishments. Indeed, Cialdini and his colleagues (Cialdini, Borden, Thorne, Walker, Freeman, & Sloan, 1976) have shown that persons whose self-esteem has been lowered temporarily are more likely to point out their association to a "winner" than are persons whose self-esteem had not been lowered.[1]

The reflection process depends on two things: the psychological *closeness* of another person and the *performance* of that other person. The closeness variable in the SEM model is very much like Heider's (1958) unit relation: To the extent that two persons are in a unit relation, they are close. Thus closeness increases with things like similarity, physical proximity, and common origins. In addition, just as one can distinguish sentiment relations from unit relations, one can distinguish attraction from closeness. Although these is a tendency for interpersonal liking to be associated with closeness, this will not always be the case. The performance variable is concerned with the quality of another's performance. Given that people often use their own performance as a standard in evaluating the performance of others, the quality of another's performance, from a particular individual's perspective, is usually *relative* (to the perceiver's own performance).

Closeness and performance combine interactively to determine reflection. If someone is not close, if one has no association with him or her, one's self-evaluation will not be raised by the reflection of his or her performance, even if he or she is a Nobel laureate. Similarly, if the other person's performance is mediocre, one's self-evaluation will not be raised by reflection regardless of how close one is to the other. Thus reflection depends on both closeness *and* good performance.

Comparison Process

I have argued that being in a close relationship with another person who performs well can raise one's self-evaluation (the reflection process). How-

---

[1]Incidentally, associating oneself with a so-called winner might be a good strategy for affecting others' opinions. For example, Sigall and Landy (1973) found that impressions of a male were more positive if he was seen with an attractive woman who was described as his girlfriend than if the woman was unattractive or not described as his girlfriend.

ever, one's self-evaluation may also suffer, by comparison, when one is close to someone who performs particularly well. And the comparison process (which results in a *lowered* self-evaluation) seems to depend on the same interactive combination of closeness and performance as does the reflection process (which results in a raised self-evaluation). That is, if another's performance is mediocre, then regardless of how close one is to that other, one's self-evaluation is not likely to suffer by comparison. If another's performance is very good, then the closer the person, the greater the tendency to make comparisons and the more one will suffer by comparison.

Relevance

The effects of reflection and comparison processes appear to cancel themselves out. However, these processes are not always (or even generally) equally important. According to the SEM model, their relative importance is determined by the *relevance* of the other person's performance to one's self-definition. We all recognize achievement across a wide variety of endeavors: waterskiing, novel writing, mathematics, cooking, and so on. However, our own aspirations for excellence are on a much more circumscribed set. I want to be a good social psychologist and a good cabinetmaker, and these dimensions are tied up in my self-definition. Someone else may define herself in terms of being a good lawyer, a good tennis player, and a gourmet cook. To the extent that another's performance is not on a self-defining dimension, it is not relevant to one's self-definition. Further, if the other's performance level is too much better or poorer than one's own performance, comparisons with that other are difficult (Festinger, 1954), and his or her performance would not be relevant to one's self-definition. To put it in positive terms, another's performance is relevant to one's self-definition to the extent that the performance level is not too discrepant from one's own performance level and is on a self-defining dimension.

The relevance of another's performance to one's self-definition weights the comparison process relative to the reflection process. If the performance is high in relevance to one's self-definition, the comparison process will be important and the good performance of a close other will threaten self-evaluation. If the performance is low in relevance, then the reflection process will be important and one might bask in the reflected glory of a close other's good performance.

Model Dynamics and Interpersonal Relationships

The primary assumption of the SEM model is that persons try to maintain a positive self-evaluation.[2] I have sketched out how another's closeness and

---

[2]The assumption that everyone tries to maintain a positive self-evaluation may turn out to be too strong. Despite evidence, for example, that persons who are low in self-esteem may actually

performance affect self-evaluation via reflection and comparison processes and how the relevance of another's performance to one's self-definition determines the relative importance of these processes. The description of these relationships makes clear that one can alter self-evaluation in a variety of ways: changing another's closeness, altering his or her relative performance, or changing the relevance of that performance to one's self-definition. It is these latter behaviors on which I focus and not on self-evaluation per se.

The self-evaluation construct is at the heart of the SEM model, but it is *strictly* a construct. It is not assumed to be "real" or present in any measurable form. (Indeed, in earlier work [e.g., Tesser, 1980; Tesser & Campbell, 1980] I used the term "self-esteem" to refer to this construct. I abandoned that term because it was too easy to reify and to think about the construct in terms of measurable, chronic individual differences.) The raison d'être of the self-evaluation construct is its ability to help make understandable the relations among the variables that do have empirical indicants: closeness, relevance, and performance. These three entities serve as the measured or manipulated variables in the research described later.

The SEM model is systemic. That is, each variable is both a consequence and a cause of the other two. An example will show how the model operates. Suppose Mary is interested in a career as a pianist. Joan, a girl about Mary's age, moves in next door. Joan also is a talented pianist. Since piano playing is relevant to Mary's self-definition, she is threatened by comparison. How might she deal with this threat? She could change her own self-definition and reduce relevance. This would reduce the importance of comparison and increase the importance of the reflection process. For example, she can decide that she really is not interested in the piano for a career, or she can decide she is really a jazz pianist and Joan is really a classical pianist. With such a resolution, Joan's accomplishments would not be a threat and might even be a source of gain, by reflection, for Mary.

Other resolutions include *interpersonal* strategies. Mary can somehow reduce Joan's closeness or somehow affect the difference in the quality of their performances to Mary's own benefit. Given that a major focus of this volume is on interpersonal relations, I have more to say about each of these strategies but will reserve those comments for later discussion. The point I wish to make here is that because the model is systemic, a change in any variable affects the entire system. Further, unless two of the variables are "fixed," there is no way to predict which variable Mary will choose to change. Thus experiments conducted to test the model control (fix) two of

engage in SEM processes more than do persons high in self-esteem (see Tesser & Campbell, 1982b), the same processes may not be observed among certain clinical populations such as depressives.

the variables at different levels and observe their effects on the third variable. Correlational studies must take combinations of two of the variables to make predictions about the third.

Later I describe how performance is jointly affected by closeness and relevance and how interpersonal closeness is jointly affected by performance and relevance. In each section I review some experimental research designed to test the predictions.

On Helping and Hurting Others: Operating on Performance

Despite the song title which suggests that "you always hurt the one you love," common wisdom suggests that one is more likely to help and less likely to hurt persons who are close. The SEM model suggests that both the song and the common wisdom are correct but that they are correct under different circumstances.

If another is performing on a dimension that is relevant to one's self-definition, then comparison processes will be important. The closer the other person, the more threatening will be that other's good performance.[3] One way to reduce the threat is to prevent the other person's good performance. Therefore, when another is performing on a dimension relevant to one's self-definition, the song should be correct: The closer the other person, the more interference and hindrance of the other's performance we would expect to be forthcoming. Now suppose that the other person's performance is on an irrelevant dimension. Rather than being threatened by comparison, one can benefit by the reflection of a close other's good performance. When relevance is low, the folk wisdom should be correct: The closer one is to another person, the more one should aid or help that other person's performance.

Smith and I (Tesser & Smith, 1980) tested these hypotheses experimentally. We had two pairs of male friends (the pairs were unacquainted with each other) report to the laboratory for a verbal task. For half the sessions, the task was described so as to make it relevant to their self-definition—that is, it presumably measured verbal intelligence, managerial potential, and so on. For the remaining sessions, it was described so as to make it low in relevance—that is, it was described as a game in which success does not tell us anything important about the person. The task involved each person guessing several target words from clues provided by the other three participants from a list of clues graded in difficulty. One person from each friend-

---

[3]It is worth noting that sometimes persons may work so closely that their performance and the outcomes of their performance may be inseparable. Under such circumstances this assumption would not be expected to hold.

ship pair played first. The feedback was arranged so that neither did very well but so that each had a personal benchmark by which to judge the subsequent performance of the remaining two participants (one friend and one stranger to each). If they wanted one or both of the remaining players to do well, they could select easy clues. If they wanted one or both players to do poorly, they could select difficult clues.

The results provided support for the model. First, when the task is relevant, we expect that participants would not want to be outperformed. Indeed, participants selected harder clues for the others when the task was more relevant than when it was less relevant. What about the differences between close (friends) and distant (strangers) others? When the task was low in relevance, just as common wisdom predicts, participants helped their friends more than the stranger by giving their friend easier clues than those they gave the stranger. Not only was this trend attenuated with high relevance, it was reversed. In the high relevance condition, as the song suggests, the participants actually gave easier clues to the stranger than they did to their friend.

Although Berndt (1981) did not manipulate relevance, he did observe the extent to which kindergarten, second-grade, and fourth-grade children actually helped a close friend and an acquaintance. The children were given rewards for coloring pictures. One child was given a crayon at the start of each trial. The amount of time the child shared the crayon was the index of helping. Berndt found that girls did not differ in the extent to which they shared the crayon with the friend and the acquaintance: Second- and fourth-grade boys, on the other hand, actually shared the crayon more with the acquaintance than with the friend. Berndt suggests that boys may be more competitive than girls. It is possible, however, that the task was simply more relevant to the boys than to the girls.

Persons may distort the performance of close and distant others in the interest of self-evaluation maintenance. Evidence from the literature on psychological projection is consistent with this idea. For example, Secord, Backman, and Eachus (1964) gave subjects convincing feedback that they possessed a negatively evaluated characteristic. Then they measured the extent to which this characteristic was projected onto a friend and a nonfriend. From the present perspective, the feedback lowered the relative performance of the subject on a relevant dimension. Given that there is a greater threat, via comparison, from the close person than from the distant person, the model predicts more projection of the negative attribute onto the close person than onto the distant person. This is what Backman et al. (1964) found: Subjects came to see the negative attribute as more characteristic of their friend than of the nonfriend.

The projection literature is suggestive, but it was not collected specifically to test the SEM model, and its support is based on post hoc interpretation. Also, it does not vary the relevance of performance to the subject's self-definition. Campbell and I (Tesser & Campbell, 1982a) tried to correct these deficits in a comprehensive study that varied both the relevance of the performance dimension and the quality of the subjects' own performance on the task. To accomplish this, two pairs of female friends (the pairs were unacquainted) reported for an experiment on "first impressions." Each subject was given the opportunity to tell a little about herself to the others. Then each subject went to a separate booth to work with a microcomputer. The computer presented each subject with items from a "social sensitivity test" and items from an "aesthetic judgment test" which the subject had to answer. For each item, the computer indicated to the subject whether her answer was correct—the computer was preprogrammed to give positive feedback on half the items and negative feedback on half the items. It then prompted the subject to "guess" how her friend (close other) would respond to the item *or* how one of the women she had just met (distant other) would respond to the item. Finally, subjects indicated whether social sensitivity or aesthetic judgment was more relevant to their self-definition. In sum, subjects were given the opportunity to project onto a friend and onto a stranger good performance (positive feedback) or poor performance (negative feedback) on a high or low relevance dimension.

The SEM model predicts a complex interaction. Let us focus on net positivity in projection—that is, number of projections of correct answers less the number of projections of incorrect answers. On a high-relevance dimension, a close other's good performance is threatening, by comparison, so we expect relatively less positivity in projection for a close other than for a distant other. On the other hand, for a low-relevance dimension, a close other's good performance is beneficial, by reflection, so we expect relatively more positivity in projection for a close other than for a distant other. This was precisely the experiment's outcome: It turned out this way among women for whom social sensitivity was more relevant than aesthetic judgment and also among women for whom aesthetic judgment was more relevant than social sensitivity.

An important aspect of interpersonal relationships is the extent to which individuals help or harm one another as each tries to perform the tasks that are personally important. The SEM model suggests that helping another through actual behavioral means or even through perceptual distortion of that other's performance is dependent not only on one's relationship to that other (i.e., closeness) but also on the relevance of that other's performance to one's self-definition. Thus, from the present perspective, helping is not simply a function of characteristics of the potential target or characteristics of the potential helper, but an interactive function of both.

The Closeness of Interpersonal Relationships: Some Effects
of Relevance and Performance

A central aspect of an interpersonal relationship is the closeness of that relationship. In the previous paragraphs I have tried to show how closeness (along with relevance) can affect interpersonal helping—that is, relative performance. Here I use the SEM model to focus on the determinants of the closeness of relationships.

The pattern for making predictions is already familiar. For a particular configuration of relevance and performance, we simply use the model to determine the extent to which a close relationship would result in high or low self-evaluation: To the extent that a close relationship would result in high self-evaluation, we predict a close relationship; to the extent that a close relationship would result in low self-evaluation, we predict a distant or less close relationship. Suppose the performance dimension is highly relevant to one's self-definition. The better another performs, the more threat to self-evaluation, by comparison, associated with a close relationship. Thus, when the performance dimension is relevant, the better another's performance, the less close we expect the relationship to be. On the other hand, if the performance dimension is low in relevance to one's self-definition, the better the other's performance, the more to be gained, by reflection, from a close relationship. Thus, when the performance dimension is low in relevance, the better another's performance, the closer we expect the relationship to be.

Pleban, and I (Pleban & Tesser, 1981) tested this set of hypotheses by inviting pairs of male college students to participate in a "college bowl"-like quiz. Before the quiz, each participant filled out a questionnaire designed to measure the personal relevance of a variety of topics, including news events, rock music, and photography. For half the participants, the quiz was on a high-relevance topic; for the remaining participants, the quiz was on a low-relevance topic. One of the participants in each pair was an experimental confederate who knew the answers to all the questions. He was trained to vary his own performance by making it worse, about the same, or better than the real subject's performance. At the end of the quiz, each participant was told that he had performed at about the 50th percentile. The confederate's performance, however, varied: 20th, 40th, 60th, or 80th percentile.

There were several indexes of closeness. Participants were asked to fill out a questionnaire in another room. The confederate was in the room before the subject arrived, and the physical distance the subject sat from the confederate served as a behavioral index of closeness. Another index of closeness was derived from subjects' willingness to work with the confederate again. A third index was constructed from the extent to which the subject felt he and the confederate had things in common. Finally, an affective index of closeness was based on the subject's liking for the confederate.

Recall the specific predictions from the SEM model. When the confederate's performance is highly relevant to the subject's self-definition, the better the confederate's performance, the more the subject would distance himself from the confederate. When the confederate's performance is low in relevance, the better the confederate's performance, the closer the subject would move toward the confederate. The results provided partial support for the hypotheses. When the confederate's performance was poorer than that of the subject, there were no differences between conditions. However, as the confederate's performance became increasingly better than the subject's performance, closeness *increased* if the performance was low in relevance, and closeness *decreased* if the performance was high in relevance. This relationship held on three of the four measures of closeness. Recall that in defining closeness, I distinguished closeness from liking or affect. In this case, it was the affective index of closeness that was unaffected by the experimental manipulations.

Although little experimental evidence exists of the hypothesized effects of relevance and performance on interpersonal closeness, the data we have collected suggest that the distinction between closeness and attraction may be a useful one. They also suggest that the way one defines oneself (in combination with another's performance) will have an affect on the closeness of one's relationship with that other. Finally, the data suggest that closeness of relationships may be at least partly understandable from the perspective of self-evaluation maintenance.

PSYCHOLOGICAL DEVELOPMENT AND THE SEM MODEL

I have attempted to explain the SEM model and how it operates. The research I have described dealt with adults, but now I would like to turn my attention to the developing child. SEM processes may be important to child development in two ways: First, the child's environment and interactions with others will be structured by the playing out of the SEM processes in others. That is, the child will serve in others' attempts to maintain their own self-evaluation. Second, the way in which the child's own self-evaluation maintenance processes unfold and change throughout the life span are of interest. I discuss the developing child's changing role as a foil in the SEM processing of others and also a bit about the development of SEM processes in the child.

Some Developmental Changes in One's Role as an Object of Others' SEM Processes

Who are the "others" who can "use" the child in maintaining their own self-evaluation? For present purposes, I believe it is sufficient to delineate three others: parents, siblings, and peers. The role the developing child is likely to play as these others attempt to maintain their own self-evaluation is subsequently described.

Parents

Consider the newborn. At birth, the neonate's "performance" takes place on dimensions that are not relevant to the self-definition of his or her parents. Parents generally do not define themselves in terms of gurgling, grasping, sucking, smiling, and general infantile cuteness. Because relevance is low, comparison processes will be unimportant and reflection processes will be important. Parents should bask in the reflected glory of the new child. To the extent that the child makes the appropriate noises, grimaces, and so on, there will be a strong tendency for the parents to increase closeness through affection and public displays of closeness: "That's *my* baby!" There should also be a tendency to facilitate and positively distort the child's performance: "Doesn't my child smile beautifully?"

Through the middle childhood and early adolescent years, the child may begin to perform on dimensions having to do with the parents' self-definition. However, the discrepancy between the child's performance and the parents' performance is likely to be so large that the child's performance remains low in relevance. Thus the child should continue to be the object of the parents' *reflection* processes until maturity; parents should continue to increase closeness for good performance. However, not only will parents feel good about the accomplishments of their offspring, but the child's poor or unwarranted performance can also reflect negatively on the parents. To the extent that the child fails on important tasks or violates important norms, the parent should try to minimize the importance of the task and the severity of the violation and/or distort the child's performance in the socially desirable direction. The parent may also, or alternatively, try to reduce closeness to the child by withdrawing affection and/or publicly disclaiming association: "No child of mine acts that way."

When the child reaches maturity, there is a *potential* for comparison processes to become important for the parent. For example, the child may select the same occupation as the parent. In this case, the child's performance is relevant to the parent's self-definition. If the child's performance exceeds the performance of the parent on a dimension that is relevant to the parent's self-definition, then the parent will suffer by comparison. One way to reduce this threat is for the parent to distance him- or herself from the child.

I have collected some data related to this point about well-known scientists and their fathers (Tesser, 1980). According to these data, when the child performs extremely well—well enough to be reported in a standard biographical directory—the more similar his occupation to that of his father, the more distant the relationship between father and son. On an anecdotal level, following a colloquium describing the SEM model, an attractive young woman told me that when men became more interested in her, her relationship with her mother cooled. Her account was reminiscent of Snow White. She said that her mother's self-definition was tied up in being physically attractive, and when her mother started to suffer by comparison to her daughter, there was a resulting change in the relationship.

From a theoretical perspective, a parent threatened by comparison not only may operate on closeness to the child but could also change his or her own self-definition to make the child's performance less relevant. Or the parent could interfere actively with or lower cognitively the child's performance. In general, my guess is that cases in which the child's performance is relevant to the parent's self-definition are relatively rare, particularly for parents of opposite gender to that of the child. In those instances where there is a threat to the parent by comparison with the child, I think it unlikely that the parent will change his or her own self-definition or interfere actively with the child's performance.

Siblings—The Effects of Age

In order to look at the developmental sequence with siblings, I believe it is necessary to distinguish between siblings who are close in age to the child and those who are a good deal older than the child. The course of events for the sibling who is substantially older than the child will be much like that of the parents. The child's performances will have little relevance to the much older sib's self-definition until the child reaches maturity. For example, even if the child chooses to play soccer and soccer is important to the self-definition of the much older sib, it is unlikely that the much younger child's performance—even if it is very good—will even approach that of the much older sibling. Only at maturity, then, will there be the possibility that the child is performing on dimensions or at levels that are relevant to the older sib's self-definition. Thus with one exception, until the child reaches maturity, he or she is likely to serve as the object of the much older sib's reflection processes.[4] That is, the older sib will want the child to do well and will

[4]There is the possibility for an interesting kind of asymmetry here. Although the younger child is unlikely to be a comparison person for the older child, it is possible that the older child

reward good performance with public and private displays of closeness. The much older sib will attempt to minimize poor performance and distance himself or herself from the child for the child's poor performance.

For purposes of this discussion, however, the much older sib differs from the parent in at least one important respect. In most instances the self-definition of older sibs, like that of the child, will be tied up, to some degree, in gaining the affection and approval of their parents. To the extent that even the immature child is more successful in gaining that approval, the older child will suffer by comparison, and the mechanisms for dealing with such threats are likely to be brought to bear on the child.

Aside from the importance of parental approval, the case for a sib relatively close in age to the child is likely to be different from that of the much older sib. At early stages of the child's development, the child's performance is likely to be relevant to the self-definition of a similar-aged sib. It will be easy for parents (and the sib) to draw comparisons between the child and the sib on such things as obedience and neatness. And even subtle distinctions that result in greater parental attention and affection may be detected by the sib. Similar-aged sibs will be in school at the same time and bring home report cards at the same time. In the early stages of development, when the similar-aged sib's self-definition is relatively diffuse and not specialized, the child's performance will almost certainly be relevant to the sib's self-definition. As the sib develops and as his or her own self-definition becomes better articulated, differentiated, and more complex, the similar-aged child's self-definition and range of performance are also becoming more differentiated and complex. With this increasing complexity comes an increasing *possibility* that the performances of the child will be less relevant to the self-definition of the sib. That is, with greater complexity, there are more dimensions to choose from with a smaller possibility of both sibs choosing the same ones. However, the *potential* remains high throughout their life span for the child's performance to be relevant to the similar-aged sib's self definition.

Again, to the extent that the relevance of the child's performance to the sib's self-definition is high, the comparison process will be more important than the reflection process: The child's good performance will cause the sib to suffer by comparison. There are several things the similar-aged sib can do to relieve this suffering. He or she can reduce closeness, for example, by withdrawing affection or by increasing physical separation; he or she can disregard the child's accomplishments or try to interfere with the child's performance by, for example, fighting with the child or destroying the

---

may serve, in a sense, as a comparison person for the younger child. That is, the parent could compare the younger child's performance to the older child's performance when he or she was the same age.

child's "products." As the sib's own self-definition becomes better articulated, the sib can change his or her own self-definition so as to make the
child's performance less relevant.

One specific hypothesis that falls out of this line of reasoning is that
siblings who are close in age should get along less well than siblings who are
quite different in age. I (Tesser, 1980) divided a sample of young adult
respondents with one sibling into those whose sibling was more than 3 years
discrepant in age and those whose sibling was less than 3 years discrepant in
age.[5] More sibling friction was reported by the latter group than by the
former.

Sibs who are close in age to the child differ from sibs who are distant in
age from the child not only with respect to the dynamics of age-related
changes in the relevance of the child's performance for their self-definition,
but also in a more static way: namely, in closeness. Sibs who are closer in
age to the child are also closer in terms of the model's closeness parameter.
This implies that when the child's performance is on a dimension that is
irrelevant to the sib's self-definition, a close-aged sib will profit more by
basking in the reflected glory of the child's outstanding performance and
will suffer more (by reflection) for the child's poor performance than will a
sib who is substantially different in age. What are the implications of closeness in age when the child's performance is better than a sib's on a relevant
dimension? Given that suffering by comparison increases with closeness,
siblings who are close in age should feel more threatened by comparison and
should engage in SEM strategies more than do children who are different in
age.

Fortunately, some data were obtained to support this set of hypotheses. In
the study just mentioned (Tesser, 1980), college student respondents with
one sibling were partitioned with respect to whether their sib was close in
age (less than 3 years apart) or distant in age (more than 3 years apart) and
whether the sib outperformed the respondent or the respondent outperformed the sib on a highly relevant dimension. This last partition was based
on responses to the question, "During the time you spent at home, how
successful was your brother/sister in such things as popularity, skills, pos-
sessions, and appearance?" The SEM model suggested that two ways in
which sibs might deal with comparison problems are by changing their
closeness to the child or by interfering with the child's performance. These
two dimensions were combined in this study into a "sibling friction" index,
which included items asking about sibling friction, sibling arguments and

---

[5]The design of the study was actually more complex. Subjects' gender and birth order were
taken into account, and there were three levels of performance. The interested reader is referred
to Tesser (1980) for a fuller account.

fights, feelings of sibling competition, lack of help or sibling interest, lack of happiess in home, and hostility or strain in sibling relations.

Again, as the child's relevant performance exceeds that of the sib, the threat by comparison should increase, *particularly for sibs close in age.* Thus as the child's relevant performance exceeds that of the sib, there should be relatively more friction with sibs close in age than sibs less close in age. This was the case for both male and female respondents and for first-born respondents and second-born respondents. When the respondent was outperformed by his or her sib, respondents close in age to the sib reported more friction than did respondents distant in age. And this closeness effect was attenuated when the respondent outperformed his or her sib.

Another way of dealing with a child's threats by comparison is for the sib to reduce the relevance of the child's performance to the sib's self-definition. If the sib can make him- or herself different from (i.e., not identify with) the child in terms of his self-definition, then relevance would be reduced and comparison processes would be less important. Again, the threat via comparison should be greater to the closer (in age) sib than to the more distant sib, so there should be a greater tendency for close sibs to reduce identification as a result of comparison threats than for distant sibs to do so. The respondents described earlier (Tesser, 1980) also indicated the extent to which they identified with their sib in skills and abilities and ways of acting in social situations. Closeness in age did not affect reported identification of female respondents. The expected effects did, however, emerge for males. When a respondent was outperformed by his or her sib (high threat via comparison), the closer in age the respondent was to the sib, the *less* he or she identified with the sib. When the respondent outperformed the sib (low threat via comparison), the closer in age the respondent was to the sib, the *more* he or she identified with the sib.

Siblings—The Effects of Gender

The gender of the child's sibling(s) will also have an impact on the role the child is likely to play in the sibling's SEM processes. Let us focus first on the child at maturity. When the child is mature, his or her good performances are less likely to be on dimensions that are highly relevant to an opposite-gender sibling and more likely to be on dimensions that are relevant to a same-gender sib. What men do is more likely to be relevant to men than to women, and what women do is more likely to be relevant to women than to men. Therefore, when the child is mature, the reflection process will be relatively more important for opposite-gender sibs and the comparison process relatively more important for same-gender sibs. Opposite-gender sibs, profiting by reflection, should be more likely to respond to the child's successes with closeness and glorification of his or her accomplishments, whereas same-gender sibs, suffering by comparison, should be more likely to respond with distance and derogation of the child's success. One implication of this line of reasoning is that individuals who are constantly in trouble, unsuccessful, and so on should be helped more by their same-gender sibs than by their opposite-gender sibs. Individuals who are quite successful should be closer to their opposite-gender sib than their same-gender sib.

The effect of sibling gender on how the *developing* child is treated is conditioned by the age discrepancy between the child and the sibling. When the sibling is much older than the child, the gender of the sibling will make little difference in determining the relevance of the child's performance. Relevance will be low until the child is mature (see the foregoing discussion).

When the sibling is close in age, the gender of the sibling will have implications for the relevance of the child's performance at an early age. At the very earliest stages of development, prior to 2 or 3 years of age (Thompson, 1975; Bell, Weller, & Waldrop, 1971; Kagan, 1971), gender roles are irrelevant to one's sense of self, but by 4 or 5 years of age, children know their parents' expectations regarding gender roles (Fauls & Smith, 1956), and by 6 and 7 years, they have acquired the concept of gender constancy (e.g., Masters & Wilkinson, 1976). Thus the close-aged sib does not have to be very old to discriminate behaviors that differ with respect to relevance for his or her own gender identity. By the time close-aged sibs reach 7 or 8 years of age (Suls & Sanders [1982] suggest 9 years), same-gender and different-gender sibs are likely to be quite different in the extent to which the child's performance is relevant to their own self-definition: The child's performance should be more relevant to the same-gender sib than to the opposite-gender sib; the child is more likely to have a role in the playing out of the comparison process at the hands of same-gender sibs and the reflection process[6] at the hands of opposite-gender sibs.

Sibling gender can also index closeness. That is, a child who is of the same gender as a sib, from the perspective of the model, is closer to the sib. Suppose it is possible to hold the relevance of the child's performance for the sib's self-definition constant, regardless of the sib's gender. If it is true that same-gender sibs are closer than opposite-gender sibs, then suffering by comparison to the *relevant* performance of the child should be greater for a same-gender sib than for an opposite-gender sib. On the other hand, the accomplishments of the child on an *irrelevant* dimension should bring more

---

[6]This statement is strongly made for clarity. In line with my previous discussion on the effects of age, I expect that sibs who are close in age always have the potential for comparison processes and that gender role differences allow for the possibility of decreased relevance.

in the way of reflected glory to the same-gender sib than to the opposite-gender sib. (However, as noted earlier, it is likely that the child's performance will not be on a dimension that is irrelevant to the same-gender sib.)

Peers

The child may also serve as a foil in the self-evaluation maintenance processes of peers. Obviously, however, if the child is serving as a foil for a peer, the peer is also serving as a foil for the child. In this section I talk about the SEM processes among peers without making an arbitrary distinction between peer and child. That is, I recognize that the child and his or her peer are equal co-conspirators in these processes.

Naively, one might think that peers are important only after the child begins school, but this is not the case. According to Parten and Newhall (1943), by 5 years of age, nursery school children are engaging in cooperative play with elements of division of labor, group censorship, and the subordination of individual needs to group goals. Further, Wright's (1967) data suggest that by 5 years of age, more than 30% of the behavioral episodes in a child's daily life are with peers. This percentage increases to approximately 50% by age 11. Even preschool children, 3 or 4 years old, can, in interaction with peers, already be classified as sociometric stars, isolates (neglectees), or rejectees (Gottman, 1977). This implies that even young children are exercising choice with respect to the closeness of particular peers.

The school, however, is a convenient site for studying SEM behaviors. There are semi-captive collections of children available, and their performance is rather public (Levine, 1983). Also, school tends to be relevant to most children's self-definition, and it is possible to track the closeness of peers through similarity of gender, race, and class assignments. Thus this discussion focuses on peer effects in a school context.

Smith, Campbell, and I (Tesser *et al.*, in press) began analyzing some data collected among fifth and sixth graders that illustrate the playing out of SEM processes among peers. We focused on children who are chosen or rejected by their peers. The SEM model suggests that a child who performs (1) better than the peer on a dimension that is irrelevant to the peer's self-definition but (2) not as well as the peer on a dimension that is relevant to the peer's self-definition will be chosen by the peer. In this case, the peer can bask in the reflected glory of the child's better performance on the irrelevant dimension and look good by comparison to the child's poorer performance on the relevant dimension.

To test this hypothesis, we approached our young respondents on two occasions. On the first occasion, each was given a list of activities, including arithmetic, reading, football, checkers, and singing. From this list each indicated his or her most relevant activity, that is, the one at which it was most important to do well—and the least important activity—that is, the one at which it was least important to do well. They were also asked to name the child in the class to whom they were closest—that is, the one with whom they most liked to spend time—and the child to whom they were most distant—that is, the one with whom they least liked to spend time. Finally, on a second occasion, each respondent rated his or her own, the close child's, and the distant child's performance on the activities the respondent had indicated previously were most and least relevant to his or her own self-definition.

The results of the study are intriguing. First, on the *average* (across relevant and irrelevant activities), the respondent judged his or her own performance and that of the close child to be virtually identical. Second, the respondent rated him- or herself and the close child as performing better on the respondent's relevant activity than on his or her irrelevant activity. At first glance these data suggest that respondents select close others who are similar to themselves. Selected children perform at the same overall level as the respondent and are good at what the respondent is good at. In addition, these data do not appear particularly consistent with the SEM model hypothesis. Deeper analysis of the data, however, reveals strong support for the SEM prediction.

Although the respondent rated the close child's performance to be better on the (respondent's) relevant dimension than on his or her irrelevant dimension, the respondent rated his or her *own* performance to be better than that of the close child on the relevant dimension and his or her *own* performance to be poorer than that of the close child on the irrelevant dimension. Thus the respondent could indeed gain by comparison to the close child's good (though poorer than his or her own) performance on a dimension relevant to the respondent's self-definition. The possibility for basking in the reflected glory of the close child's better performance on the irrelevant dimension is also present.

The results for the distant child can be summarized easily: The respondent rated the distant child's performance as poorer than his or her own and poorer than the close child's performance on both the relevant and irrelevant dimensions.

Because all these results are based on ratings made by the child's peer, the question of accuracy becomes important. Are children selected because their *actual* performances conform to a particular pattern, or because their peers have made distorted judgments of the children's performances? We (Tesser *et al.,* in press) were able to address this question by comparing the respondent's judgments of the performance of close and distant children with the teacher's judgments. Presumably the teacher, being out of the peer network, is unbiased (or has a set of biases that are unrelated to that averaged over the collection of children) in making her judgments.

Using teacher judgment as a standard of accuracy leads to the conclusion that there is at least some distortion. Compared to the teacher ratings, the distant child's performance was severely underestimated on both relevant and irrelevant attributes. Distortion of own and the close child's performance was not univalent. The respondent distorted his or her own performance upward on the relevant activity and downward on the irrelevant activity. Distortion of the close child's performance was the complement of distortion of own performance. Performance on the relevant dimension (to the respondent) was underestimated, and performance on the irrelevant attribute was overestimated. From the teacher's perspective, the respondent and the close child are indistinguishable in terms of their performance, and both perform better than the distant child, particularly on the relevant attribute.

In sum, the extent to which children choose one another is determined by their judgment of one another's performance. If, from the chooser's perspective, another child does not perform as well on a relevant dimension but performs better on an irrelevant dimension, that other child is more likely to be chosen.

We have seen how SEM processes among children can affect who is chosen as a friend (closeness). The model suggests that the children may play other roles in the SEM processing of one another. Suppose the child is close to a peer and outperforms the peer in a particular domain. There are two things the peer can do to avoid the prospect of suffering by comparison: (1) reduce the relevance of the performance domain to his or her own self-definition and thereby bask in the reflected glory of the close child's good performance, or (2) try to operate on the performance differential by, for example, working harder in that performance domain to improve his or her own performance.

We (Tesser, Campbell, & Campell, in preparation) have found evidence for both of these processes among adolescents (high school seniors). Closeness was indexed in this study by similarity of gender–race. The importance of school performance to our sample of adolescents' self-definition was associated more strongly with their relative performance among close others (i.e., same gender and race) than among distant others (i.e., different race and gender). School became less relevant to their self-definition as others outperformed them, and this relationship was stronger when the others were close (same gender–race).

In an additional analysis, we divided this sample into those who said that school was relevant to their self-definition and those who said that school was not relevant. (There were two indexes of school relevance: desire for more education and course interest. Hence there were two conceptual replications.) For each respondent we recorded the grade point average of a classmate the respondent designated as a friend and a nonfriend of the same gender and race as the friend. Then, among school–relevant respondents and among school-irrelevant respondents we correlated the respondent's own grade point average with the grade point average of his or her friend and also with the grade point average of his or her nonfriend. We reasoned that where school is highly relevant to the respondent's self-definition, the better the respondent's friend does, the better the respondent had better do or suffer by comparison. To the extent that school is less relevant, and/or to the extent that the other is not close, the respondent should suffer less by comparison to a good performer. Thus the correlation between respondent's grade point average and another's grade point average should be higher among school-relevant respondents and their friends than in any of the other three combinations: school-relevant with nonfriends, school-irrelevant with friends, and school-irrelevant with nonfriends. This appeared to be the case in both conceptual replications.

Children usually cannot exert control over the particular peers with whom they find themselves in close contact in school. School policy regarding such things as "mainstreaming," "tracking" and desegregation have an affect on children via SEM processes. These impacts may be easiest to see among so-called special children—those who are intellectually gifted or those who have learning difficulties. Children who have learning difficulties and are mainstreamed for the most part will be close to children who outperform them, and their self-evaluation should suffer by comparison. Indeed, underachievers who are mainstreamed tend to have lowered self-esteems (e.g., Fink, 1962) than do students with average achievement. Suppose, however, the handicapped child is put into a special classroom with other slow learners. In this case they are less likely to suffer by comparison.

Strang, Smith, and Rogers (1978), at the beginning of the academic year, measured the self-concept of 8- and 9-year-olds who were enrolled in special classes for the academically handicapped. All of their subjects were mainstreamed for part of the day. Salience of the mainstream or special class was the important imdependent variable. Six weeks after this partial mainstreaming began, half of the subjects were removed from their special classes and asked to fill out the self-concept measure a second time. Half of the subjects were removed from their mainstream classroom, and their membership in the class was made salient to them before filling out the self-concept measure the second time. One might think that because there is a stigma associated with the special class and no stigma associated with the mainstream class, those for whom the mainstream class was salient would feel best about themselves. This was not the case, as the SEM model[7] might anticipate. The self-concept of the academically handicapped children whose special class was salient became *more* positive, whereas the self-concept of those for whom the mainstream class was salient became *less* positive.

The case for the academically gifted child is the mirror image of that for the handicapped child. When the gifted child is mainstreamed, he or she is likely to be performing better academically than most of his or her peers with little threat by comparison. When any particular gifted child is segregated to special classrooms for the gifted, however, he or she is less likely to be at the top of the class. To the extent that school is relevant to his or her self-definition, the gifted child in the segregated class is likely to be threatened by comparison. Smith and Johnson (1981) collected relevant self-concept data on both learning-disabled and gifted children. Their 9- to 12-year-old subjects were classified into four groups: The learning-disabled had been in special classes for at least 1 year; the "regular class failing" group were normal intellectually in a regular class but were failing academically; the "regular class average" group were normal intellectually and average or better on grades; the "talented" group were nominated by their teachers for a special enrichment class and participated in that special class with other talented children twice a week. Learning-disabled and talented children responded to a self-concept measure within the context of their special classes. The regular class failing and regular class average students responded to the measure in small groups outside of their regular classes. The results were interesting: The learning-disabled students, tested in their special group, and the regular class average students did not differ in the positivity of their self-concept. In contrast, the talented students, tested in the context of their special class, and the regular class failing students had significantly less favorable self-concepts than did the regular class average students. These data fit nicely with the idea that one's performance relative to that of close others is more consequential than is absolute performance.

It is sometimes easier to see the playing out of SEM processes when there is an abrupt change in the person to whom a child is close. Just such a natural experiment was carried out when U.S. schools became desegregated. Black and white children were forced into close contact with one another. Prior to desegregation, the testimony of social scientists in *Brown* vs *Board of Education* (1955) implied that desegregation would raise black self-es-

---

[7]The self-concept measure (Piers, 1969) used by Smith and his colleagues is essentially a measure of self-esteem that has specific components dealing with school. Strictly speaking, the SEM model treats self-evaluation as a hypothetical, unmeasured variable and makes no predictions about self-esteem measures. However, I could find no research that addresses this point as well, with measures of school relevance or performance.

teem and increase academic achievement. The social scientists were only half right. Stephan's (1978) review of desegregation research concluded that although desegregation affected black achievement positively, it rarely caused increases in black self-esteem and was more often associated with decreases in self-esteem. Although decreases in self-esteem and increases in achievement appear contradictory, they are consistent with the notion that the child's performance relative to those who are close (i.e., classmates) is an important determinant of self-evaluation. For most black students, desegregation caused them to suffer by comparison. It had the effect of putting them in close contact with others (whites) whose school performance—a presumably relevant dimension—was better than their own.

The Ontogeny of SEM Processes

In the first section of the chapter I described the SEM model and reviewed some experimental evidence for its role in social relationships. In the previous section, I focused on how the developing child might serve others in others' attempts at self-evaluation maintenance. In this section I speculate on the development of SEM processes.

In order to deal with the ontogenic unfolding of SEM processes, I believe that an understanding of the differentiation of self is crucial. There are really two tasks involved in distinguishing the self, and these two tasks are, I believe, the antecedents of SEM processes. The first, and perhaps most primitive, is the task of distinguishing the self as a separate entity, different from other entities, having its own, separate physical boundaries. I believe this task plays a role in the development of the closeness variable and the reflection process. The second task is the development of an identity as a distinctive person among persons. I believe this task is related to the comparison process. These two tasks are similar to what psychoanalyst Mahler (1968) refers to as *separation* and *individuation*.

Closeness and the Reflection Process

In the beginning, the infant's world is an amorphous jumble of sights, sounds, and touches. It has no shape, no boundaries. It is all one, including the individual. The infant's first task is to distinguish (or construct) important invariances, to recognize boundaries, to develop object (Piaget, 1954) and person permanence (Fraiberg, 1969)—and, within all this, to distinguish himself or herself from objects and other persons.

In a sense, everything starts out as part of the self and must be distinguished from the self. This is particularly true of persons who interact most with the infant—for example, the child's mother. The infant must distinguish the mother from him- or herself. In a sense, however, the mother, having been differentiated from the self, always remains part of the self. Soon the infant can distinguish a familiar person from a stranger (e.g., Bronson, 1972). The familiar person is more a part of the self than the stranger. The separation of the self from the rest of the social world continues as the child matures. Soon he or she makes distinctions on the basis of physical attributes such as age, physical size, and then gender (Lewis & Brooks-Gunn, 1979) and skin color (Proshansky, 1966). At some point the child uses more abstract dimensions, such as religion, values, and social class. In every instance, the more familiar or similar person is more a part of the self and, from the perspective of the model, closer to the child.

To the extent that another is part of the self, that other's positive affect–successes are the self's positive affect–successes; that other's negative affect–failures are the self's negative affect–failures. Thus a primitive version of the *reflection process* is in place almost at birth, and its developmental course is the course described by (1) the development of separation of the self from other social entities and, of course, (2) the development of the cognitive apparatus to recognize achievement.

In the earliest stages, the reflection process is no more than empathic emotional responses made to close others. Hoffman (1976) argued that empathic distress responses, based on conditioning, are available to the infant within the first few weeks of life, even before the infant has developed a sense of self or other. Indeed, during the first year of life, the infant may not differentiate who is experiencing distress and may behave as if another's distress were his or her own. With maturity, the empathic response is transformed into sympathetic distress, a genuine concern for the other. Hoffman (1976) states it as follows:

> Since the young child experiences a global empathic distress which fuses his own feelings with his impressions of another, it seems reasonable to assume that his undifferentiated unpleasant feelings, wishes, and images would be subsequently transferred to both the separate "self" and "other" which emerge from the global self later in development. That is, the properties of the whole become the properties of its emerging parts [p. 135].

Hoffman argues that the reason sympathetic concern continues even after the child clearly distinguishes between self and other is that the child recognizes a "oneness" with others. I would add that the feeling of oneness is more likely with others who are close to the child.

Self-Definition and the Comparison Process (Emotional versus Performance Dimensions)

The comparison process is coordinated to *individuation,* the development of the individual's separate identity. I believe that the course of individuation is determined by differential reinforcement and differential feedback regarding one's competence. In developing this line of argument, it is necessary to distinguish two types of behavioral dimensions: emotional dimensions and performance dimensions (Tesser, 1980). Emotional dimensions are not individuating, but performance dimensions are individuating.

There are a variety of behaviors that on an individual basis, are not *differentially* valued. For example, everyone in the same family can have similar preferences about food and religion. They can all be emotionally expressive or reserved. To the extent that there is a correct or better performance on these emotional dimensions, it lies not in distinguishing oneself from close others but in behaving in a modal fashion. For a variety of reasons, very early in the child's development he or she will begin to adopt the behavior of persons close to him or her on emotional dimensions. First, such expressive behaviors tend to be more affective than cognitive. Thus the child, even without well-developed cognitive skills, is *able* to adopt them. Second, the behavior will be rather commonly *available* for modeling. And because modal behavior is rewarded, there will be multiple models exhibiting the behavior. Finally, because modal behavior is valued, the child will be *reinforced* for adopting such behaviors. It is important to note, however, that although adoption of these behaviors helps to develop the child's sense of self, it does *not* individuate the child with respect to those close to him or her. Indeed, it makes the child more like those close to him or her even while it may distinguish him or her from distant others.

The second set of behavioral dimensions—performance dimensions—are particularly important from the perspective of the SEM model. They are the dimensions on which reflection and comparison processes take place. Performance dimensions are dimensions that engage skilled behavior that is valued. It is possible to order individuals in terms of competence on performance dimensions. Indeed, good performance is often defined as a performance that is better than someone else's performance. For example, it is generally better to be faster or smarter or prettier than others. On such dimensions, modal behavior does not receive praise, recognition, general approbation, or certification of competence. Rather, it is *atypical* behavior, behavior that is better than another's that leads to public and private recognition of competence. It is clear, then, that people will, almost by necessity, be differentially reinforced on performance dimensions. And that differential feedback will be clearest and easiest to see among close others.

It is on performance dimensions that individuation takes place. On performance dimensions the developing child begins to acquire that part of his or her self-definition to which another's performance may be relevant. What does all this mean in process terms? The account is quite straightforward: The child is motivated toward self-enhancement. He or she tries out a variety of activities. To the extent that someone else is better at the activity—particularly someone who is close (i.e., similar age–gender)—self-enhancing feedback will not be forthcoming. Unless the developing child chooses to perform on activities that are different from those close to him or her, the child's performance is not likely to be more successful than those close to him or her, since those close others are likely to be older and more practiced.[8] Thus in terms of performance dimensions, the child will tend to develop an individuated or unique self-definition.[9]

In a real sense, certification of excellence at a particular activity becomes more and more like a zero-sum game as the actors become closer and closer. To the extent that persons are in close proximity (e.g., same household), to the extent they are similar on important background variables such as age and gender, it will be easier to compare their performance on a particular dimension and differentially reinforce them. Indeed, where there is formal recognition of achievement, often there is also formal recognition of categories such as gender and age *within* which there is differential feedback. Thus to the extent that one's own unique sense of self is tied to a particular performance dimension, a better performance, *particularly by a close other*, will be threatening. This set of relations is the genesis of the comparison process.

The genesis of the comparison process is different from the reflection process in several ways. The reflection process occurs developmentally prior to the comparison process. It has a more affective, less cognitive base. The reflection process is based on the lack of a distinction between self and others (a distinction that takes time to make) and an almost automatic empathic process. The comparison process, on the other hand, depends on the development of several rather subtle distinctions. The child (1) must have an idea of his or her own self-definition, (2) must be able to distinguish grades of performance, and (3) must be able to compare performances at least on dimensions relevant to his or her own self-definition.

Some systematic research has been conducted on the development of social comparison processes. For example, Suls and Mullen (1982) offered a life-span developmental theory about the use of similar others, dissimilar others, and the self at a previous time as comparison persons. But more pertinent for present purposes is research on the origins of social comparison processes. Although Masters (1971) has shown that even nursery school-aged children are sensitive to the differential reinforcement of peers

---

[8]Obviously, this will not always be the case. For example, young children are better at being "cute" than are older children.

[9]I have not traced the importance of distinctiveness across the life span. Suls and Mullen (1982) have attempted to do this. In an intriguing set of arguments they suggest that distinctiveness may peak during middle age (35–50 years).

(cf. Hook & Cook, 1979), Ruble and her associates (Boggiano & Ruble, 1979; Ruble, Boggiano, Feldman, & Loeble, 1980; Ruble, Parsons, & Ross, 1976) found that social comparison information does not affect self-evaluations until around 7 to 8 years of age. Other research suggests that by age 5 years, children show less distortion in their perception of their relative rank among peers in running (Morris & Nemcek, 1981) and in "toughness" (Edelman & Omark, 1973). However, accuracy in estimating class rank in reading does not emerge until age 9 years (Nicholls, 1978). Taken together, this research suggests that social comparison processes, *on experimenter-defined dimensions,* although somewhat variable, arrive relatively late— somewhere between 7 and 8 years of age.

Although this research is important and interesting, it is only partially relevant to the particular comparison process associated with the SEM model. That is, the research cited does not deal with variations in the relevance of the performance dimension to the child's self-definition or to variations in the closeness of the comparison children.

I suspect that full-blown, veridical social comparison processes come relatively late in the developmental sequence, but the beginnings of such processes are present even with the emergence of language. At first any concrete, quantitative dimension begins to take on performance-like qualities. And preschoolers, for whom home and parents occupy a large part of their self-definition, can be heard to tell one another, "My dad is bigger than your dad," or "My mom is older than your mom." Indeed, there is evidence that even though preschoolers are not accurate about performance ranking, they systematically distort their own performance upward (e.g., Morris & Nemcek, 1981). In their own homes, even very young children can detect changes in the attention or affection they receive from parents, particularly with the arrival of a new child. One attempt to cope with this change is to perform like the new child by regressing (i.e., bed-wetting, baby talk, etc.). Such regression does not result in development of a unique self, and it is generally punished and drops out. However, the attempt to perform like the baby does show a form of awareness of changes in reward as the result of *another's* performance that results in a change in own performance. In sum, although the comparison process is rather late in developing, its antecedents are present relatively early.

The relevance of another's performance to one's self-definition determines the importance of the social comparison process. Although the cognitive apparatus for full-blown comparison processes are in place by 7 to 8 years of age, one's self-definition remains fluid throughout the life span (e.g., Erikson, 1972). For any particular individual, the *substance* of the comparison process will be fluid throughout the life span.

SUMMARY

A self-evaluation maintenance (SEM) model based on two opposing processes—reflection and comparison—was described. To the extent that a psychologically close other performs well, the reflection process results in an increment in self-evaluation, and the comparison process results in a decrement in self-evaluation. The importance of the comparison process relative to the reflection process varies directly with the relevance of the performance dimension to the individual's self-definition. By assuming that individuals wish to maintain a positive self-evaluation, it was possible to make predictions about when they would be helpful and harmful to others and when they would reduce or increase the closeness of interpersonal relationships. Some experimental evidence bearing on these predictions was reviewed.

Two aspects of child development related to the SEM model were discussed. First, the developing child may serve as a foil in the SEM strategies of others. In this context, the role of the child's parents, siblings, and peers was discussed. Second, the child's own acquisition of SEM behaviors was discussed. It was suggested that the reflection process develops from primitive, affective empathic behavior and that the comparison process develops from more cognitive, differential learning processes.

REFERENCES

Bell, R. Q., Weller, G. M., & Waldrop, M. F. Newborn and preschooler: Organization of behavior and relations between periods. *Monographs of the Society for Research in Child Development*, 1971, *36*(1–2, serial no. 142).

Berndt, T. Effects of friendship on prosocial intentions and behavior. *Child Development*, 1981, *52*, 636–643.

Boggiano, A. K., & Ruble, D. N. Competence and the overjustification effect: A developmental study. *Journal of Personality and Social Psychology*, 1979, *37*, 1462–1468.

Bronson, G. W. Infants' reactions to unfamiliar persons and novel objects. *Monographs of the Society for Research in Child Development*, 1972, *47*(3, serial no. 148).

Brown v. Board of Education of Topeka, 98F. Supp. 797 (1951), 347 U.S. 483 (1954), 349 U.S. 294 (1955).

Cialdini, R. B., Borden, R. J., Thorne, A., Walker, M. R., Freeman, S., & Sloan, L. R. Basking in reflected glory: Three (football) field studies. *Journal of Personality and Social Psychology*, 1976, *34*, 366–375.

Edelman, M. S., & Omark, D. R. Dominance hierarchies in young children. *Social Science Information*, 1973, *12*, 103–110.

Erikson, E. H. Eight stages of man. In C. S. Lavatelli & F. Stendler (Eds.), *Readings in child behavior and child development*. New York: Harcourt Brace Jovanovich, 1972.

Fauls, L. B., & Smith, W. D. Sex-role learning of five-year-olds. *Journal of Genetic Psychology*, 1956, *89*, 105–117.

Festinger, L. A theory of social comparison processes. *Human Relations,* 1954, *7,* 117–140.

Fink, M. B. Self-concept as it relates to academic achievement. *California Journal of Educational Research,* 1962, *13,* 57–62.

Fraiberg, S. Libidinal object constancy and mental representation. *Psychoanalytic Study of the Child,* 1969, *24,* 9–47.

Gottman, J. M. Toward a definition of social isolation in children. *Child Development,* 1977, *48,* 513–517.

Heider, F. *The psychology of interpersonal relations.* New York: Wiley, 1958.

Hoffman, M. L. Empathy, role taking, guilt, and development of altruistic motives. In T. Lickona (Ed.), *Moral development and behavior: Theory, research, and social issues.* New York: Holt, Rinehart & Winston, 1976.

Hook, J. G., & Cook, T. D. Equity theory and the cognitive ability of children. *Psychological Bulletin,* 1979, *86,* 429–445.

Kagan, J. *Change and continuity in infancy.* New York: Wiley, 1971.

Levine, J. M. Social comparison and education. In J. M. Levine & M. C. Wang (Eds.), *Teacher and student perceptions: Implications for learning.* Hillsdale, NJ: Erlbaum, 1983.

Lewis, M., & Brooks-Gunn, J. *Social cognition and the acquisition of self.* New York: Plenum, 1979.

Mahler, M. S. *On human symbiosis and the vicissitudes of individuation* (Vol. 1): *Infantile psychosis.* New York: International Universities Press, 1968.

Masters, J. C. Social comparison in young children. *Young Children,* 1971, *27,* 37–60.

Masters, J. C., & Wilkinson, A. Consensual and discriminative stereotyping of sex-role judgments by parents and children. *Child Development,* 1976, *47,* 208–217.

Morris, W. N., & Nemcek, D. *The development of social comparison motivation among preschoolers: Evidence of a stepwise progression.* Unpublished manuscript, Dartmouth College, Hanover, NH, 1981.

Nicholls, J. G. The development of concepts of effort and ability, perception of academic attainment and the understanding that difficult tasks require more ability. *Child Development,* 1978, *49,* 800–814.

Parten, M., & Newhall, S. W. Social behavior of preschool children. In R. G. Barker, J. S. Kounin, & H. F. Wright (Eds.), *Child behavior and development.* New York: McGraw-Hill, 1943.

Piaget, J. *The construction of reality in the child.* New York: Basic Books, 1954.

Piers, E. V. *Manual for the Piers-Harris Children's Self-Concept Scale.* Nashville, TN: Counselor Recordings and Tests, 1969.

Pleban, R., & Tesser, A. The effects of relevance and quality of another's performance on interpersonal closeness. *Social Psychology Quarterly,* 1981, *44,* 278–285.

Proshansky, H. M. The development of intergroup attitudes. In L. W. Hoffman & M. L. Hoffman (Eds.), *Review of child development research* (Vol. 2). New York: Russell Sage, 1966.

Ruble, D. N., Boggiano, A. K., Feldman, N. S., & Loebl, J. H. Developmental analysis of the role of social comparison in self-evaluation. *Developmental Psychology,* 1980, *16,* 105–115.

Ruble, D. N., Parson, J. E., & Ross, J. Self-evaluative responses of children in an achievement setting. *Child Development,* 1976, *47,* 990–997.

Secord, P. F., Backman, C. W., & Eachus, H. T. Effects of imbalance in the self-concept on the perception of persons. *Journal of Abnormal and Social Psychology,* 1964, *68,* 442–446.

Sigall, H., & Landy, D. Radiating beauty: The effects of having a physically attractive partner on person perception. *Journal of Personality and Social Psychology,* 1973, *28,* 218–224.

Smith, M. D., & Johnson, D. *Social comparison and self-concept in academic environments.* Unpublished manuscript, Vanderbilt University, Nashville, TN, 1981.

Stephan, W. School desegregation: An evaluation of predictions made in *Brown* v. *Board of Education. Psychology Bulletin,* 1978, *85,* 217–238.

Strang, L., Smith, M. D., & Rogers, C. M. Social comparison, multiple reference groups, and the self-concepts of academically handicapped children before and after mainstreaming. *Journal of Educational Psychology,* 1978, *70,* 487–497.

Suls, J., & Mullen, B. From the cradle to the grave: Comparisons and self-evaluation across the life-span. In J. Suls (Ed.), *Psychological perspectives on the self* (Vol. 1). Hillsdale, NJ: Erlbaum, 1982.

Suls, J., & Sanders, G. S. Self-evaluation through social comparison: A developmental analysis. In L. Wheeler (Ed.), *Review of personality and social psychology* (Vol. 3). Beverly Hills, CA: Sage, 1982.

Tesser, A. Self-esteem maintenance in family dynamics. *Journal of Personality and Social Psychology,* 1980, *39,* 77–91.

Tesser, A., & Campbell, J. Self-definition: The impact of the relative performance and similarity of others. *Social Psychology Quarterly,* 1980, *43,* 341–347.

Tesser A., & Campbell, J. Self-evaluation maintenance and the perception of friends and strangers. *Journal of Personality,* 1982, *50,* 261–279. (a)

Tesser, A., & Campbell, J. *Self-evaluation maintenance processes and individual differences in self-esteem.* Paper presented at the Symposium on Functioning and Measurement of Self-Esteem, American Psychological Association, Washington, DC: 1982. (b)

Tesser, A., Campbell, J., & Campbell, B. Some relationships among performance, interests, and friendships. In preparation.

Tesser, A., Campbell, J., & Smith, M. Friendship choice and performance: Self-evaluation maintenance in children. *Journal of Personality and Social Psychology,* in press.

Tesser, A., & Smith, J. Some effects of friendship and task relevance on helping: You don't always help the one you like. *Journal of Experimental Social Psychology,* 1980, *16,* 582–590.

Thompson, S. K. Gender labels and early sex-role development. *Child Development,* 1975, *46,* 339–347.

Wright, H. F. *Recording and analyzing child behavior.* New York: Harper & Row, 1967.

Author Index

Subject Index

G

General exchange perspective, in social exchange process, 164–170

Genotype–environment correlation, reactive vs. passive, 164

Given matrix, in social exchange process, 169

Group decision making, communal vs. exchange relationships in, 252–254

Group discussions, *see also* Peer group influence

in children's moral decisions, 195–217

developmental theory and, 201–203

Group influences

information exchange and, 216

positive and negative views of, 196–197

Group polarization, in adult groups, 204–205

Group shifts

altruism dilemma and, 208–212

honesty dilemma and, 206–212

social comparison theory in, 208–209

H

Handicapped children, self-evaluation maintenance processes for, 291

Heart rate, in emotional responsiveness, 96

Honesty dilemma

in children's groups, 206–212

discussion variables in, 210

Hullian behavior theory, 6

Hurting others, in SEM model, 276–278

Husbands' emotional maturity, wives' rating of, 73

Husband–wife cooperativity, in social exchange process, 80–82, 168–169

Husband–wife interaction, distinctive element in, 78–79, *see also* Marital interaction

I

IBI, *see* Interbeat interval

Identity relationship, 173

Individual relationships, functional significance of, 12

Individuation, comparison process and, 293–294

Infant–caretaker interactions, *see* Caretaker–infant interactions

Inferences

developmental patterns and, 224–226

knowledge and, 226–229

Influence processes, assessment of, 216, *see also* Peer group influence

Information exchange, group influences and, 216

Insider–outsider differences, in personal relationships research, 24–25

Instruct–Help code, 155

Intensive case study technique, 11

Interactional system, wholeness or unity of, 73

Interaction patterns, in marital adjustment, 73

Interbeat interval, in emotional responsiveness, 96

Interpersonal relationships

closeness of, 273, 279–280

knowledge and, 235–236

Interpersonal strategies, 275–276

Intra-individual structure, microsocial variables and, 55

Intrapersonal correlations, knowledge and, 235–236

Irritability, dyadic trait for, 60–61

Irritability measures, validity of, 61–64

Irritability scores, for mother–child dyads, 57–61

K

Knowledge

assessment of, 233–237

categories of, 234–235

common vs. program-specific, 227

of common goals, 236

as error variance or variable, 233–234

general vs. task-specific, 235

inferences and, 226–229, 233–235

social experiences and, 229

uses of, 229–233

Knowledge assessment

pitfalls in, 237

social inferences and, 233–235

Knowledge-deficiency view, of young viewers' comprehension difficulties, 230